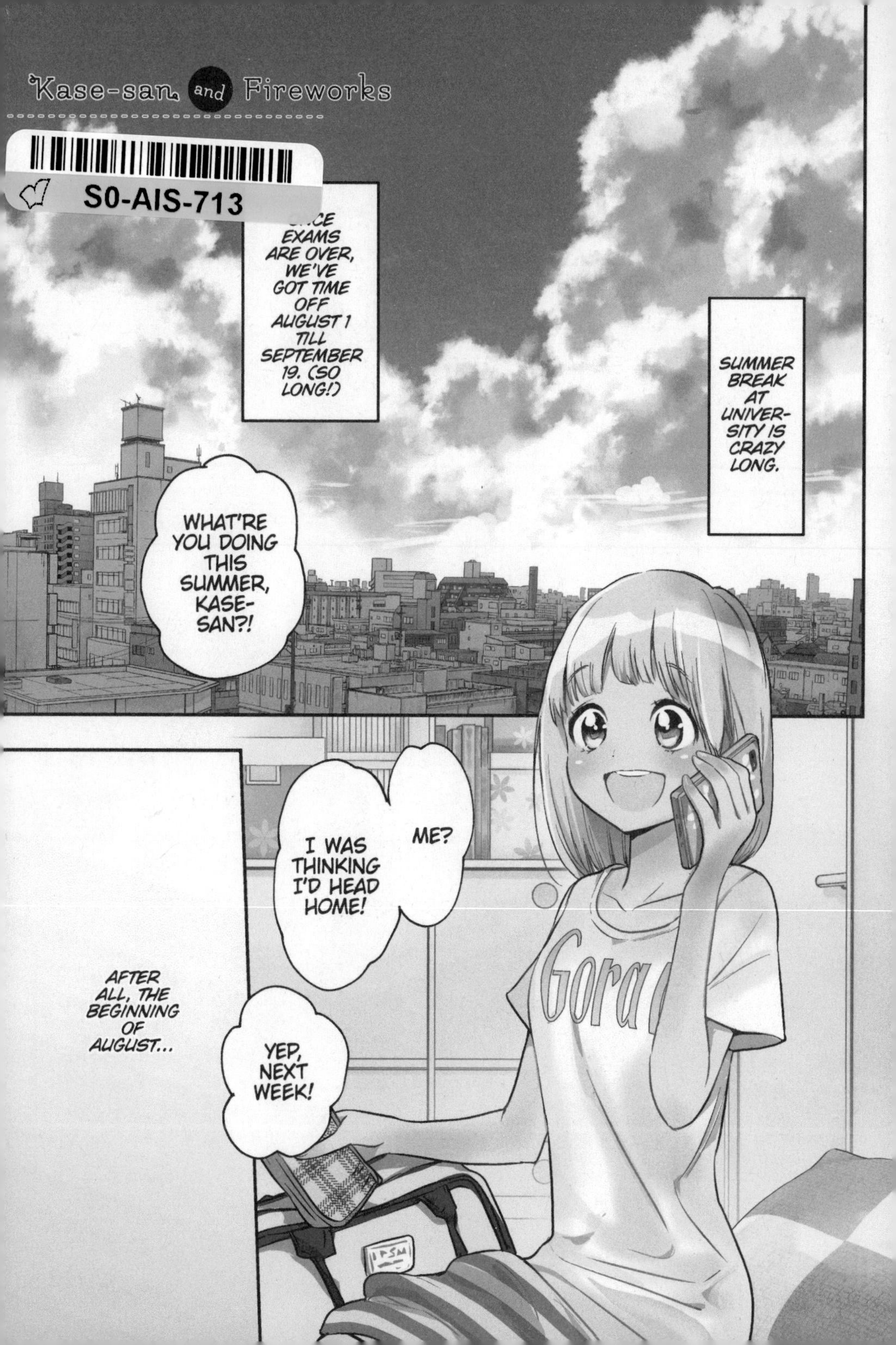
Kase-san and Fireworks
SUMMER BREAK AT UNIVERSITY IS CRAZY LONG.
ICE EXAMS ARE OVER, WE'VE GOT TIME OFF AUGUST 1 TILL SEPTEMBER 19. (SO LONG!)
WHAT'RE YOU DOING THIS SUMMER, KASE-SAN?!
ME?
I WAS THINKING I'D HEAD HOME!
YEP, NEXT WEEK!
AFTER ALL, THE BEGINNING OF AUGUST...

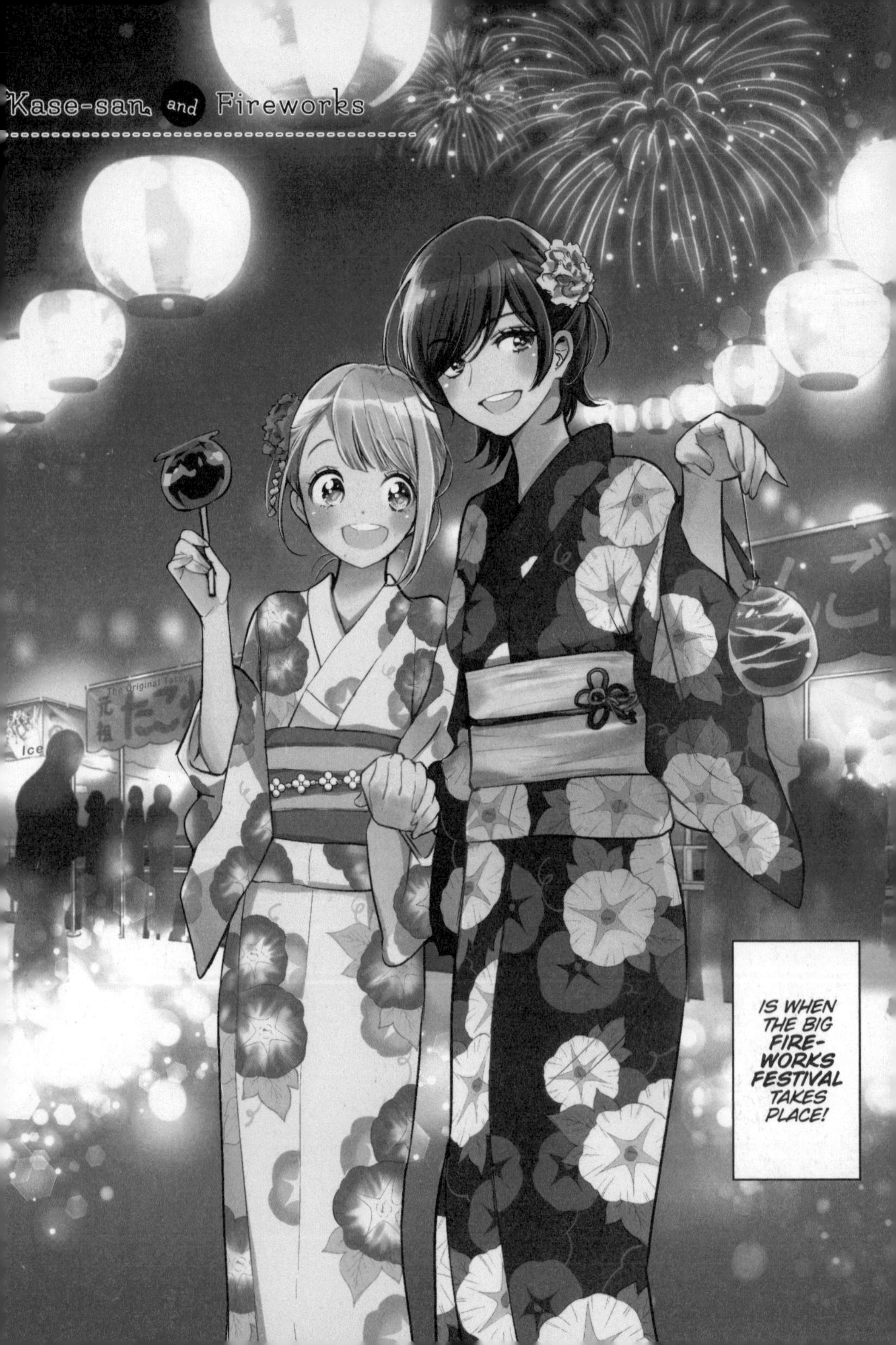
Kase-san and Fireworks
IS WHEN THE BIG FIRE-WORKS FESTIVAL TAKES PLACE!
Ice

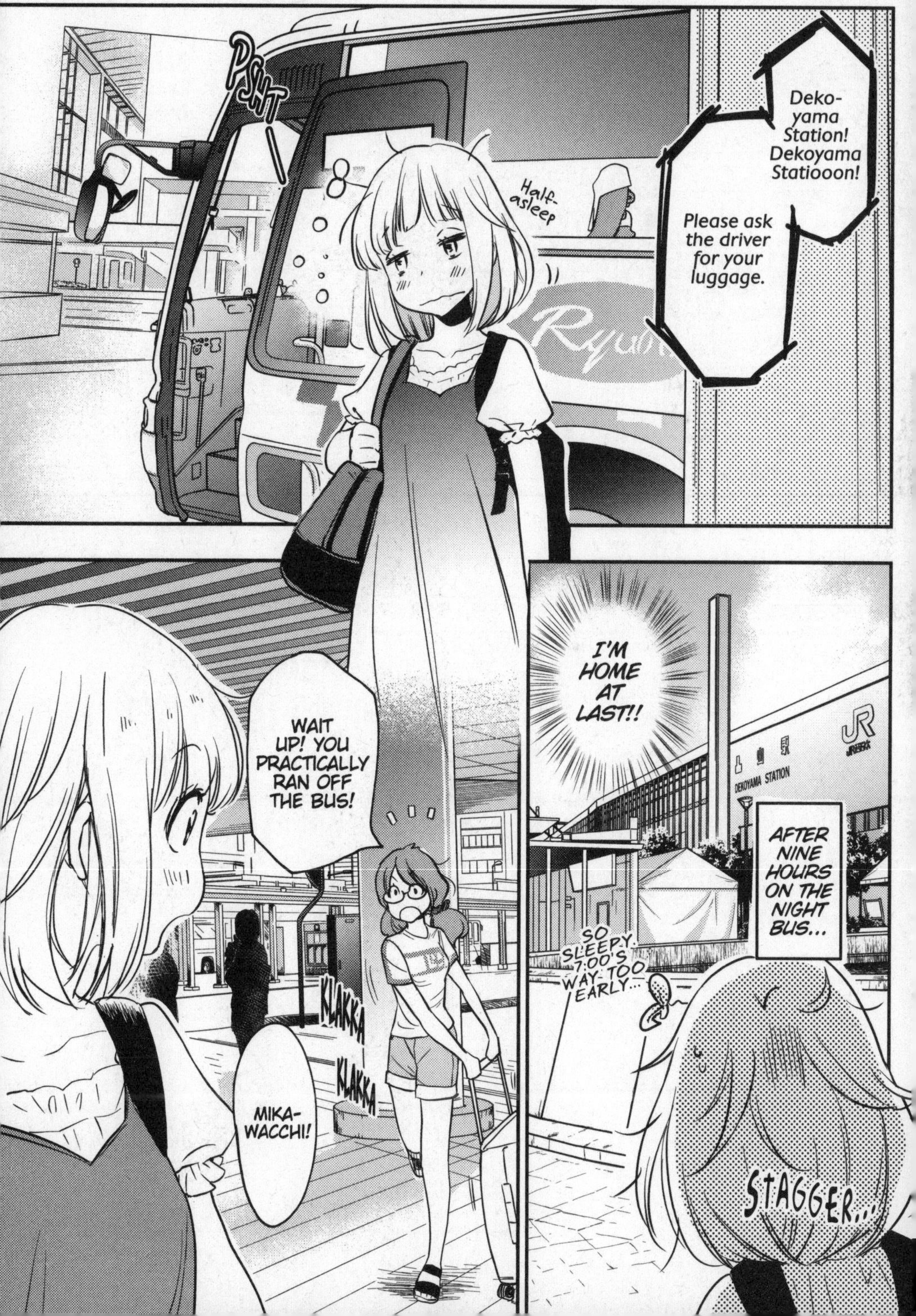
Dekoyama Station! Dekoyama Statiooon!
Please ask the driver for your luggage.
Half-asleep
PSHT
I'M HOME AT LAST!!
DEKOYAMA STATION
AFTER NINE HOURS ON THE NIGHT BUS...
SO SLEEPY. 7:00'S WAY TOO EARLY...
STAGGER...
WAIT UP! YOU PRACTICALLY RAN OFF THE BUS!
KLAKKA
KLAKKA
MIKA-WACCHI!

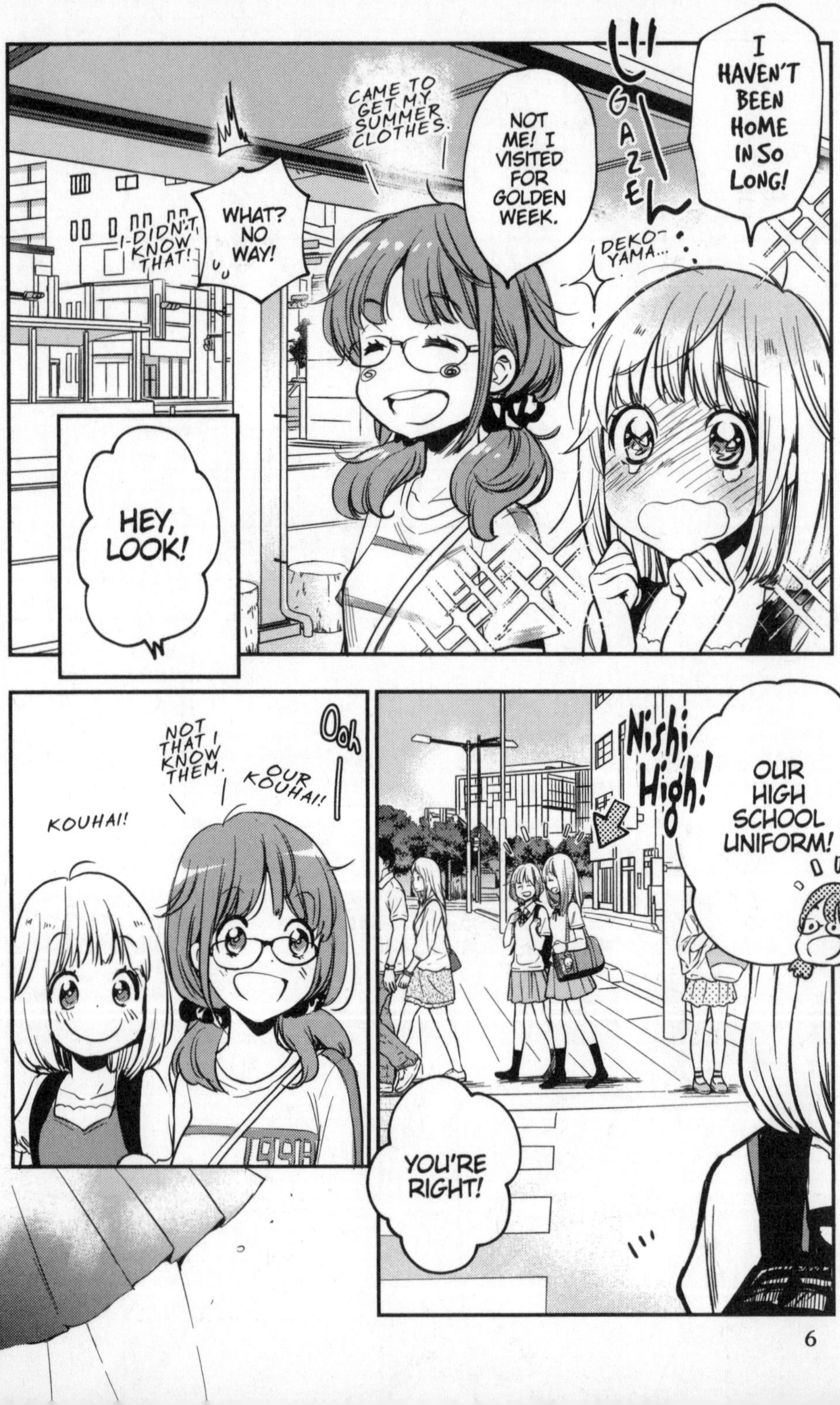
I HAVEN'T BEEN HOME IN SO LONG!
GAZE
DEKOYAMA...
NOT ME! I VISITED FOR GOLDEN WEEK.
CAME TO GET MY SUMMER CLOTHES.
WHAT? NO WAY!
I-DIDN'T KNOW THAT!
HEY, LOOK!
Nishi High!
OUR HIGH SCHOOL UNIFORM!
YOU'RE RIGHT!
Ooh
OUR KOUHAI!
NOT THAT I KNOW THEM.
KOUHAI!

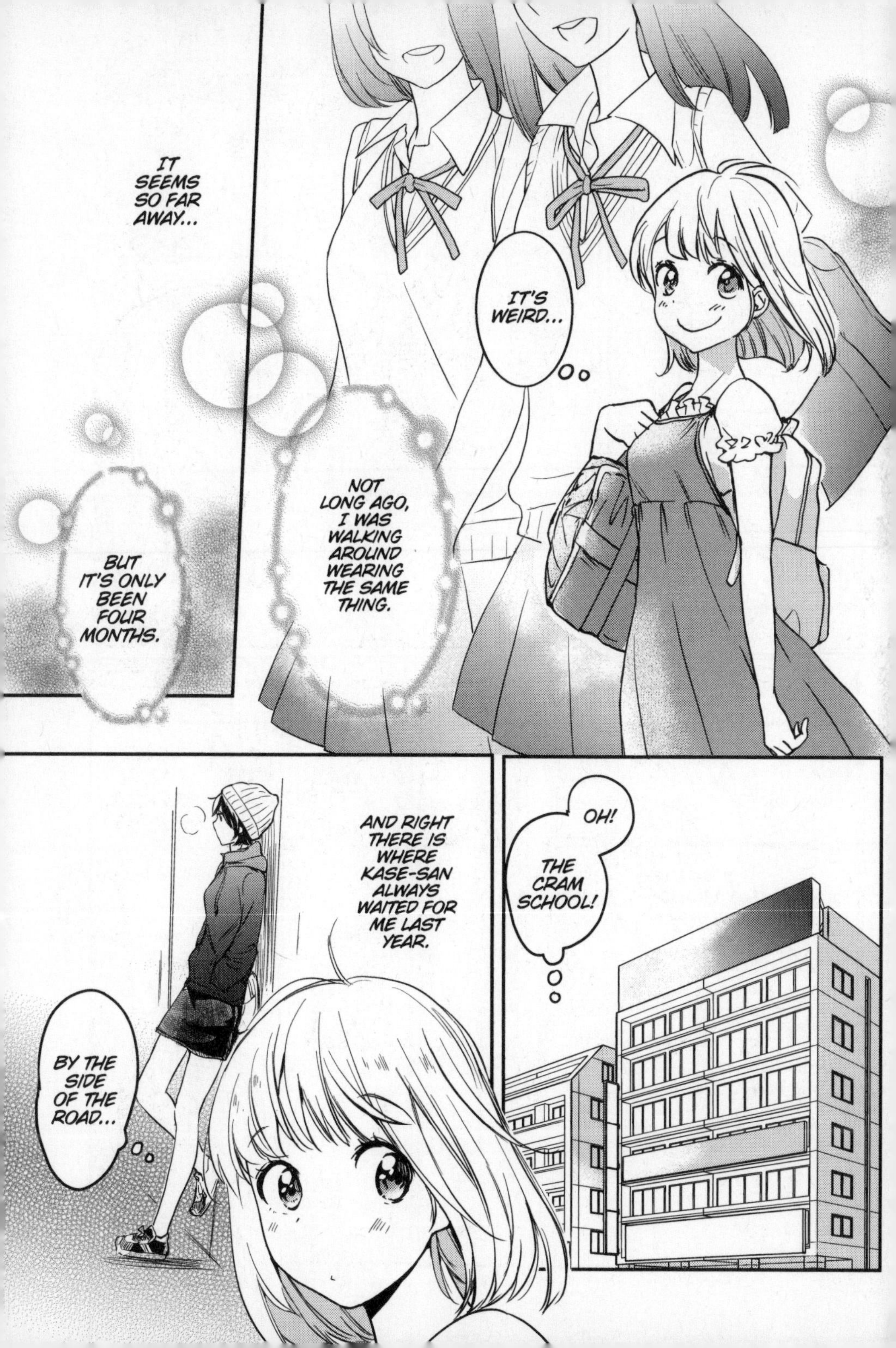
IT'S WEIRD...
NOT LONG AGO, I WAS WALKING AROUND WEARING THE SAME THING.
IT SEEMS SO FAR AWAY...
BUT IT'S ONLY BEEN FOUR MONTHS.
OH!
THE CRAM SCHOOL!
AND RIGHT THERE IS WHERE KASE-SAN ALWAYS WAITED FOR ME LAST YEAR.
BY THE SIDE OF THE ROAD...

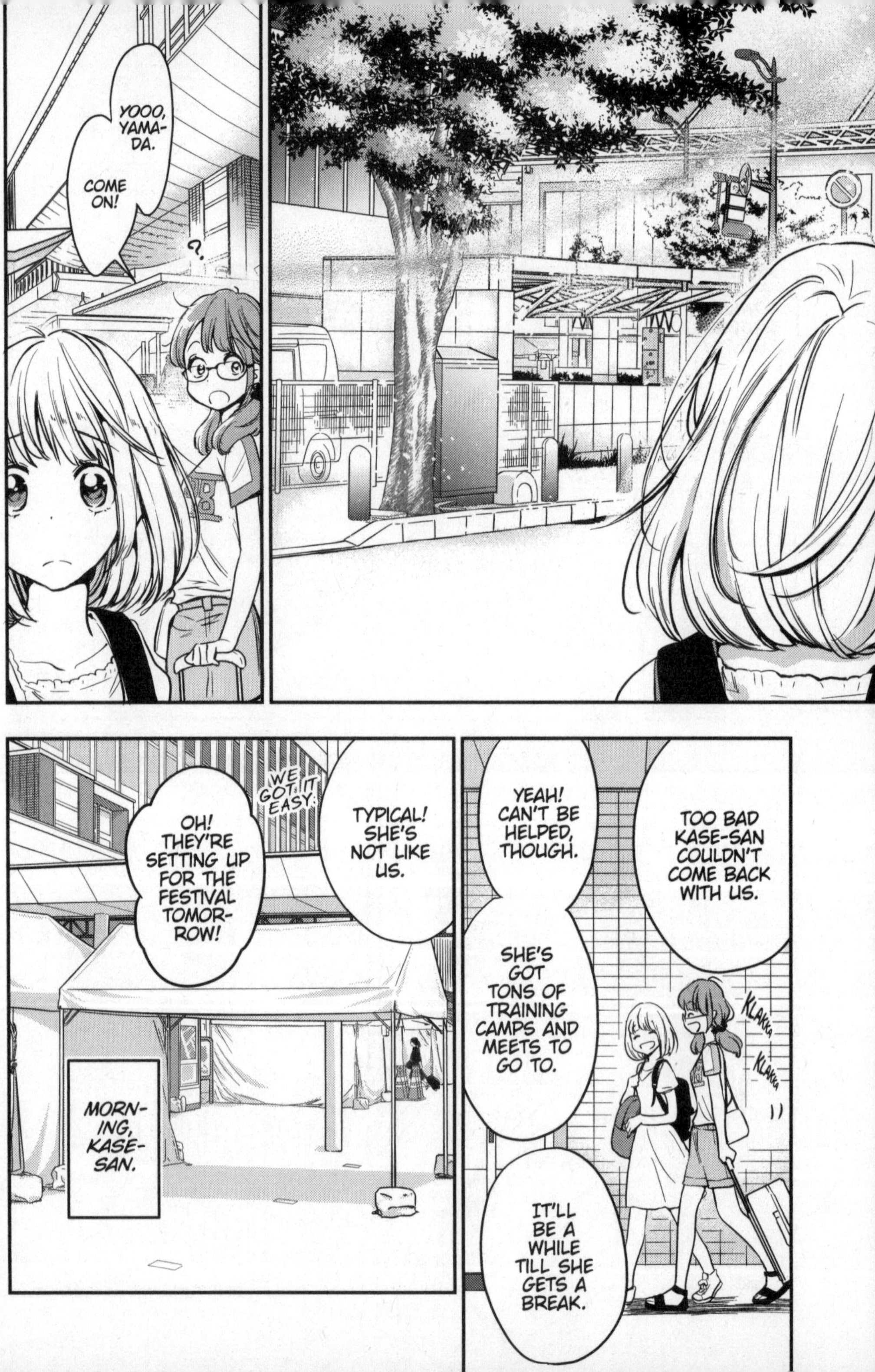
YOOO, YAMADA.
COME ON!
?
TOO BAD KASE-SAN COULDN'T COME BACK WITH US.
YEAH! CAN'T BE HELPED, THOUGH.
SHE'S GOT TONS OF TRAINING CAMPS AND MEETS TO GO TO.
KLAKKA
KLAKKA
IT'LL BE A WHILE TILL SHE GETS A BREAK.
TYPICAL! SHE'S NOT LIKE US.
WE GOT IT EASY.
OH! THEY'RE SETTING UP FOR THE FESTIVAL TOMORROW!
MORNING, KASE-SAN.

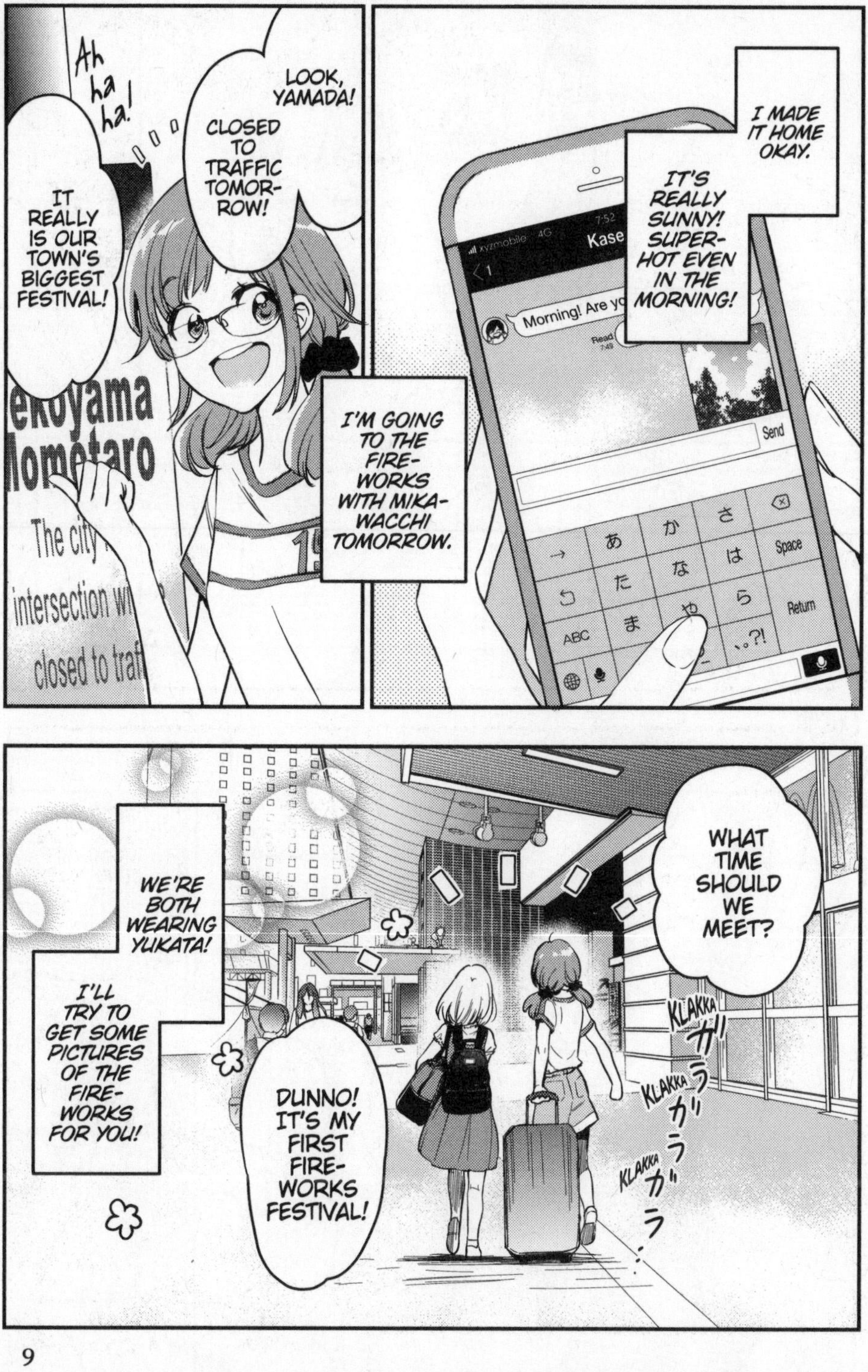
I MADE IT HOME OKAY.
IT'S REALLY SUNNY! SUPER-HOT EVEN IN THE MORNING!
Kase
Morning! Are yo
Send
Space
Return
ABC
I'M GOING TO THE FIRE-WORKS WITH MIKA-WACCHI TOMORROW.
LOOK, YAMADA! CLOSED TO TRAFFIC TOMOR-ROW!
Ah ha ha!
IT REALLY IS OUR TOWN'S BIGGEST FESTIVAL!
WHAT TIME SHOULD WE MEET?
KLAKKA ガラ
KLAKKA ガラ
KLAKKA ガラ
WE'RE BOTH WEARING YUKATA!
I'LL TRY TO GET SOME PICTURES OF THE FIRE-WORKS FOR YOU!
DUNNO! IT'S MY FIRST FIRE-WORKS FESTIVAL!

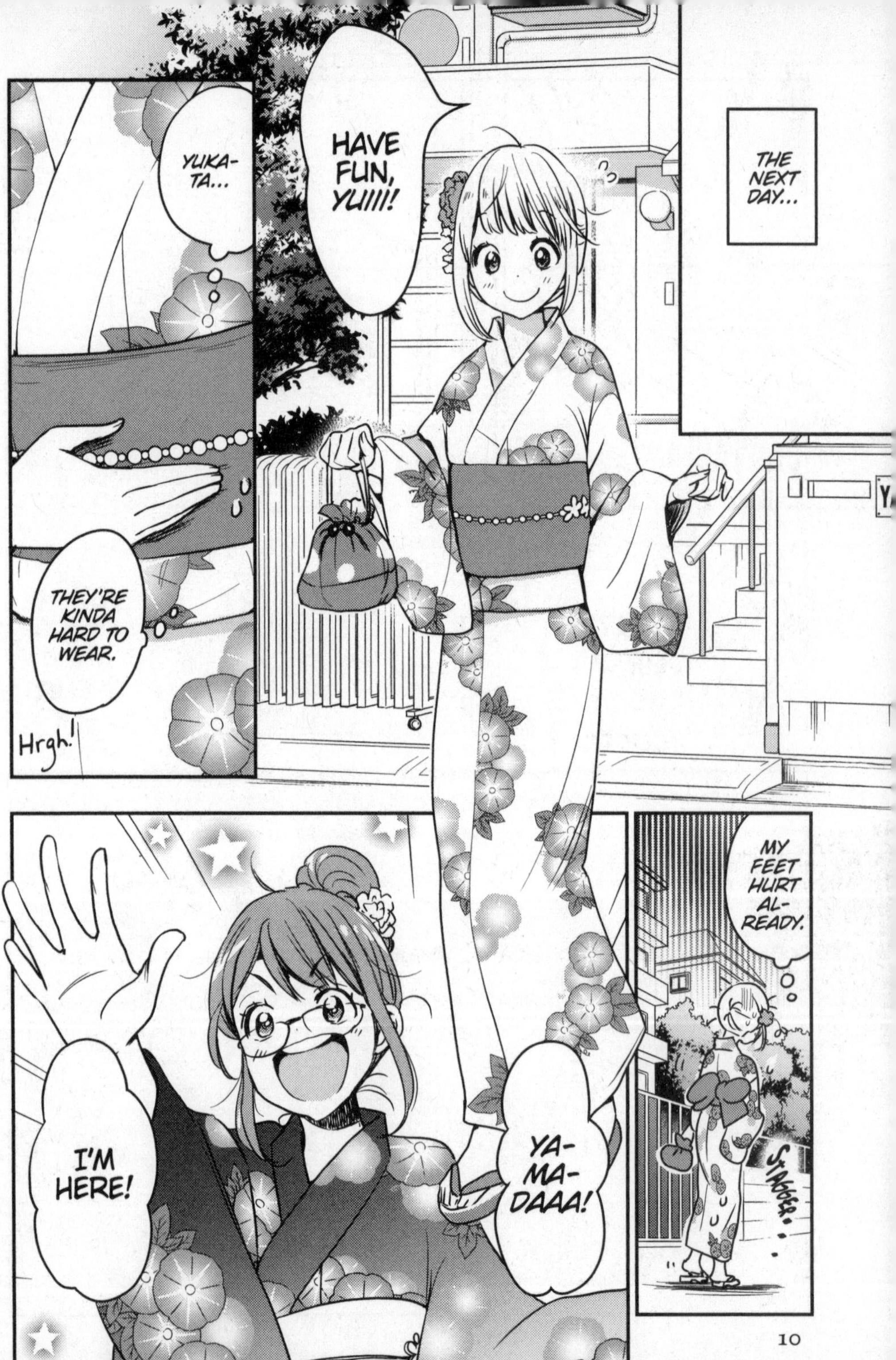
THE NEXT DAY...
HAVE FUN, YUIIII!
YUKA-TA...
THEY'RE KINDA HARD TO WEAR.
Hrgh!
MY FEET HURT AL-READY.
STAGGER...
YA-MA-DAAA!
I'M HERE!

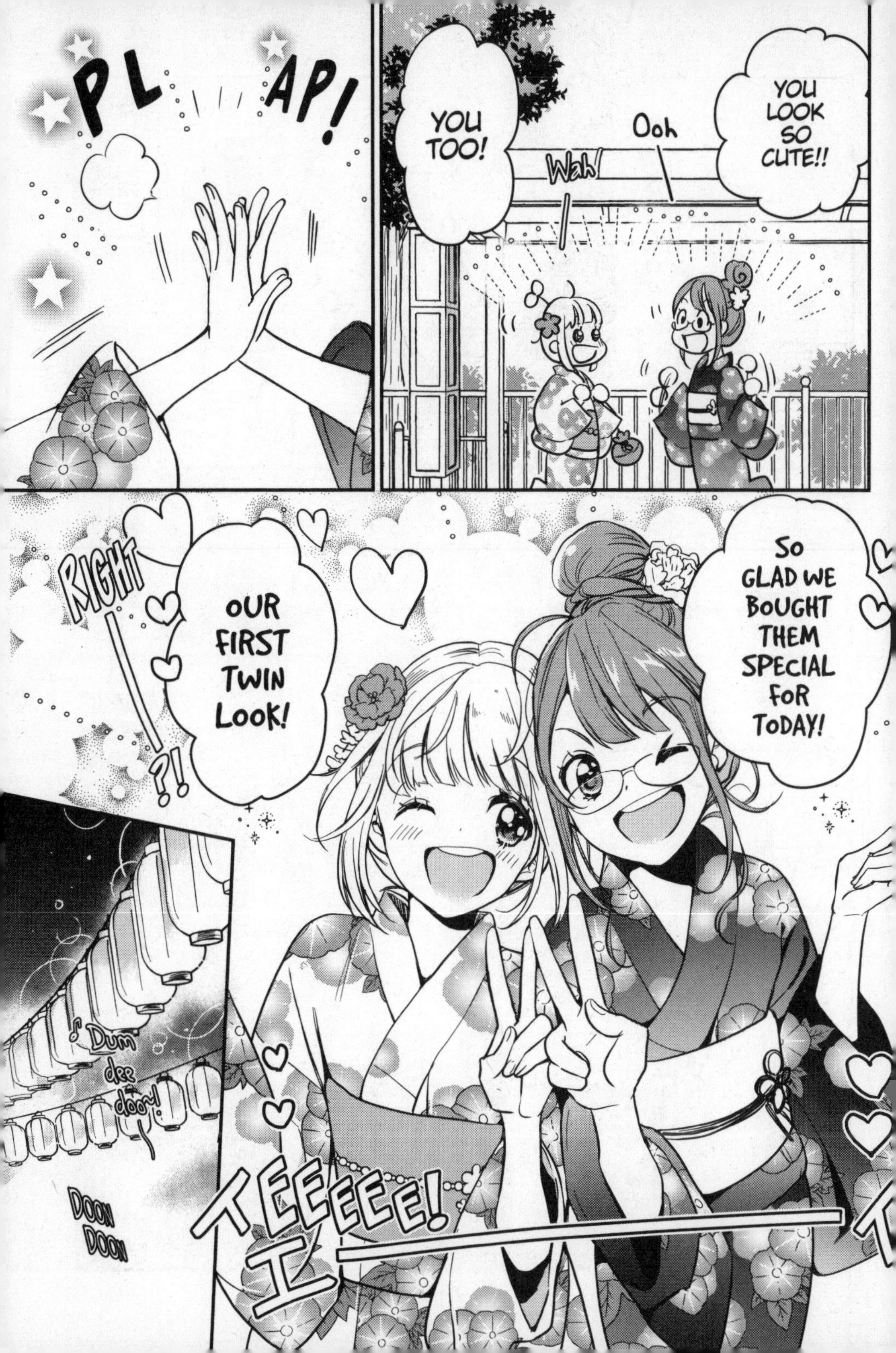
YOU LOOK SO CUTE!!
Ooh
Wah!
YOU TOO!
PL AP!
So GLAD WE BOUGHT THEM SPECIAL FoR TODAY!
OUR FIRST TWIN LooK!
RIGHT ?!
EEEEE!
Dum dee doo~!
DOON DOON

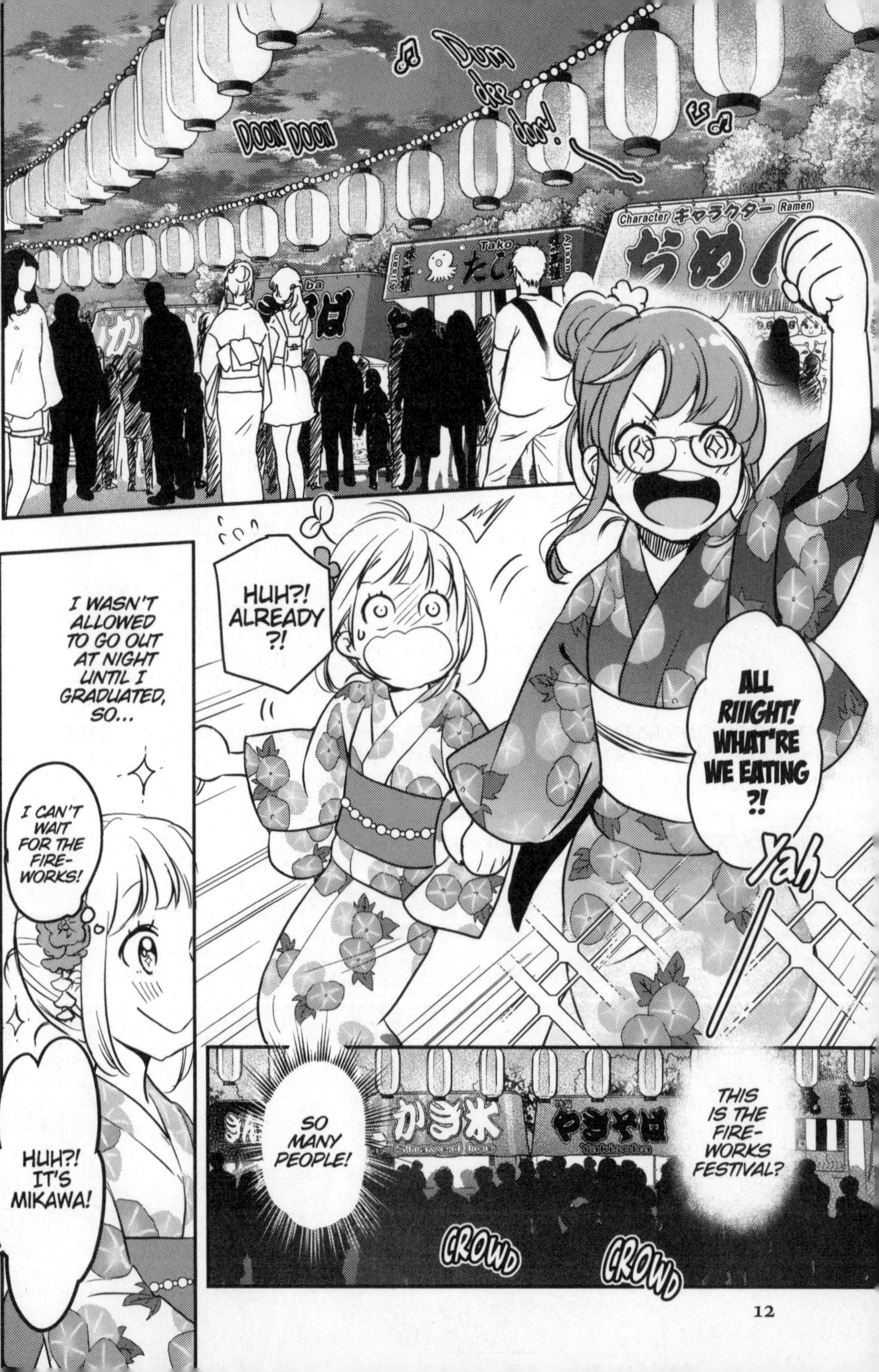
♫ Dum dee doo! ♫
DOON DOON
Character キャラクター Ramen
Tako たこ
Aisan
Soba
ALL RIIIGHT! WHAT'RE WE EATING?!
Yah
HUH?! ALREADY?!
THIS IS THE FIRE-WORKS FESTIVAL?
SO MANY PEOPLE!
かき氷 Shaved Ice
やきそば Yakisoba
CROWD
CROWD
I WASN'T ALLOWED TO GO OUT AT NIGHT UNTIL I GRADUATED, SO...
I CAN'T WAIT FOR THE FIRE-WORKS!
HUH?! IT'S MIKAWA!

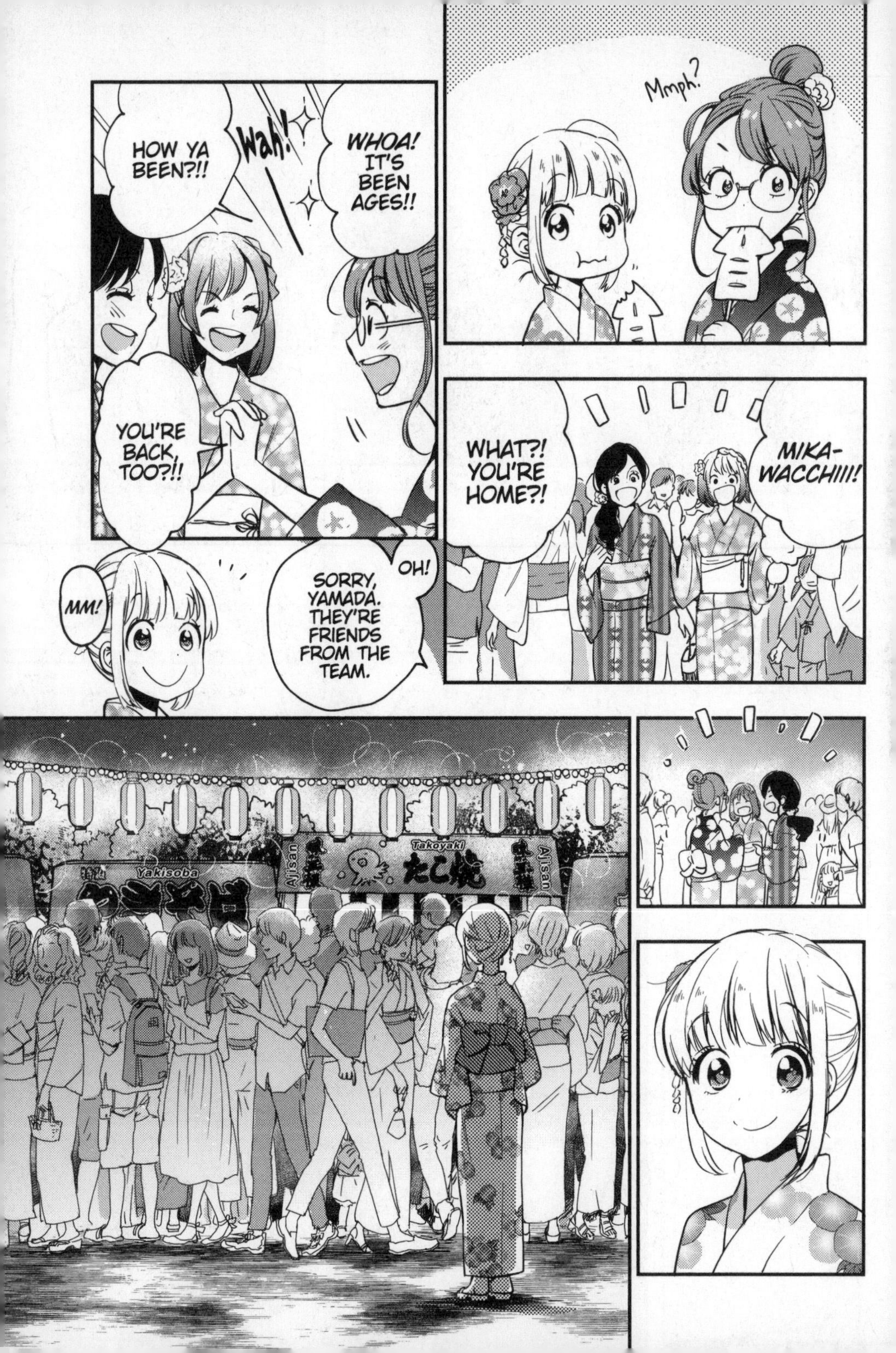
Mmph?
MIKA-WACCHI!!!!
WHAT?! YOU'RE HOME?!
WHOA! IT'S BEEN AGES!!
Wah!
HOW YA BEEN?!!
YOU'RE BACK, TOO?!!
OH!
SORRY, YAMADA. THEY'RE FRIENDS FROM THE TEAM.
MM!
Ajisan
Takoyaki
たこ焼
Ajisan
Yakisoba

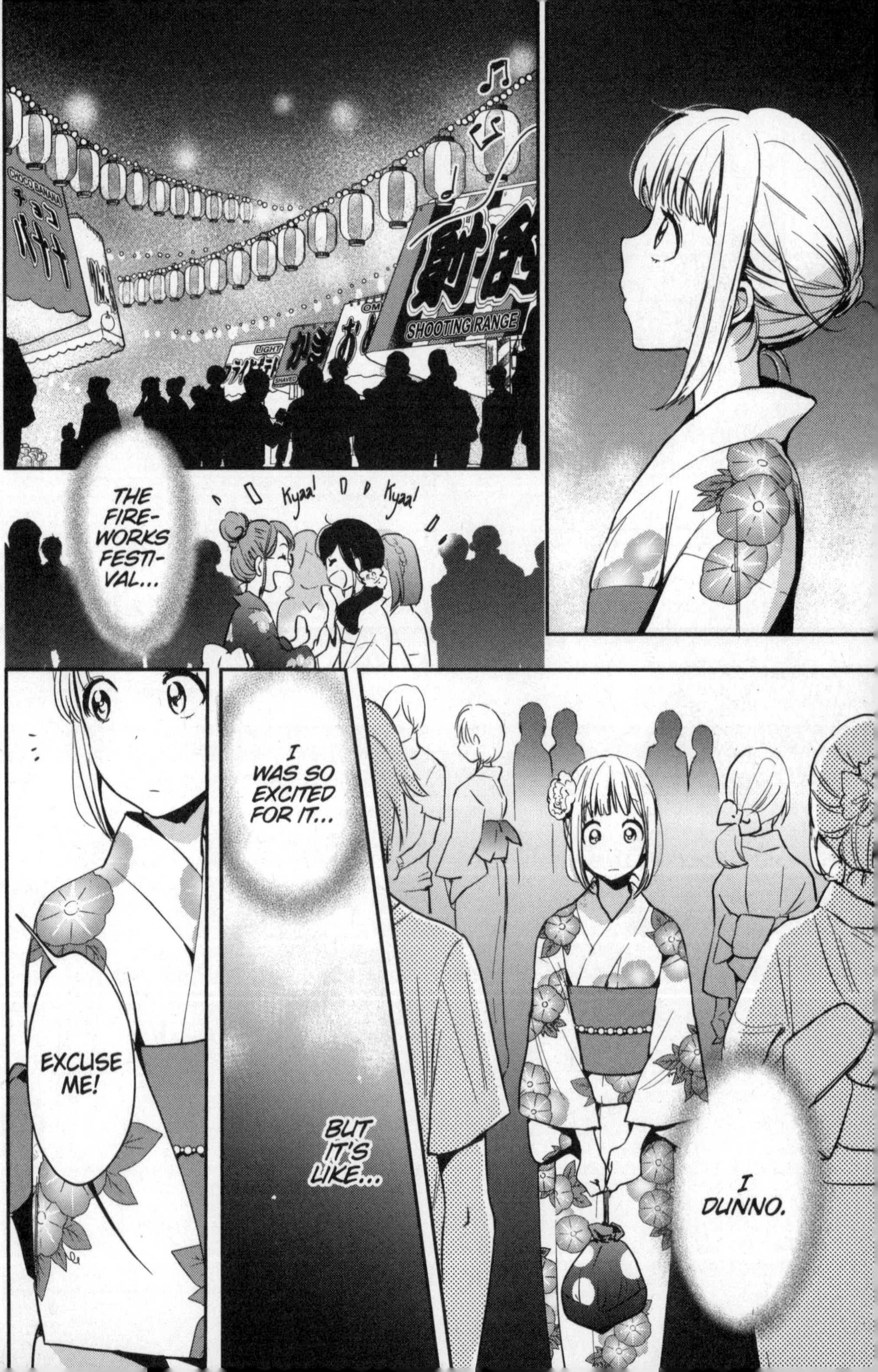
CHOCO BANANA
LIGHT
SHAVED
OM
SHOOTING RANGE
THE FIRE-WORKS FESTI-VAL...
Kyaa!
Kyaa!
I DUNNO.
I WAS SO EXCITED FOR IT...
BUT IT'S LIKE...
EXCUSE ME!

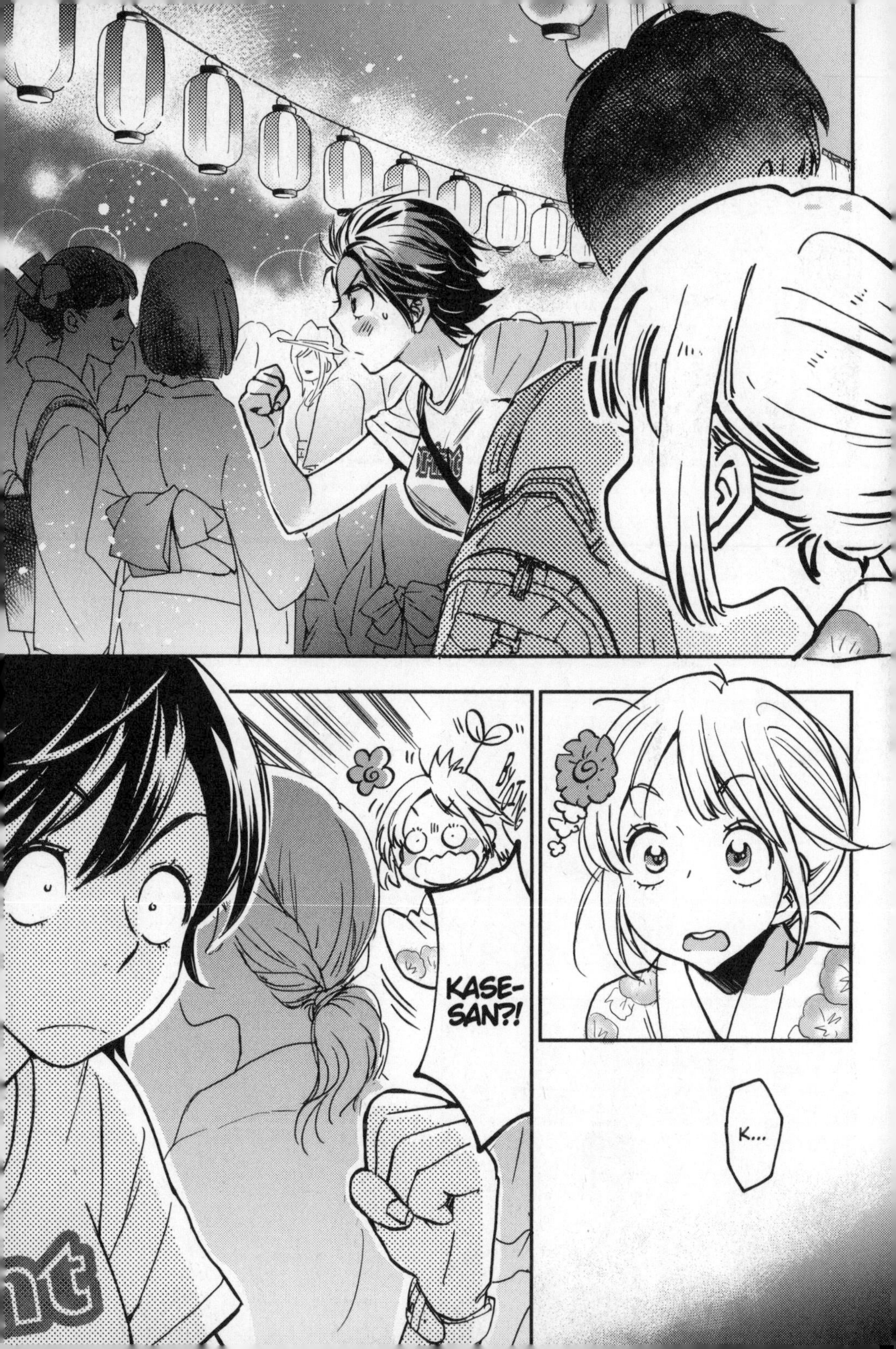
K...
BYOING
KASE-SAN?!

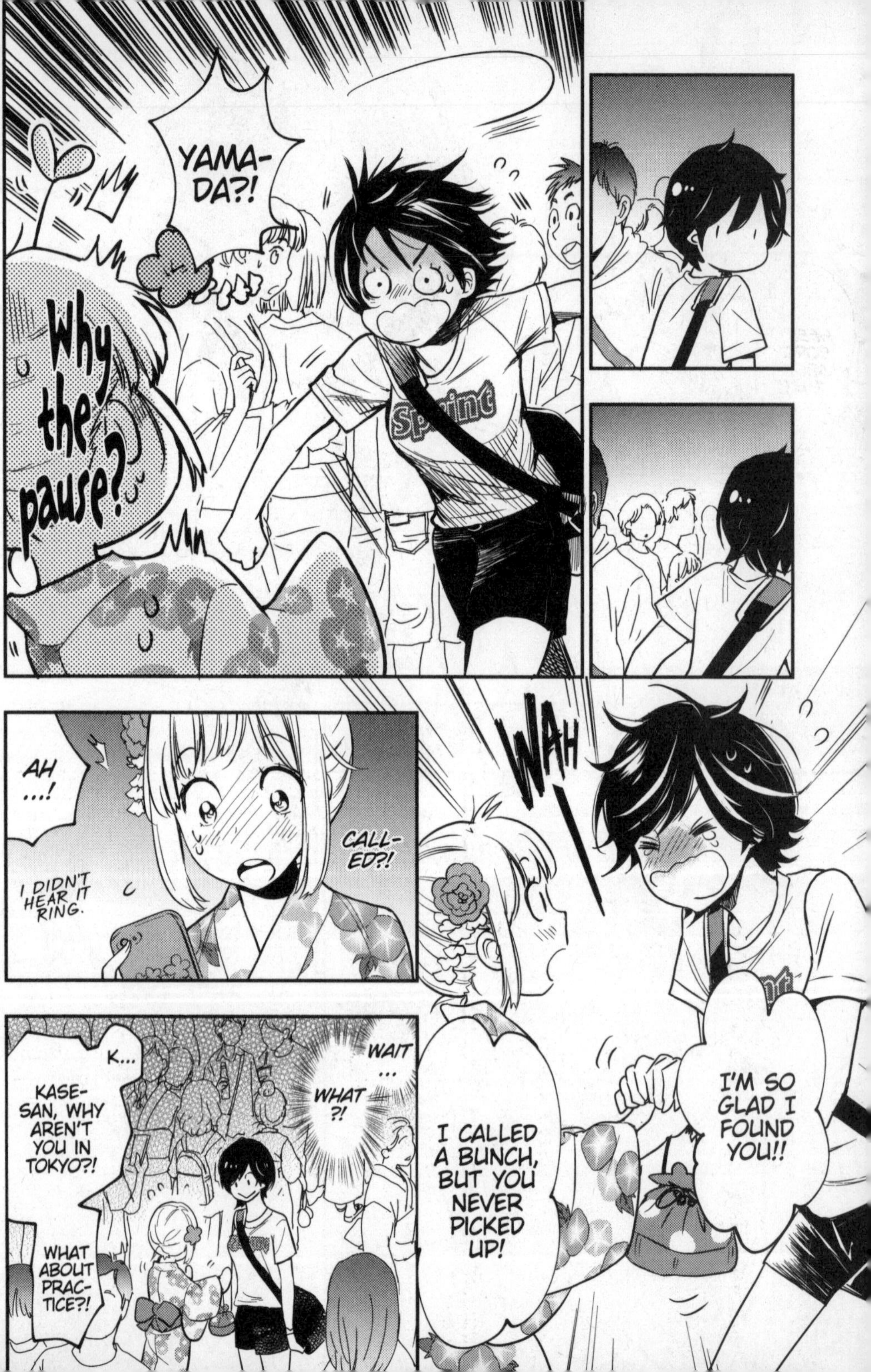
YAMA-DA?!
Why the pause?
WAH
I'M SO GLAD I FOUND YOU!!
I CALLED A BUNCH, BUT YOU NEVER PICKED UP!
CALL-ED?!
AH ...!
I DIDN'T HEAR IT RING.
WAIT ...
WHAT ?!
K...
KASE-SAN, WHY AREN'T YOU IN TOKYO?!
WHAT ABOUT PRAC-TICE?!

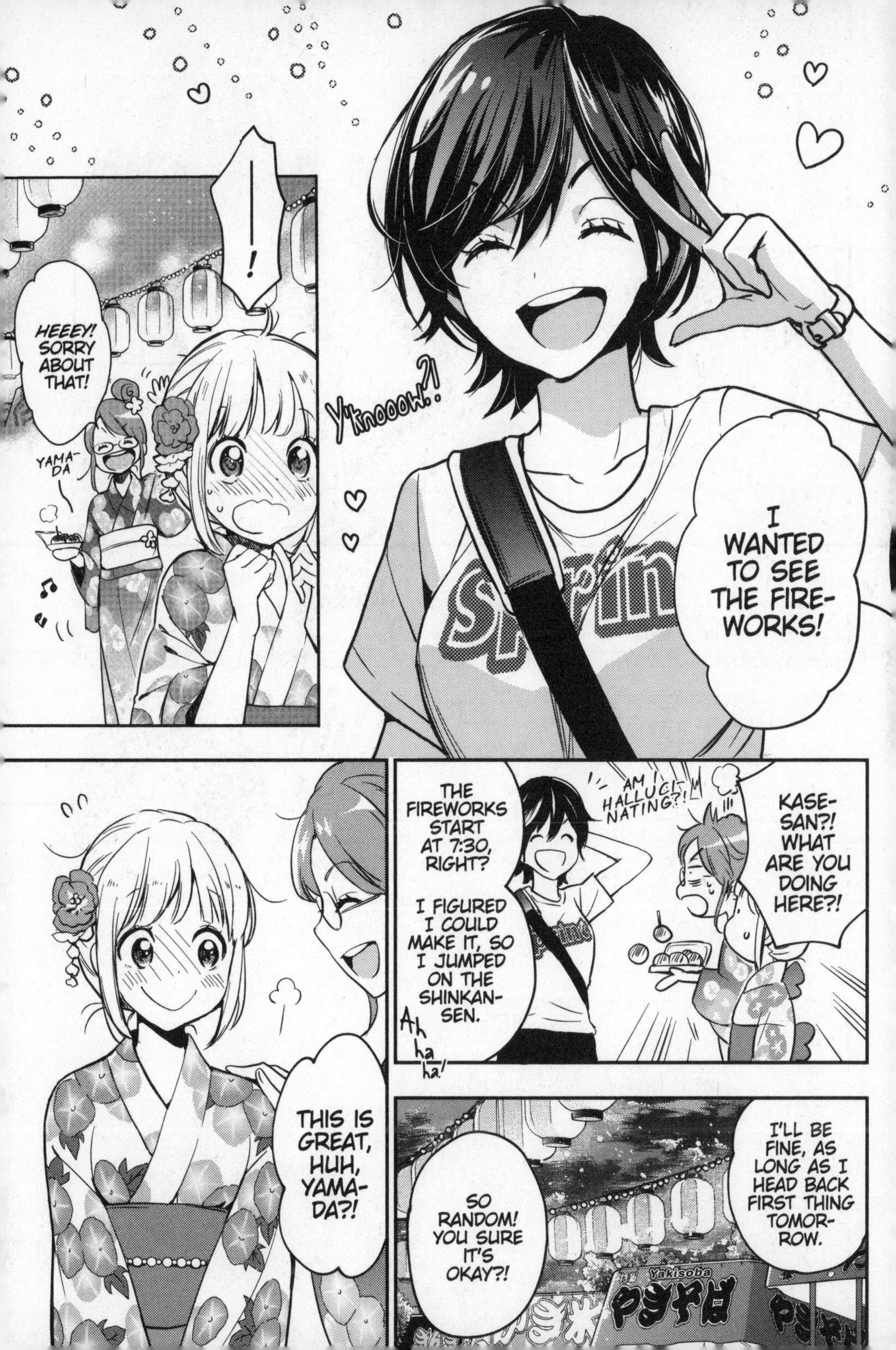
Y'knooow?!
I WANTED TO SEE THE FIRE-WORKS!
!!
HEEEY! SORRY ABOUT THAT!
YAMADA
KASE-SAN?! WHAT ARE YOU DOING HERE?!
AM I HALLUCI-NATING?!
THE FIREWORKS START AT 7:30, RIGHT?
I FIGURED I COULD MAKE IT, SO I JUMPED ON THE SHINKAN-SEN.
Ahhaha!
I'LL BE FINE, AS LONG AS I HEAD BACK FIRST THING TOMOR-ROW.
SO RANDOM! YOU SURE IT'S OKAY?!
Yakisoba
THIS IS GREAT, HUH, YAMA-DA?!

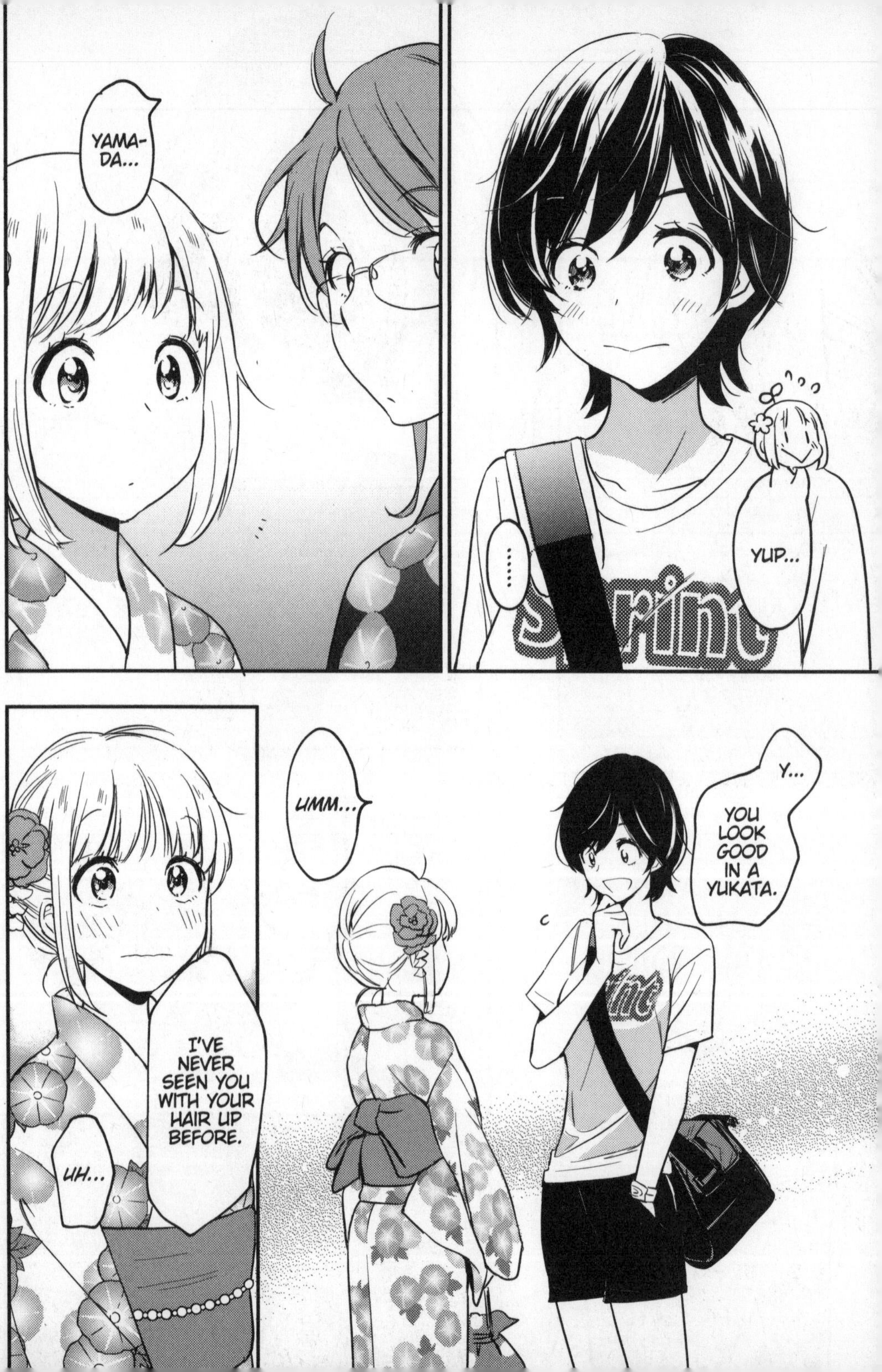
YUP...
......
YAMA-DA...
Y...
YOU LOOK GOOD IN A YUKATA.
UMM...
I'VE NEVER SEEN YOU WITH YOUR HAIR UP BEFORE.
UH...

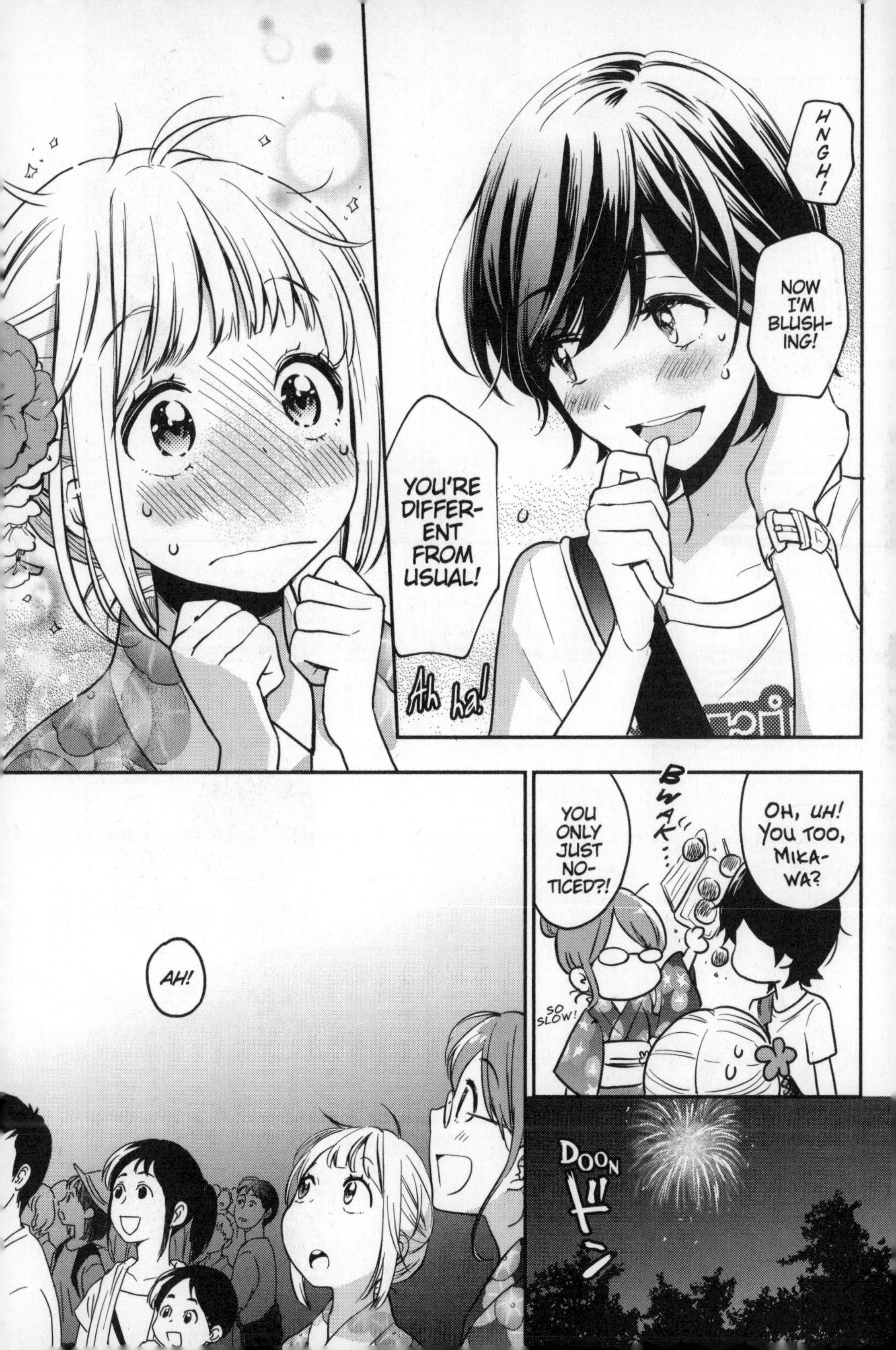
HNGH!
NOW I'M BLUSH-ING!
YOU'RE DIFFER-ENT FROM USUAL!
Ah ha!
OH, UH! YOU TOO, MIKA-WA?
BWAK...
YOU ONLY JUST NO-TICED?!
SO SLOW!
AH!
DOON
ドーン

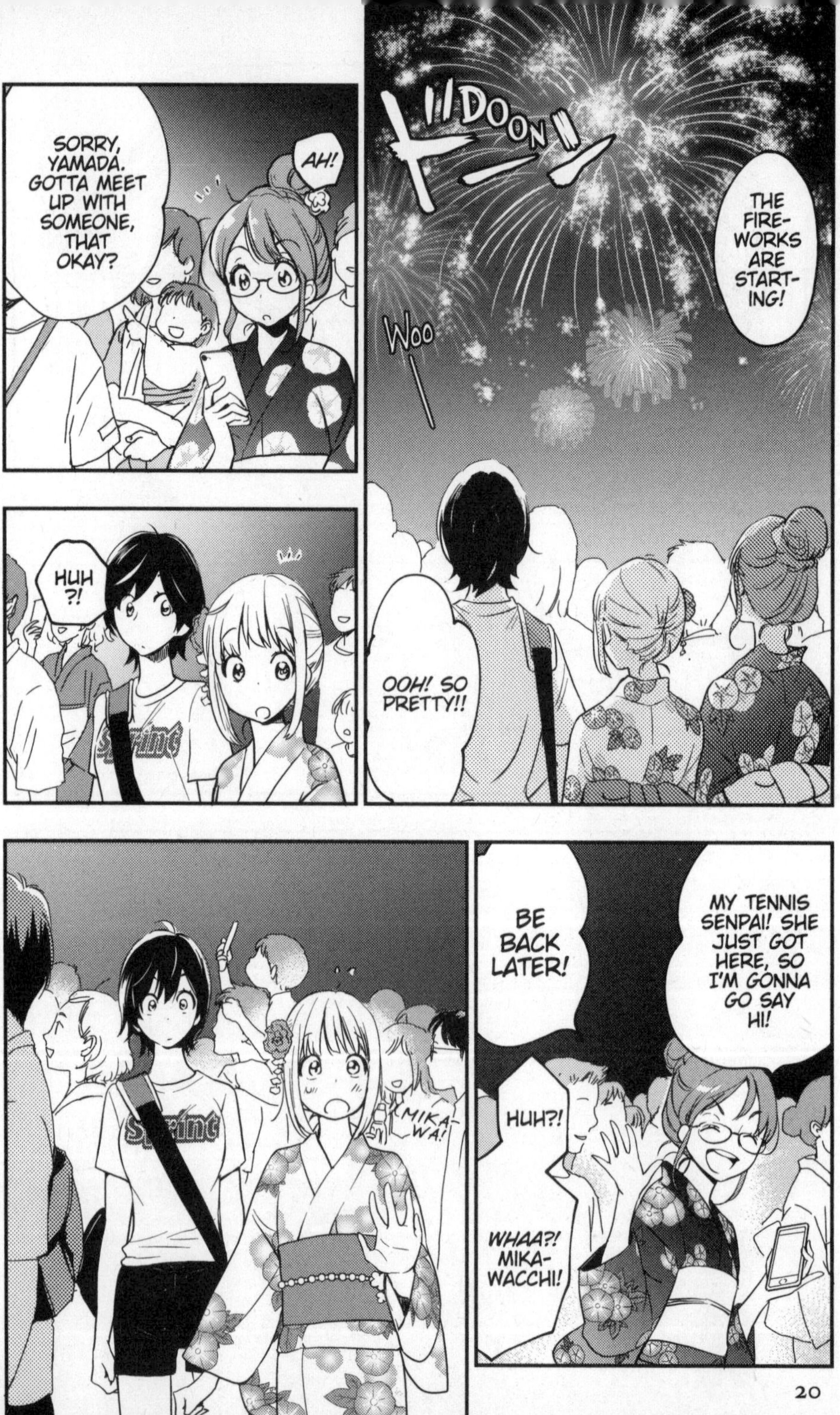

DOON
THE FIRE-WORKS ARE START-ING!
Woo
OOH! SO PRETTY!!
AH!
SORRY, YAMADA. GOTTA MEET UP WITH SOMEONE, THAT OKAY?
HUH?!
MY TENNIS SENPAI! SHE JUST GOT HERE, SO I'M GONNA GO SAY HI!
BE BACK LATER!
HUH?!
WHAA?! MIKA-WACCHI!
MIKA-WA!

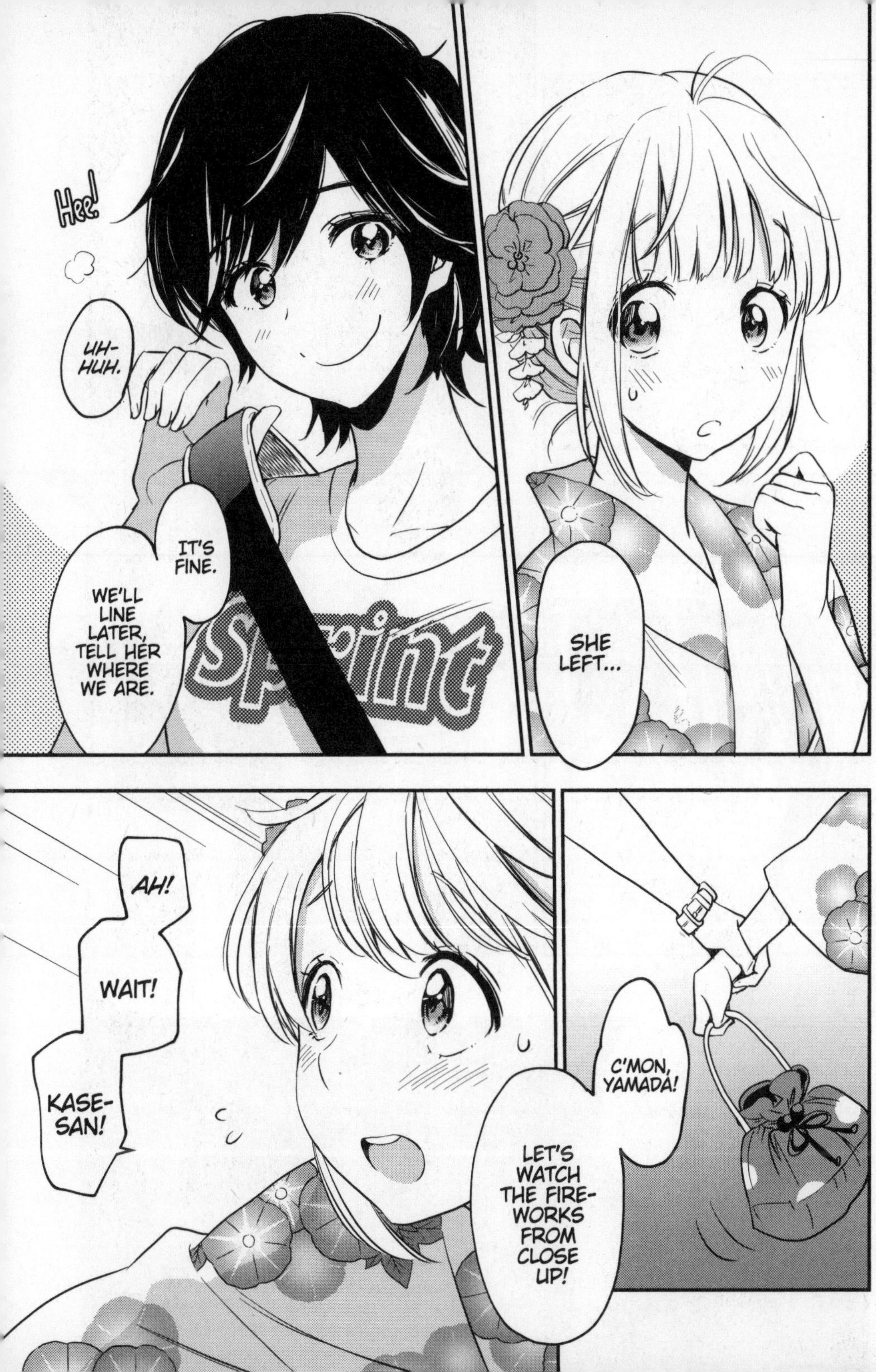
SHE LEFT...
Hee!
UH-HUH.
IT'S FINE.
WE'LL LINE LATER, TELL HER WHERE WE ARE.
C'MON, YAMADA!
LET'S WATCH THE FIRE-WORKS FROM CLOSE UP!
AH!
WAIT!
KASE-SAN!

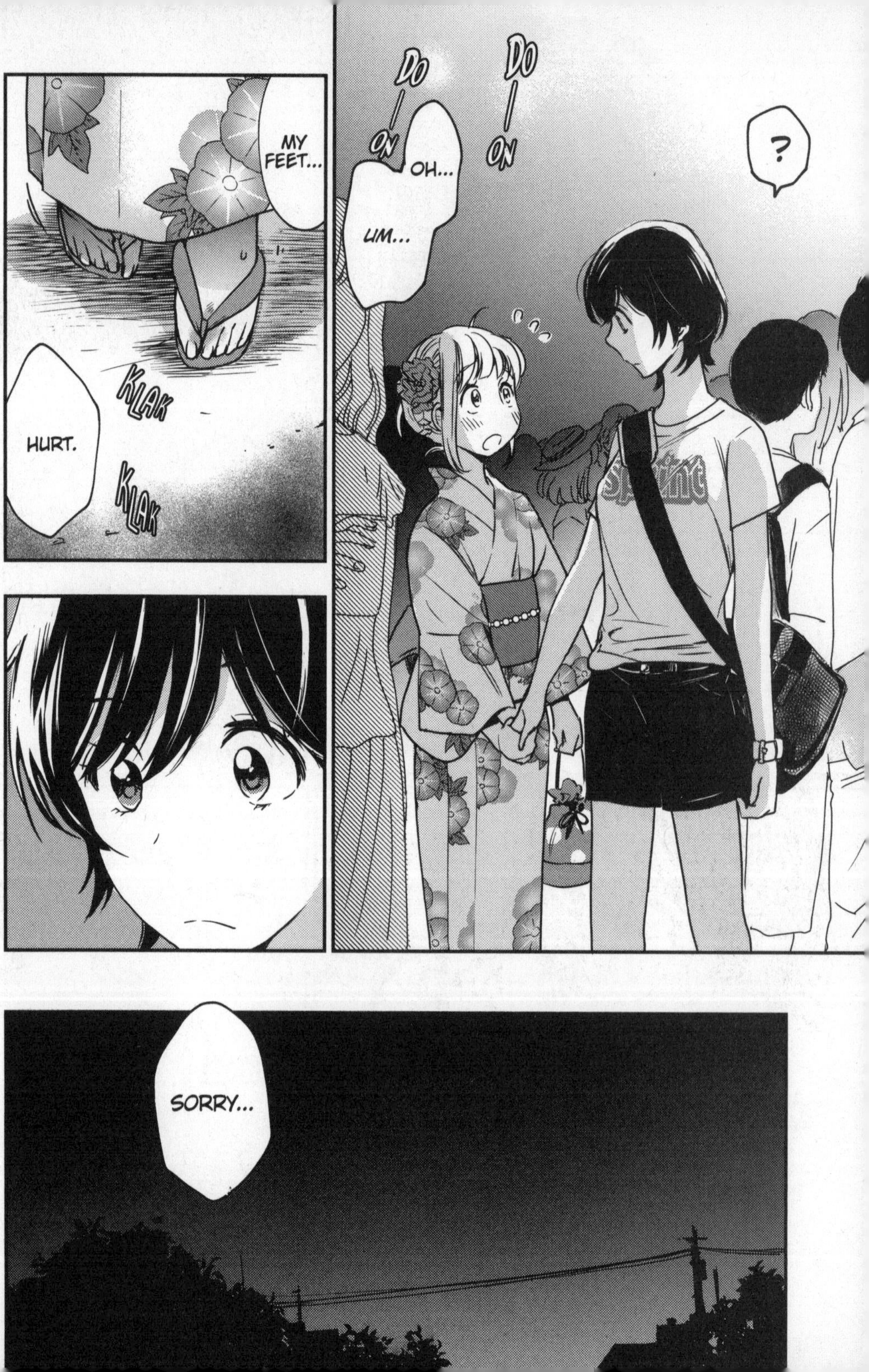
?
DO-ON
DO-ON
OH...
UM...
MY FEET...
KLAK
KLAK
HURT.
SORRY...

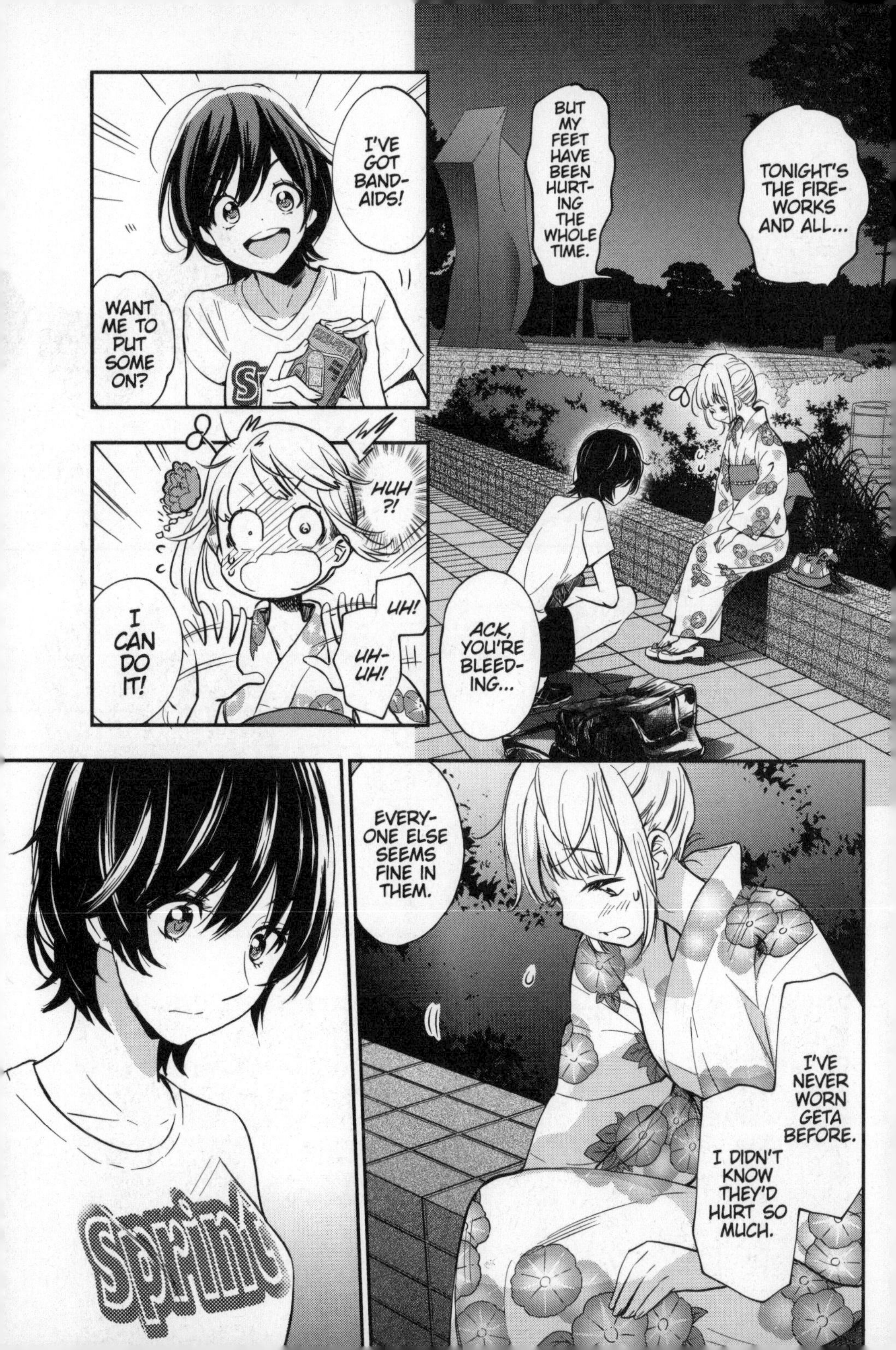
TONIGHT'S THE FIRE-WORKS AND ALL...
BUT MY FEET HAVE BEEN HURT-ING THE WHOLE TIME.
ACK, YOU'RE BLEED-ING...
I'VE GOT BAND-AIDS!
WANT ME TO PUT SOME ON?
HUH?!
UH!
UH-UH!
I CAN DO IT!
EVERY-ONE ELSE SEEMS FINE IN THEM.
I'VE NEVER WORN GETA BEFORE.
I DIDN'T KNOW THEY'D HURT SO MUCH.
Sprint

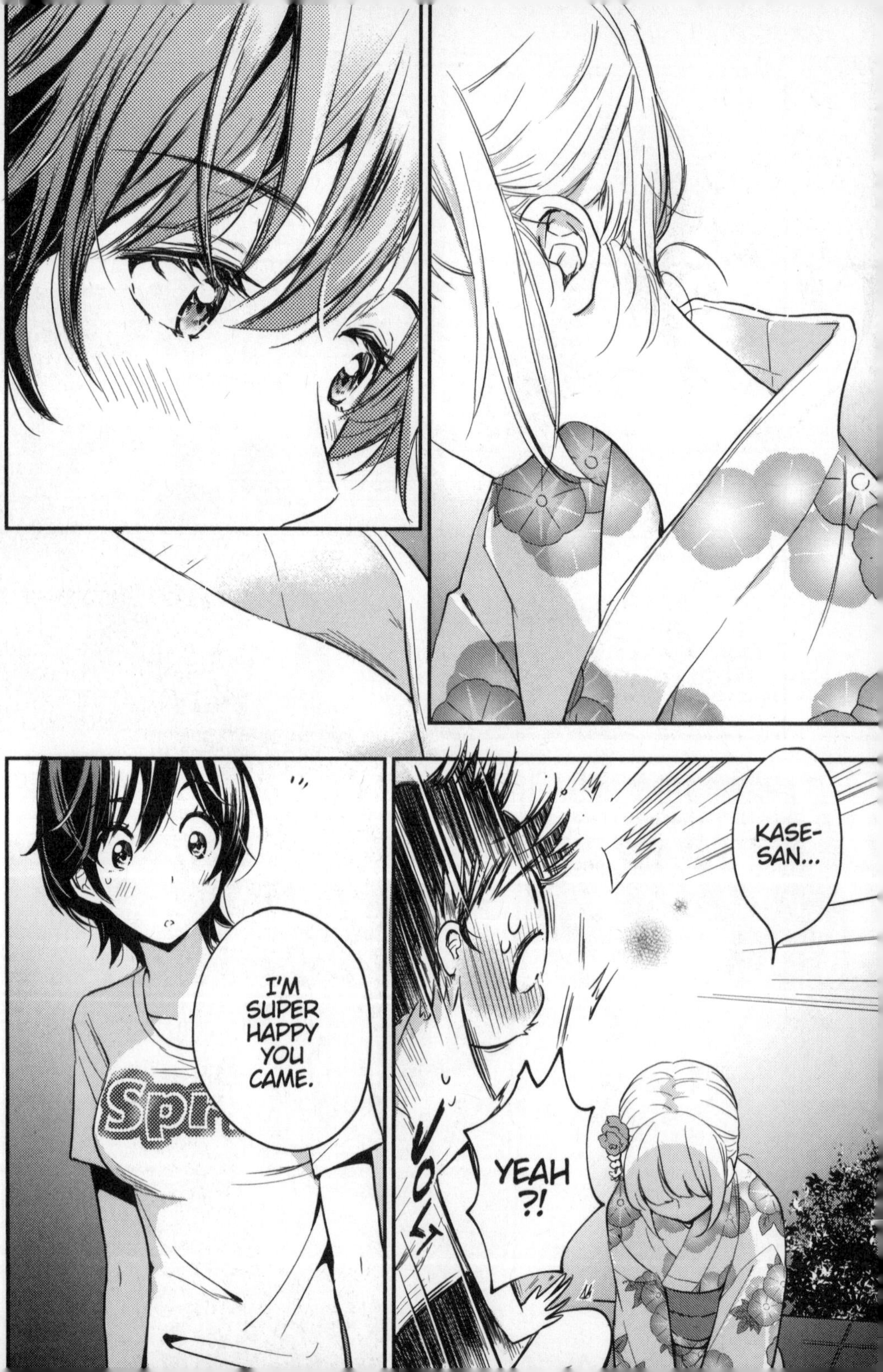
KASE-SAN...
YEAH ?!
JOLT
I'M SUPER HAPPY YOU CAME.

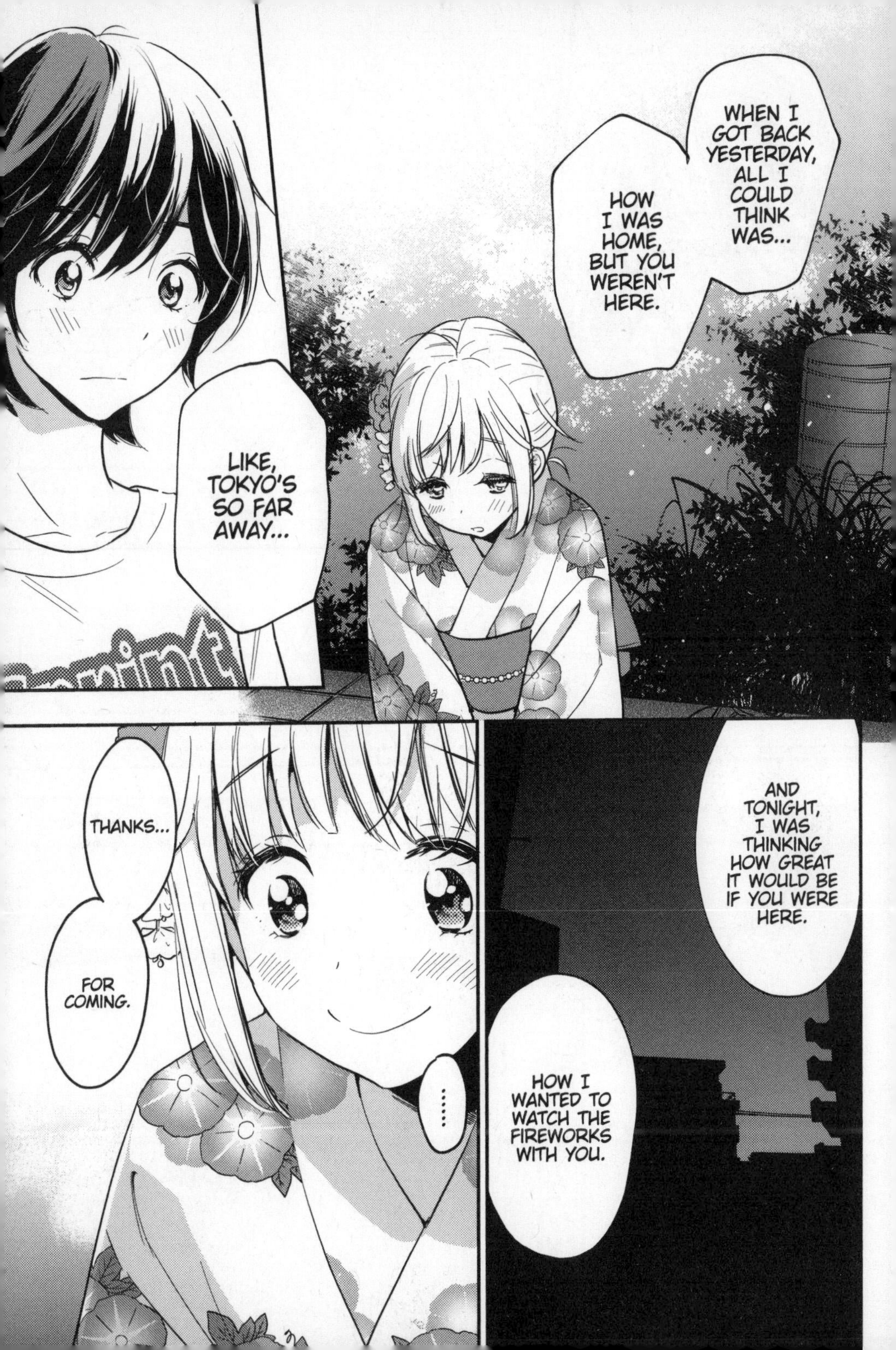

WHEN I GOT BACK YESTERDAY, ALL I COULD THINK WAS...
HOW I WAS HOME, BUT YOU WEREN'T HERE.
LIKE, TOKYO'S SO FAR AWAY...
AND TONIGHT, I WAS THINKING HOW GREAT IT WOULD BE IF YOU WERE HERE.
HOW I WANTED TO WATCH THE FIREWORKS WITH YOU.
......
THANKS...
FOR COMING.

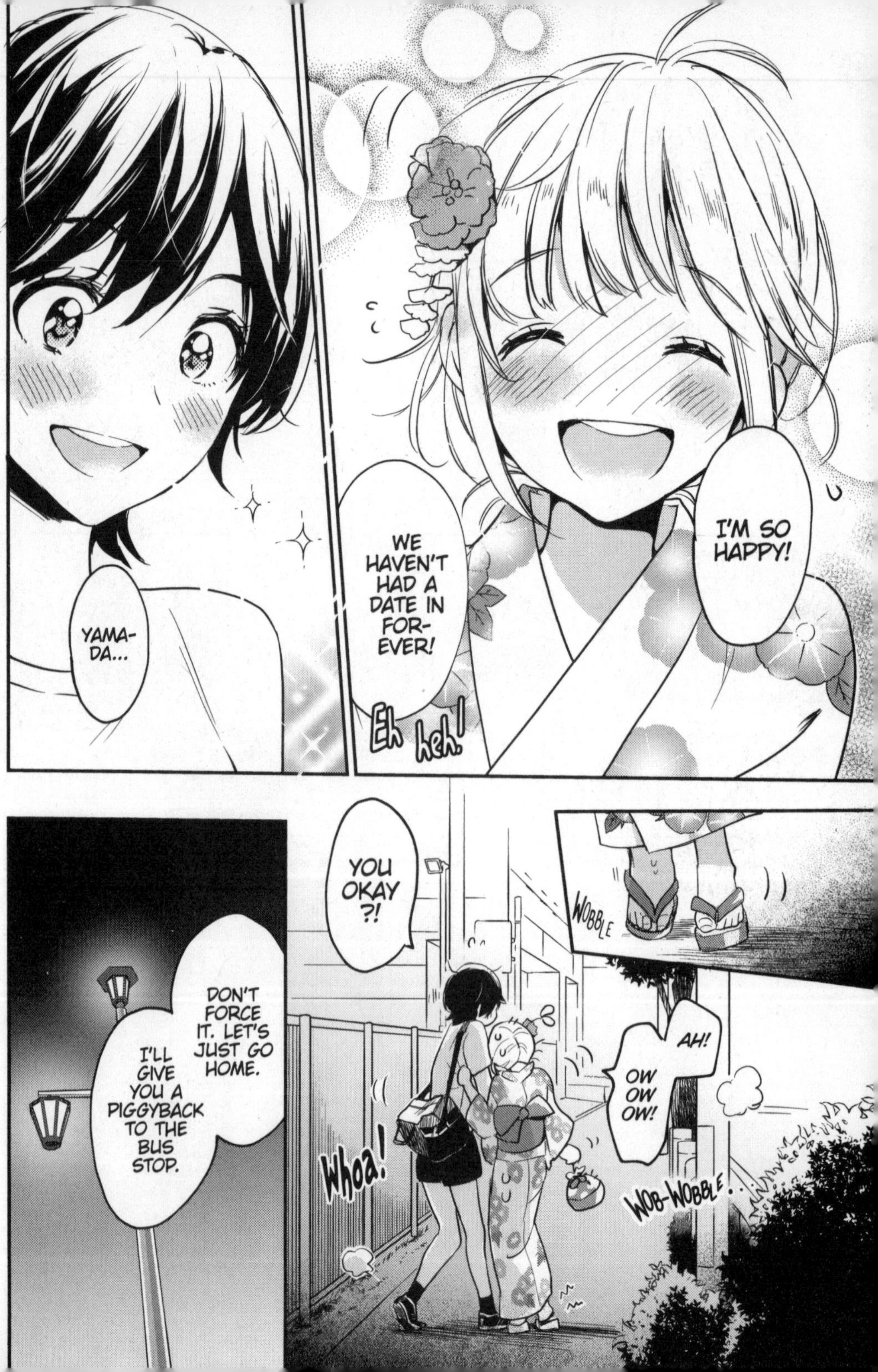
I'M SO HAPPY!
WE HAVEN'T HAD A DATE IN FOR-EVER!
Eh heh!
YAMA-DA...
WOBBLE
AH! OW OW OW!
WOB-WOBBLE...
YOU OKAY?!
Whoa!
DON'T FORCE IT. LET'S JUST GO HOME.
I'LL GIVE YOU A PIGGYBACK TO THE BUS STOP.

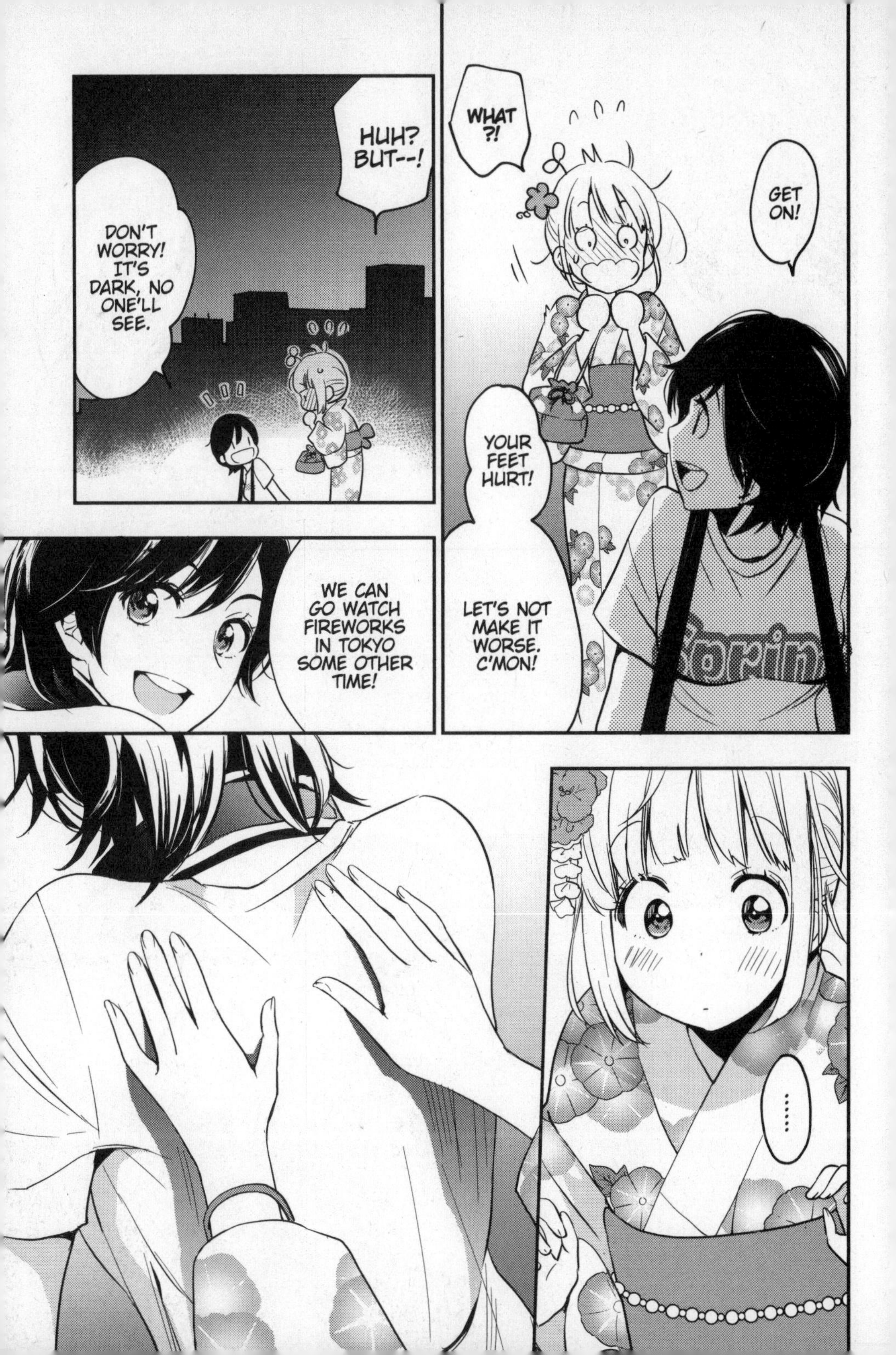

GET ON!
WHAT ?!
YOUR FEET HURT!
LET'S NOT MAKE IT WORSE. C'MON!
HUH? BUT--!
DON'T WORRY! IT'S DARK, NO ONE'LL SEE.
WE CAN GO WATCH FIREWORKS IN TOKYO SOME OTHER TIME!
......

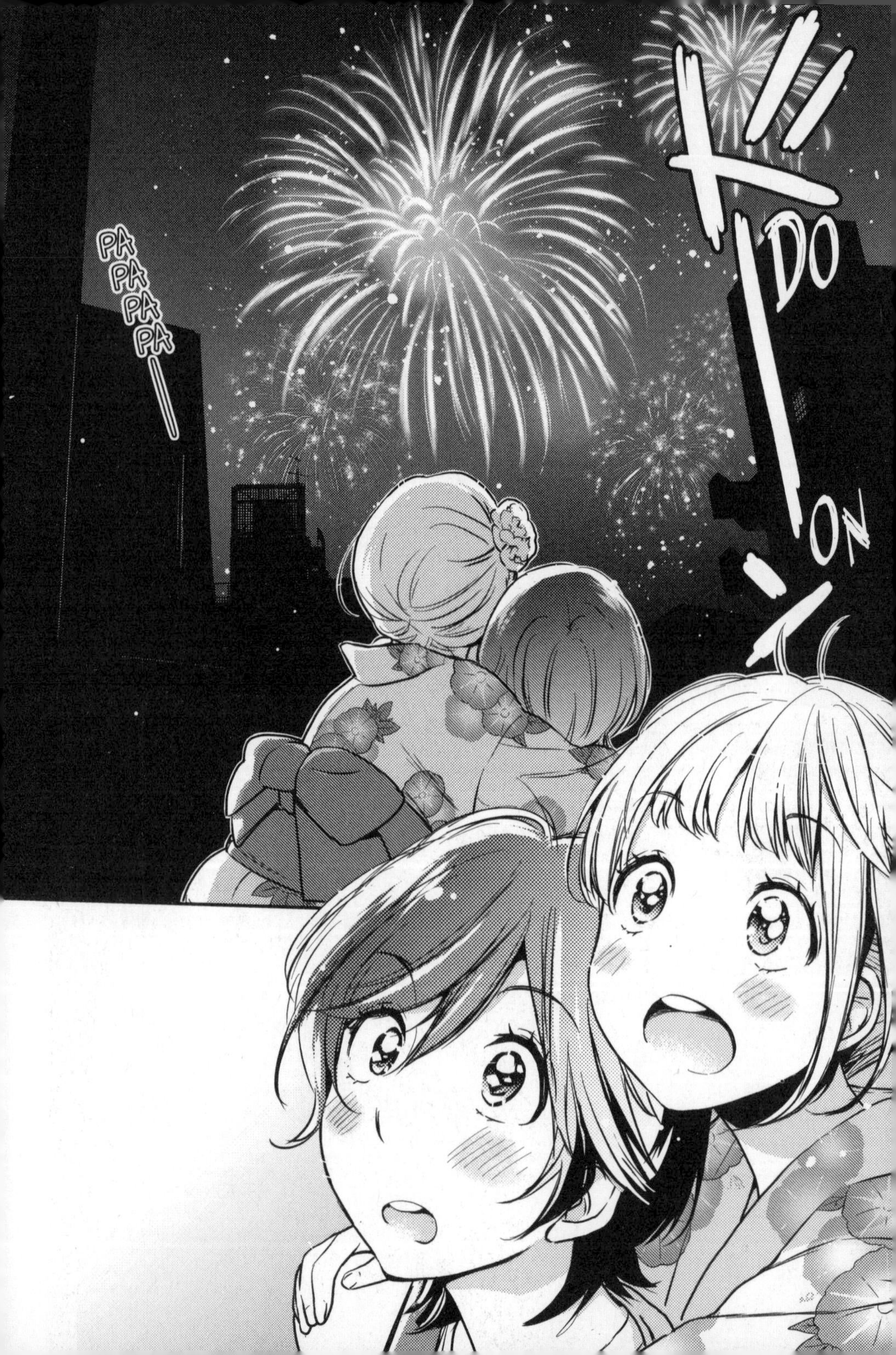
DO ON
PA PA PA PA

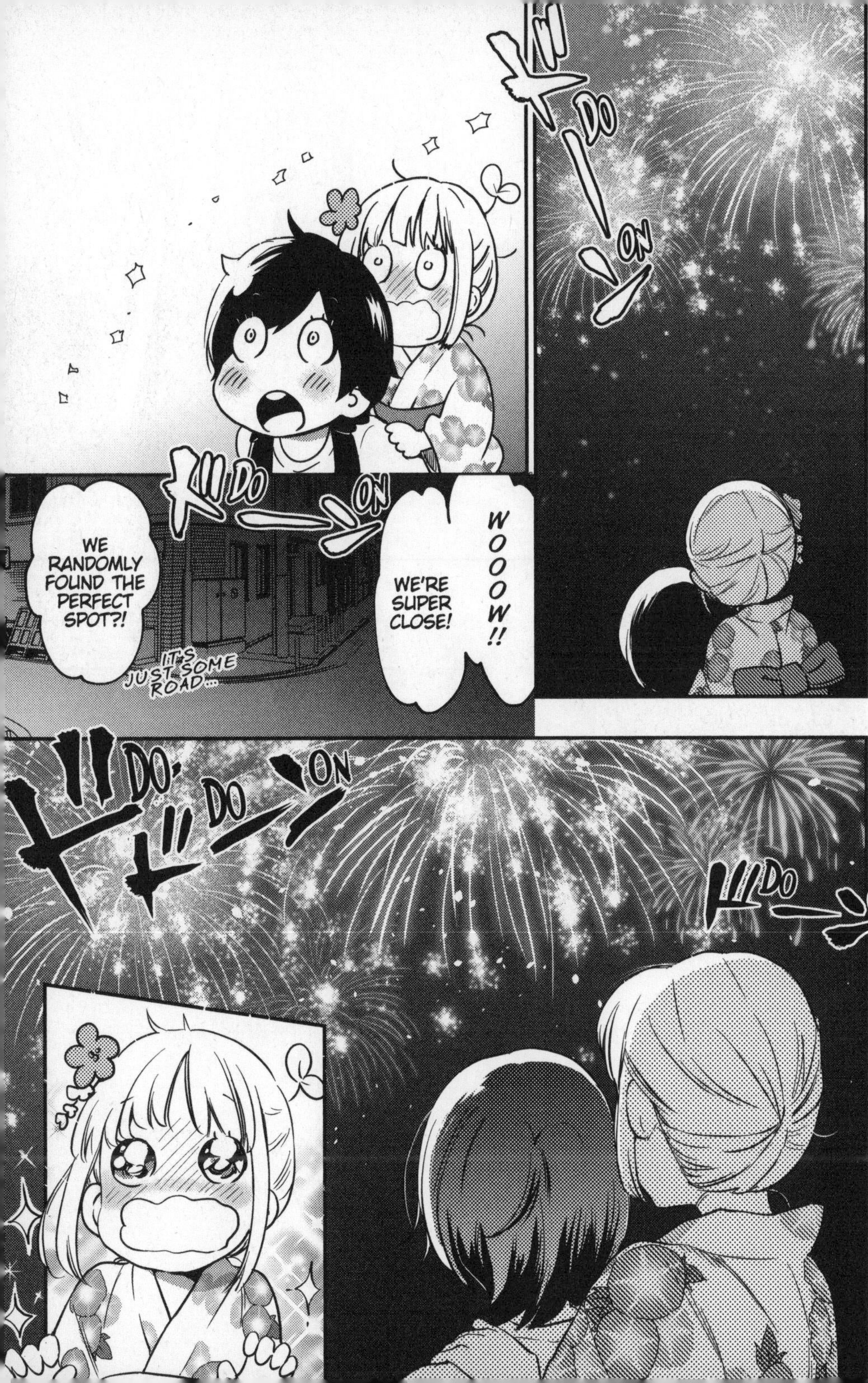
DO ON
DO ON
WOOOOW!!
WE'RE SUPER CLOSE!
WE RANDOMLY FOUND THE PERFECT SPOT?!
IT'S JUST SOME ROAD...
DO ON
DO DO ON

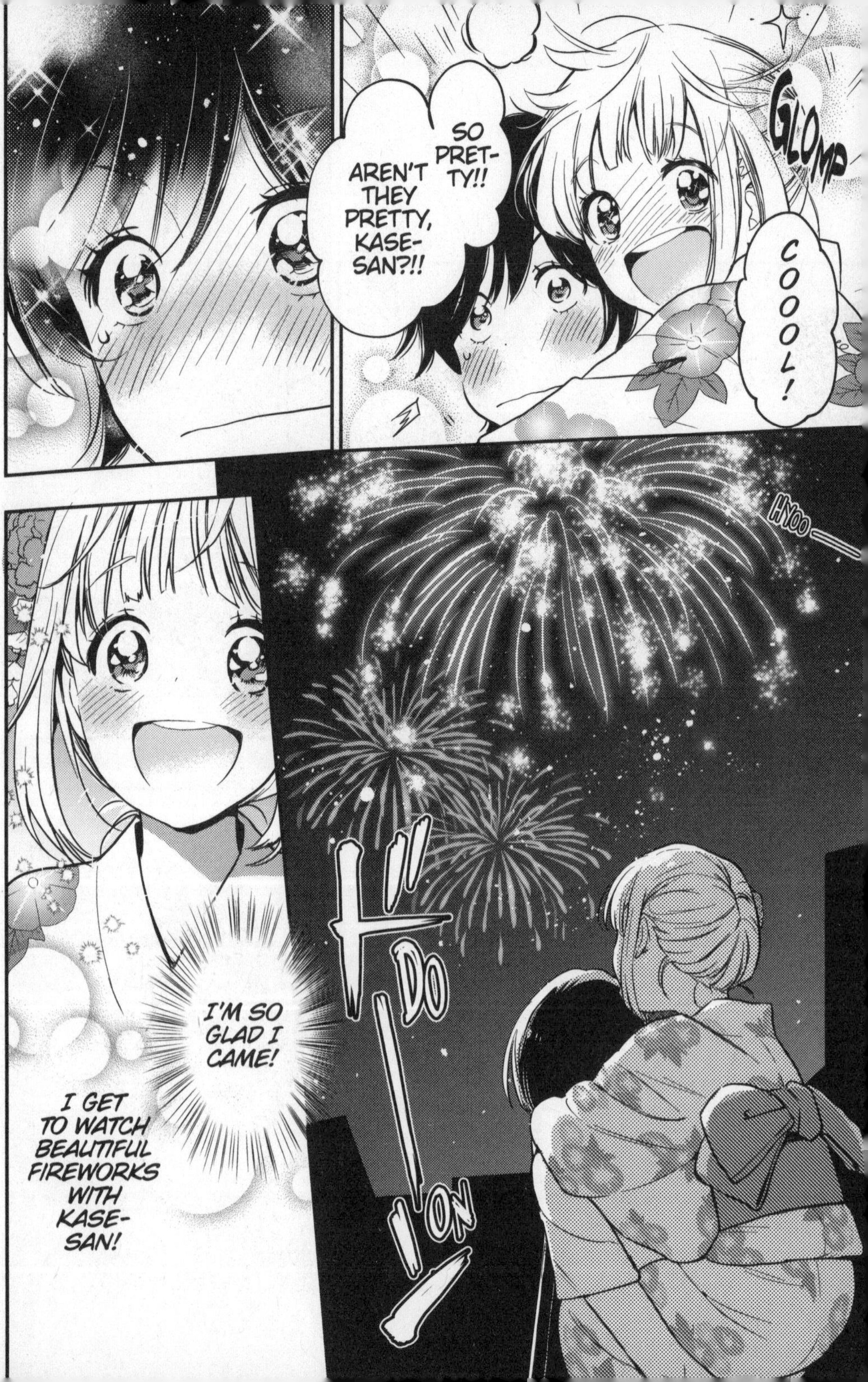
GLOMP
COOOOL!
SO PRETTY!!
AREN'T THEY PRETTY, KASE-SAN?!!
HYOO——
DOOOON
I'M SO GLAD I CAME!
I GET TO WATCH BEAUTIFUL FIREWORKS WITH KASE-SAN!

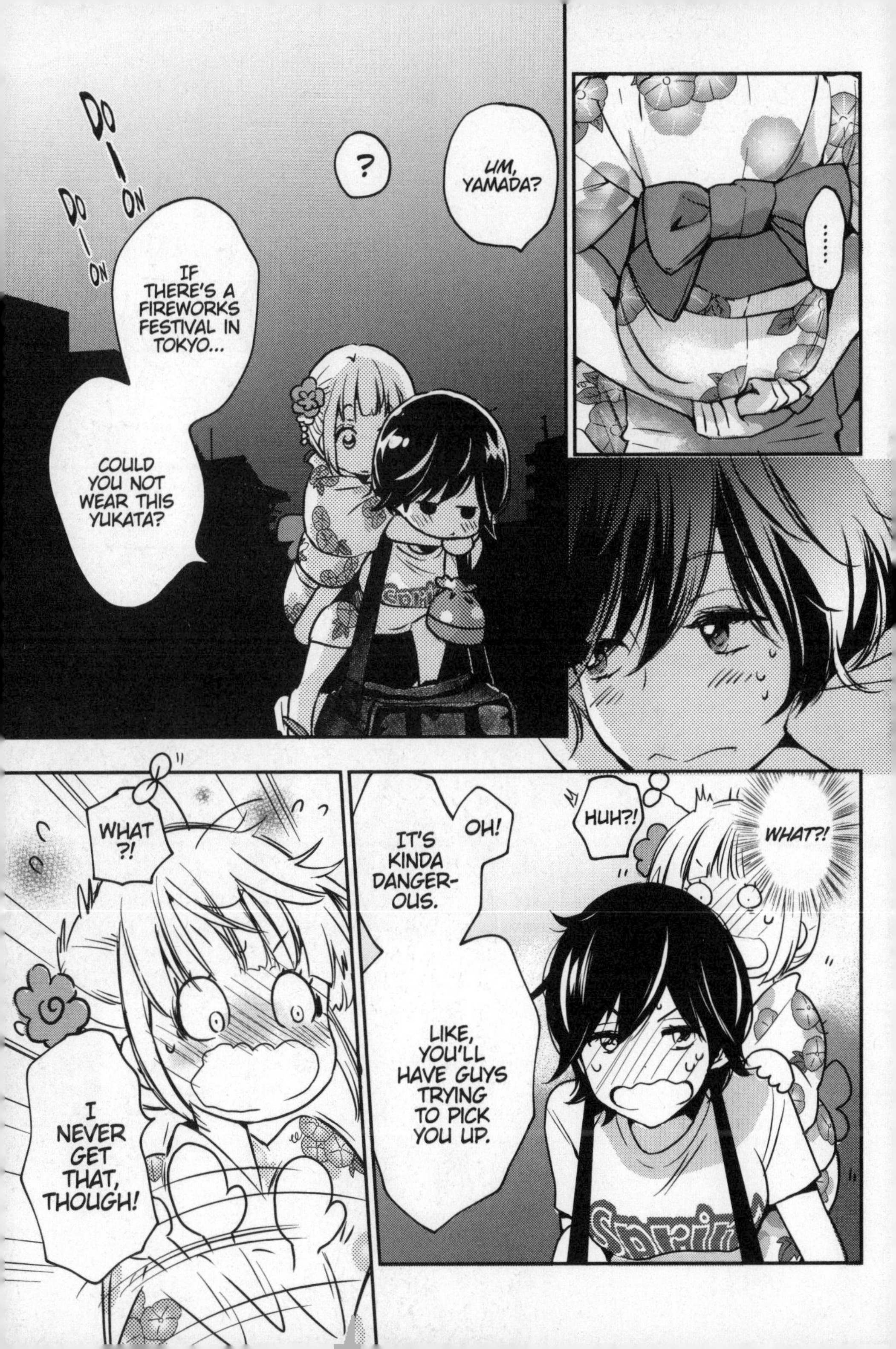

......
UM, YAMADA?
?
DO I ON
DO I ON
IF THERE'S A FIREWORKS FESTIVAL IN TOKYO...
COULD YOU NOT WEAR THIS YUKATA?
WHAT?!
HUH?!
OH!
IT'S KINDA DANGER-OUS.
LIKE, YOU'LL HAVE GUYS TRYING TO PICK YOU UP.
WHAT ?!
I NEVER GET THAT, THOUGH!

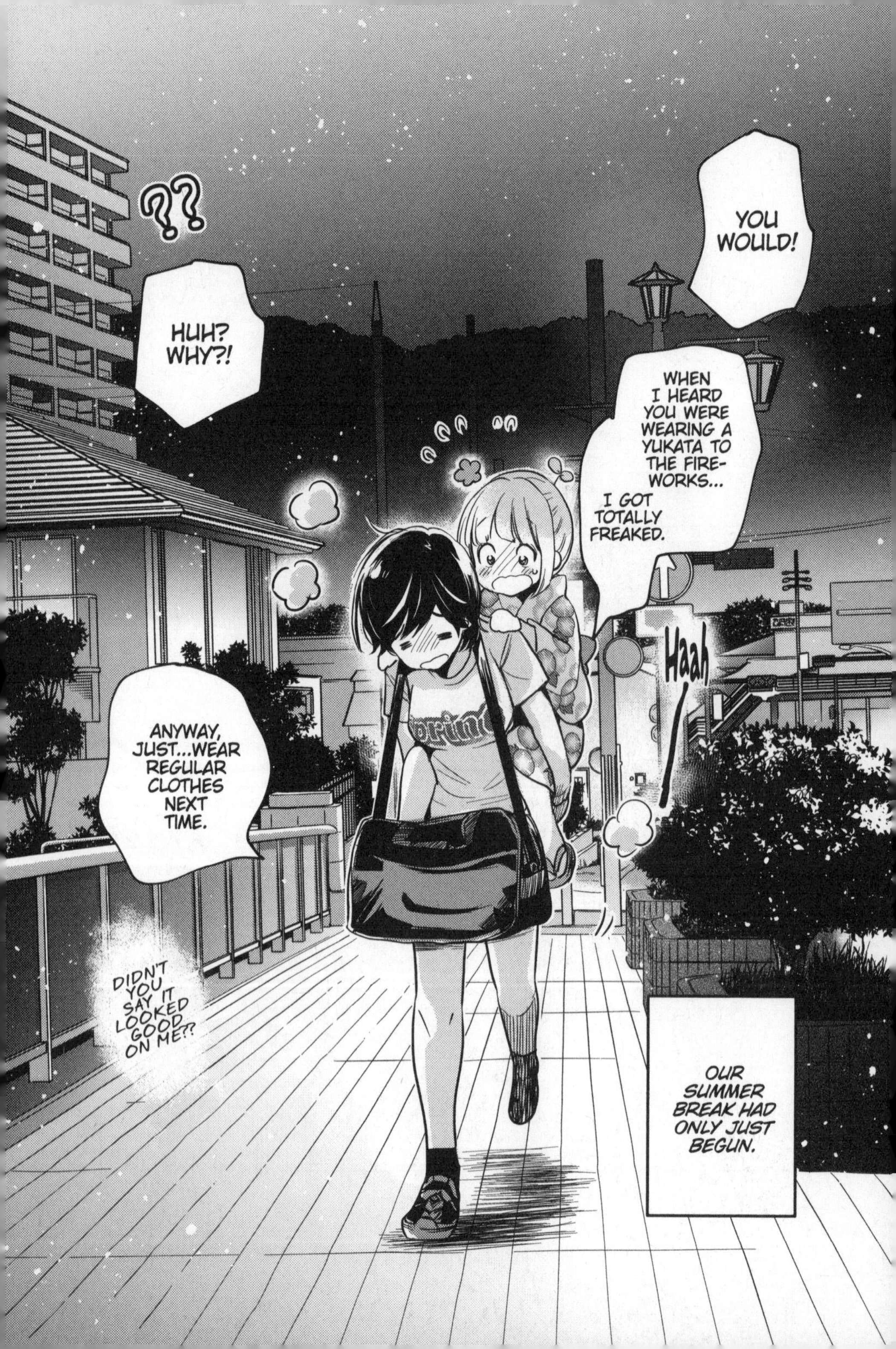
YOU WOULD!
??
HUH? WHY?!
WHEN I HEARD YOU WERE WEARING A YUKATA TO THE FIRE-WORKS... I GOT TOTALLY FREAKED.
Haah
ANYWAY, JUST...WEAR REGULAR CLOTHES NEXT TIME.
DIDN'T YOU SAY IT LOOKED GOOD ON ME??
OUR SUMMER BREAK HAD ONLY JUST BEGUN.

# Kase-san and Bubble Tea

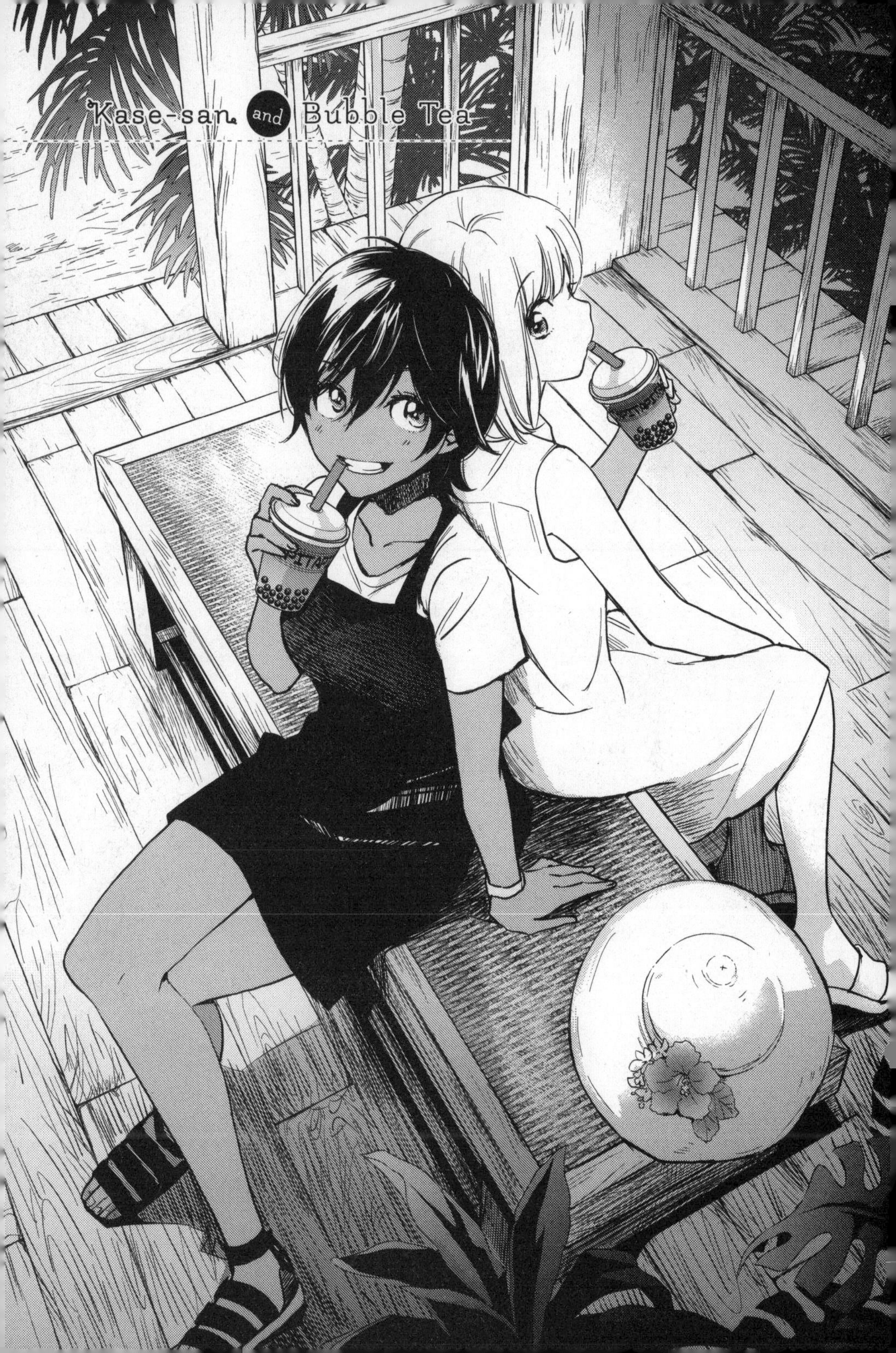

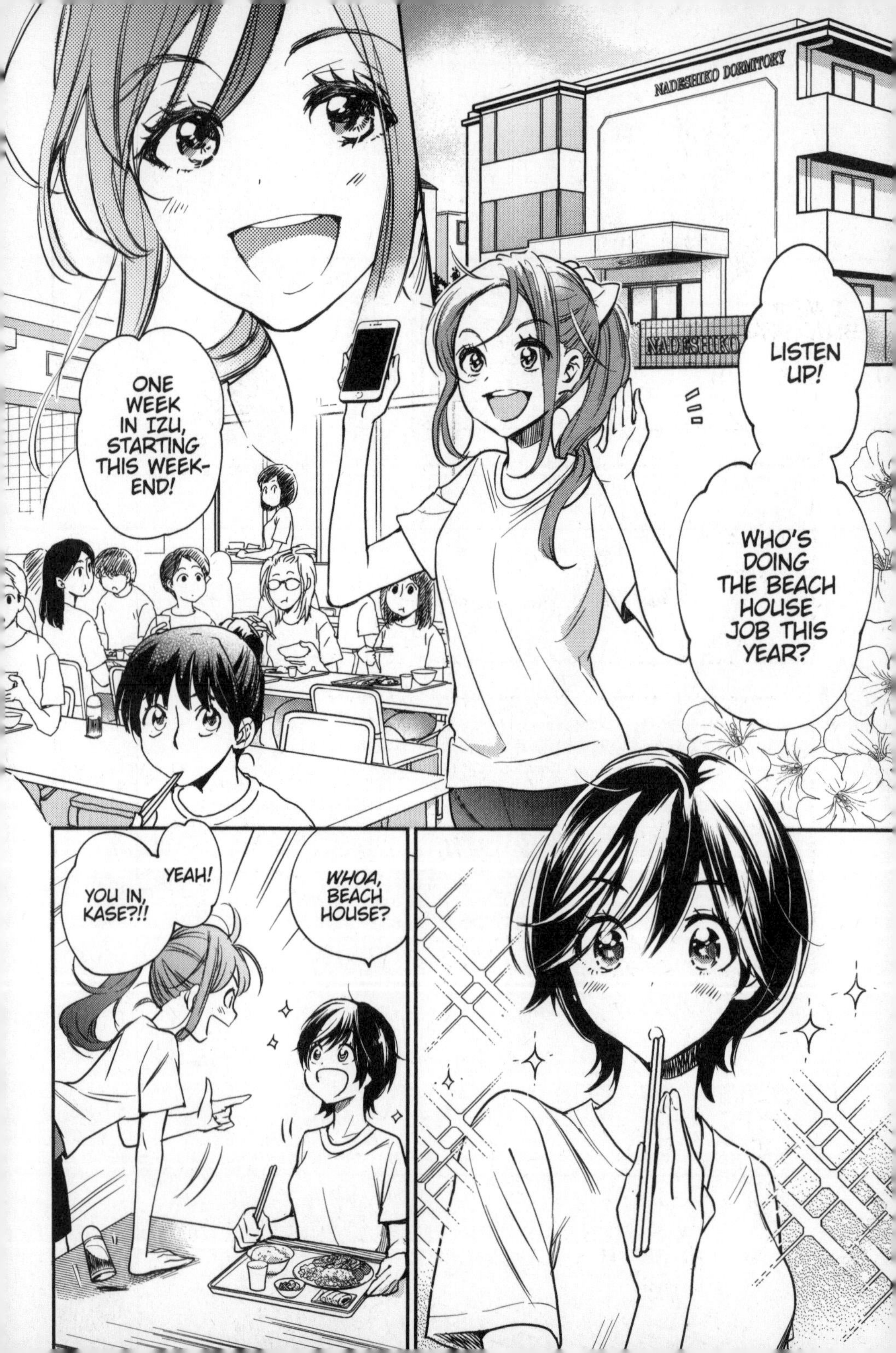
NADESHIKO DORMITORY
NADESHIKO
LISTEN UP!
WHO'S DOING THE BEACH HOUSE JOB THIS YEAR?
ONE WEEK IN IZU, STARTING THIS WEEK-END!
WHOA, BEACH HOUSE?
YEAH! YOU IN, KASE?!!

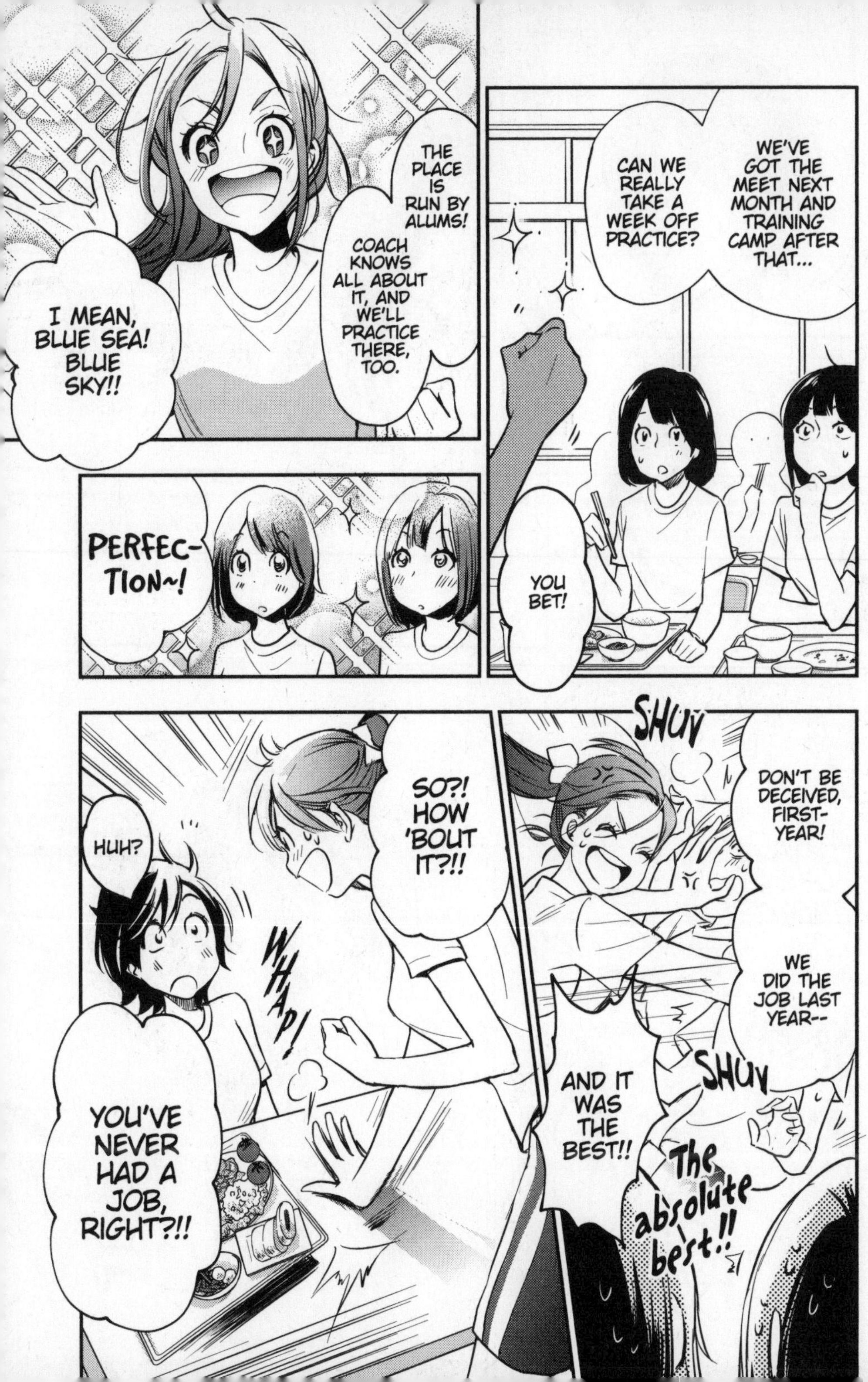
WE'VE GOT THE MEET NEXT MONTH AND TRAINING CAMP AFTER THAT...
CAN WE REALLY TAKE A WEEK OFF PRACTICE?
YOU BET!
THE PLACE IS RUN BY ALUMS!
COACH KNOWS ALL ABOUT IT, AND WE'LL PRACTICE THERE, TOO.
I MEAN, BLUE SEA! BLUE SKY!!
PERFECTION~!
SHUV
DON'T BE DECEIVED, FIRST-YEAR!
WE DID THE JOB LAST YEAR--
AND IT WAS THE BEST!!
SHUV
The absolute best!!
SO?! HOW 'BOUT IT?!!
HUH?
WHAP!
YOU'VE NEVER HAD A JOB, RIGHT?!!

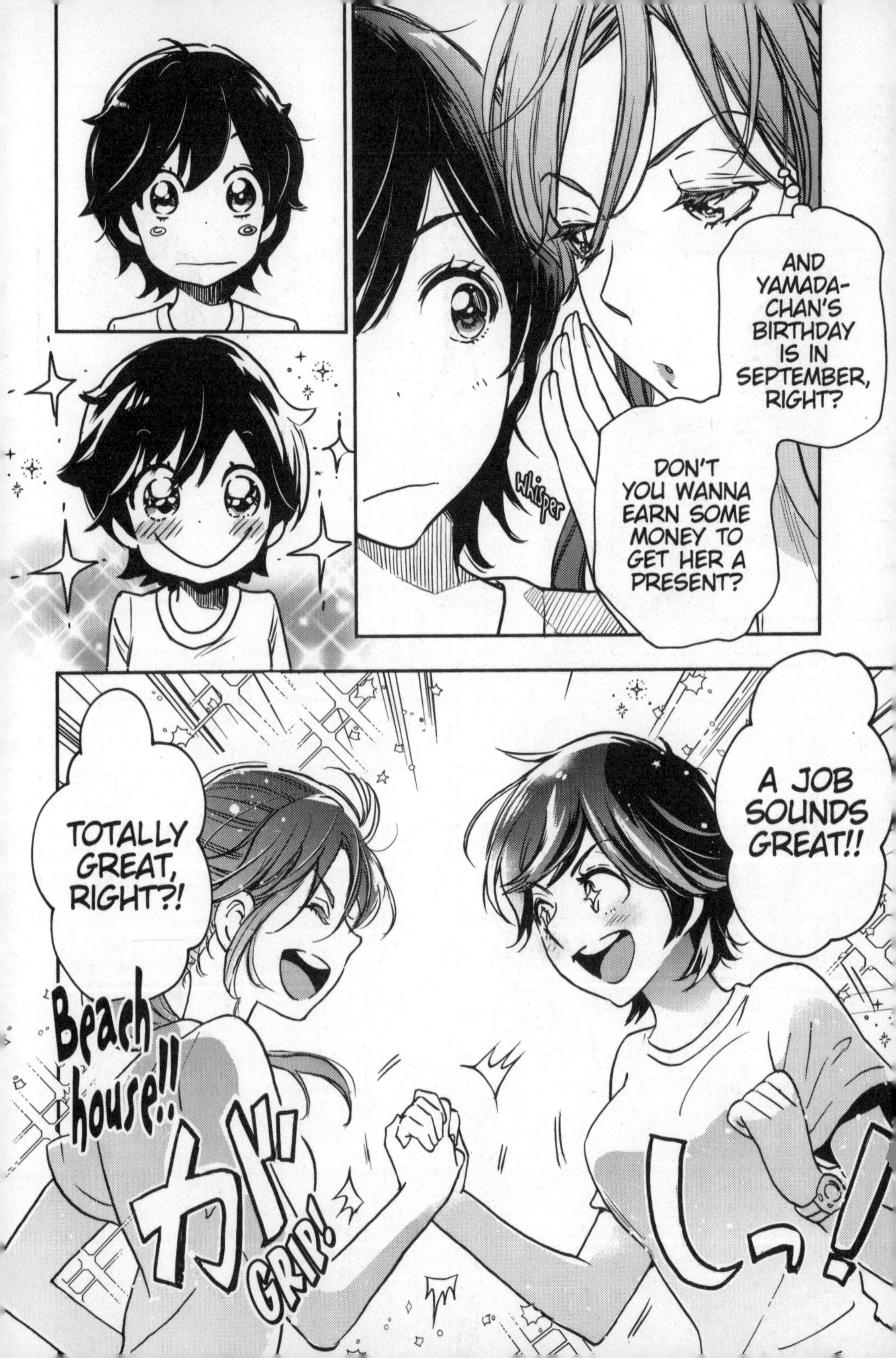

AND YAMADA-CHAN'S BIRTHDAY IS IN SEPTEMBER, RIGHT?
whisper
DON'T YOU WANNA EARN SOME MONEY TO GET HER A PRESENT?
A JOB SOUNDS GREAT!!
TOTALLY GREAT, RIGHT?!
Beach house!!
GRIP!

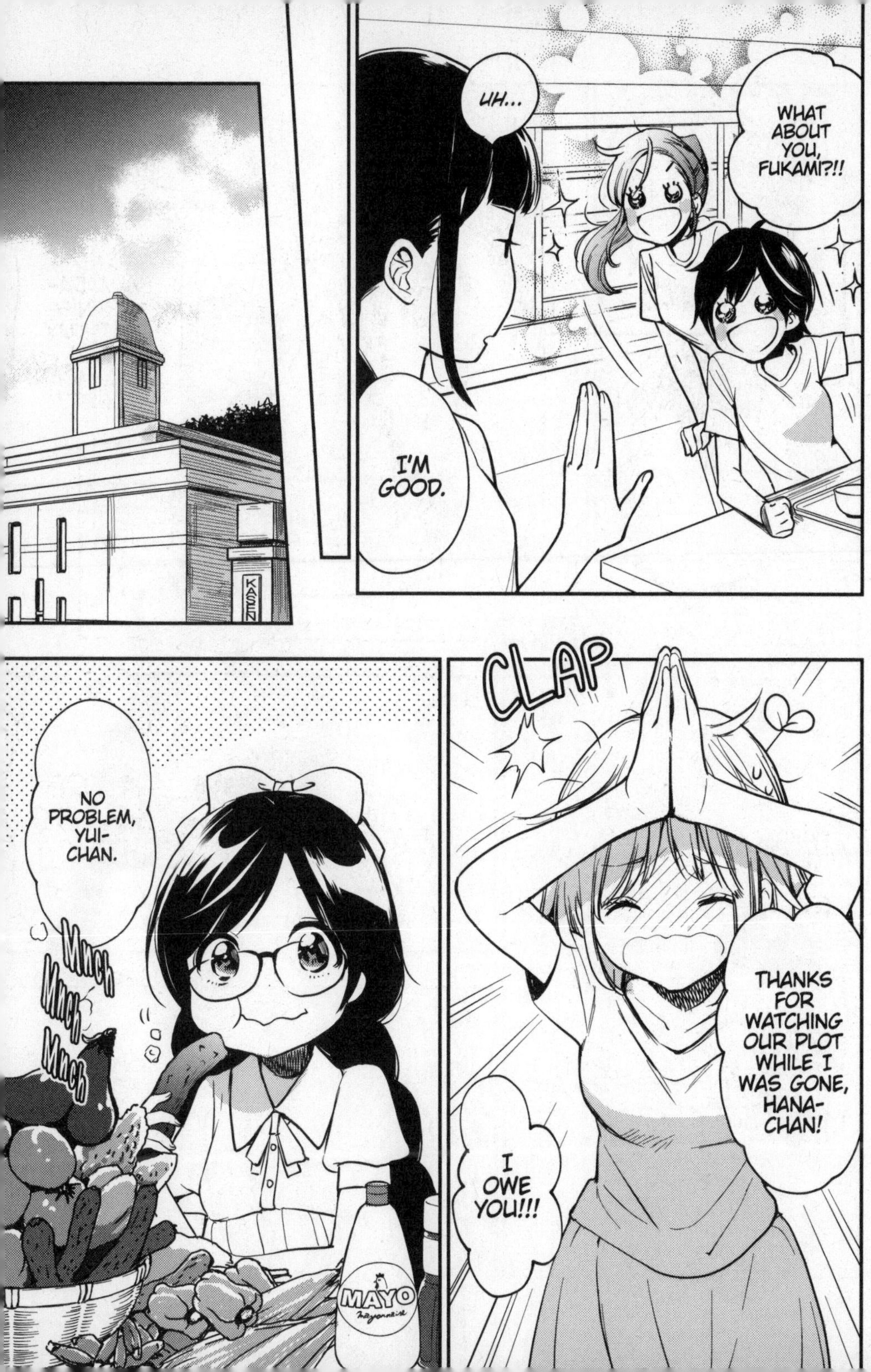
WHAT ABOUT YOU, FUKAMI?!!
UH...
I'M GOOD.
KASEN
CLAP
THANKS FOR WATCHING OUR PLOT WHILE I WAS GONE, HANA-CHAN!
I OWE YOU!!!
NO PROBLEM, YUI-CHAN.
Mnch
Mnch
Mnch
MAYO

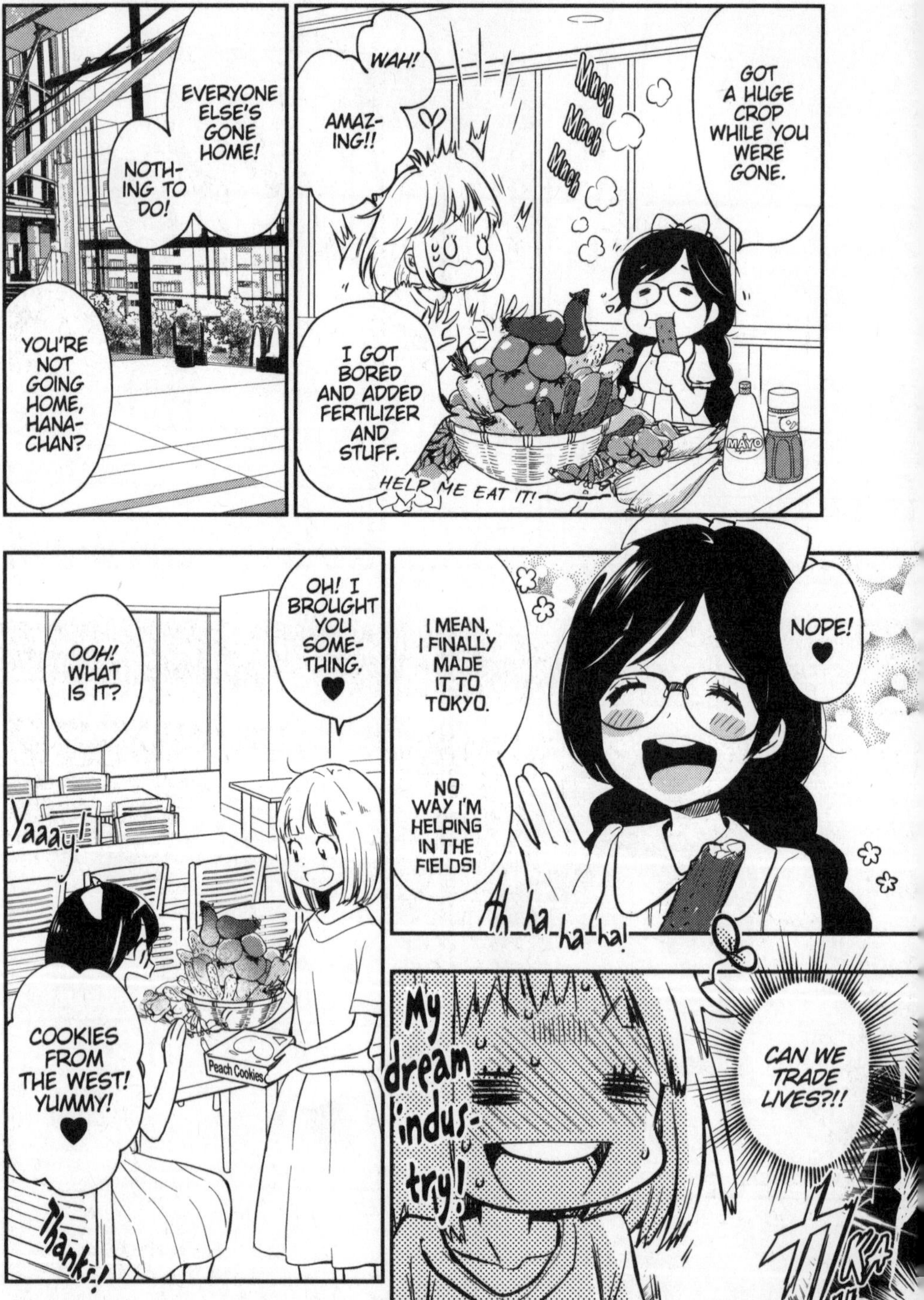
GOT A HUGE CROP WHILE YOU WERE GONE.
Munch Munch Munch
WAH!
AMAZ-ING!!
I GOT BORED AND ADDED FERTILIZER AND STUFF.
HELP ME EAT IT!
MAYO
EVERYONE ELSE'S GONE HOME!
NOTH-ING TO DO!
YOU'RE NOT GOING HOME, HANA-CHAN?
NOPE! ♥
I MEAN, I FINALLY MADE IT TO TOKYO.
NO WAY I'M HELPING IN THE FIELDS!
Ah ha-ha-ha!
CAN WE TRADE LIVES?!!
My dream indus-try!
OH! I BROUGHT YOU SOME-THING. ♥
OOH! WHAT IS IT?
Yaaay!
COOKIES FROM THE WEST! YUMMY! ♥
Peach Cookies
Thanks!

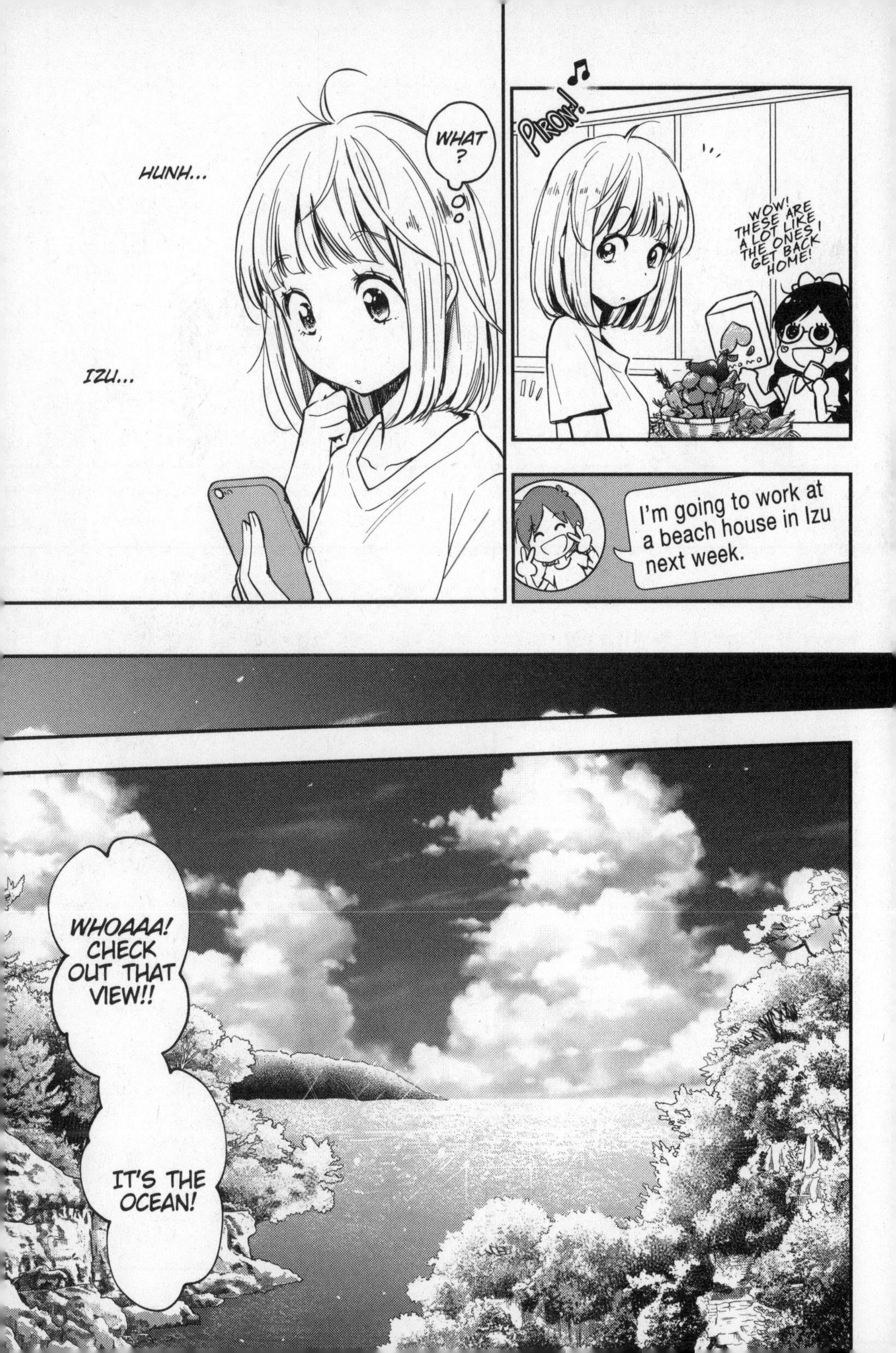
PIRON!
WOW! THESE ARE A LOT LIKE THE ONES I GET BACK HOME!
I'm going to work at a beach house in Izu next week.
WHAT?
HUNH...
IZU...
WHOAAA! CHECK OUT THAT VIEW!!
IT'S THE OCEAN!

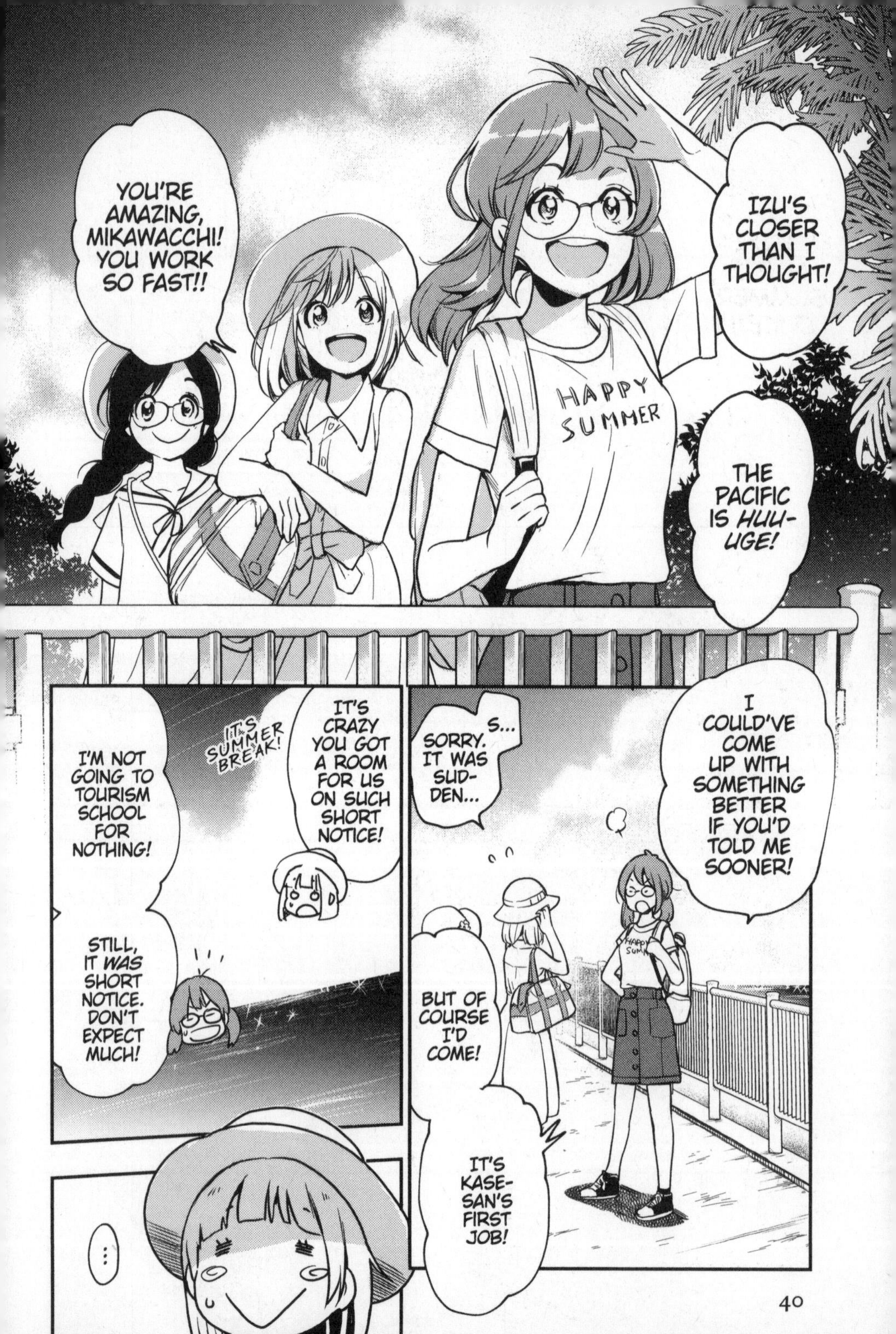
IZU'S CLOSER THAN I THOUGHT!
THE PACIFIC IS *HUU-UGE!*
YOU'RE AMAZING, MIKAWACCHI! YOU WORK SO FAST!!
I COULD'VE COME UP WITH SOMETHING BETTER IF YOU'D TOLD ME SOONER!
S... SORRY. IT WAS SUD-DEN...
BUT OF COURSE I'D COME!
IT'S KASE-SAN'S FIRST JOB!
HAPPY SUMMER
IT'S CRAZY YOU GOT A ROOM FOR US ON SUCH SHORT NOTICE!
IT'S SUMMER BREAK!
I'M NOT GOING TO TOURISM SCHOOL FOR NOTHING!
STILL, IT *WAS* SHORT NOTICE. DON'T EXPECT MUCH!
…

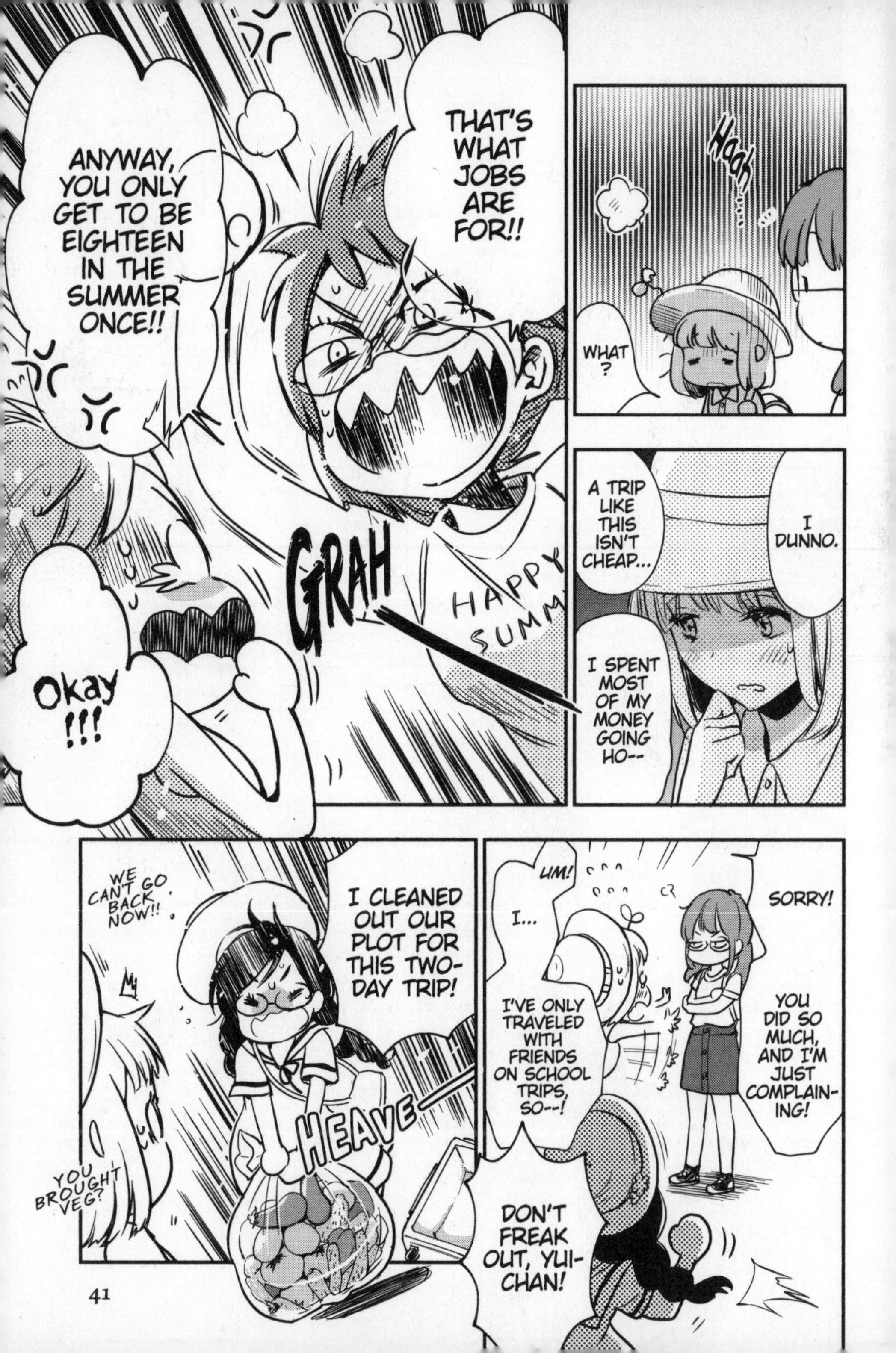
Haah...
WHAT?
I DUNNO.
A TRIP LIKE THIS ISN'T CHEAP...
I SPENT MOST OF MY MONEY GOING HO--
THAT'S WHAT JOBS ARE FOR!!
ANYWAY, YOU ONLY GET TO BE EIGHTEEN IN THE SUMMER ONCE!!
GRAH
HAPPY SUMM
Okay!!!
SORRY!
YOU DID SO MUCH, AND I'M JUST COMPLAINING!
UM!
I...
I'VE ONLY TRAVELED WITH FRIENDS ON SCHOOL TRIPS, SO--!
DON'T FREAK OUT, YUI-CHAN!
I CLEANED OUT OUR PLOT FOR THIS TWO-DAY TRIP!
WE CAN'T GO BACK NOW!!
HEAVE
YOU BROUGHT VEG?

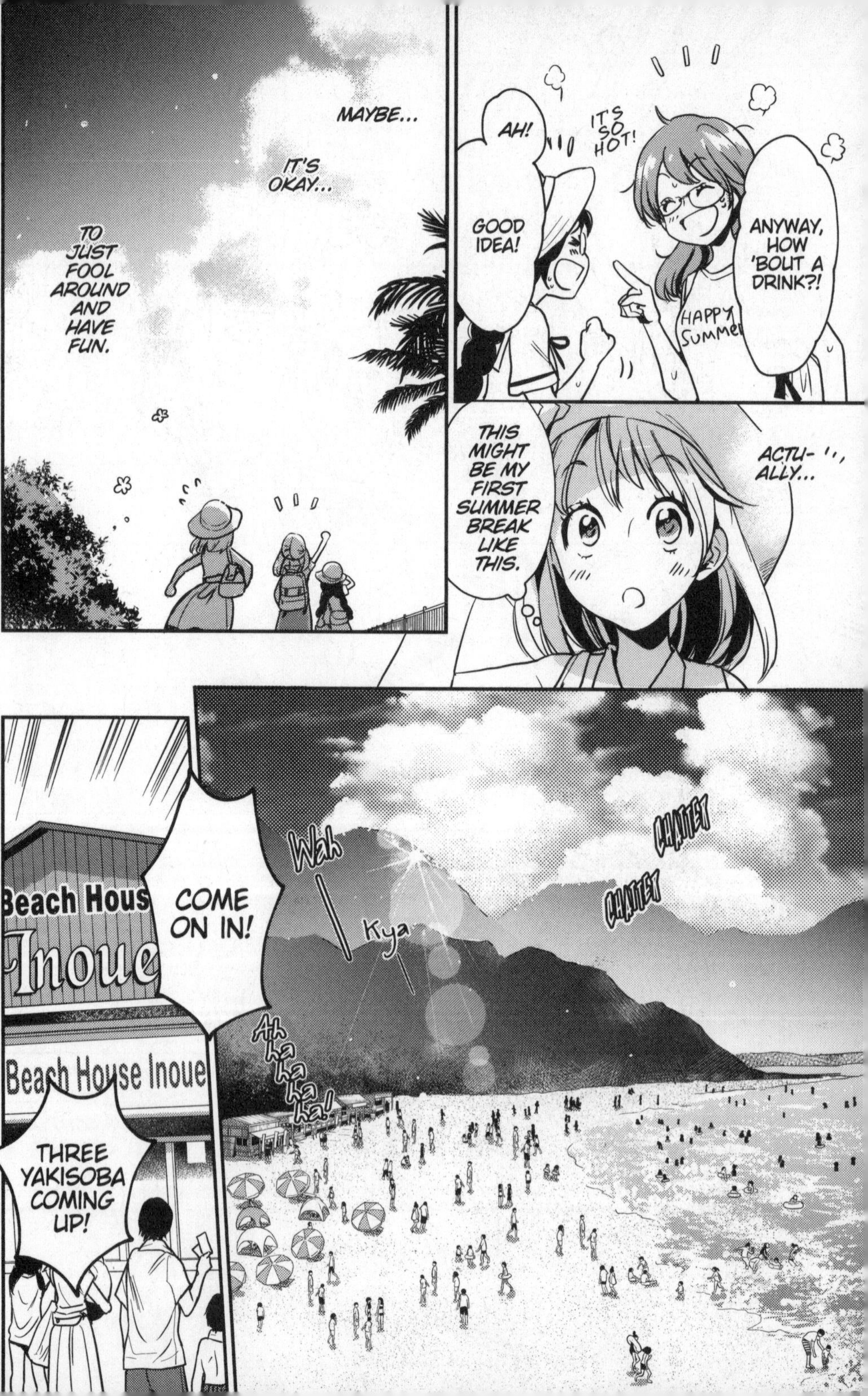
ANYWAY, HOW 'BOUT A DRINK?!
HAPPY Summe
IT'S SO HOT!
AH!
GOOD IDEA!
ACTU-ALLY...
THIS MIGHT BE MY FIRST SUMMER BREAK LIKE THIS.
MAYBE...
IT'S OKAY...
TO JUST FOOL AROUND AND HAVE FUN.
CHATTER
CHATTER
Wah
Kya
Ahahahaha!
Beach Hous
Inoue
COME ON IN!
Beach House Inoue
THREE YAKISOBA COMING UP!

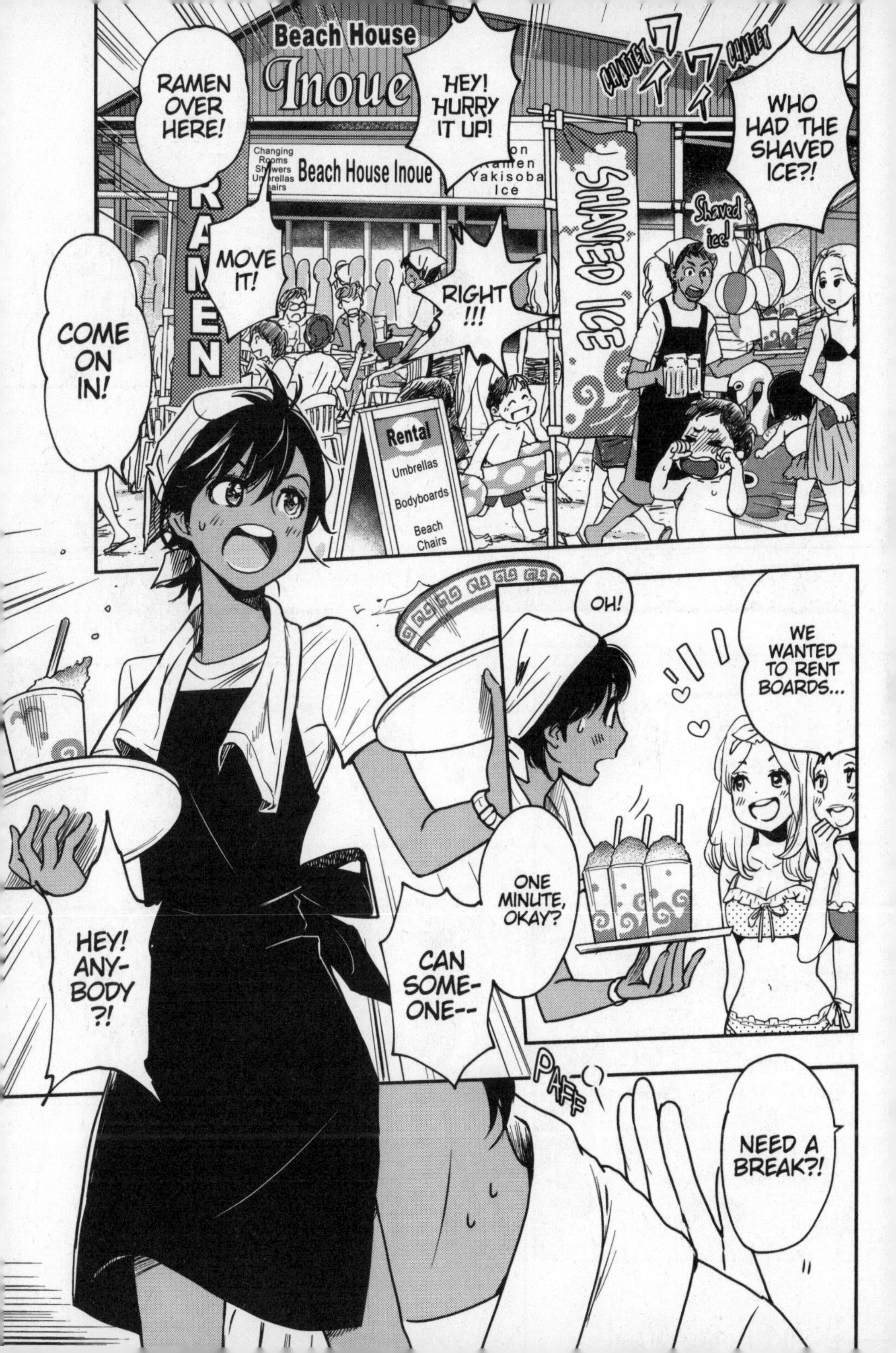
Beach House
Inoue
CHATTER
CHATTER
WHO HAD THE SHAVED ICE?!
Shaved ice!
SHAVED ICE
HEY! HURRY IT UP!
Yakisoba
Ice
Beach House Inoue
RAMEN OVER HERE!
RAMEN
RIGHT!!!
MOVE IT!
COME ON IN!
Rental
Umbrellas
Bodyboards
Beach Chairs
WE WANTED TO RENT BOARDS...
OH!
ONE MINUTE, OKAY?
CAN SOME-ONE--
HEY! ANY-BODY?!
PAFF
NEED A BREAK?!

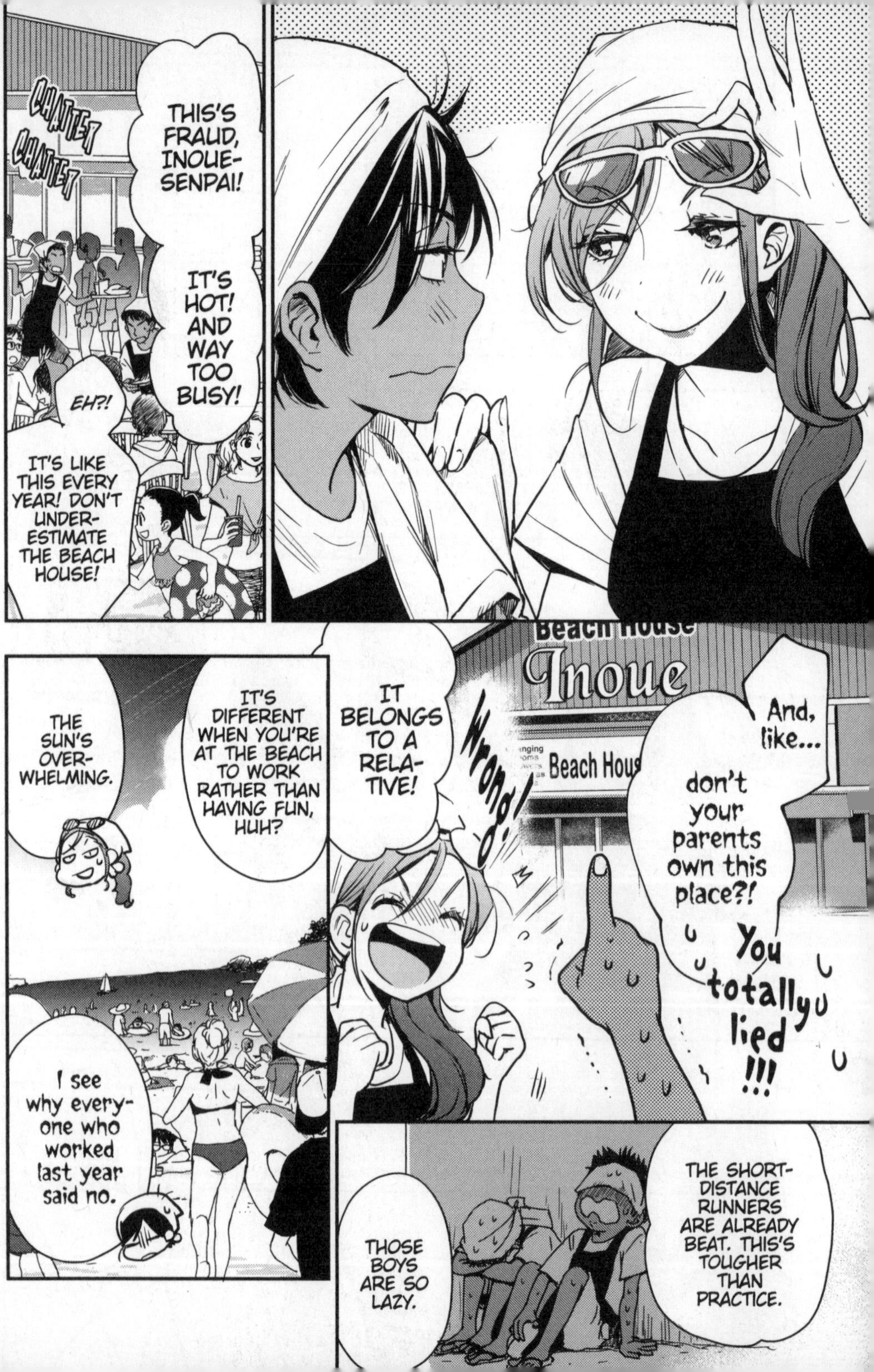
CHATTER CHATTER
THIS'S FRAUD, INOUE-SENPAI!
IT'S HOT! AND WAY TOO BUSY!
EH?!
IT'S LIKE THIS EVERY YEAR! DON'T UNDER-ESTIMATE THE BEACH HOUSE!
Beach House Inoue
Beach House
And, like...
don't your parents own this place?!
You totally lied!!!
Wrong!
IT BELONGS TO A RELATIVE!
THE SHORT-DISTANCE RUNNERS ARE ALREADY BEAT. THIS'S TOUGHER THAN PRACTICE.
THOSE BOYS ARE SO LAZY.
IT'S DIFFERENT WHEN YOU'RE AT THE BEACH TO WORK RATHER THAN HAVING FUN, HUH?
THE SUN'S OVER-WHELMING.
I see why every-one who worked last year said no.

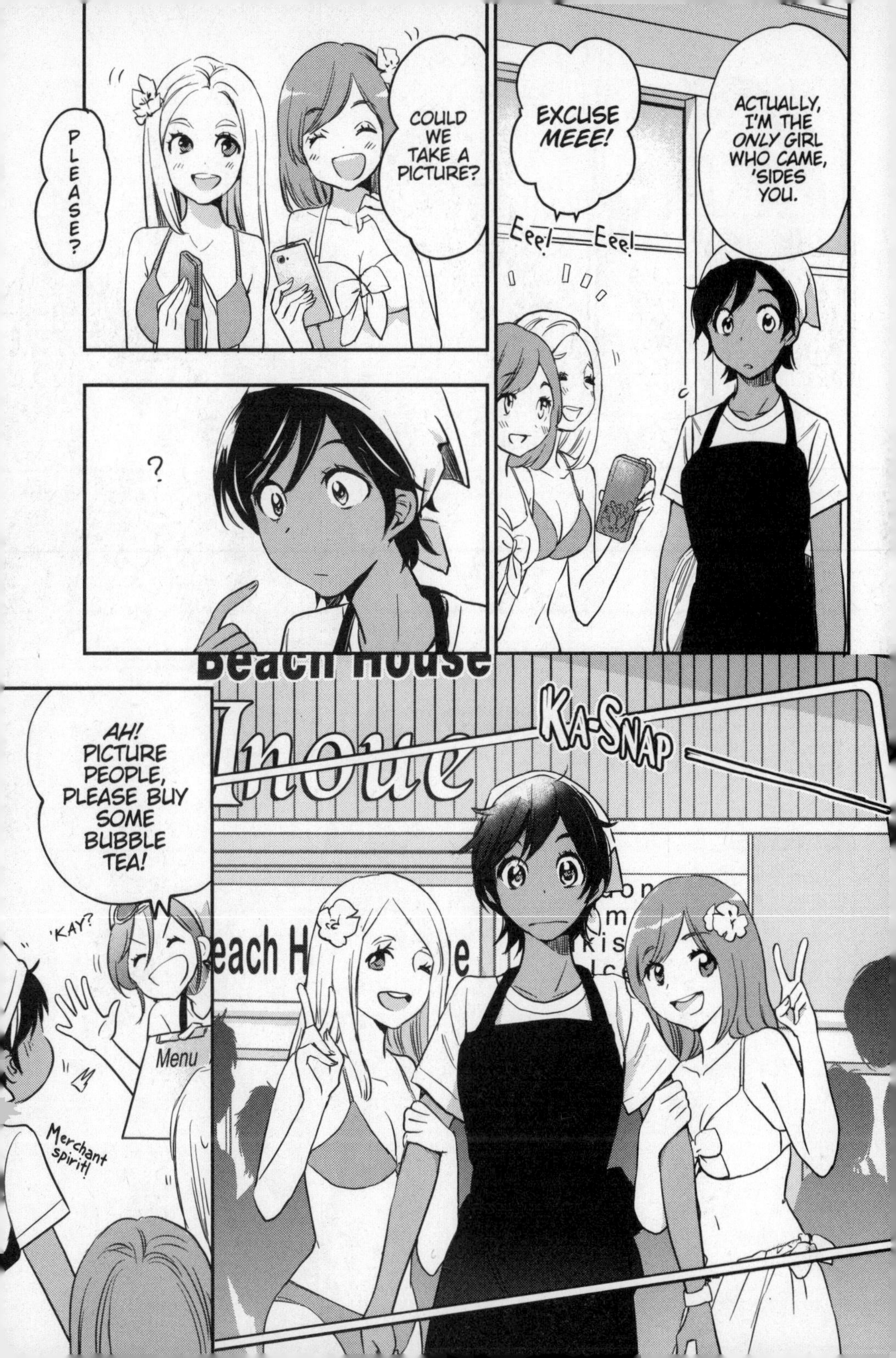
ACTUALLY, I'M THE ONLY GIRL WHO CAME, 'SIDES YOU.
EXCUSE MEEE!
Eee! Eee!
COULD WE TAKE A PICTURE?
PLEASE?
?
Beach House
Inoue
KA-SNAP
AH! PICTURE PEOPLE, PLEASE BUY SOME BUBBLE TEA!
'KAY?
Menu
Merchant spirit!

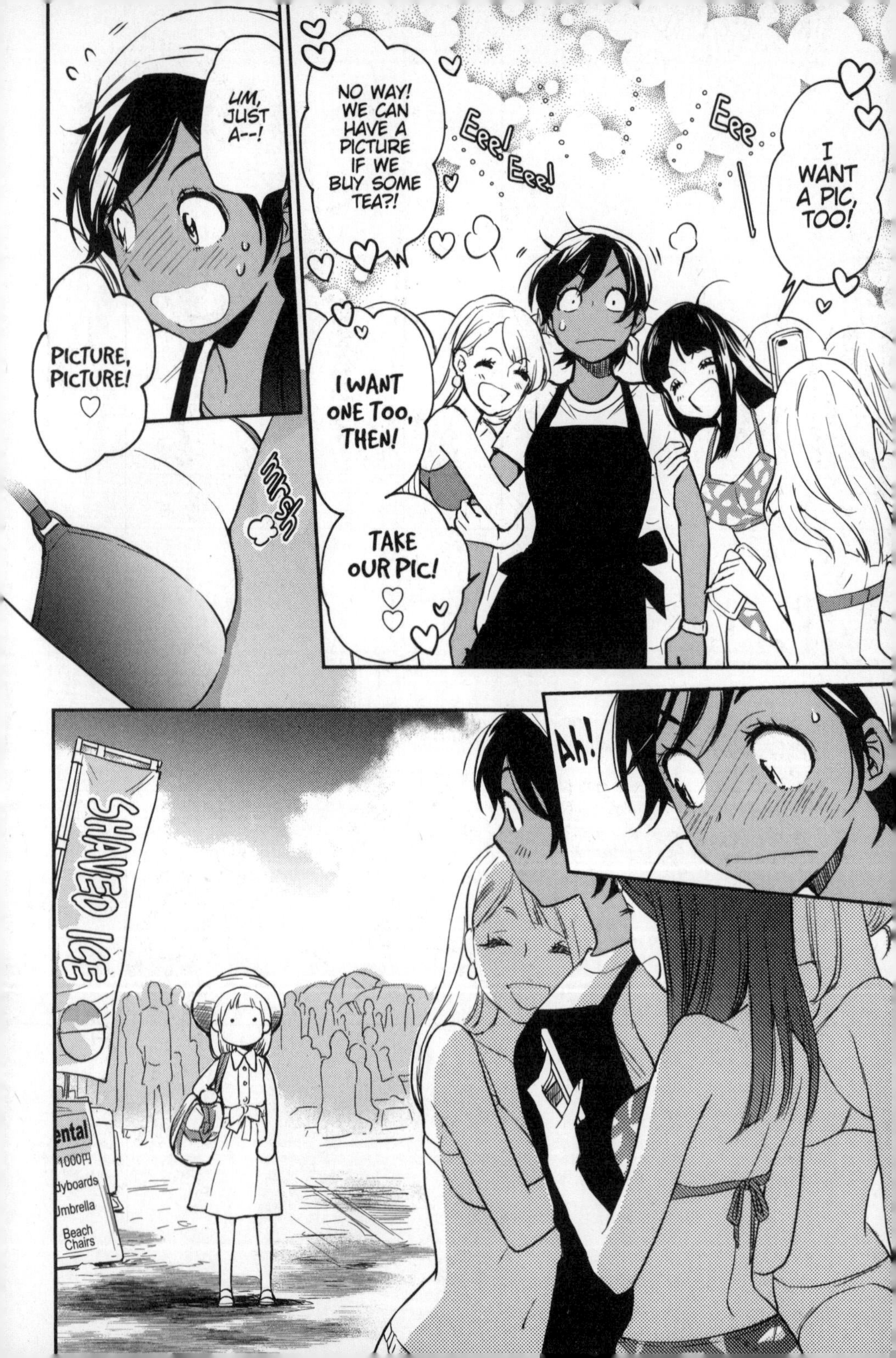
I WANT A PIC, TOO!
Eee
Eee! Eee!
NO WAY! WE CAN HAVE A PICTURE IF WE BUY SOME TEA?!
I WANT ONE TOO, THEN!
TAKE OUR PIC!
UM, JUST A--!
PICTURE, PICTURE!
mrsh
Ah!
SHAVED ICE
1000円
Umbrella
Beach Chairs

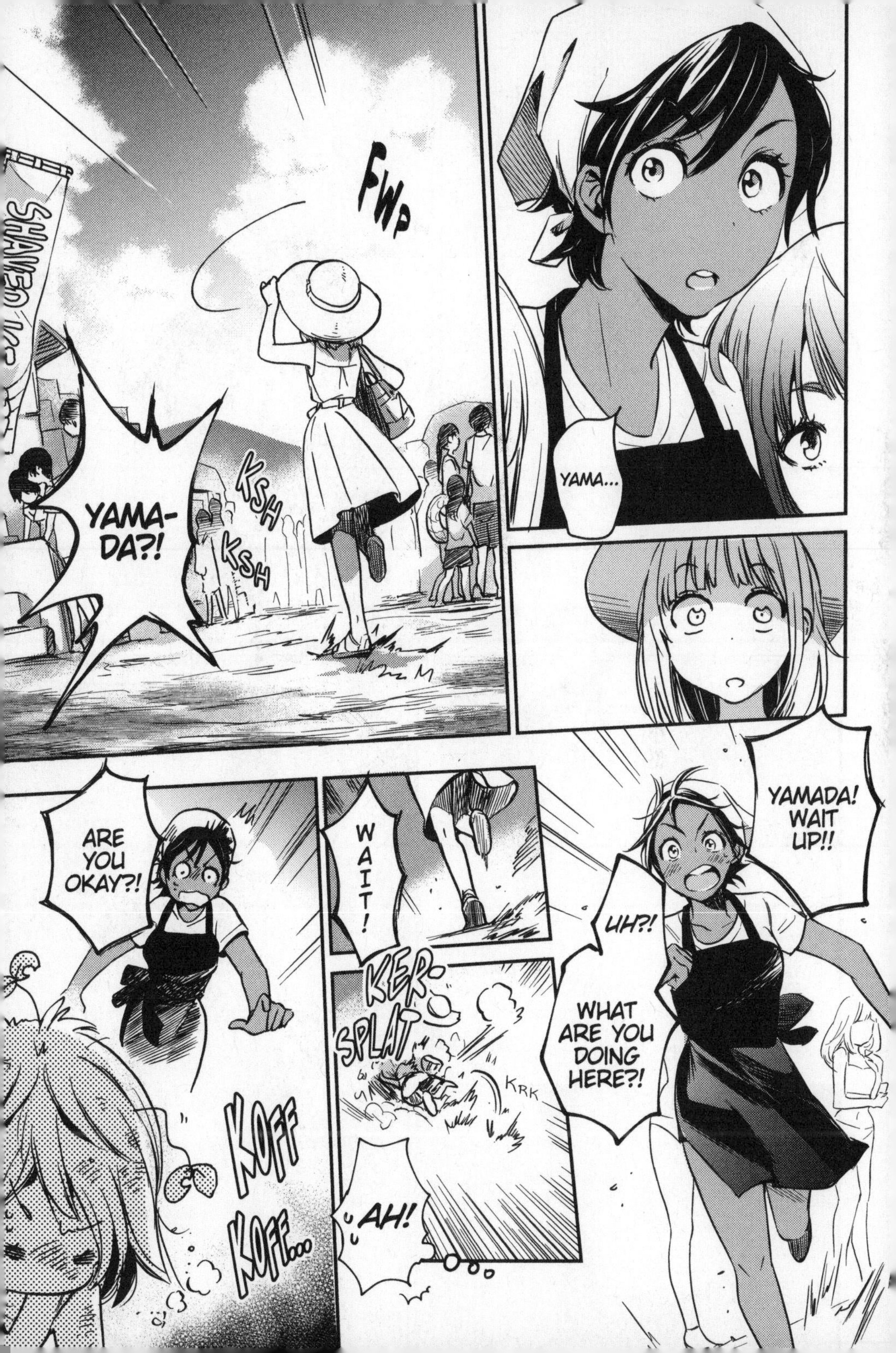
YAMA...
FWP
SHAVED
YAMA-DA?!
KSH
KSH
YAMADA! WAIT UP!!
UH?!
WHAT ARE YOU DOING HERE?!
WAIT!
KER-SPLAT
KRK
AH!
ARE YOU OKAY?!
KOFF
KOFF...

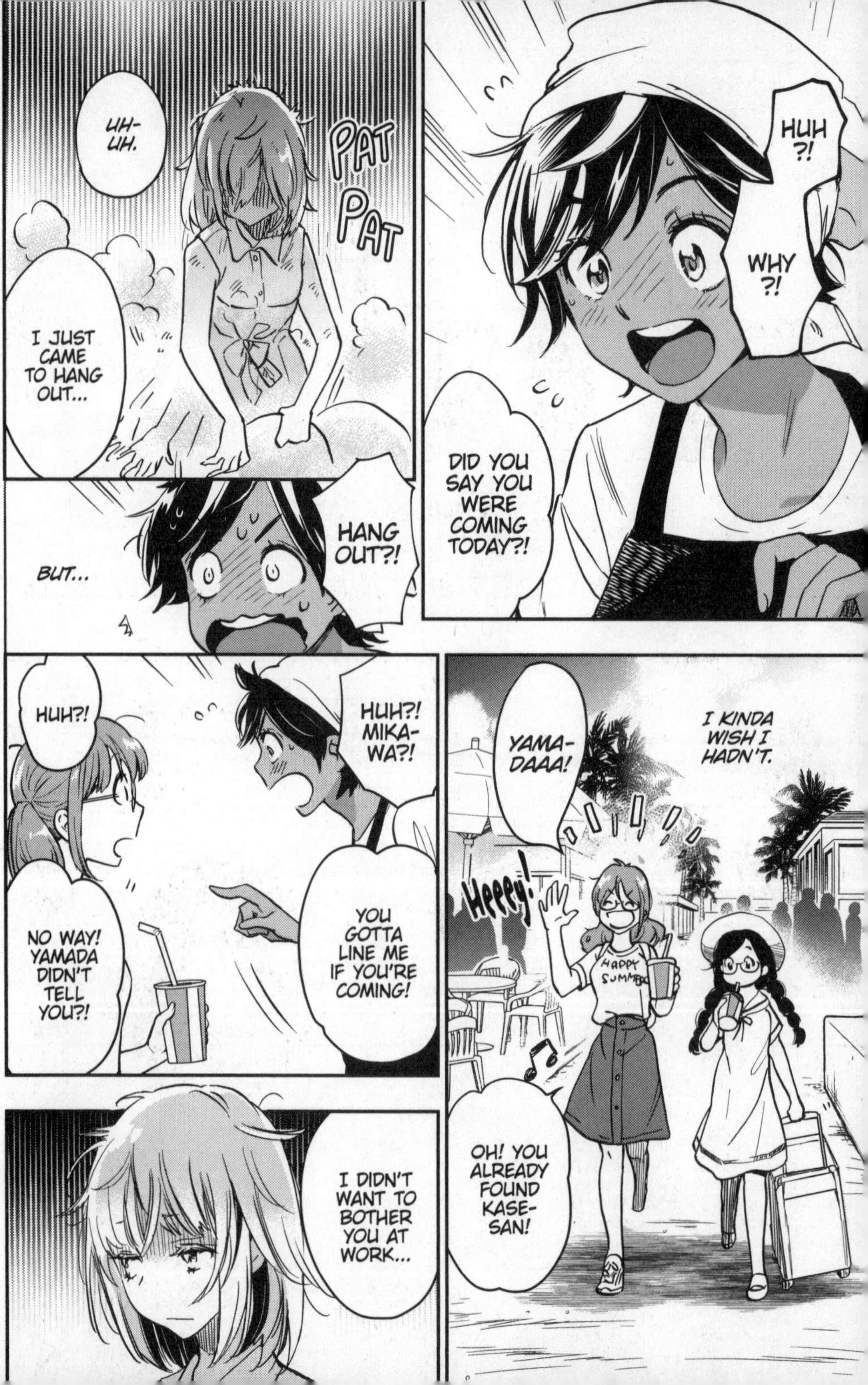
HUH ?!
WHY ?!
DID YOU SAY YOU WERE COMING TODAY?!
UH-UH.
PAT PAT
I JUST CAME TO HANG OUT...
HANG OUT?!
BUT...
I KINDA WISH I HADN'T.
YAMA-DAAA!
Heeey!
OH! YOU ALREADY FOUND KASE-SAN!
HUH?! MIKA-WA?!
HUH?!
YOU GOTTA LINE ME IF YOU'RE COMING!
NO WAY! YAMADA DIDN'T TELL YOU?!
I DIDN'T WANT TO BOTHER YOU AT WORK...

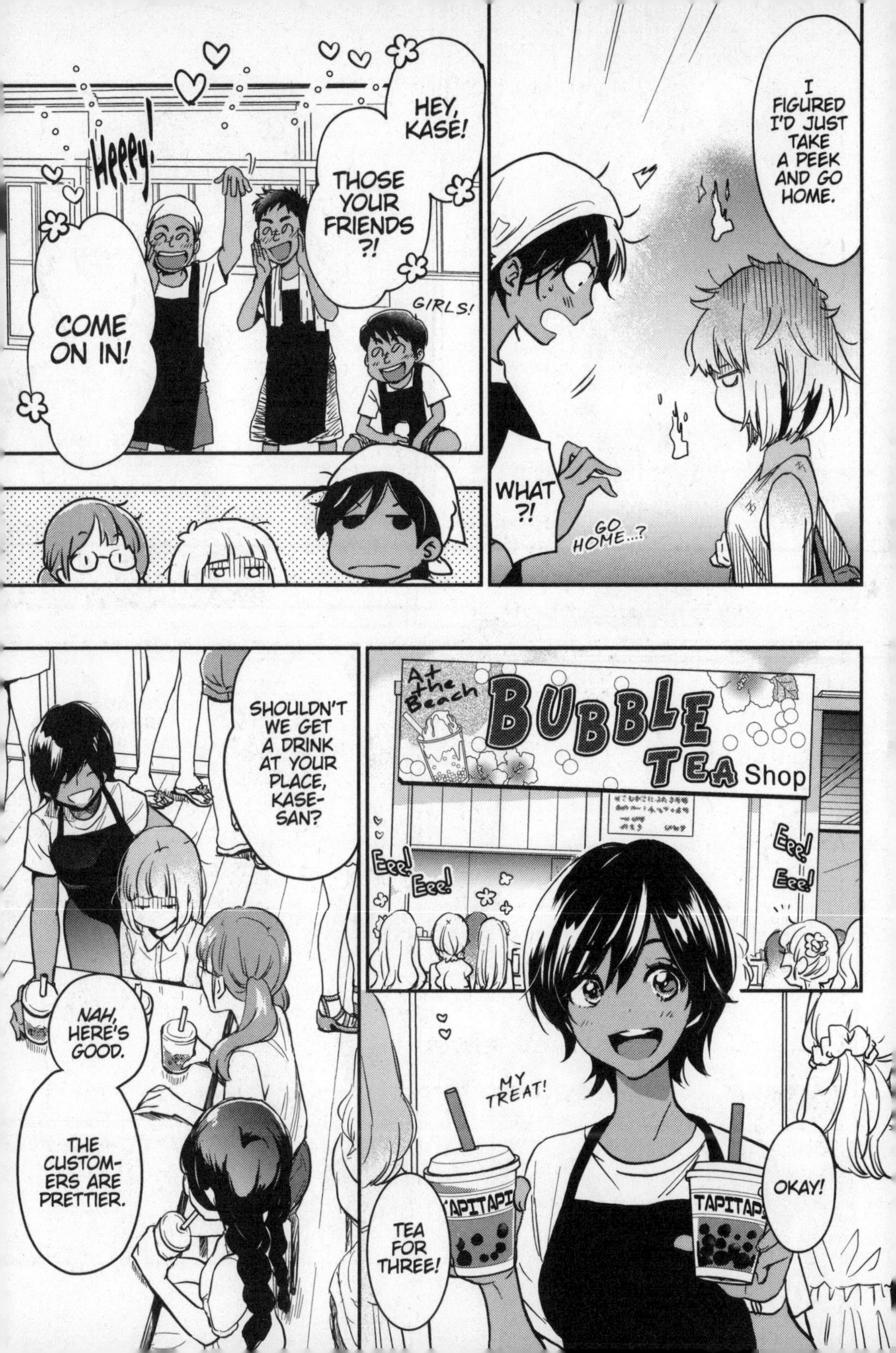
I FIGURED I'D JUST TAKE A PEEK AND GO HOME.
WHAT?!
GO HOME...?
HEY, KASE!
THOSE YOUR FRIENDS?!
Heppy!
COME ON IN!
GIRLS!
At the Beach BUBBLE TEA Shop
Eee! Eee!
Eee! Eee!
MY TREAT!
OKAY!
TAPITAPI
TAPITAPI
TEA FOR THREE!
SHOULDN'T WE GET A DRINK AT YOUR PLACE, KASE-SAN?
NAH, HERE'S GOOD.
THE CUSTOMERS ARE PRETTIER.

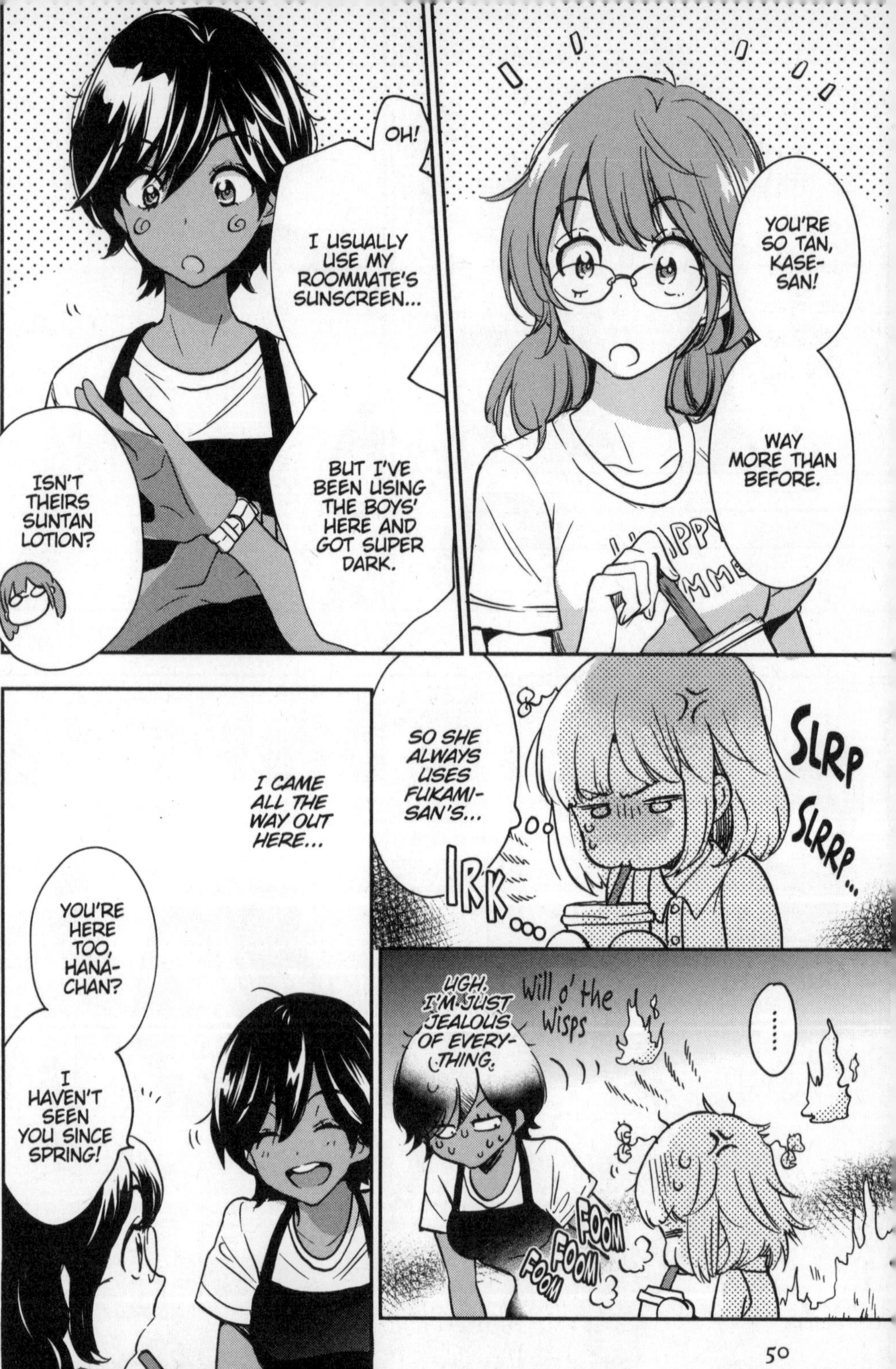
YOU'RE SO TAN, KASE-SAN!
WAY MORE THAN BEFORE.
OH!
I USUALLY USE MY ROOMMATE'S SUNSCREEN...
BUT I'VE BEEN USING THE BOYS' HERE AND GOT SUPER DARK.
ISN'T THEIRS SUNTAN LOTION?
SLRP
SLRRP...
SO SHE ALWAYS USES FUKAMI-SAN'S...
IRK...
......
Will o' the Wisps
UGH. I'M JUST JEALOUS OF EVERYTHING.
FOOM
FOOM
FOOM
I CAME ALL THE WAY OUT HERE...
YOU'RE HERE TOO, HANA-CHAN?
I HAVEN'T SEEN YOU SINCE SPRING!

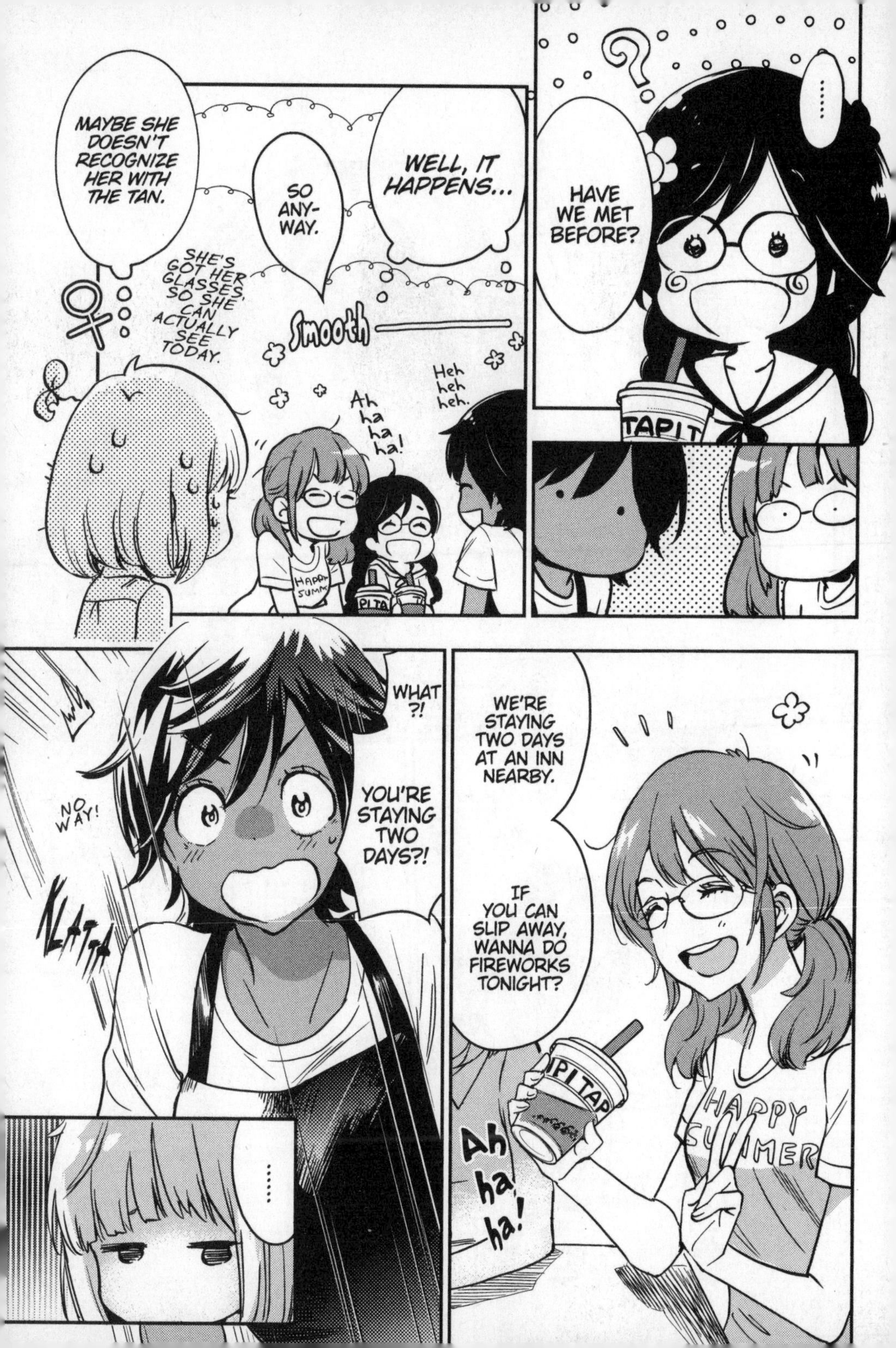

......
HAVE WE MET BEFORE?
WELL, IT HAPPENS...
SO ANYWAY.
MAYBE SHE DOESN'T RECOGNIZE HER WITH THE TAN.
SHE'S GOT HER GLASSES, SO SHE CAN ACTUALLY SEE TODAY.
Smooth
Heh heh heh.
Ah ha ha ha!
WE'RE STAYING TWO DAYS AT AN INN NEARBY.
IF YOU CAN SLIP AWAY, WANNA DO FIREWORKS TONIGHT?
Ah ha ha!
HAPPY SUMMER
WHAT?!
YOU'RE STAYING TWO DAYS?!
NO WAY!
KLATTA
......

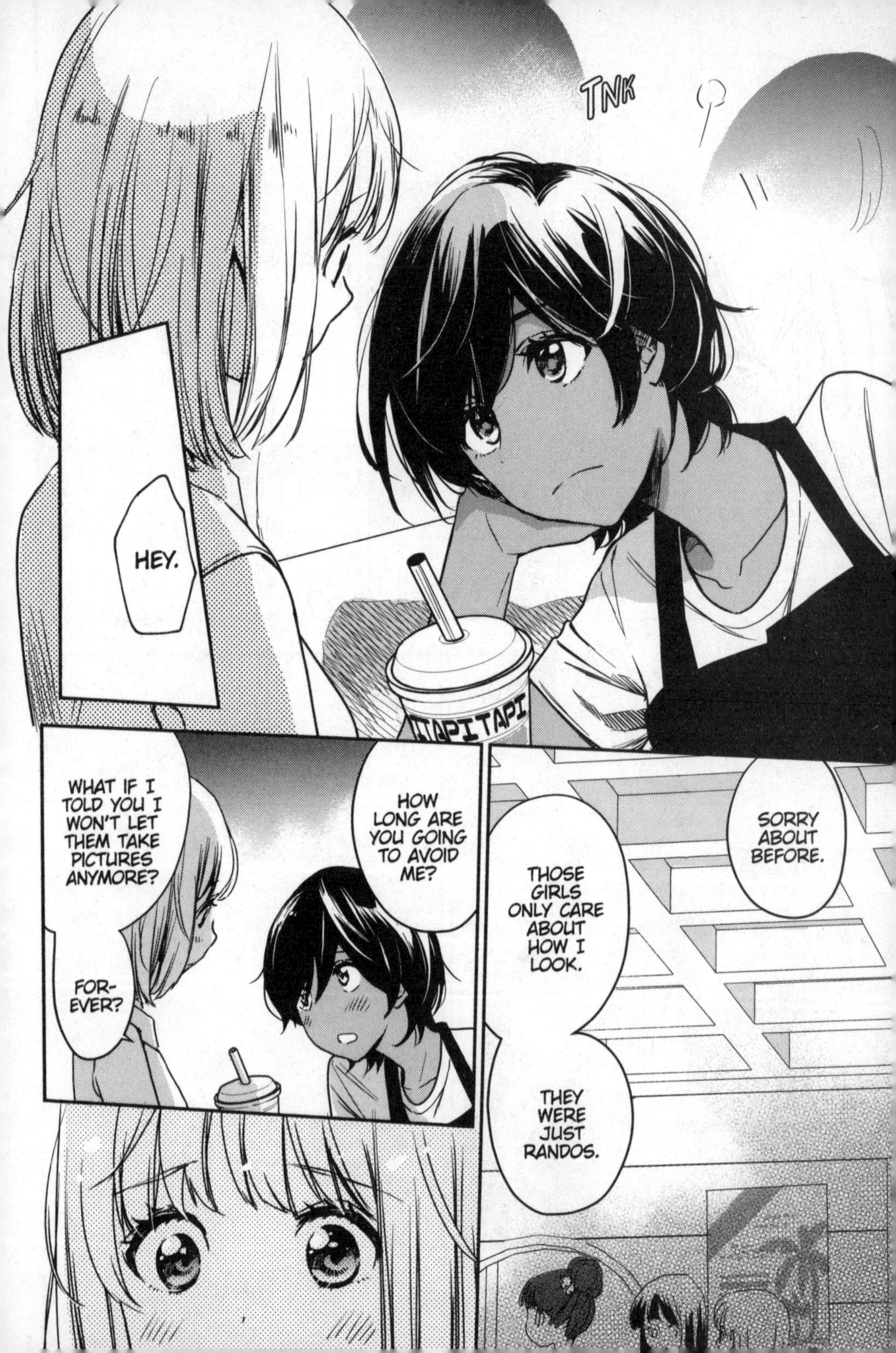
TNK
HEY.
SORRY ABOUT BEFORE.
THOSE GIRLS ONLY CARE ABOUT HOW I LOOK.
THEY WERE JUST RANDOS.
HOW LONG ARE YOU GOING TO AVOID ME?
WHAT IF I TOLD YOU I WON'T LET THEM TAKE PICTURES ANYMORE?
FOR-EVER?

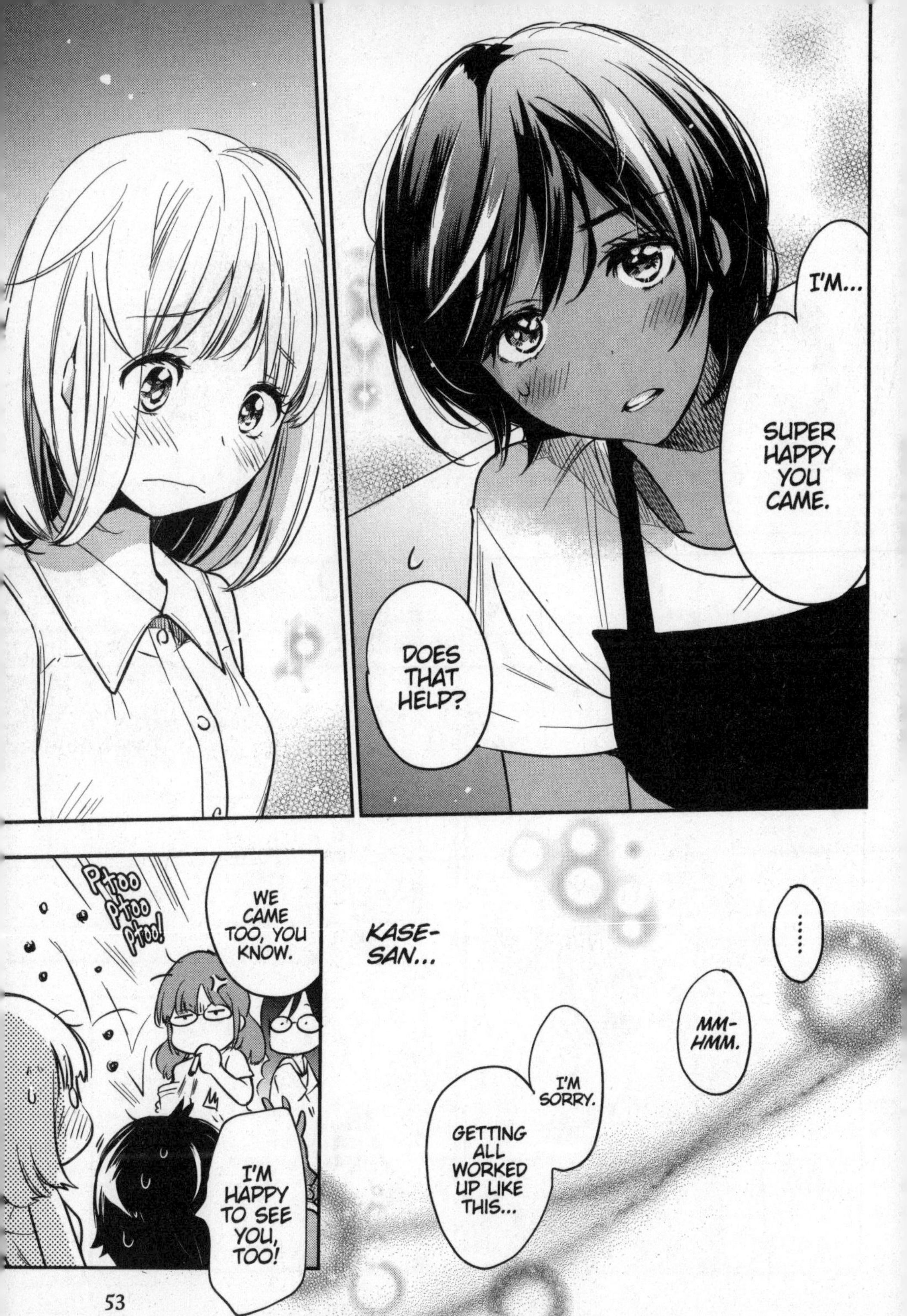
I'M...
SUPER HAPPY YOU CAME.
DOES THAT HELP?
......
KASE-SAN...
MM-HMM.
I'M SORRY.
GETTING ALL WORKED UP LIKE THIS...
WE CAME TOO, YOU KNOW.
P'too p'too p'too!
I'M HAPPY TO SEE YOU, TOO!

OKAY!
I'LL LINE YOU WHEN I GET OFF IN A BIT!
Phew!
MAYBE IT'S GOOD WE CAME.
HEY, YUI-CHAN?
I'M GLAD YOU MADE UP WITH YOUR FRIEND.
WE CAME ALL THIS WAY AND ALL.
YEAH!
I'LL EXPLAIN THINGS TO HANA-CHAN LATER.
ONCE THINGS SETTLE DOWN...

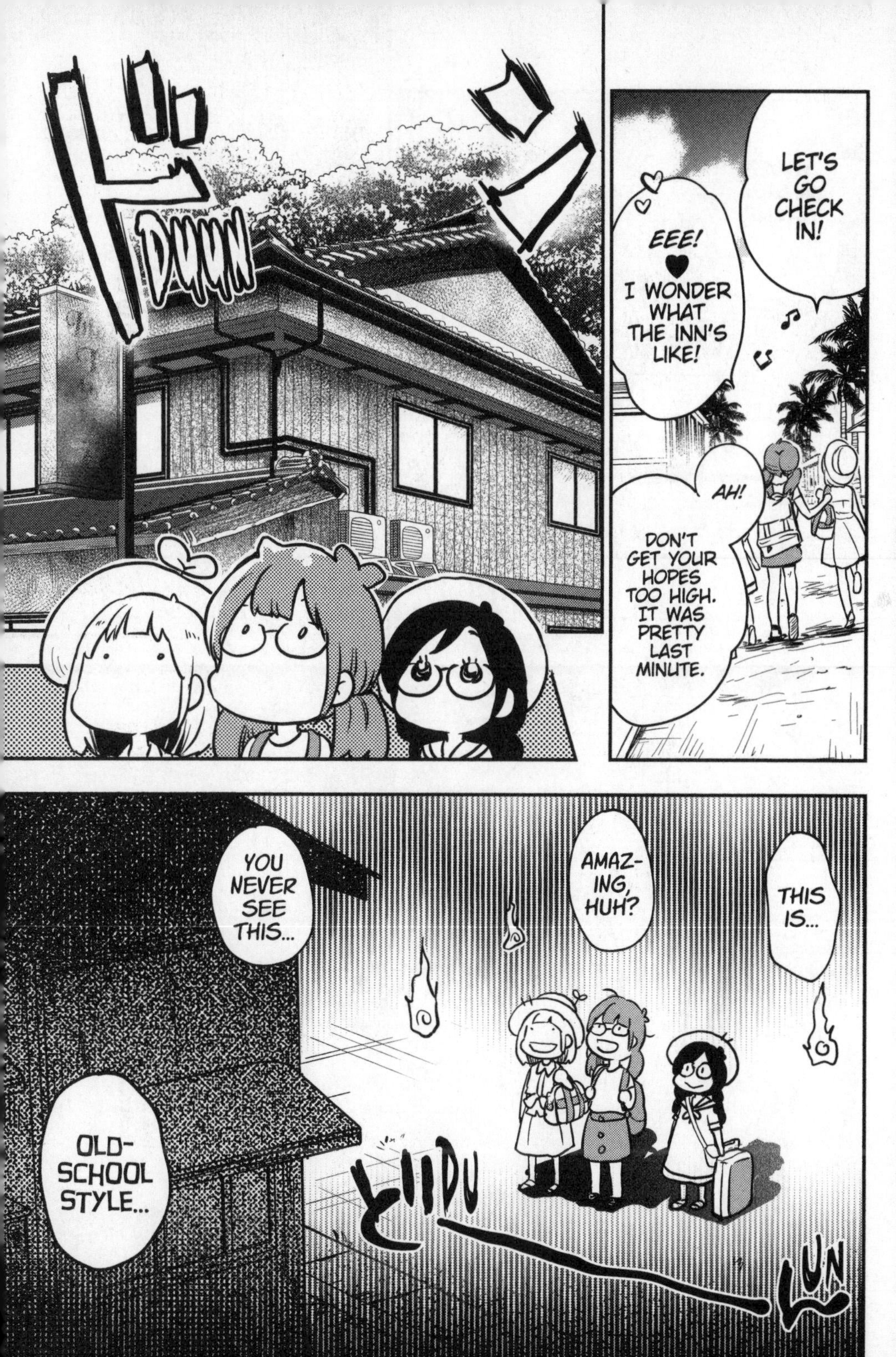
LET'S GO CHECK IN!
EEE! ♥ I WONDER WHAT THE INN'S LIKE!
AH!
DON'T GET YOUR HOPES TOO HIGH. IT WAS PRETTY LAST MINUTE.
DUUN
THIS IS...
AMAZ-ING, HUH?
YOU NEVER SEE THIS...
OLD-SCHOOL STYLE...

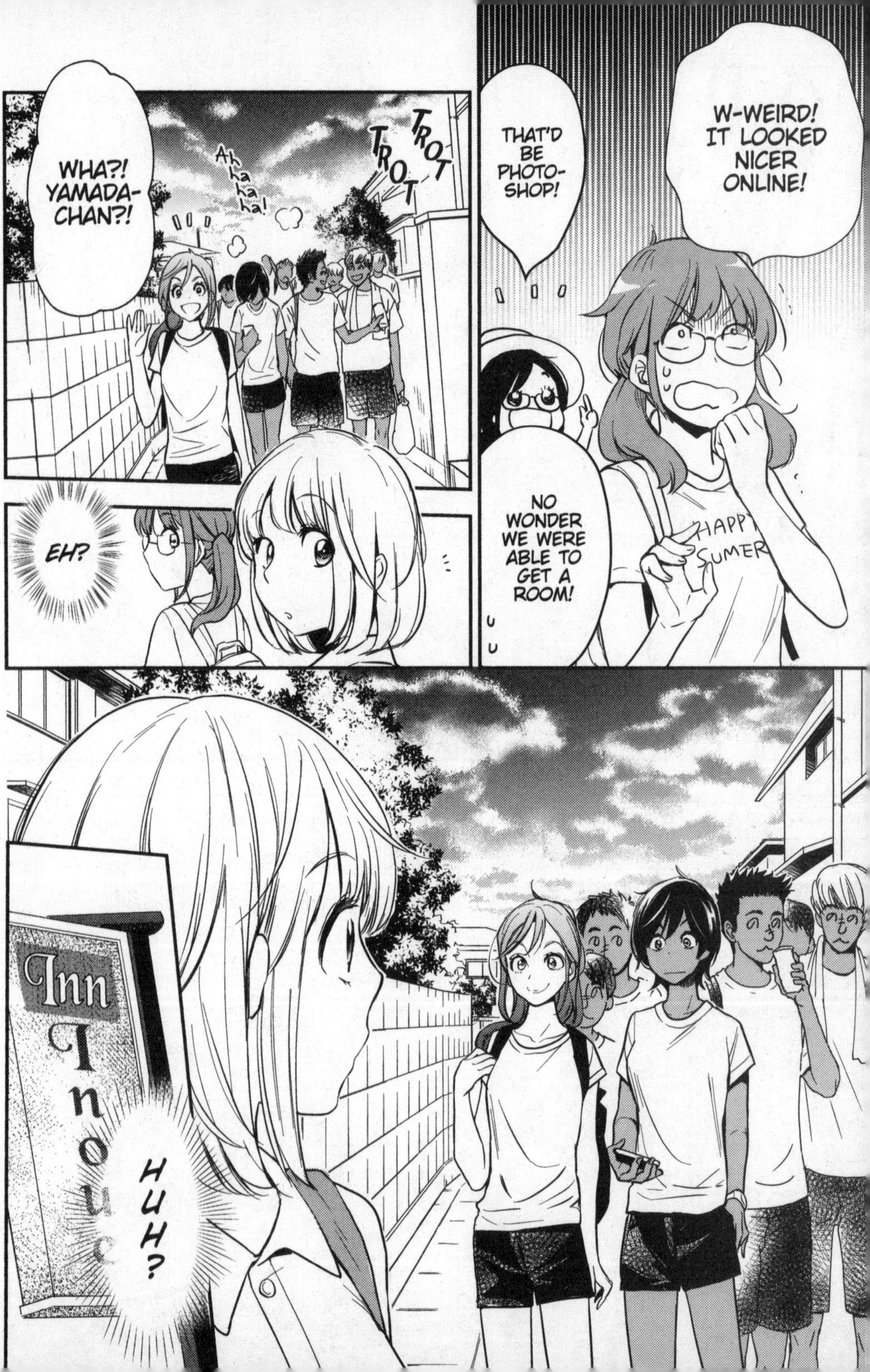
W-WEIRD! IT LOOKED NICER ONLINE!
THAT'D BE PHOTO-SHOP!
HAPPY SUMER
NO WONDER WE WERE ABLE TO GET A ROOM!
TROT TROT
Ah ha ha ha!
WHA?! YAMADA-CHAN?!
EH?
Inn
Inou
HUH?

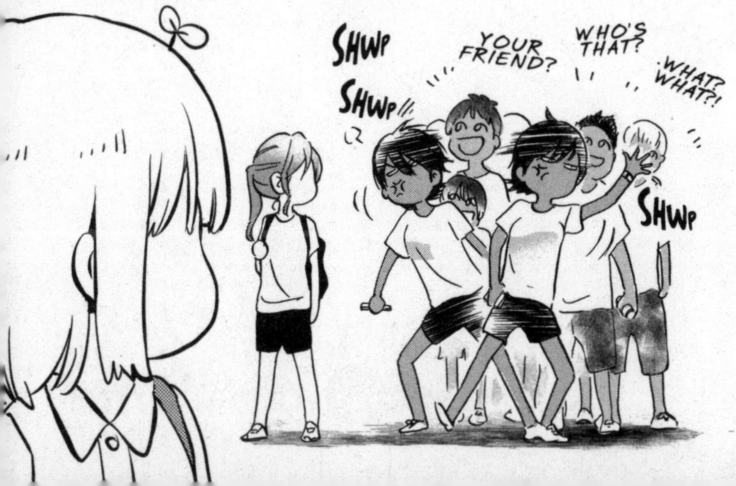
WHAT? WHAT?!
WHO'S THAT?
YOUR FRIEND?
SHWP
SHWP
SHWP

Kase-san *and* Yamada ②

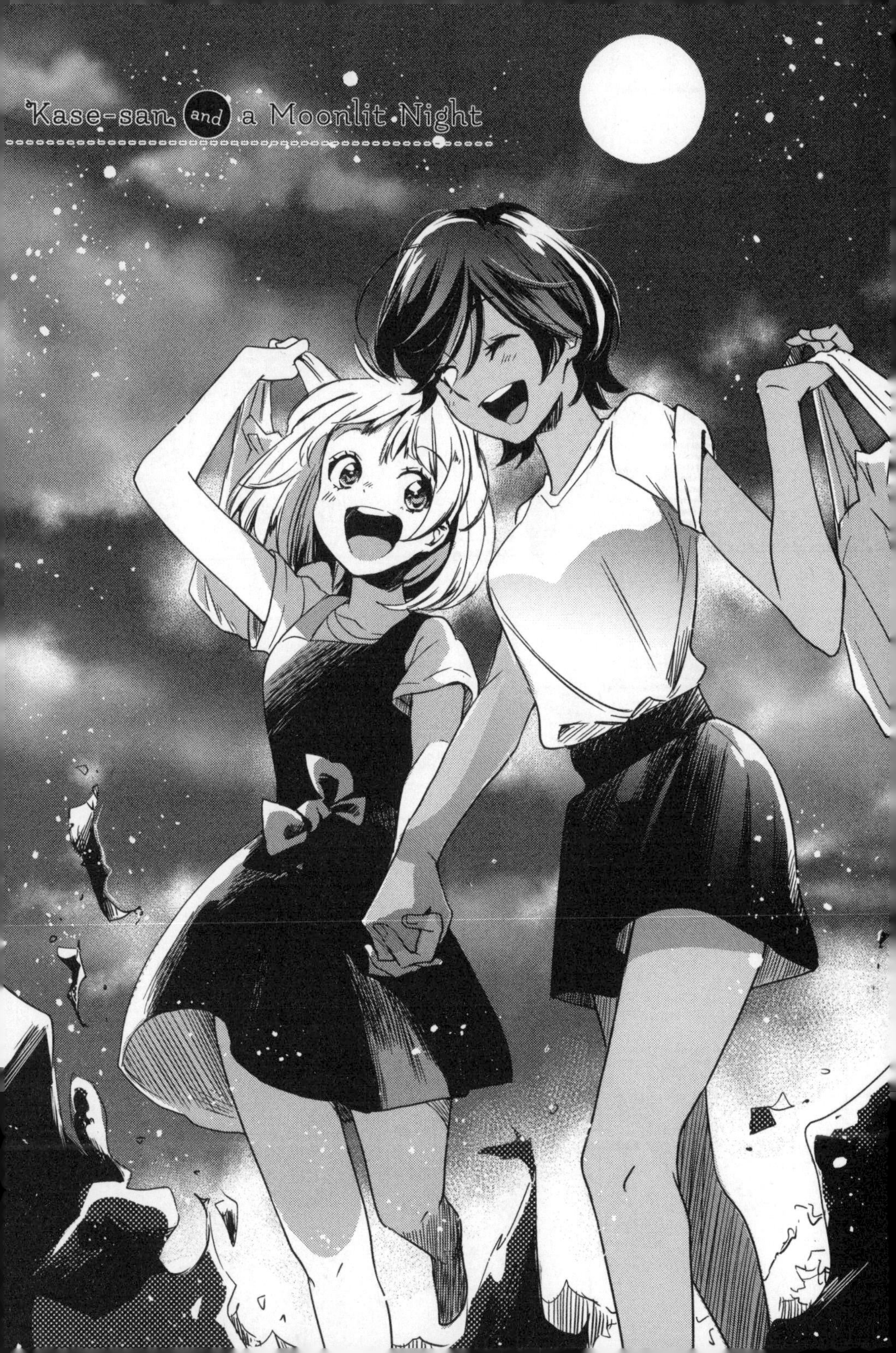
Kase-san and a Moonlit Night

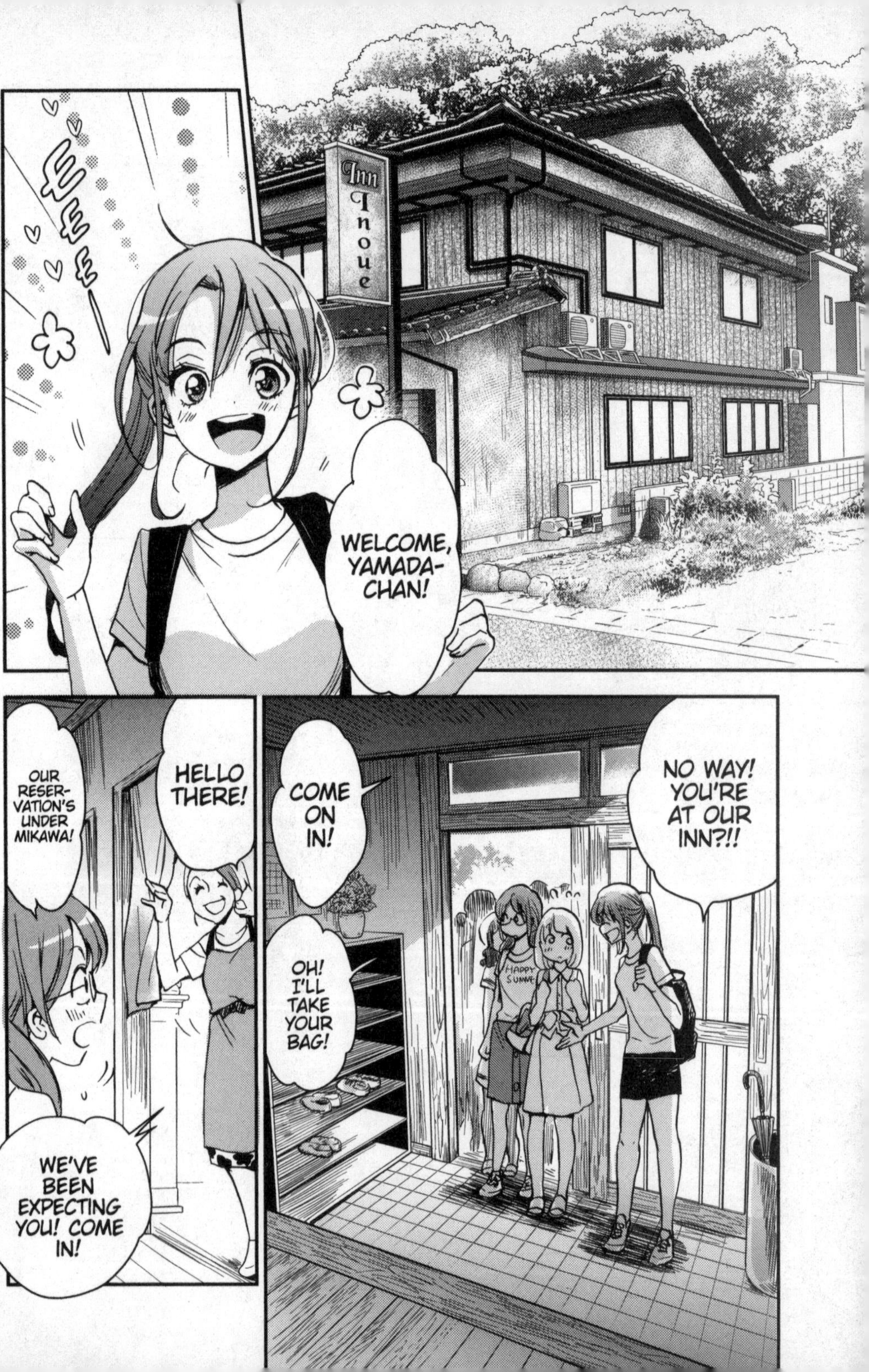
Inn Inoue
WELCOME, YAMADA-CHAN!
NO WAY! YOU'RE AT OUR INN?!!
COME ON IN!
OH! I'LL TAKE YOUR BAG!
HELLO THERE!
OUR RESER-VATION'S UNDER MIKAWA!
WE'VE BEEN EXPECTING YOU! COME IN!

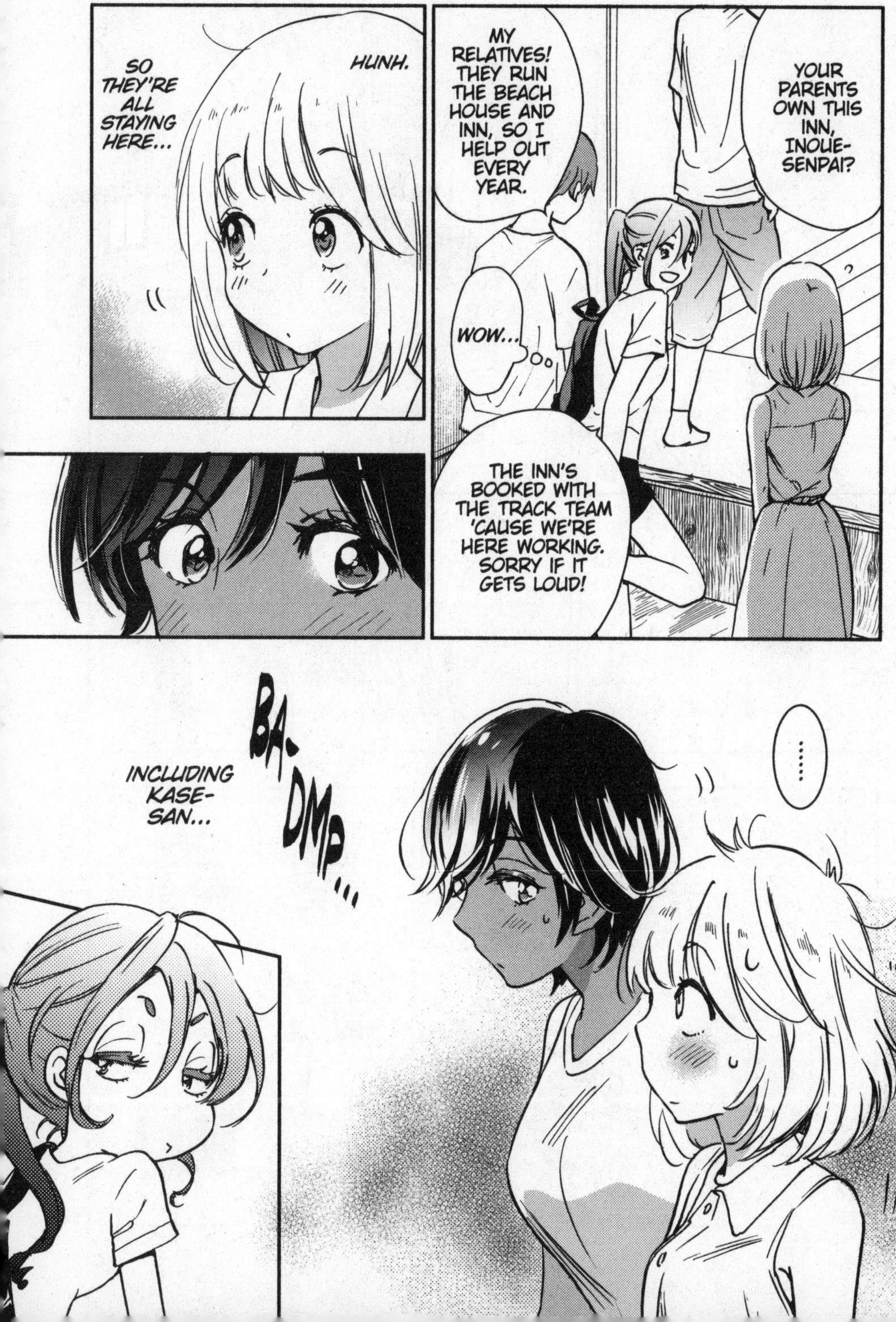
YOUR PARENTS OWN THIS INN, INOUE-SENPAI?
MY RELATIVES! THEY RUN THE BEACH HOUSE AND INN, SO I HELP OUT EVERY YEAR.
WOW...
THE INN'S BOOKED WITH THE TRACK TEAM 'CAUSE WE'RE HERE WORKING. SORRY IF IT GETS LOUD!
HUNH.
SO THEY'RE ALL STAYING HERE...
......
BA-DMP...
INCLUDING KASE-SAN...

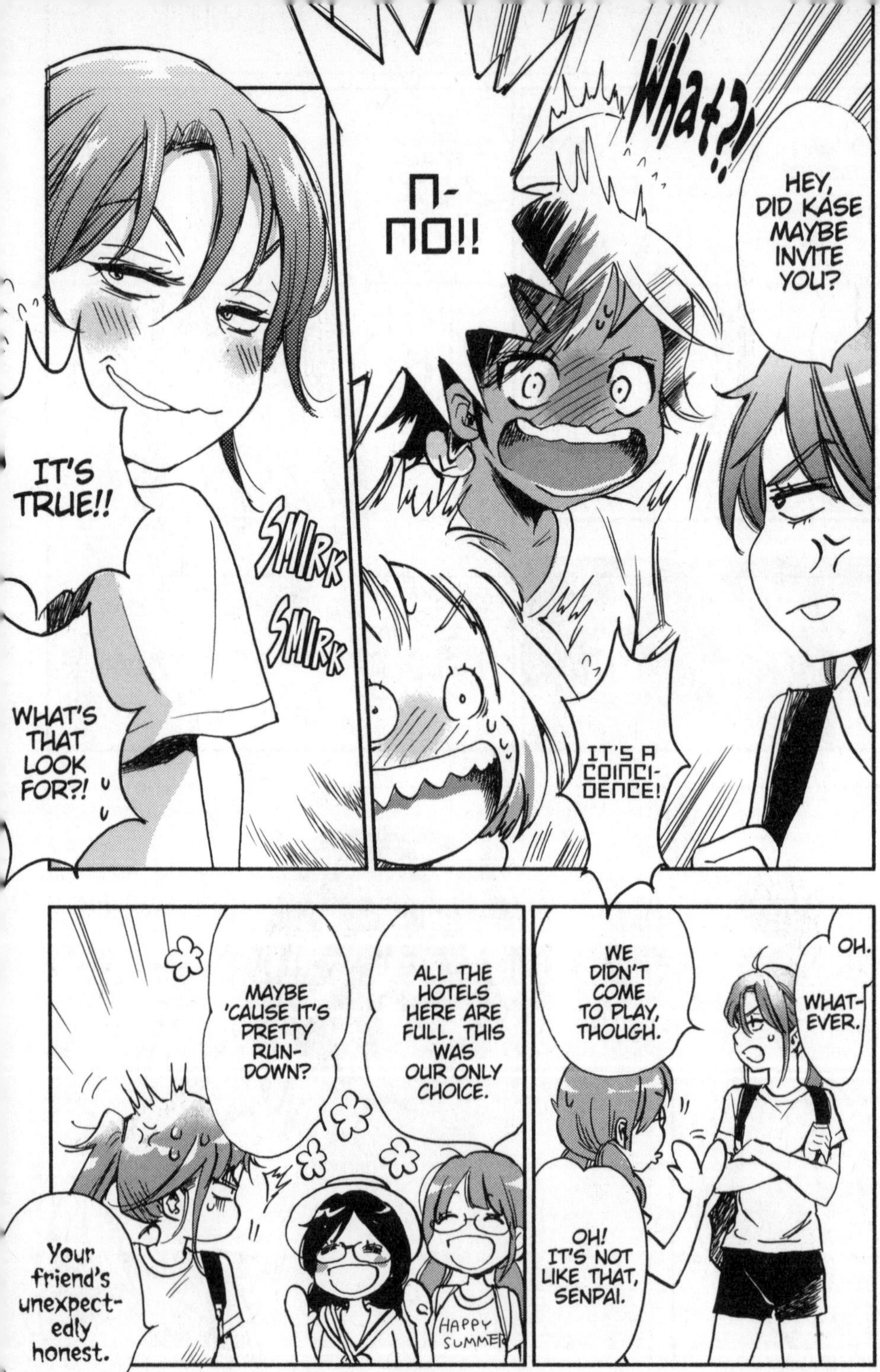
What?!
HEY, DID KASE MAYBE INVITE YOU?
N-NO!!
IT'S A COINCI-DENCE!
SMIRK
SMIRK
IT'S TRUE!!
WHAT'S THAT LOOK FOR?!
OH. WHAT-EVER.
WE DIDN'T COME TO PLAY, THOUGH.
OH! IT'S NOT LIKE THAT, SENPAI.
ALL THE HOTELS HERE ARE FULL. THIS WAS OUR ONLY CHOICE.
MAYBE 'CAUSE IT'S PRETTY RUN-DOWN?
HAPPY SUMMER
Your friend's unexpect-edly honest.

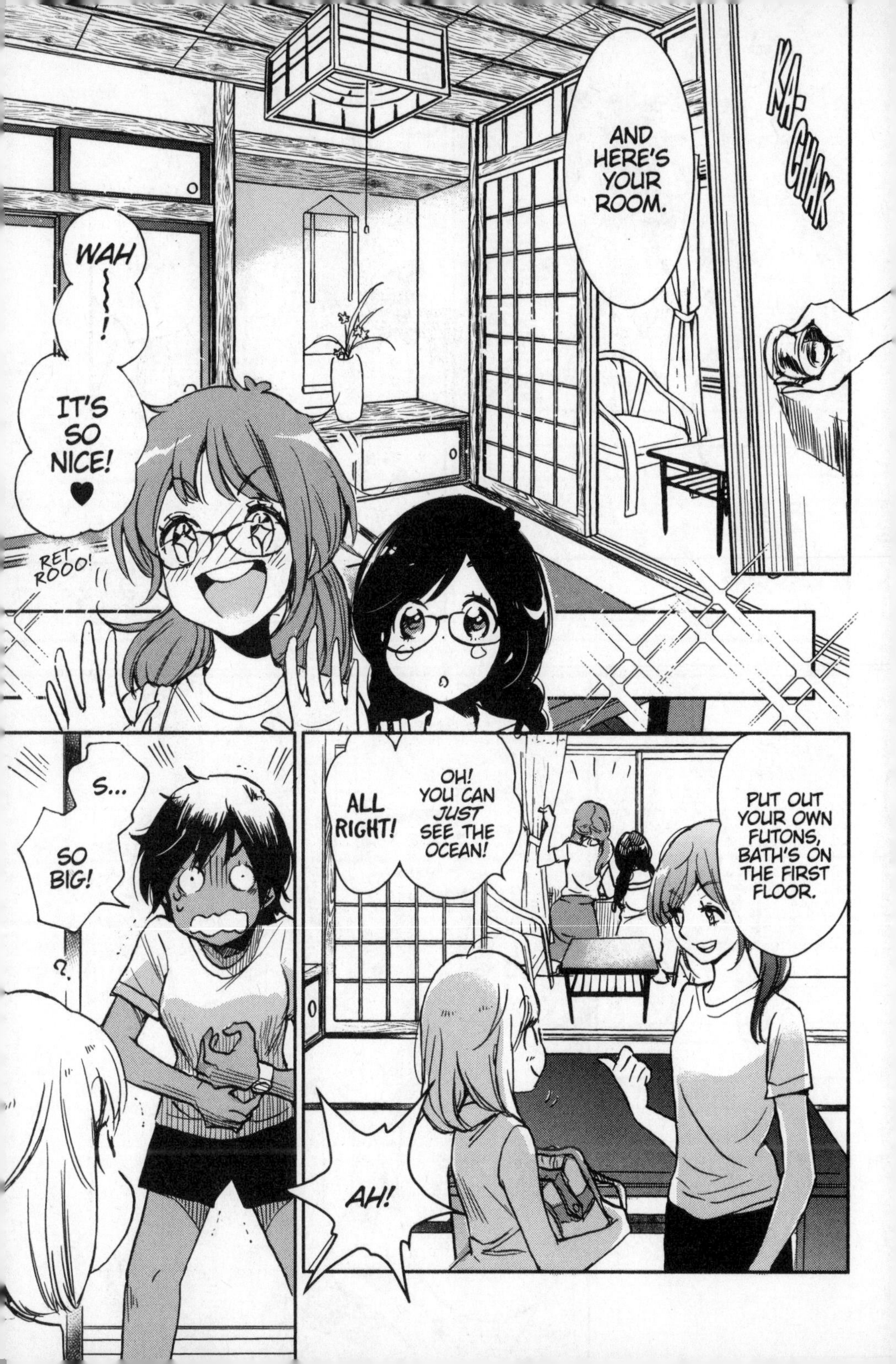
KA-CHAK
AND HERE'S YOUR ROOM.
WAH~~~!
IT'S SO NICE! ♥
RET-ROOO!
PUT OUT YOUR OWN FUTONS, BATH'S ON THE FIRST FLOOR.
OH! YOU CAN JUST SEE THE OCEAN!
ALL RIGHT!
AH!
S...
SO BIG!
?

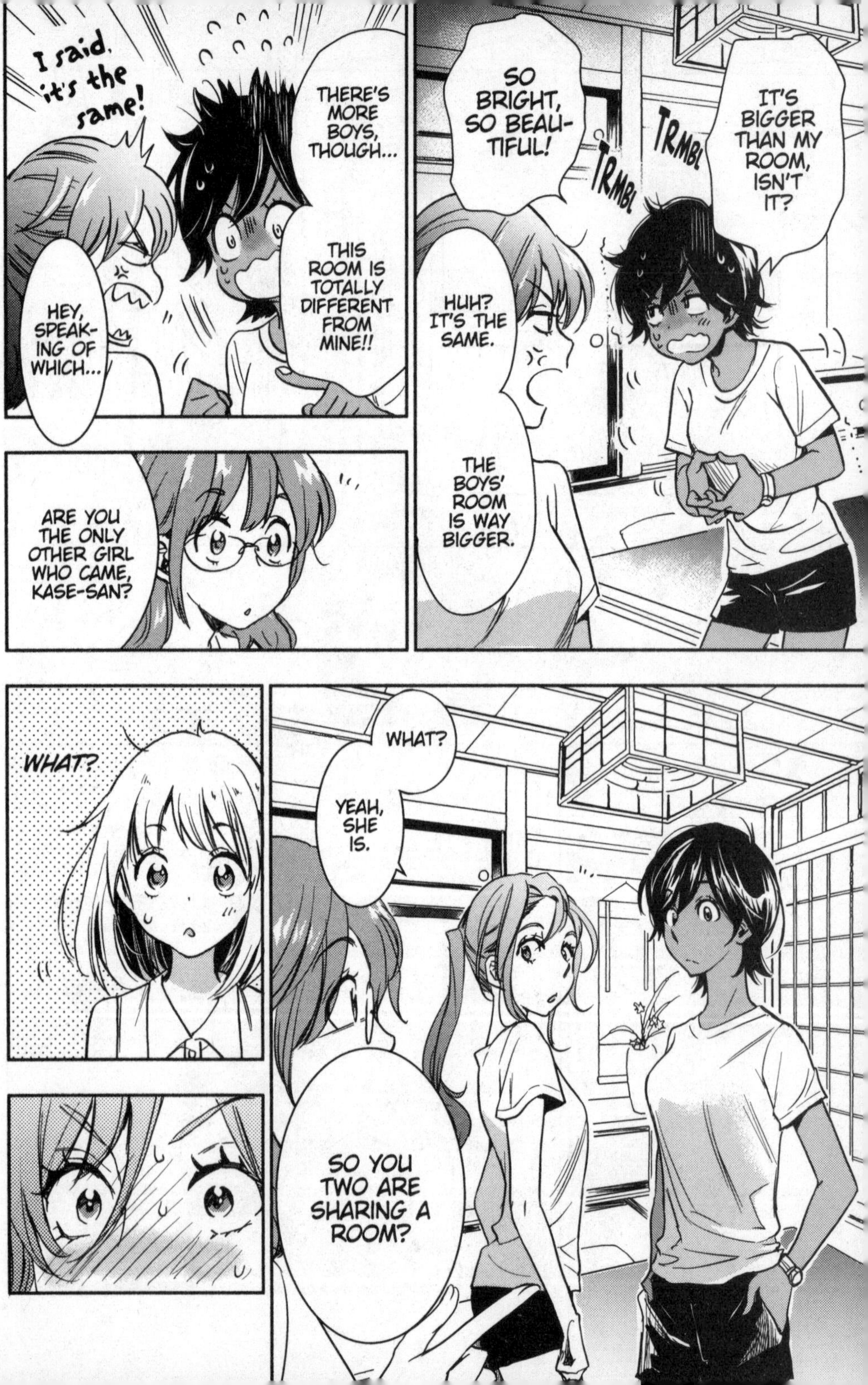
IT'S BIGGER THAN MY ROOM, ISN'T IT?
TRMBL
TRMBL
SO BRIGHT, SO BEAUTIFUL!
HUH? IT'S THE SAME.
THE BOYS' ROOM IS WAY BIGGER.
THERE'S MORE BOYS, THOUGH...
THIS ROOM IS TOTALLY DIFFERENT FROM MINE!!
I said, it's the same!
HEY, SPEAKING OF WHICH...
ARE YOU THE ONLY OTHER GIRL WHO CAME, KASE-SAN?
WHAT?
YEAH, SHE IS.
SO YOU TWO ARE SHARING A ROOM?
WHAT?

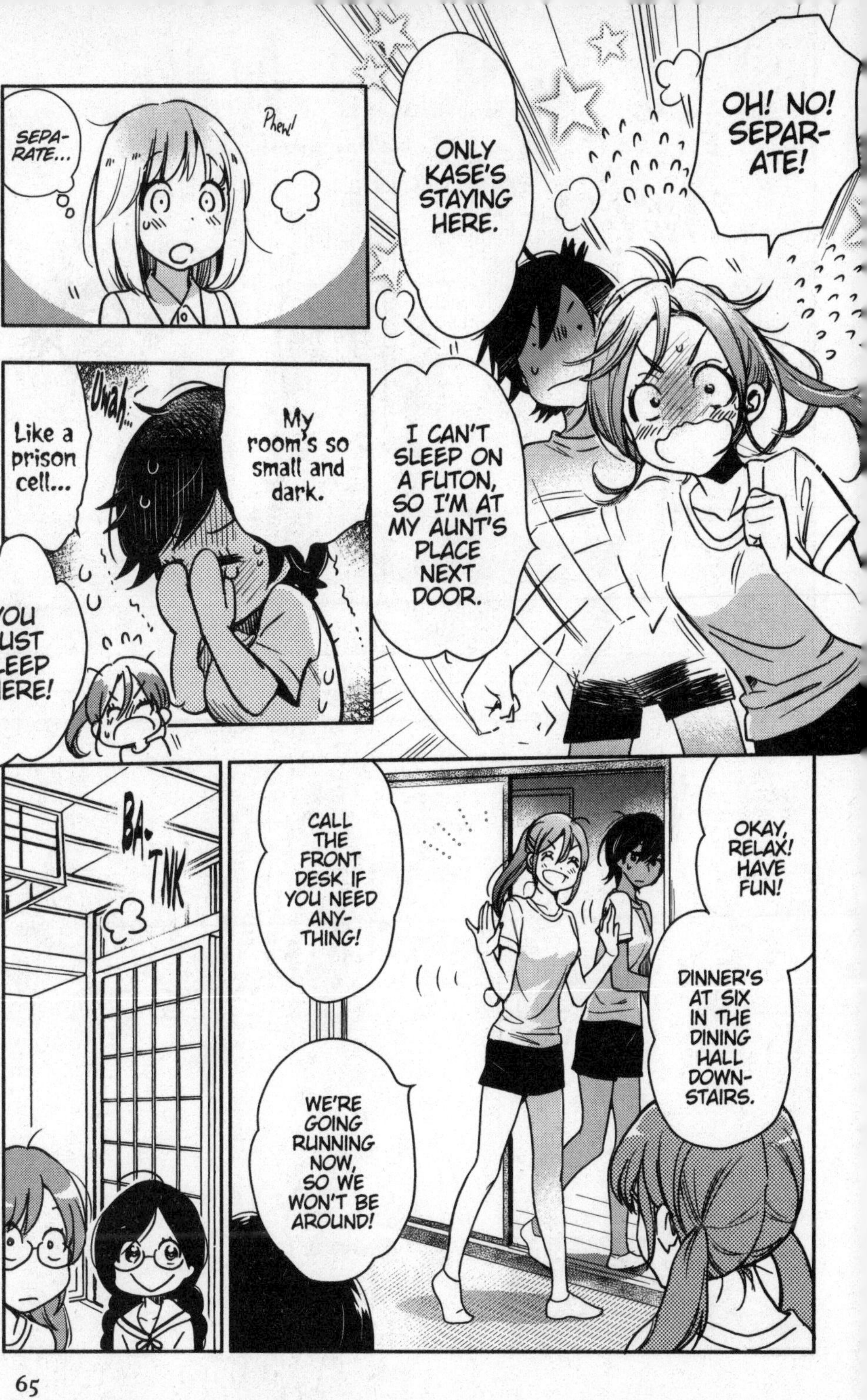
OH! NO! SEPARATE!
ONLY KASE'S STAYING HERE.
I CAN'T SLEEP ON A FUTON, SO I'M AT MY AUNT'S PLACE NEXT DOOR.
SEPARATE...
Phew!
My room's so small and dark.
Uwah...
Like a prison cell...
YOU JUST SLEEP THERE!
OKAY, RELAX! HAVE FUN!
DINNER'S AT SIX IN THE DINING HALL DOWNSTAIRS.
CALL THE FRONT DESK IF YOU NEED ANYTHING!
WE'RE GOING RUNNING NOW, SO WE WON'T BE AROUND!
BA-TNK

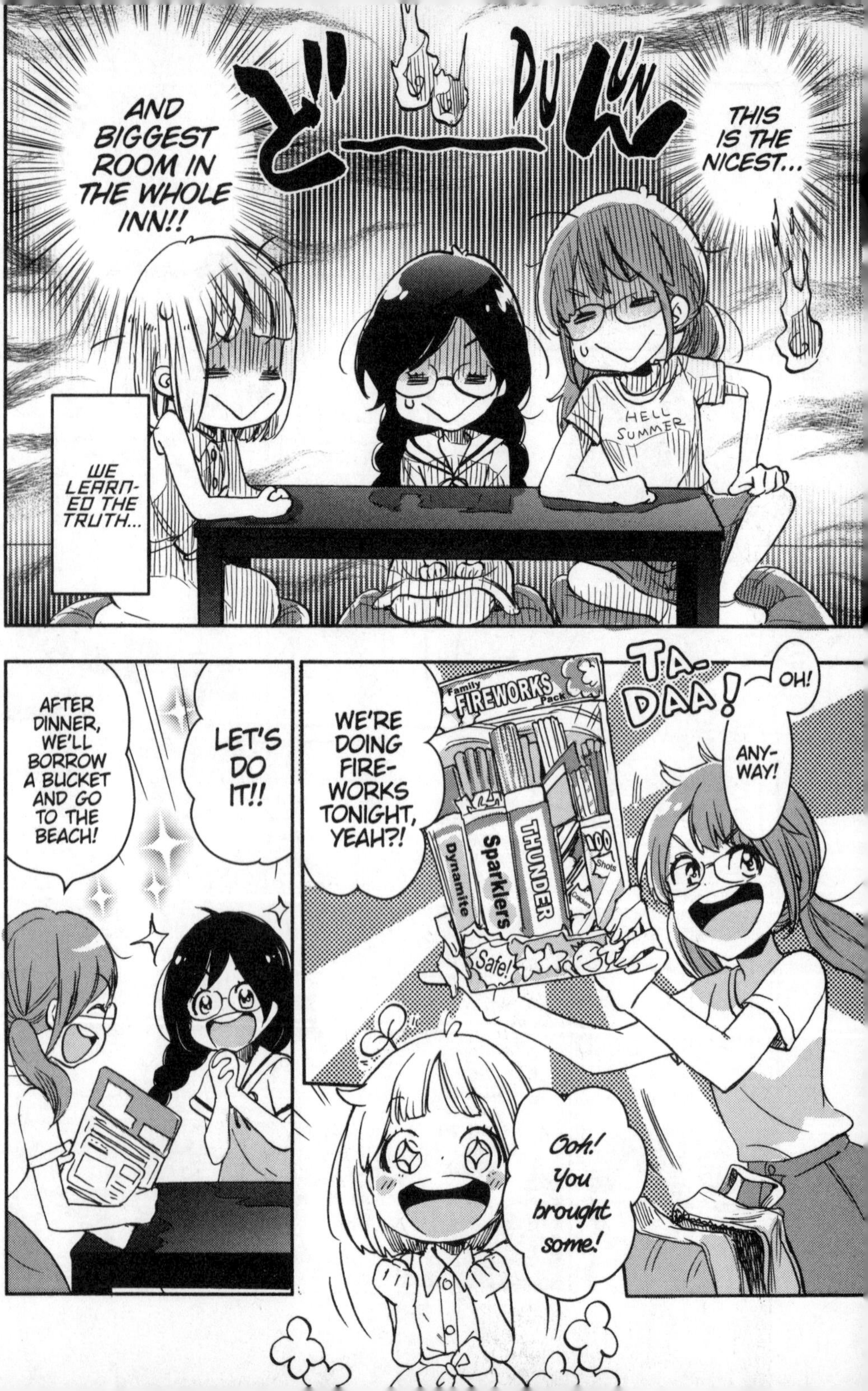
THIS IS THE NICEST...
DUUN
どーーん
AND BIGGEST ROOM IN THE WHOLE INN!!
HELL SUMMER
WE LEARNED THE TRUTH...
OH!
ANY-WAY!
TA-DAA!
WE'RE DOING FIRE-WORKS TONIGHT, YEAH?!
Family FIREWORKS Pack
Dynamite
Sparklers
THUNDER
100 Shots
Crackers
Safe!
Ooh! You brought some!
LET'S DO IT!!
AFTER DINNER, WE'LL BORROW A BUCKET AND GO TO THE BEACH!

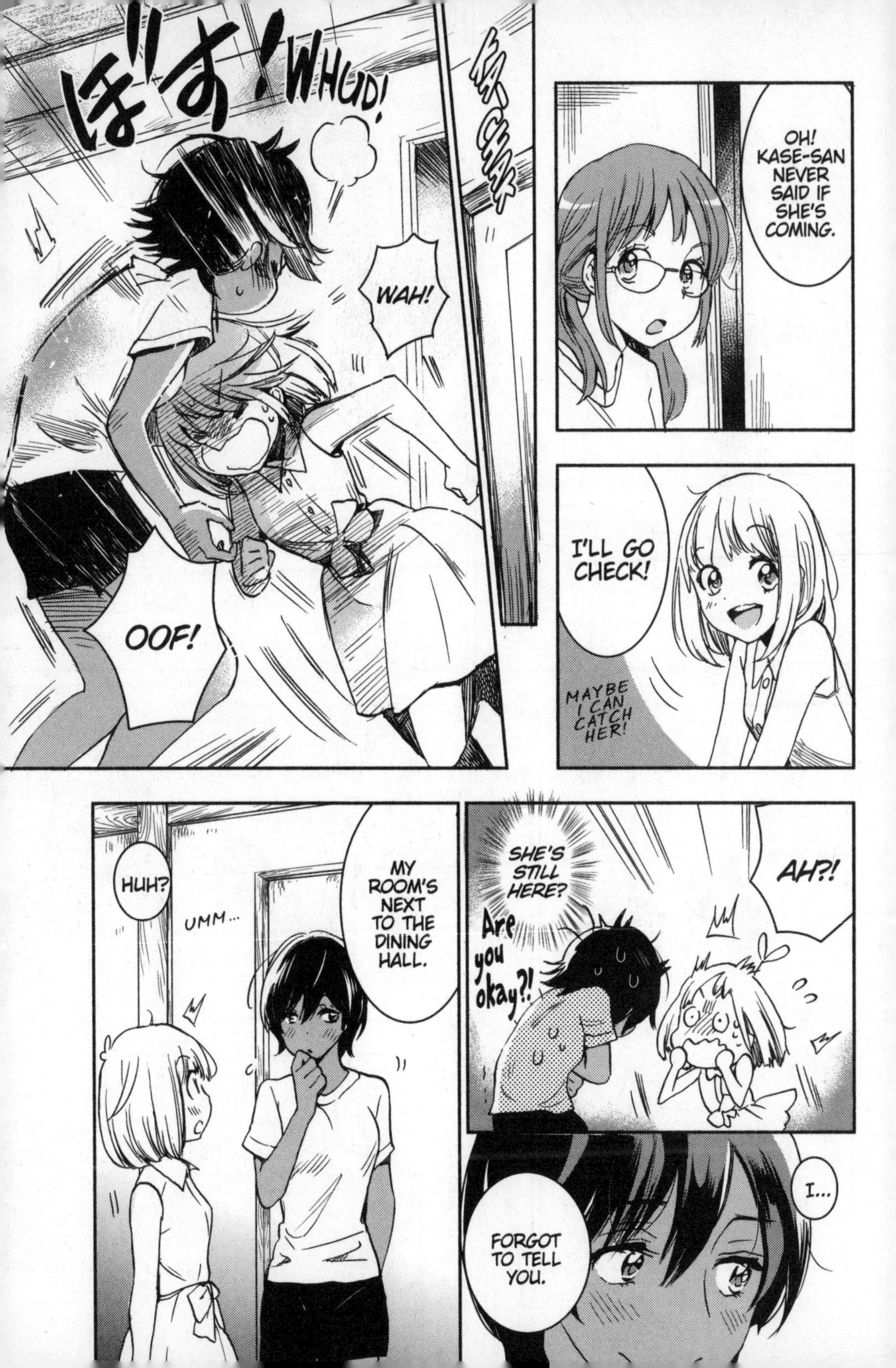
OH! KASE-SAN NEVER SAID IF SHE'S COMING.
I'LL GO CHECK!
MAYBE I CAN CATCH HER!
ぼす! WHUD!
KA-CHAK
WAH!
OOF!
AH?!
SHE'S STILL HERE?
Are you okay?!
I...
FORGOT TO TELL YOU.
MY ROOM'S NEXT TO THE DINING HALL.
UMM...
HUH?

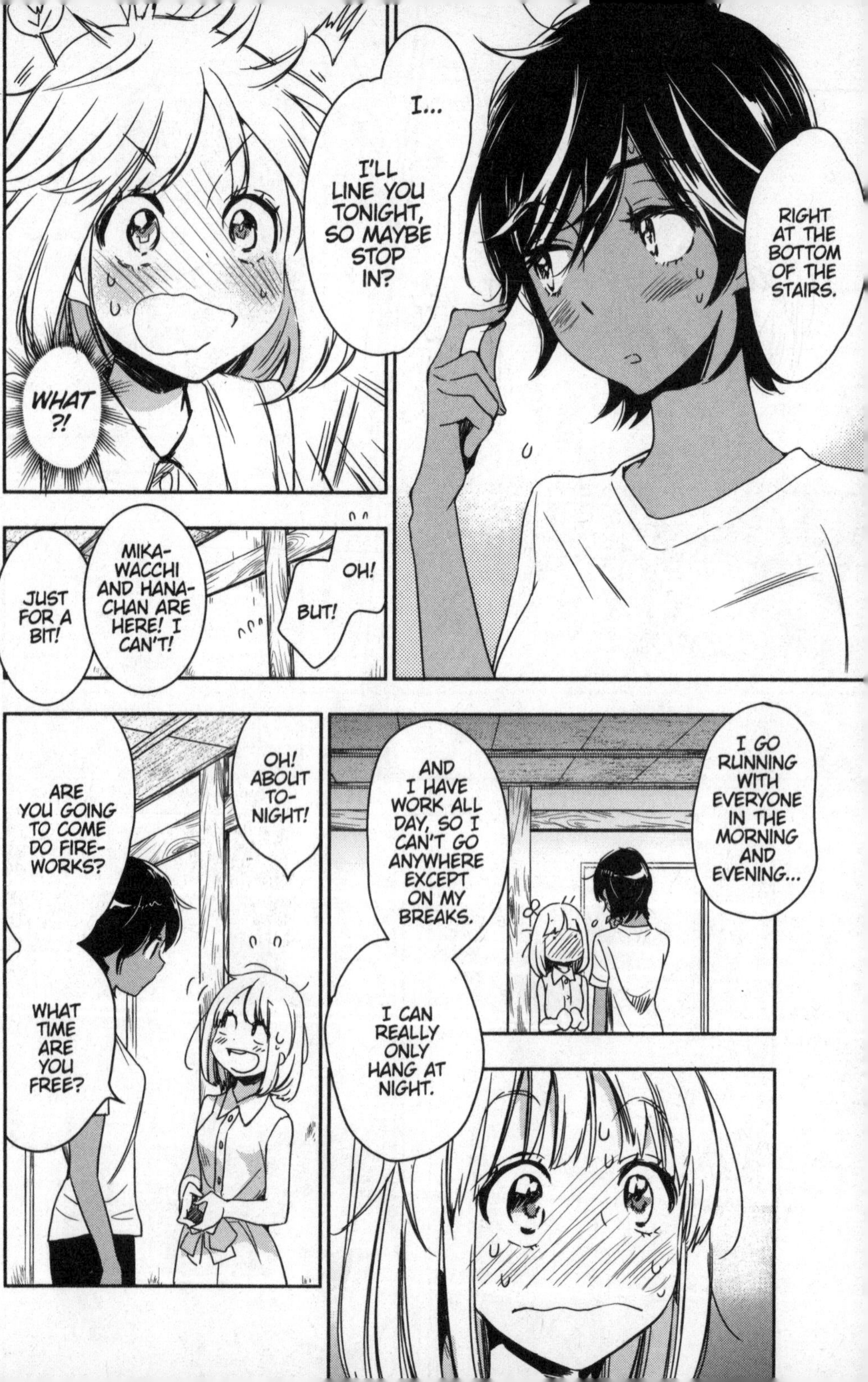
RIGHT AT THE BOTTOM OF THE STAIRS.
I...
I'LL LINE YOU TONIGHT, SO MAYBE STOP IN?
WHAT ?!
OH!
BUT!
MIKA-WACCHI AND HANA-CHAN ARE HERE! I CAN'T!
JUST FOR A BIT!
I GO RUNNING WITH EVERYONE IN THE MORNING AND EVENING...
AND I HAVE WORK ALL DAY, SO I CAN'T GO ANYWHERE EXCEPT ON MY BREAKS.
I CAN REALLY ONLY HANG AT NIGHT.
OH! ABOUT TO-NIGHT!
ARE YOU GOING TO COME DO FIRE-WORKS?
WHAT TIME ARE YOU FREE?

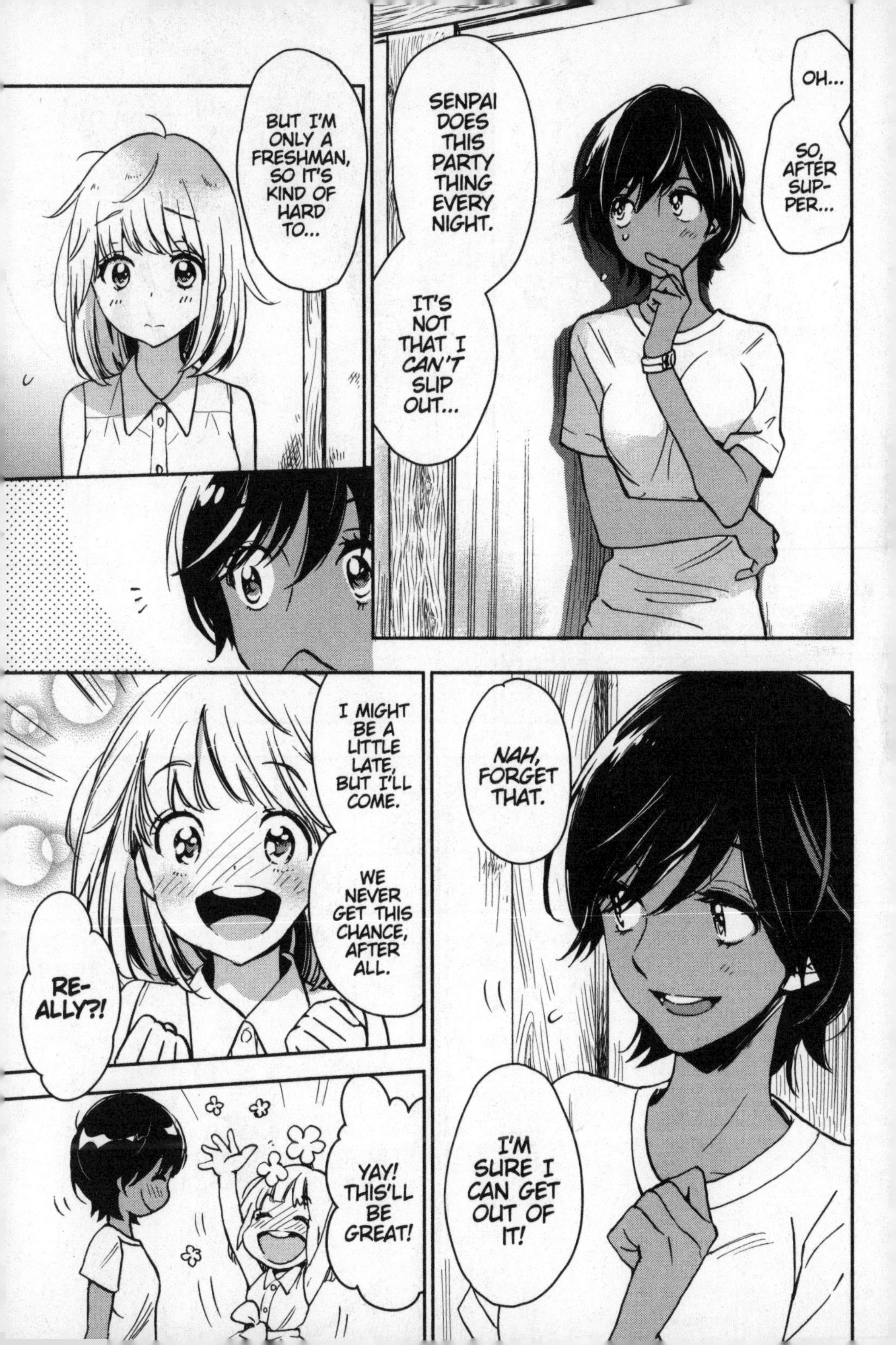
OH...
SO, AFTER SUP-PER...
SENPAI DOES THIS PARTY THING EVERY NIGHT.
IT'S NOT THAT I *CAN'T* SLIP OUT...
BUT I'M ONLY A FRESHMAN, SO IT'S KIND OF HARD TO...
*NAH,* FORGET THAT.
I'M SURE I CAN GET OUT OF IT!
I MIGHT BE A LITTLE LATE, BUT I'LL COME.
WE NEVER GET THIS CHANCE, AFTER ALL.
RE-ALLY?!
YAY! THIS'LL BE GREAT!

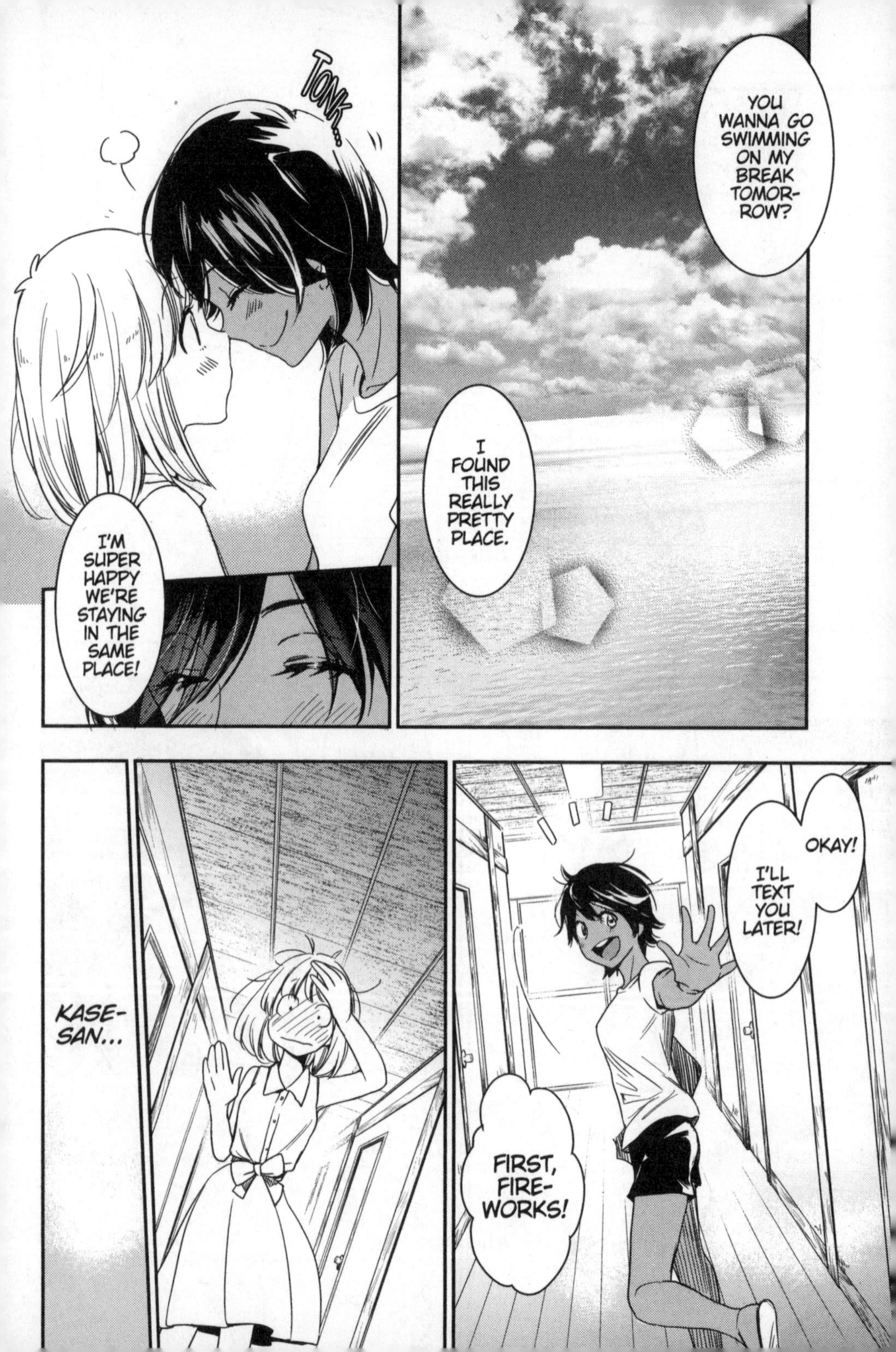
YOU WANNA GO SWIMMING ON MY BREAK TOMORROW?
I FOUND THIS REALLY PRETTY PLACE.
TONK...
I'M SUPER HAPPY WE'RE STAYING IN THE SAME PLACE!
OKAY!
I'LL TEXT YOU LATER!
FIRST, FIRE-WORKS!
KASE-SAN...

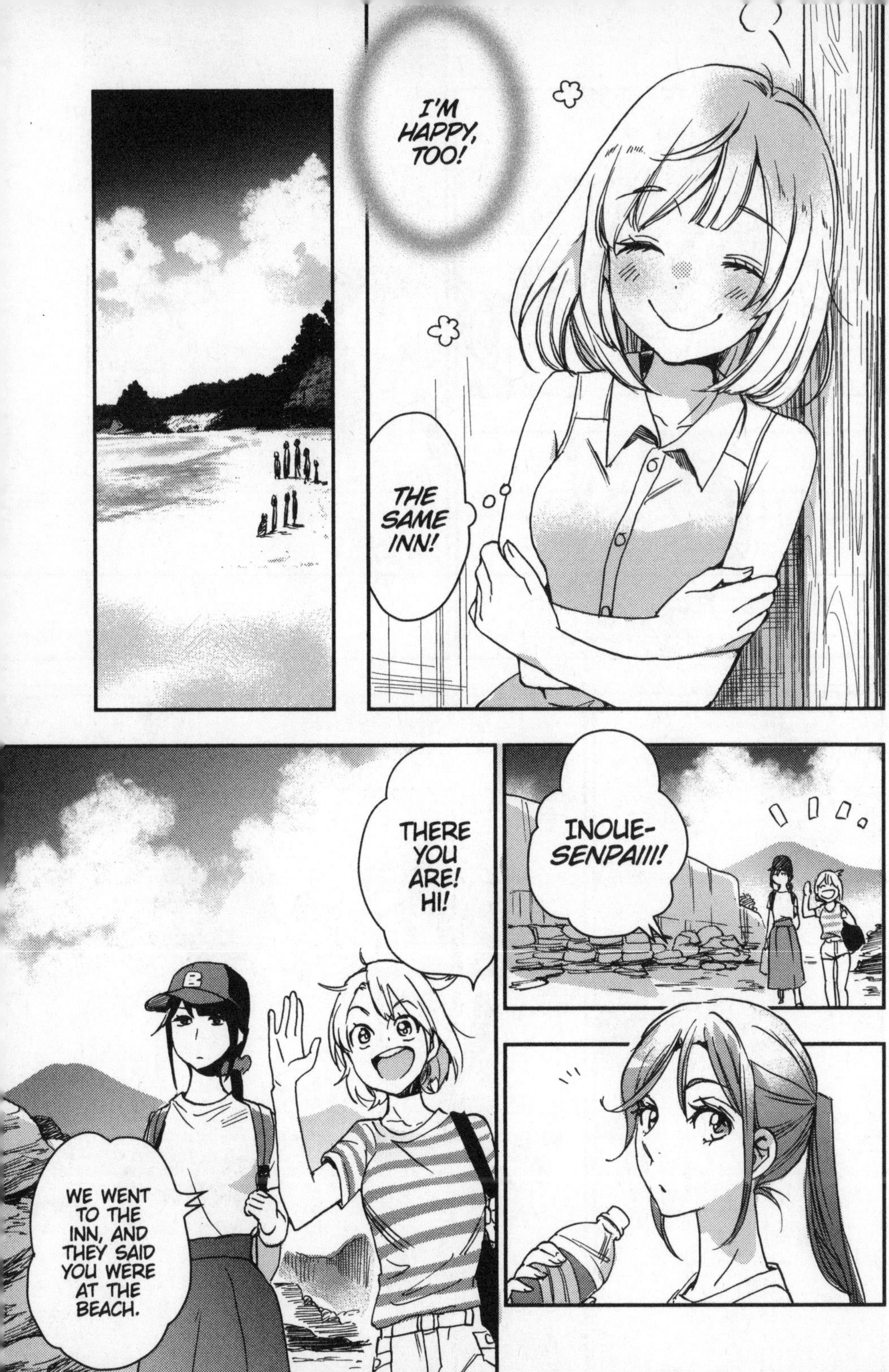
I'M HAPPY, TOO!
THE SAME INN!
INOUE-SENPAIII!
THERE YOU ARE! HI!
WE WENT TO THE INN, AND THEY SAID YOU WERE AT THE BEACH.

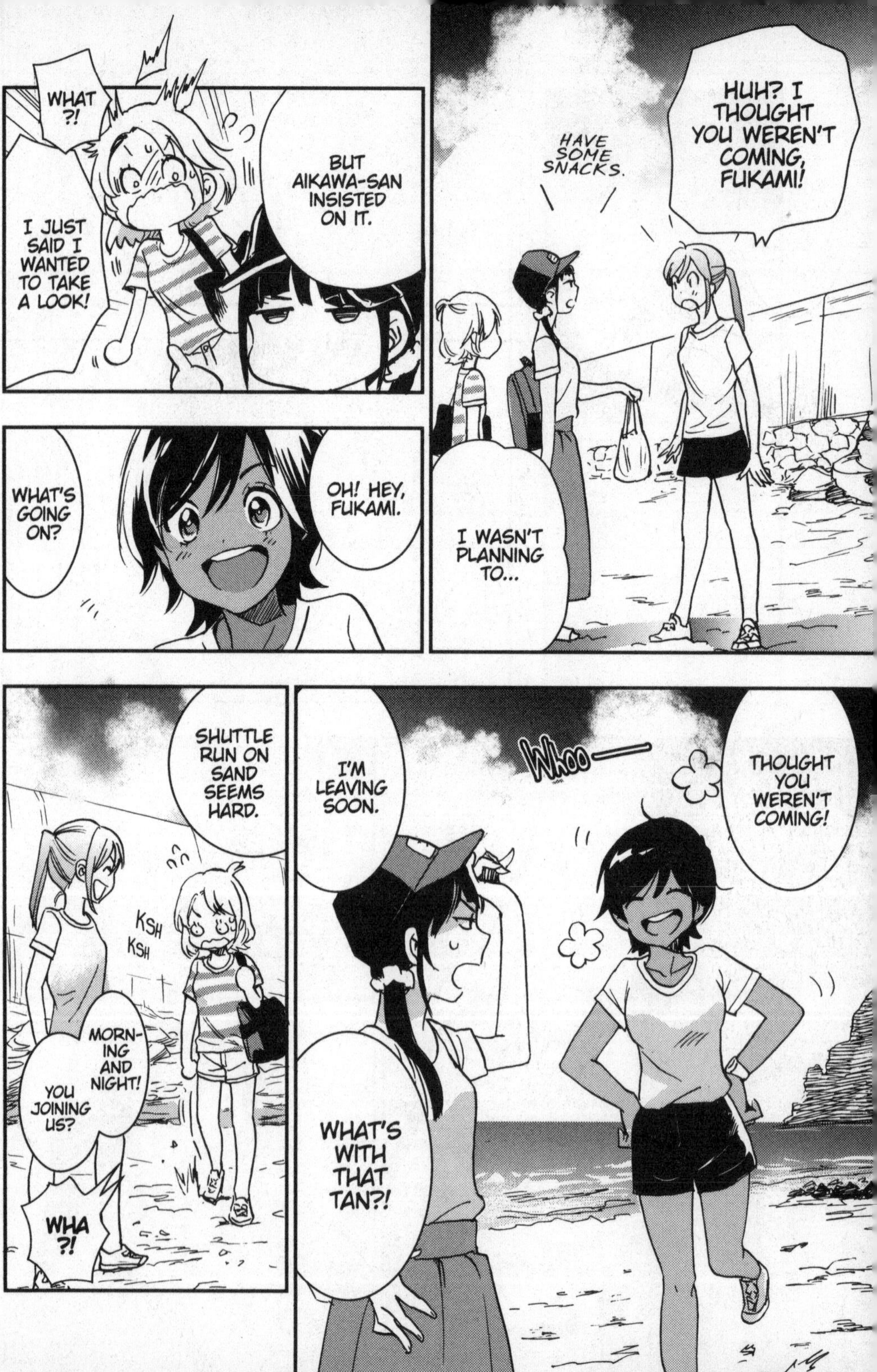
HUH? I THOUGHT YOU WEREN'T COMING, FUKAMI!
HAVE SOME SNACKS.
I WASN'T PLANNING TO...
BUT AIKAWA-SAN INSISTED ON IT.
WHAT?!
I JUST SAID I WANTED TO TAKE A LOOK!
OH! HEY, FUKAMI.
WHAT'S GOING ON?
THOUGHT YOU WEREN'T COMING!
Whoo—
I'M LEAVING SOON.
WHAT'S WITH THAT TAN?!
SHUTTLE RUN ON SAND SEEMS HARD.
KSH KSH
MORNING AND NIGHT!
YOU JOINING US?
WHA?!

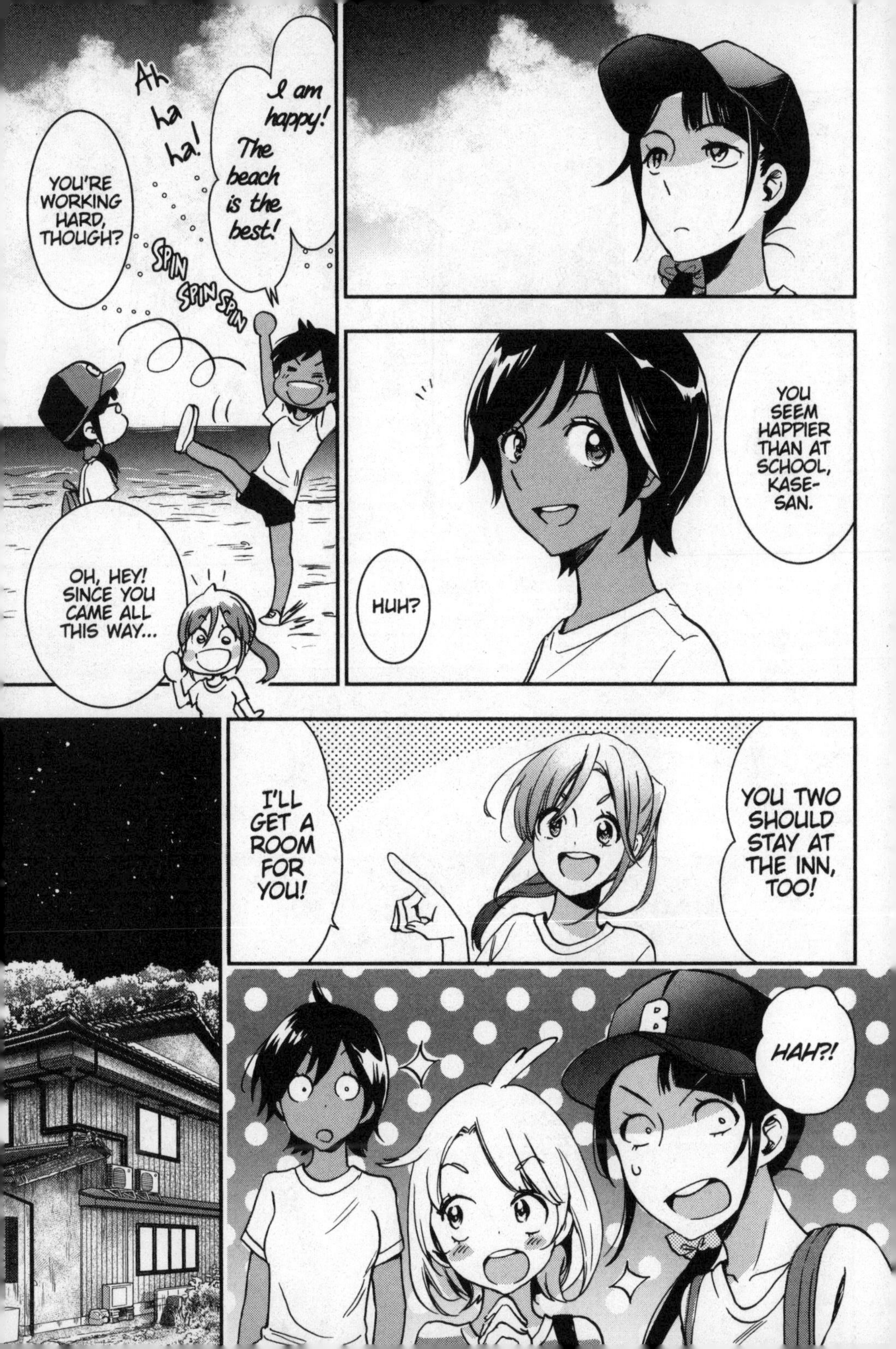

YOU SEEM HAPPIER THAN AT SCHOOL, KASE-SAN.
HUH?
I am happy! The beach is the best!
Ah ha ha!
YOU'RE WORKING HARD, THOUGH?
SPIN SPIN SPIN
OH, HEY! SINCE YOU CAME ALL THIS WAY...
YOU TWO SHOULD STAY AT THE INN, TOO!
I'LL GET A ROOM FOR YOU!
HAH?!

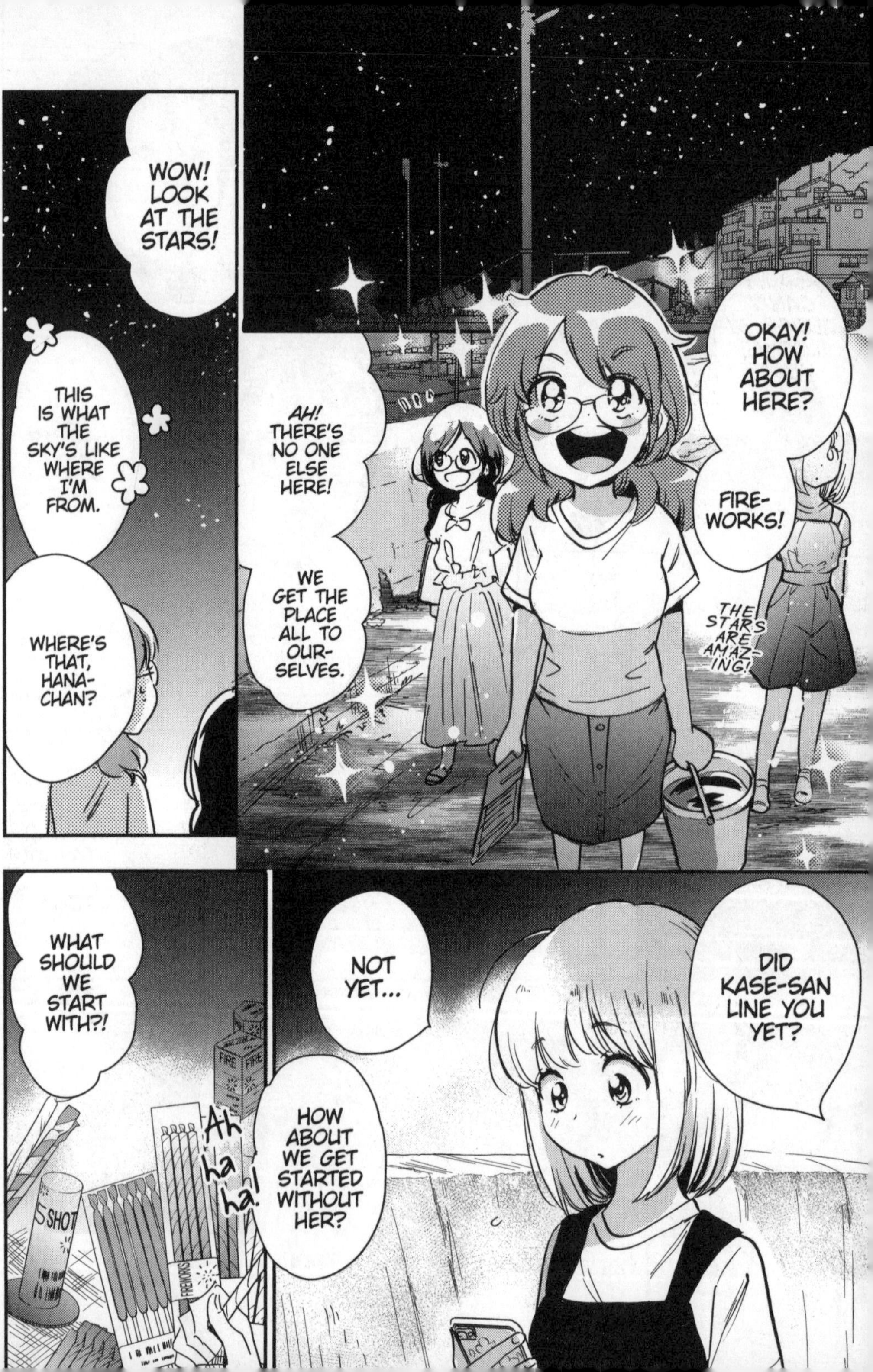
OKAY! HOW ABOUT HERE?
FIRE-WORKS!
THE STARS ARE AMAZING!
AH! THERE'S NO ONE ELSE HERE!
WE GET THE PLACE ALL TO OURSELVES.
WOW! LOOK AT THE STARS!
THIS IS WHAT THE SKY'S LIKE WHERE I'M FROM.
WHERE'S THAT, HANA-CHAN?
DID KASE-SAN LINE YOU YET?
NOT YET...
HOW ABOUT WE GET STARTED WITHOUT HER?
WHAT SHOULD WE START WITH?!
Ah ha ha!
5 SHOT
FIREWORKS
FIRE

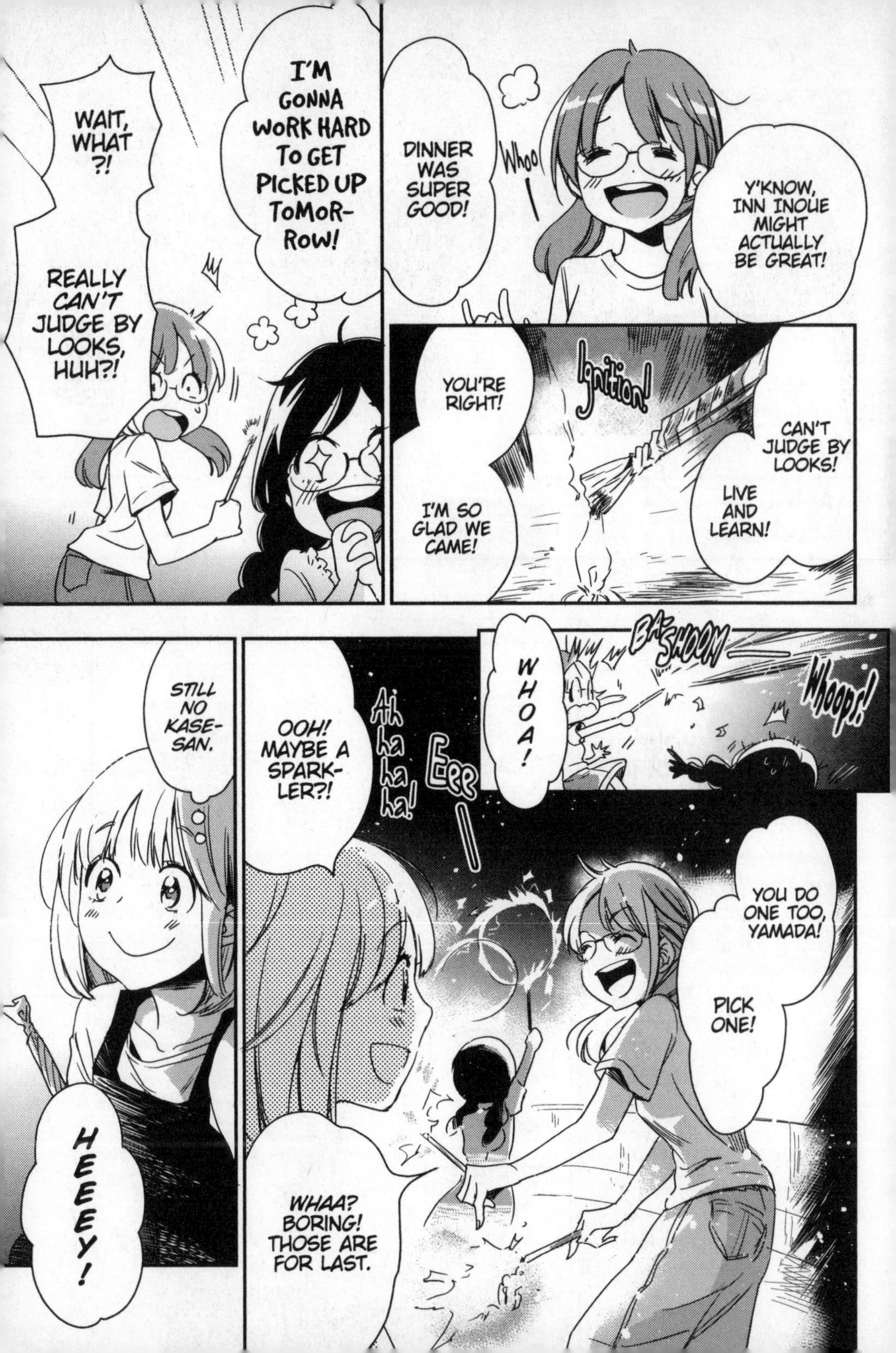

Y'KNOW, INN INOUE MIGHT ACTUALLY BE GREAT!
Whoo—
DINNER WAS SUPER GOOD!
Ignition!
CAN'T JUDGE BY LOOKS!
LIVE AND LEARN!
YOU'RE RIGHT!
I'M SO GLAD WE CAME!
I'M GONNA WORK HARD TO GET PICKED UP TOMOR-ROW!
WAIT, WHAT?!
REALLY CAN'T JUDGE BY LOOKS, HUH?!
Whoops!
BA-SHOOM—
WHOA!
YOU DO ONE TOO, YAMADA!
PICK ONE!
Eee—
Ahhahahaha!
OOH! MAYBE A SPARK-LER?!
WHAA? BORING! THOSE ARE FOR LAST.
STILL NO KASE-SAN.
HEEEY!

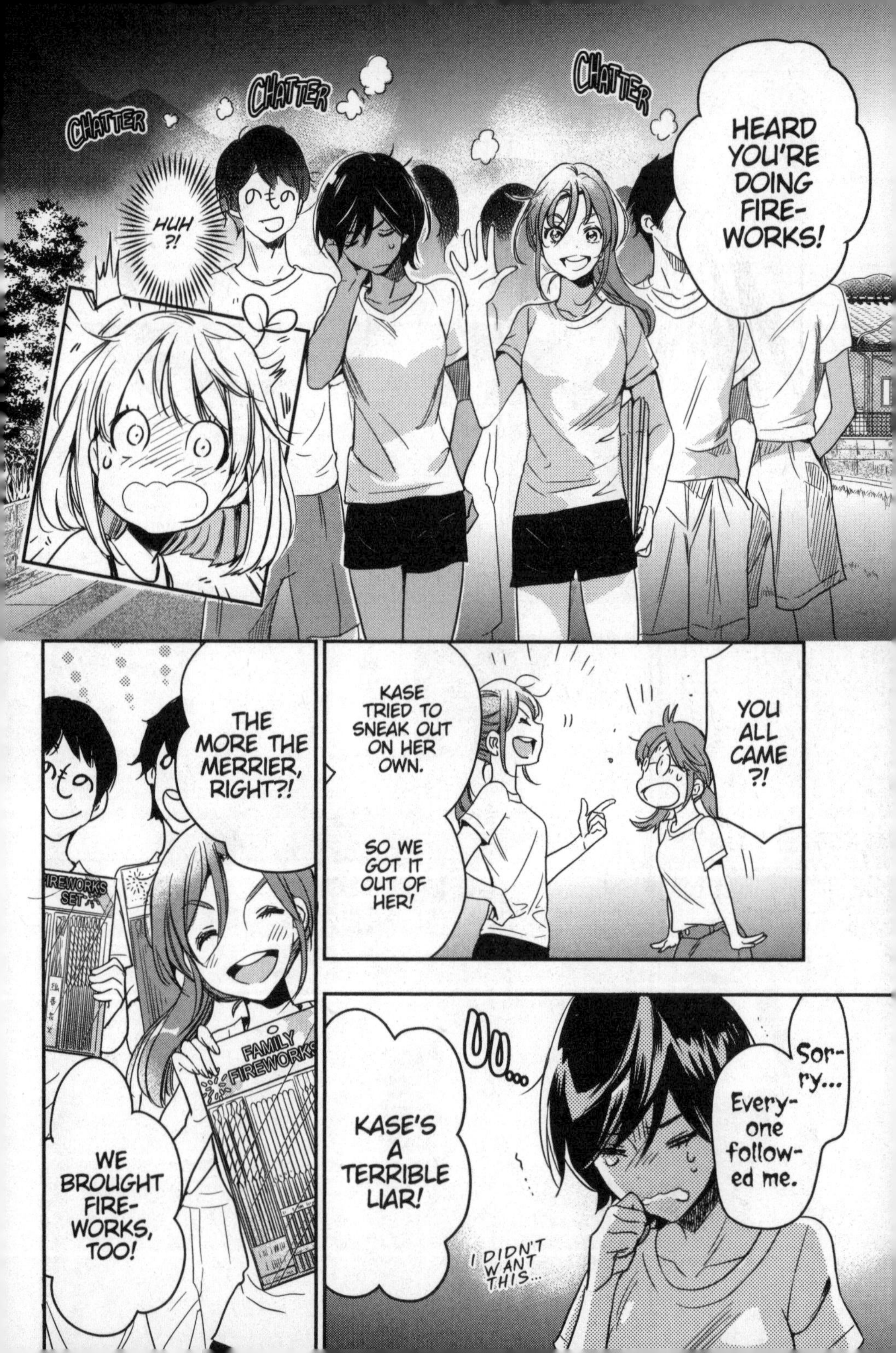
HEARD YOU'RE DOING FIRE-WORKS!
CHATTER
CHATTER
CHATTER
HUH?!
YOU ALL CAME?!
KASE TRIED TO SNEAK OUT ON HER OWN.
SO WE GOT IT OUT OF HER!
Sor-ry... Every-one follow-ed me.
UU...
KASE'S A TERRIBLE LIAR!
I DIDN'T WANT THIS...
THE MORE THE MERRIER, RIGHT?!
FIREWORKS SET
FAMILY FIREWORKS
WE BROUGHT FIRE-WORKS, TOO!

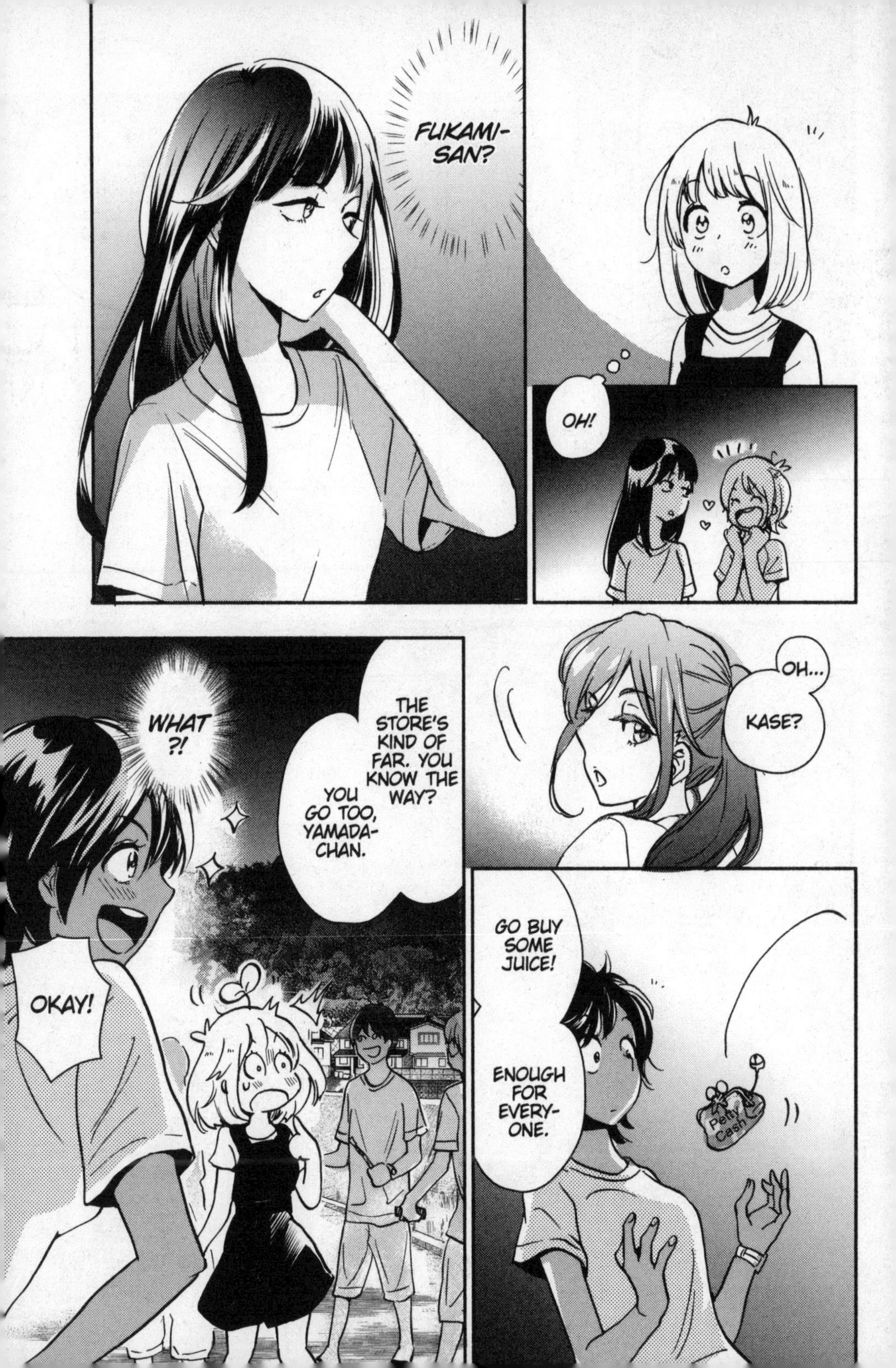
OH!
FUKAMI-SAN?
OH...
KASE?
GO BUY SOME JUICE!
ENOUGH FOR EVERY-ONE.
Petty Cash
THE STORE'S KIND OF FAR. YOU KNOW THE WAY?
YOU GO TOO, YAMADA-CHAN.
WHAT ?!
OKAY!

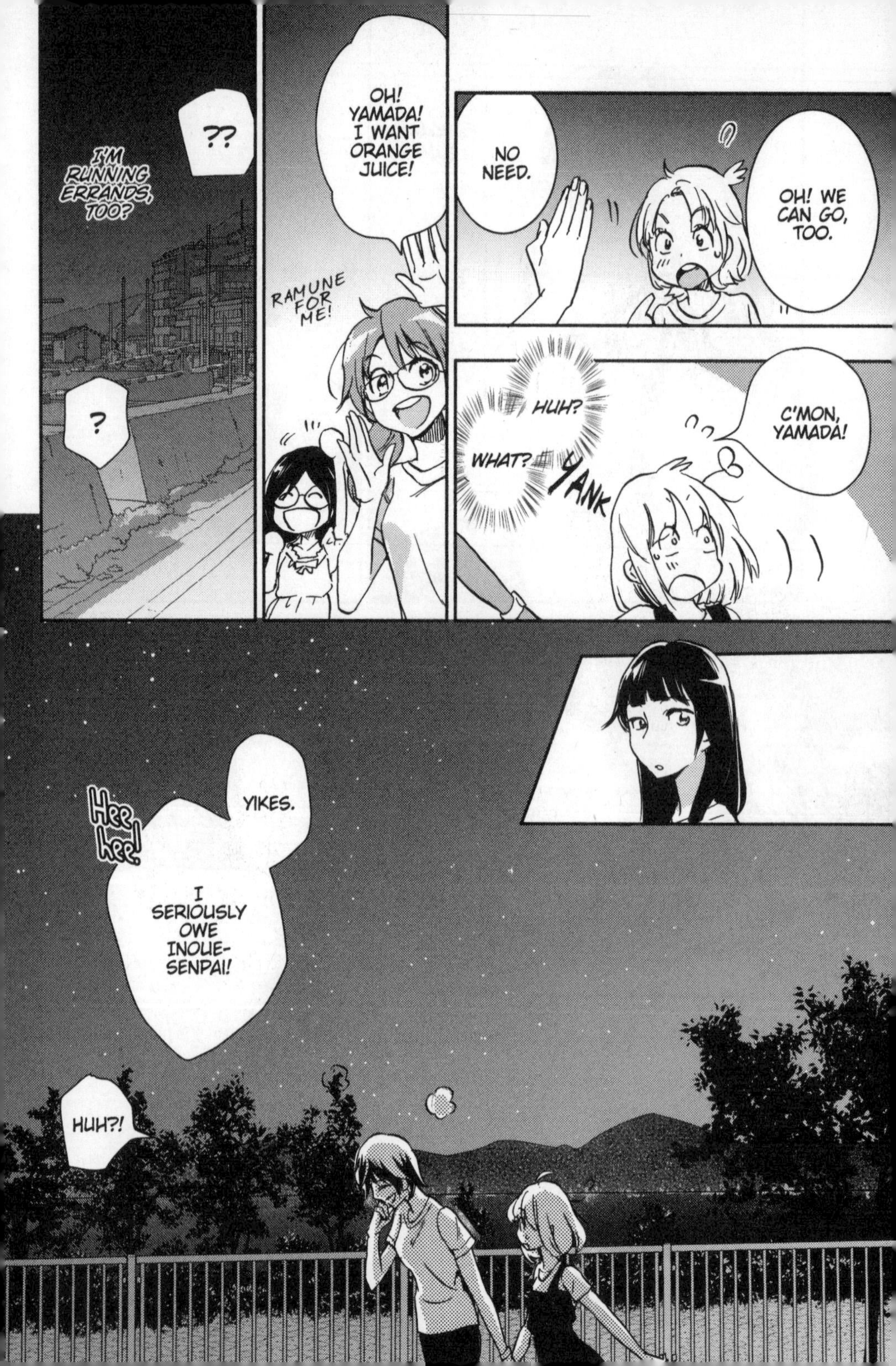
OH! WE CAN GO, TOO.
NO NEED.
C'MON, YAMADA!
YANK
HUH?
WHAT?
OH! YAMADA! I WANT ORANGE JUICE!
RAMUNE FOR ME!
??
I'M RUNNING ERRANDS, TOO?
?
YIKES.
Hee hee!
I SERIOUSLY OWE INOUE-SENPAI!
HUH?!

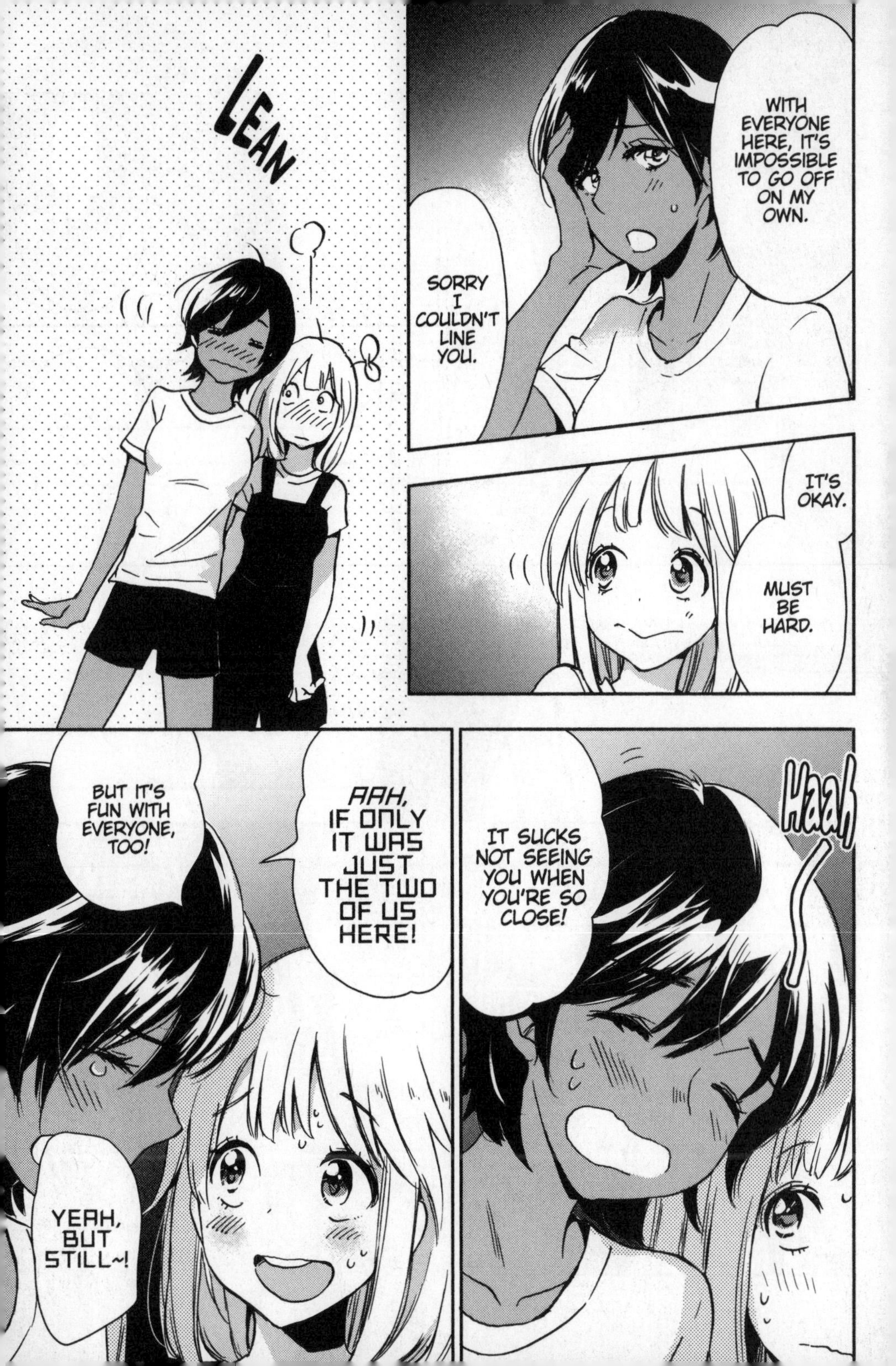
WITH EVERYONE HERE, IT'S IMPOSSIBLE TO GO OFF ON MY OWN.
SORRY I COULDN'T LINE YOU.
IT'S OKAY.
MUST BE HARD.
LEAN
Haah
IT SUCKS NOT SEEING YOU WHEN YOU'RE SO CLOSE!
AAH, IF ONLY IT WAS JUST THE TWO OF US HERE!
BUT IT'S FUN WITH EVERYONE, TOO!
YEAH, BUT STILL~!

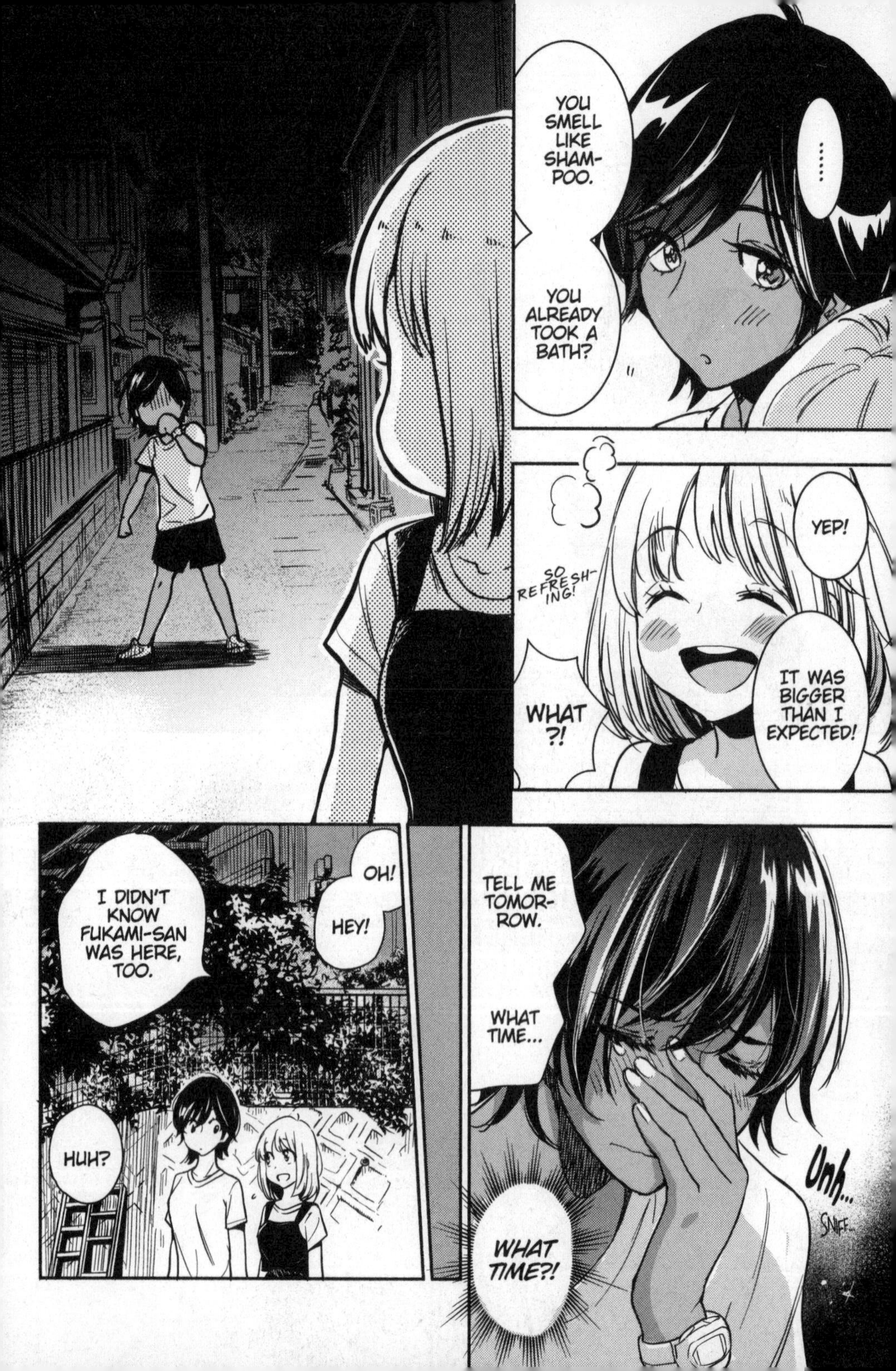
......
YOU SMELL LIKE SHAMPOO.
YOU ALREADY TOOK A BATH?
YEP!
SO REFRESHING!
IT WAS BIGGER THAN I EXPECTED!
WHAT?!
TELL ME TOMORROW.
WHAT TIME...
WHAT TIME?!
Unh...
SNIFF...
OH!
HEY!
I DIDN'T KNOW FUKAMI-SAN WAS HERE, TOO.
HUH?

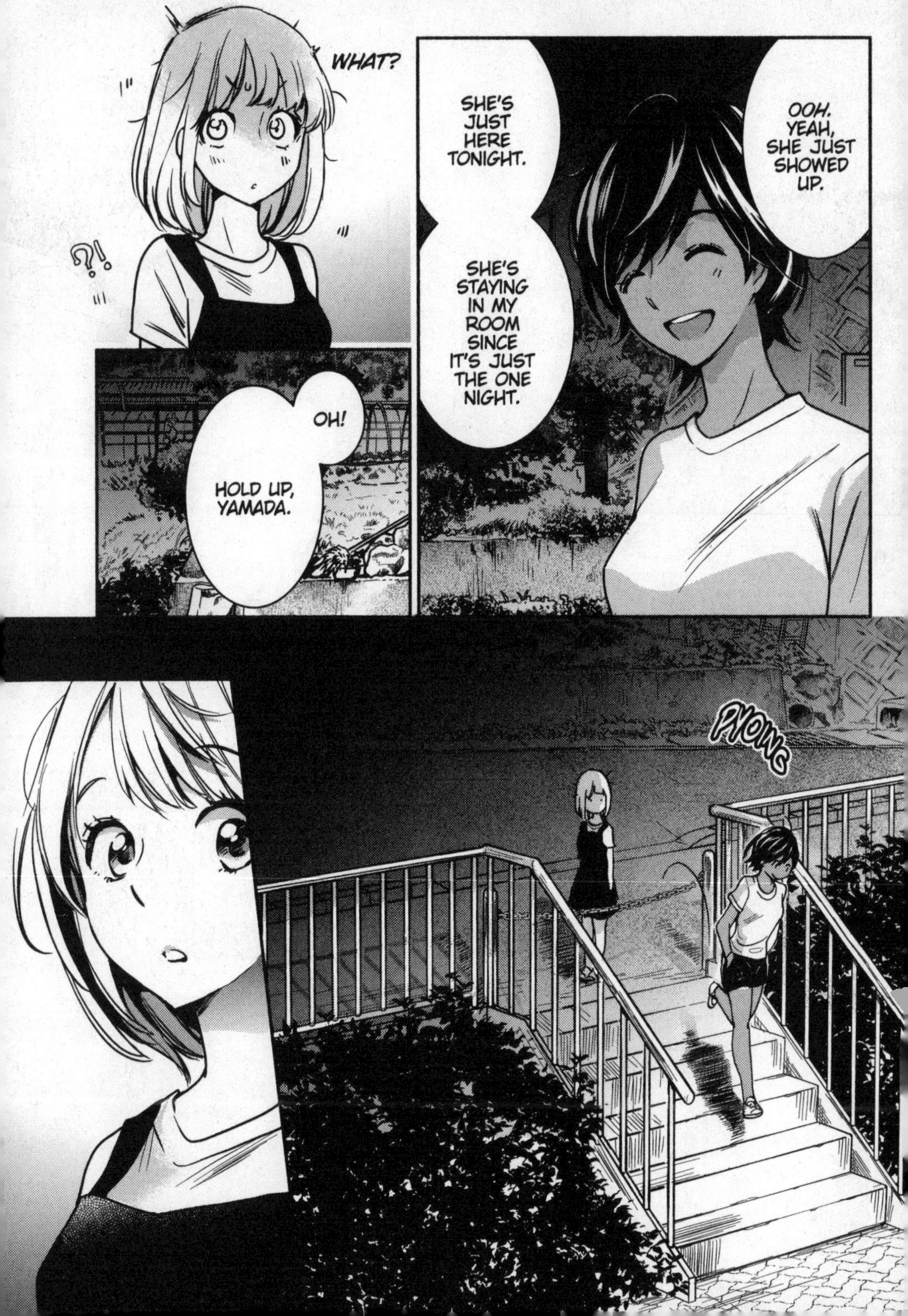

OOH. YEAH, SHE JUST SHOWED UP.
SHE'S JUST HERE TONIGHT.
SHE'S STAYING IN MY ROOM SINCE IT'S JUST THE ONE NIGHT.
WHAT?
?!
OH!
HOLD UP, YAMADA.
PYOING

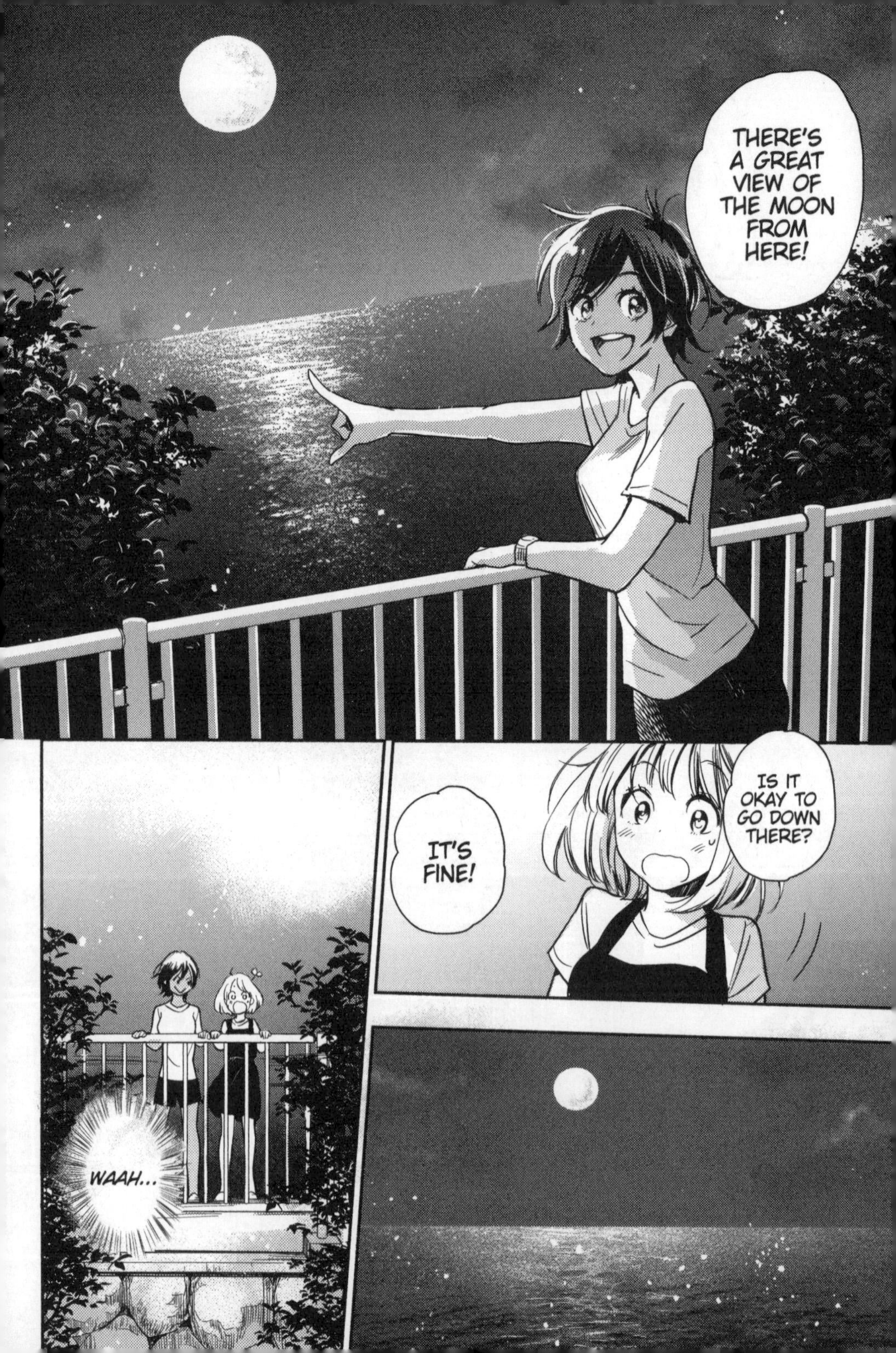
THERE'S A GREAT VIEW OF THE MOON FROM HERE!
IS IT OKAY TO GO DOWN THERE?
IT'S FINE!
WAAH...

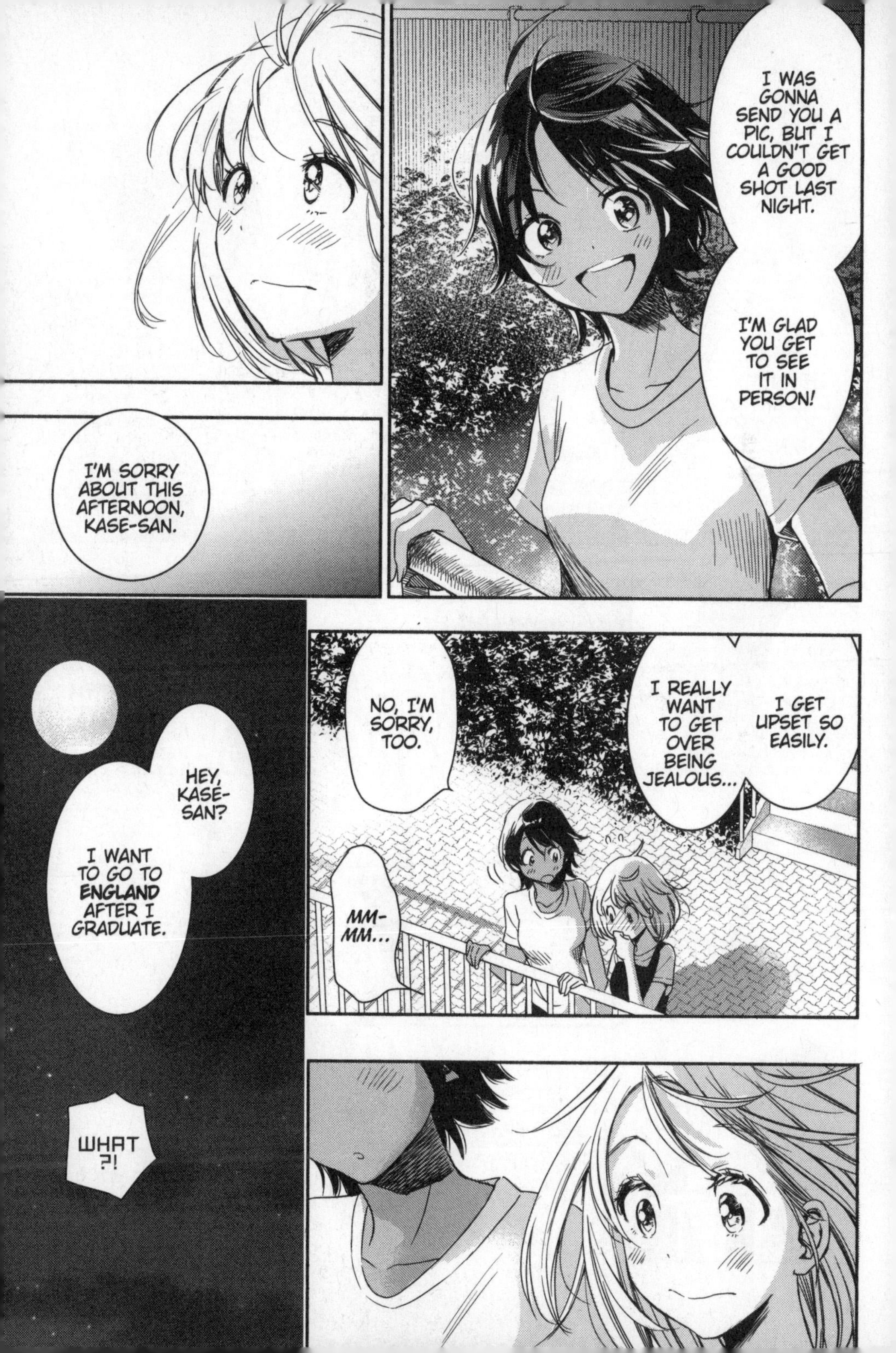
I WAS GONNA SEND YOU A PIC, BUT I COULDN'T GET A GOOD SHOT LAST NIGHT.
I'M GLAD YOU GET TO SEE IT IN PERSON!
I'M SORRY ABOUT THIS AFTERNOON, KASE-SAN.
I GET UPSET SO EASILY.
I REALLY WANT TO GET OVER BEING JEALOUS...
NO, I'M SORRY, TOO.
MM-MM...
HEY, KASE-SAN?
I WANT TO GO TO ENGLAND AFTER I GRADUATE.
WHAT ?!

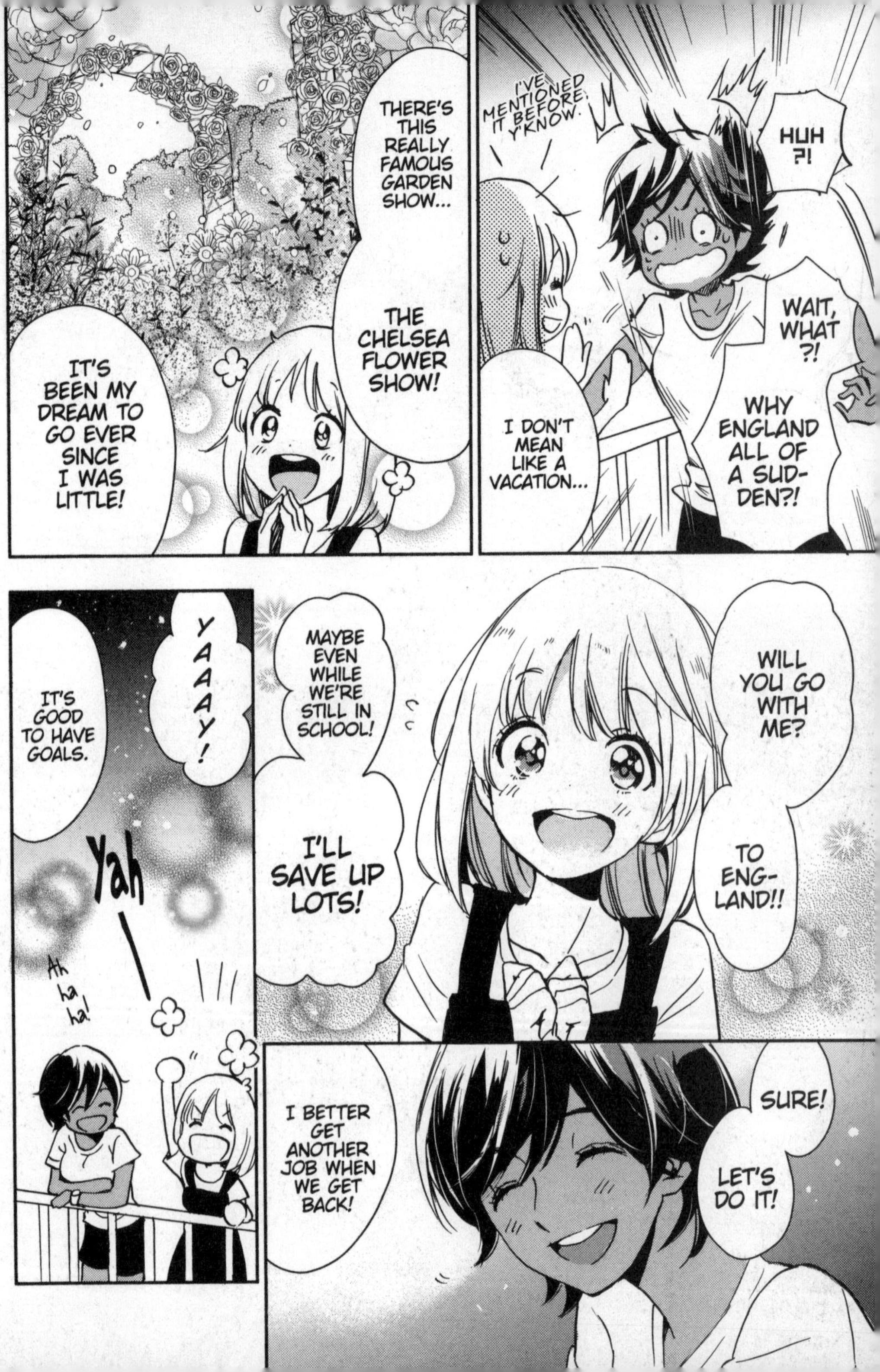
HUH ?!
I'VE MENTIONED IT BEFORE, Y'KNOW.
WAIT, WHAT ?!
WHY ENGLAND ALL OF A SUD- DEN?!
I DON'T MEAN LIKE A VACATION...
THERE'S THIS REALLY FAMOUS GARDEN SHOW...
THE CHELSEA FLOWER SHOW!
IT'S BEEN MY DREAM TO GO EVER SINCE I WAS LITTLE!
WILL YOU GO WITH ME?
TO ENG- LAND!!
MAYBE EVEN WHILE WE'RE STILL IN SCHOOL!
I'LL SAVE UP LOTS!
SURE!
LET'S DO IT!
I BETTER GET ANOTHER JOB WHEN WE GET BACK!
YAAAAY!
IT'S GOOD TO HAVE GOALS.
Yah
Ah ha ha!

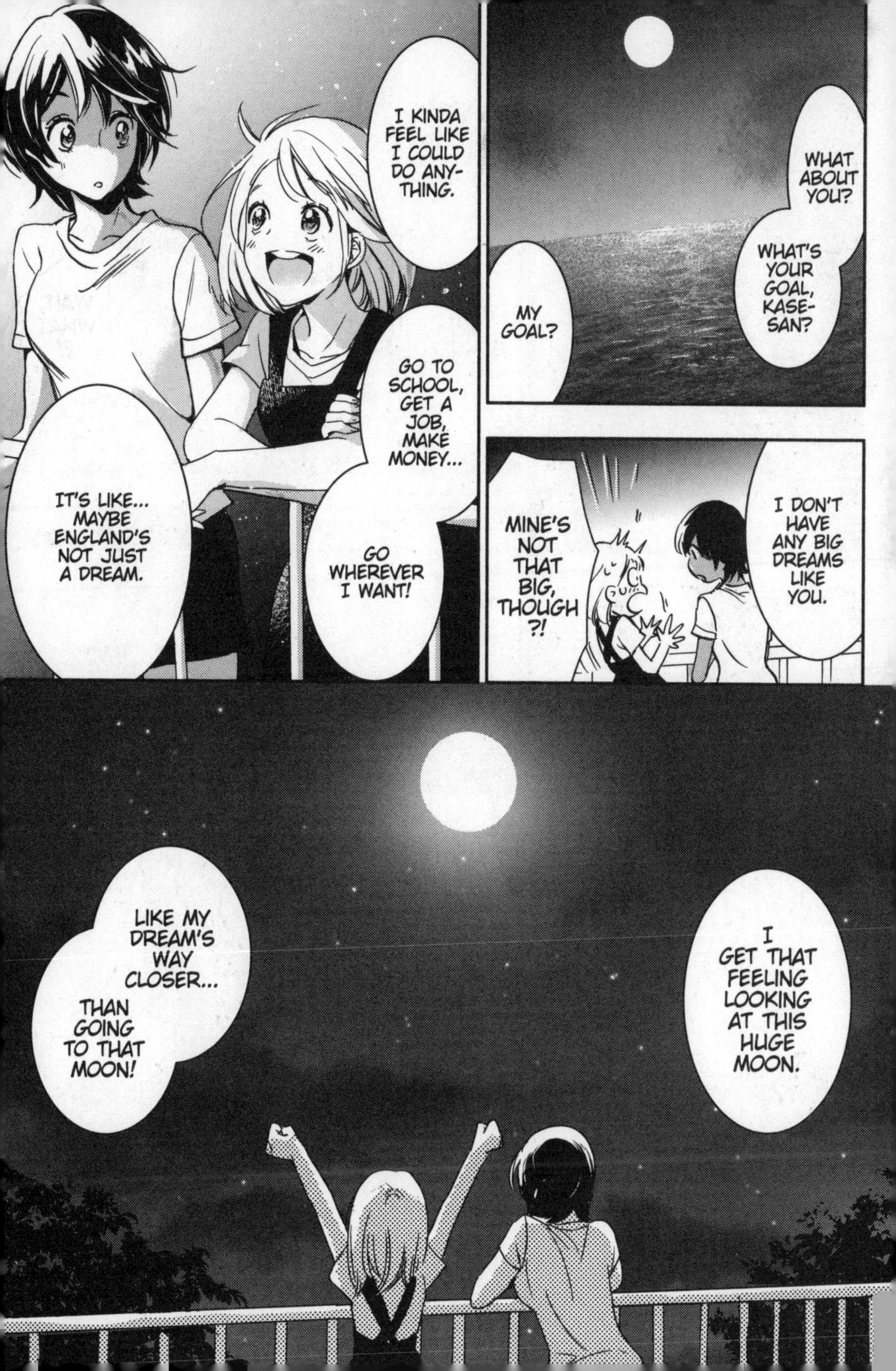
WHAT ABOUT YOU?
WHAT'S YOUR GOAL, KASE-SAN?
MY GOAL?
I DON'T HAVE ANY BIG DREAMS LIKE YOU.
MINE'S NOT THAT BIG, THOUGH?!
I KINDA FEEL LIKE I COULD DO ANY-THING.
GO TO SCHOOL, GET A JOB, MAKE MONEY...
GO WHEREVER I WANT!
IT'S LIKE... MAYBE ENGLAND'S NOT JUST A DREAM.
I GET THAT FEELING LOOKING AT THIS HUGE MOON.
LIKE MY DREAM'S WAY CLOSER...
THAN GOING TO THAT MOON!

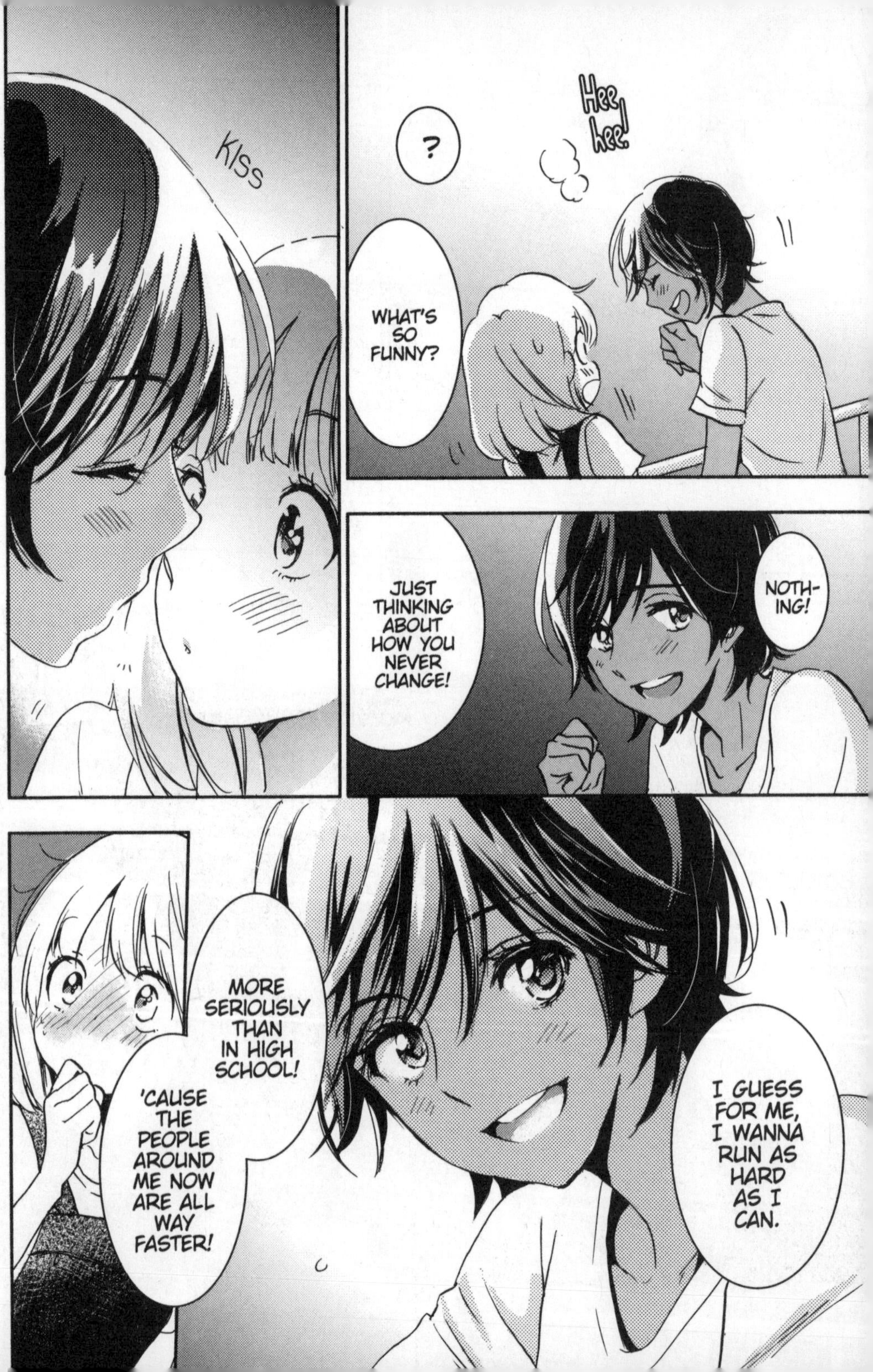
Hee hee!
?
WHAT'S SO FUNNY?
NOTH-ING!
JUST THINKING ABOUT HOW YOU NEVER CHANGE!
KISS
I GUESS FOR ME, I WANNA RUN AS HARD AS I CAN.
MORE SERIOUSLY THAN IN HIGH SCHOOL!
'CAUSE THE PEOPLE AROUND ME NOW ARE ALL WAY FASTER!

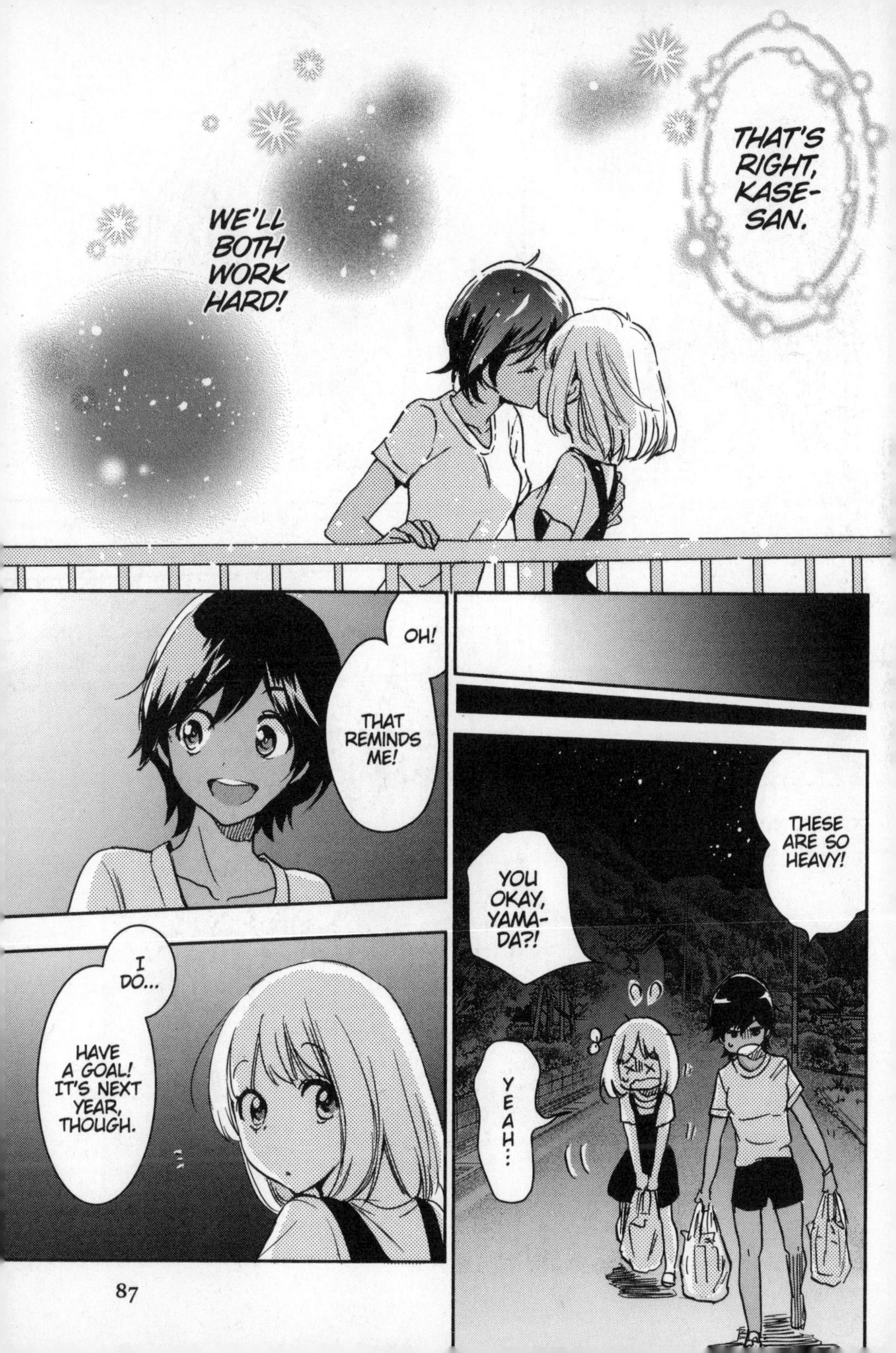
THAT'S RIGHT, KASE-SAN.
WE'LL BOTH WORK HARD!
THESE ARE SO HEAVY!
YOU OKAY, YAMADA?!
YEAH...
OH!
THAT REMINDS ME!
I DO...
HAVE A GOAL! IT'S NEXT YEAR, THOUGH.

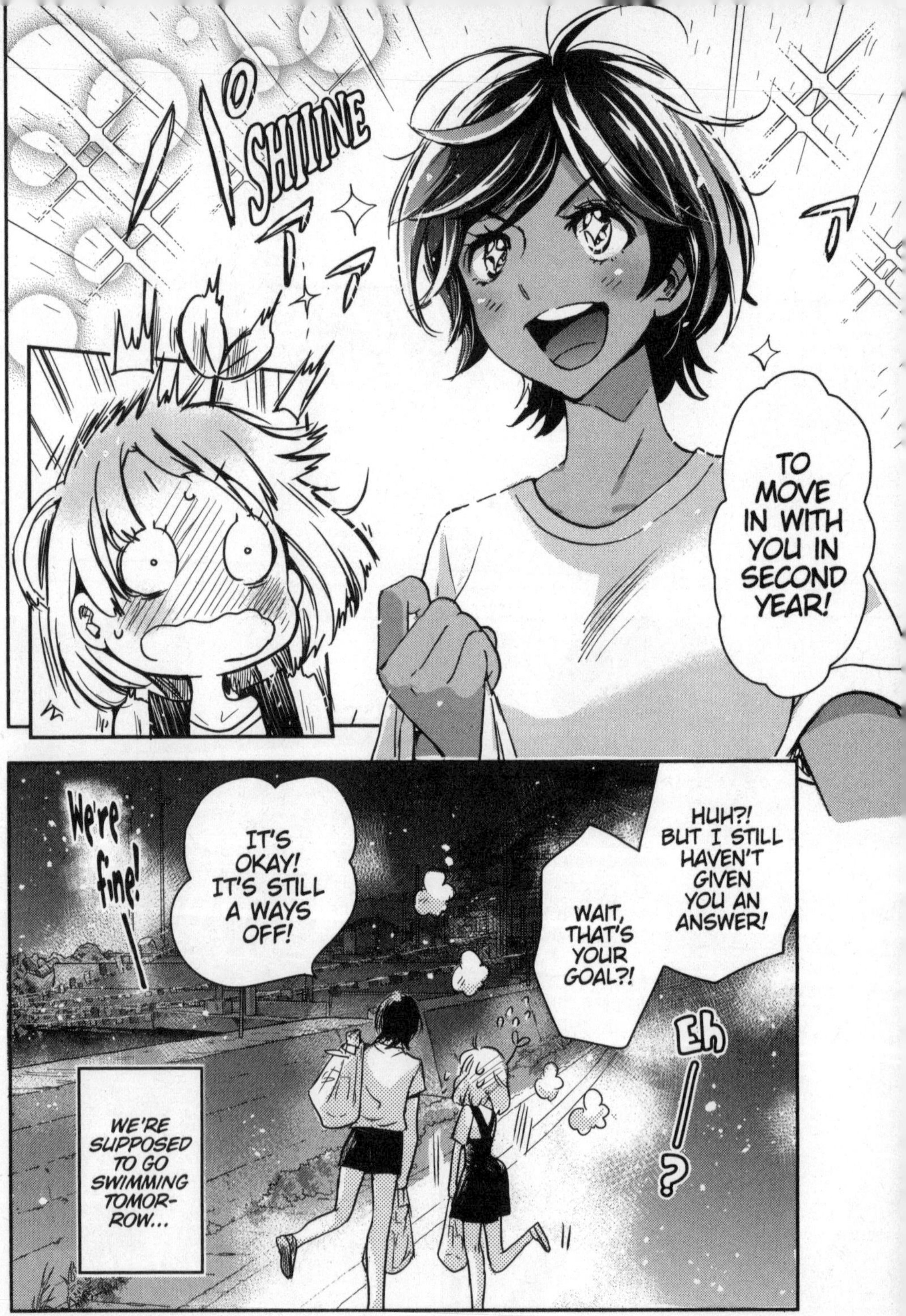
TO MOVE IN WITH YOU IN SECOND YEAR!
SHIIINE
HUH?! BUT I STILL HAVEN'T GIVEN YOU AN ANSWER!
WAIT, THAT'S YOUR GOAL?!
Eh—?
IT'S OKAY! IT'S STILL A WAYS OFF!
We're fine!
WE'RE SUPPOSED TO GO SWIMMING TOMOR-ROW...

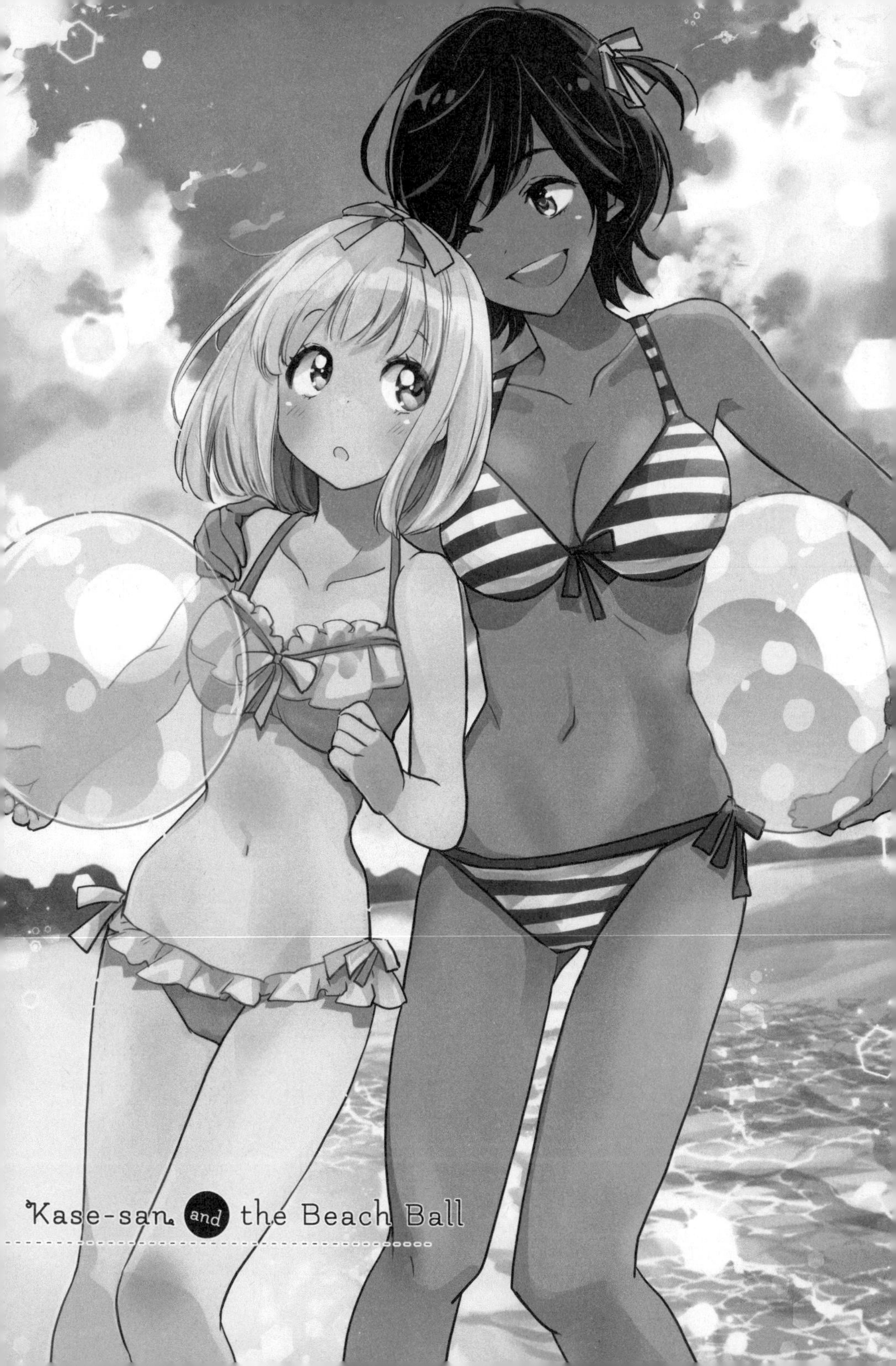
Kase-san and the Beach Ball

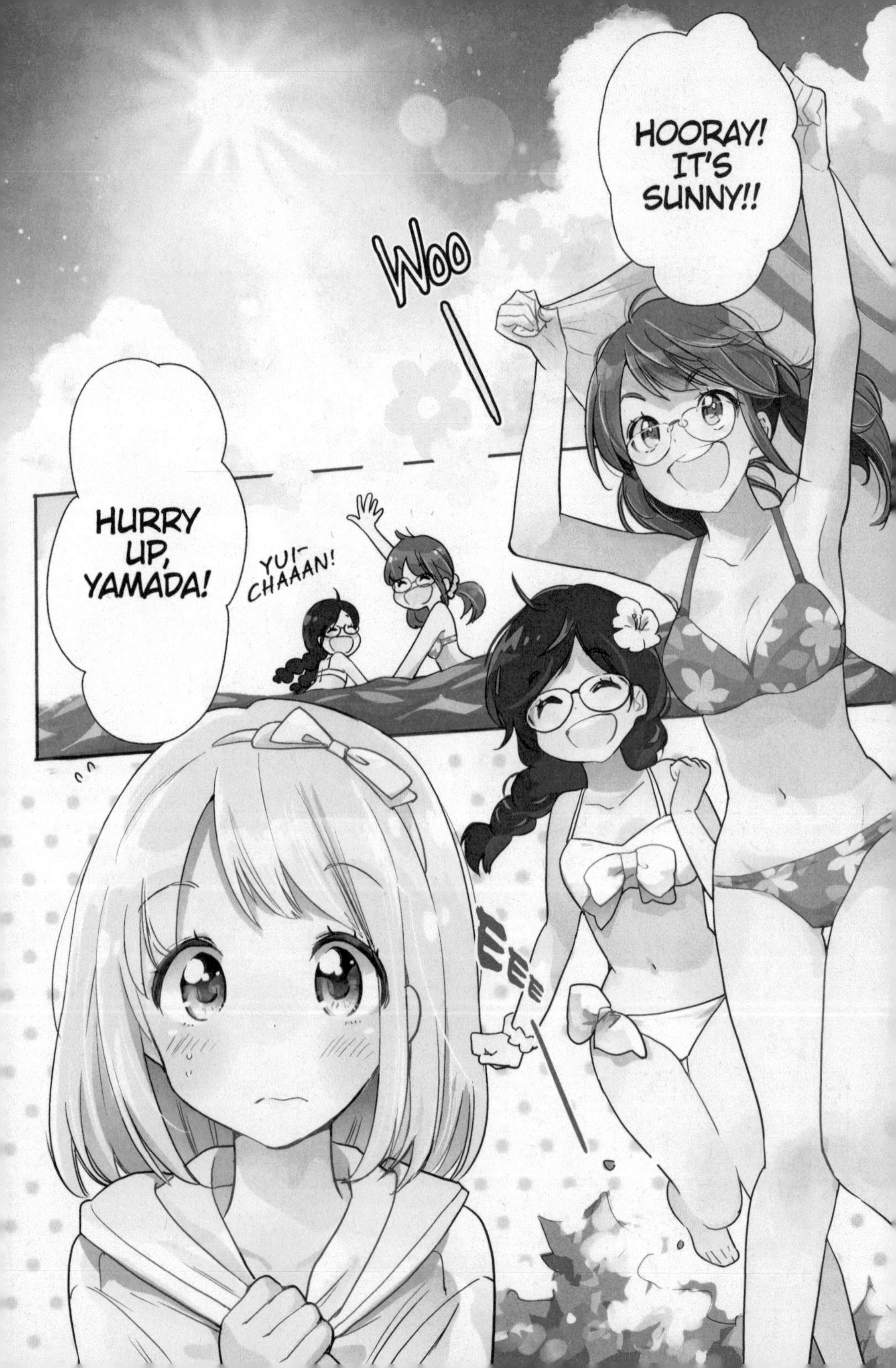
HOORAY! IT'S SUNNY!!
Woo
YUI-CHAAAN!
HURRY UP, YAMADA!
EEE

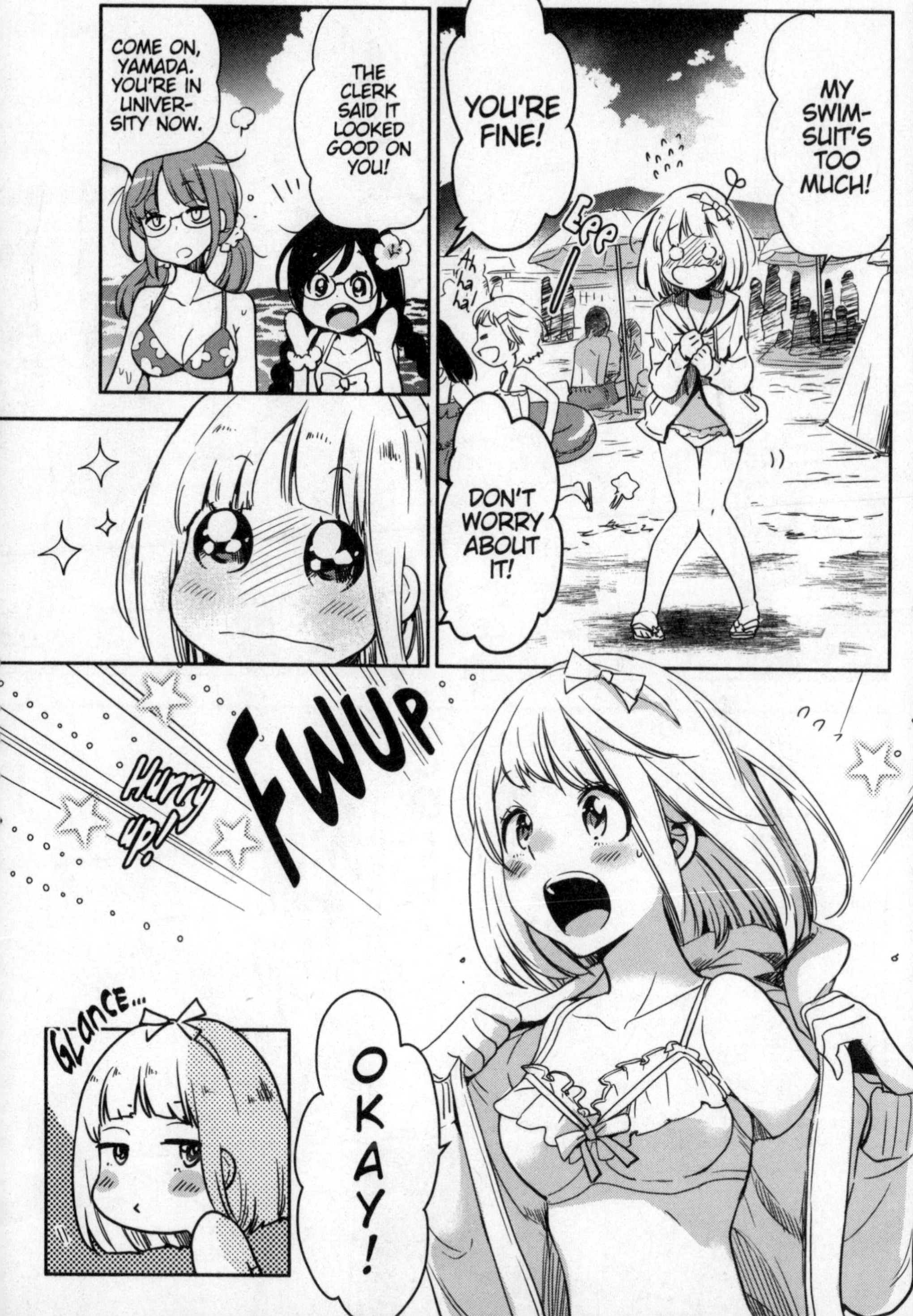
MY SWIM-SUIT'S TOO MUCH!
Eee!
YOU'RE FINE!
Ah ha ha!
DON'T WORRY ABOUT IT!
THE CLERK SAID IT LOOKED GOOD ON YOU!
COME ON, YAMADA. YOU'RE IN UNIVER-SITY NOW.
FWUP
Hurry up!
OKAY!
Glance...

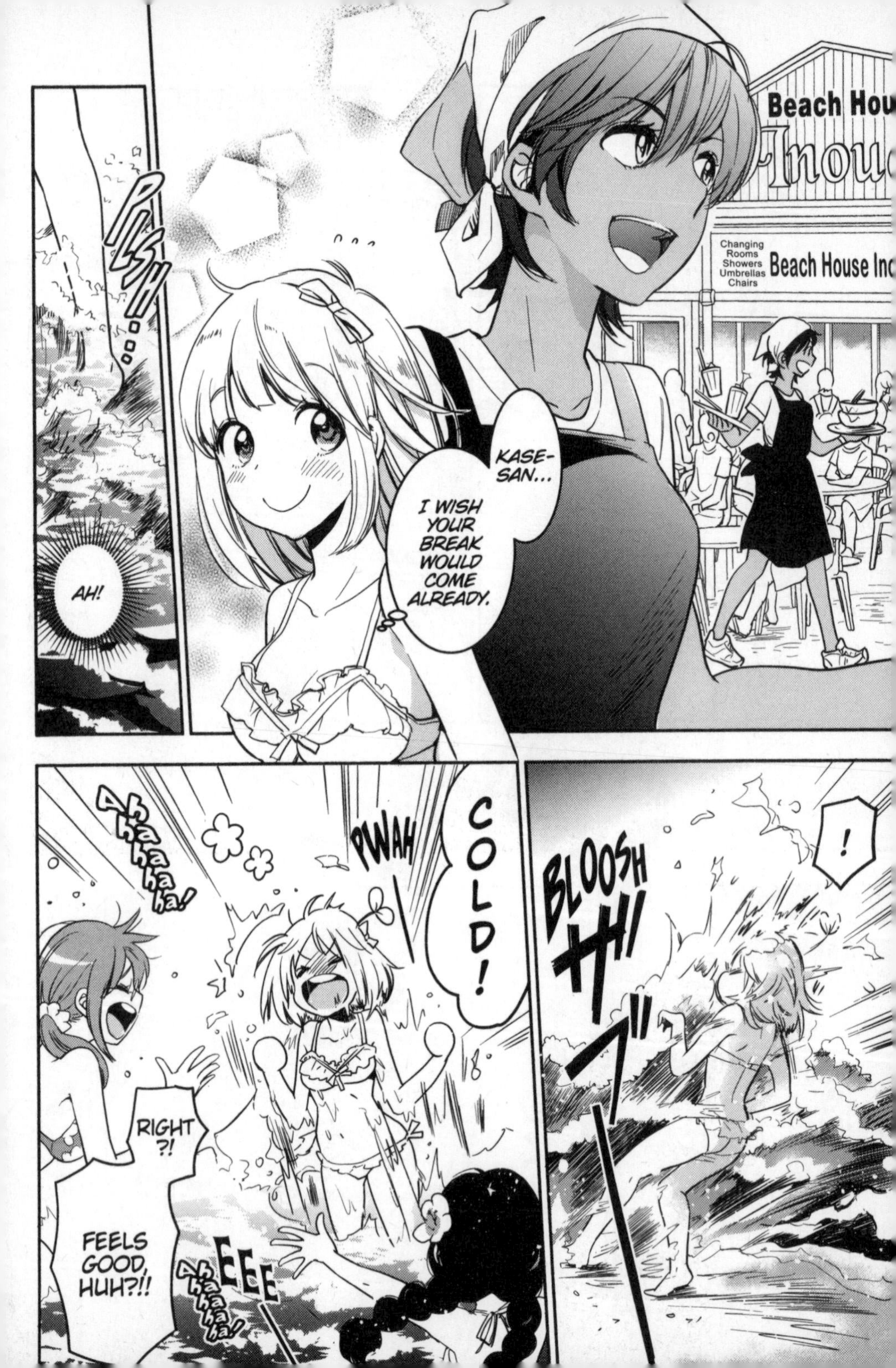
Beach Hou
Inou
Changing Rooms Showers Umbrellas Chairs
Beach House Ino
KASE-SAN...
I WISH YOUR BREAK WOULD COME ALREADY.
PISH...
AH!
!
BLOOSH
COLD!
PWAH
Ahahahaha!
RIGHT?!
FEELS GOOD, HUH?!!
EEE
Ahahahaha!

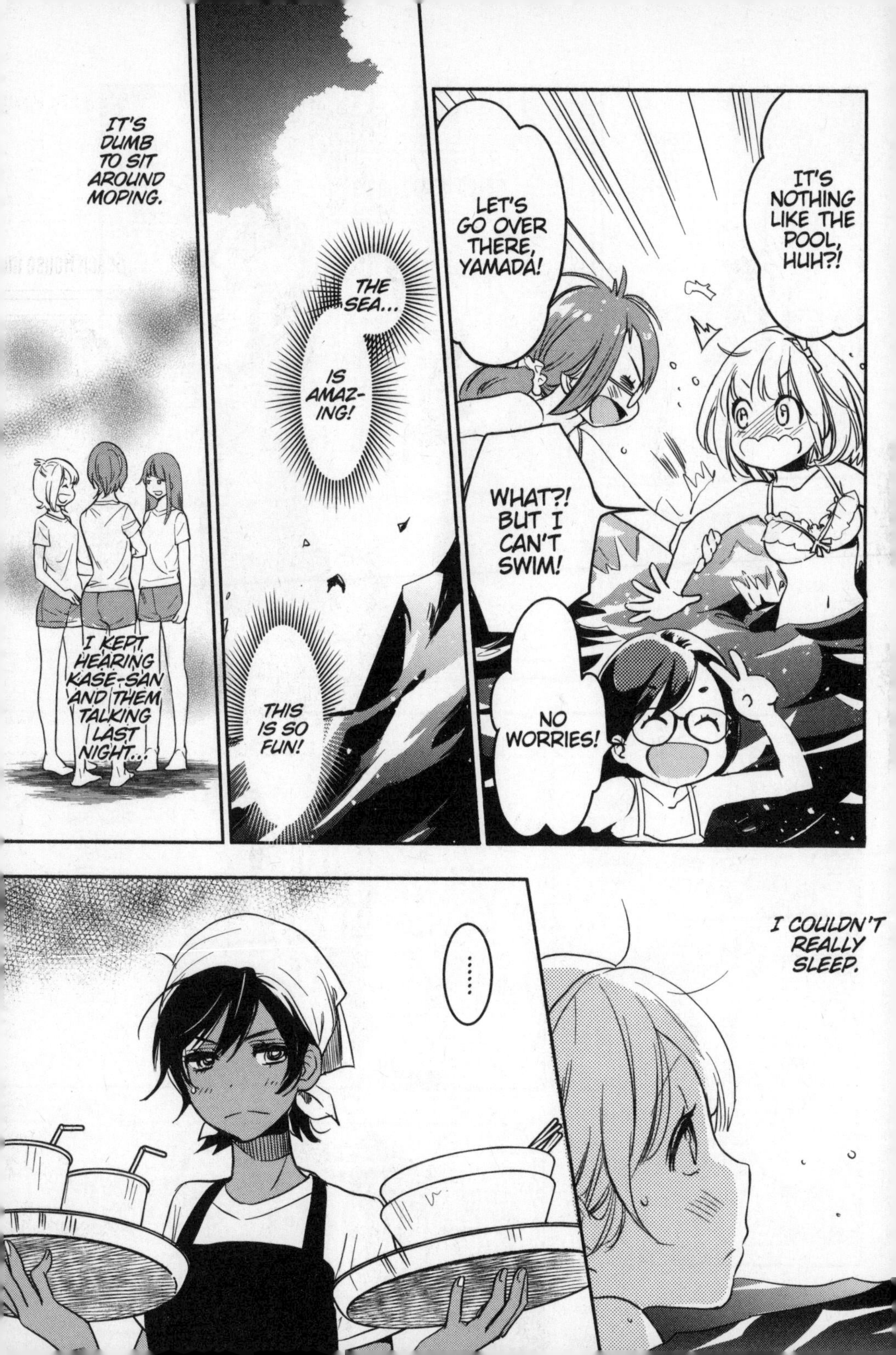
IT'S NOTHING LIKE THE POOL, HUH?!
LET'S GO OVER THERE, YAMADA!
WHAT?! BUT I CAN'T SWIM!
NO WORRIES!
THE SEA...
IS AMAZING!
THIS IS SO FUN!
IT'S DUMB TO SIT AROUND MOPING.
I KEPT HEARING KASE-SAN AND THEM TALKING LAST NIGHT...
I COULDN'T REALLY SLEEP.
......

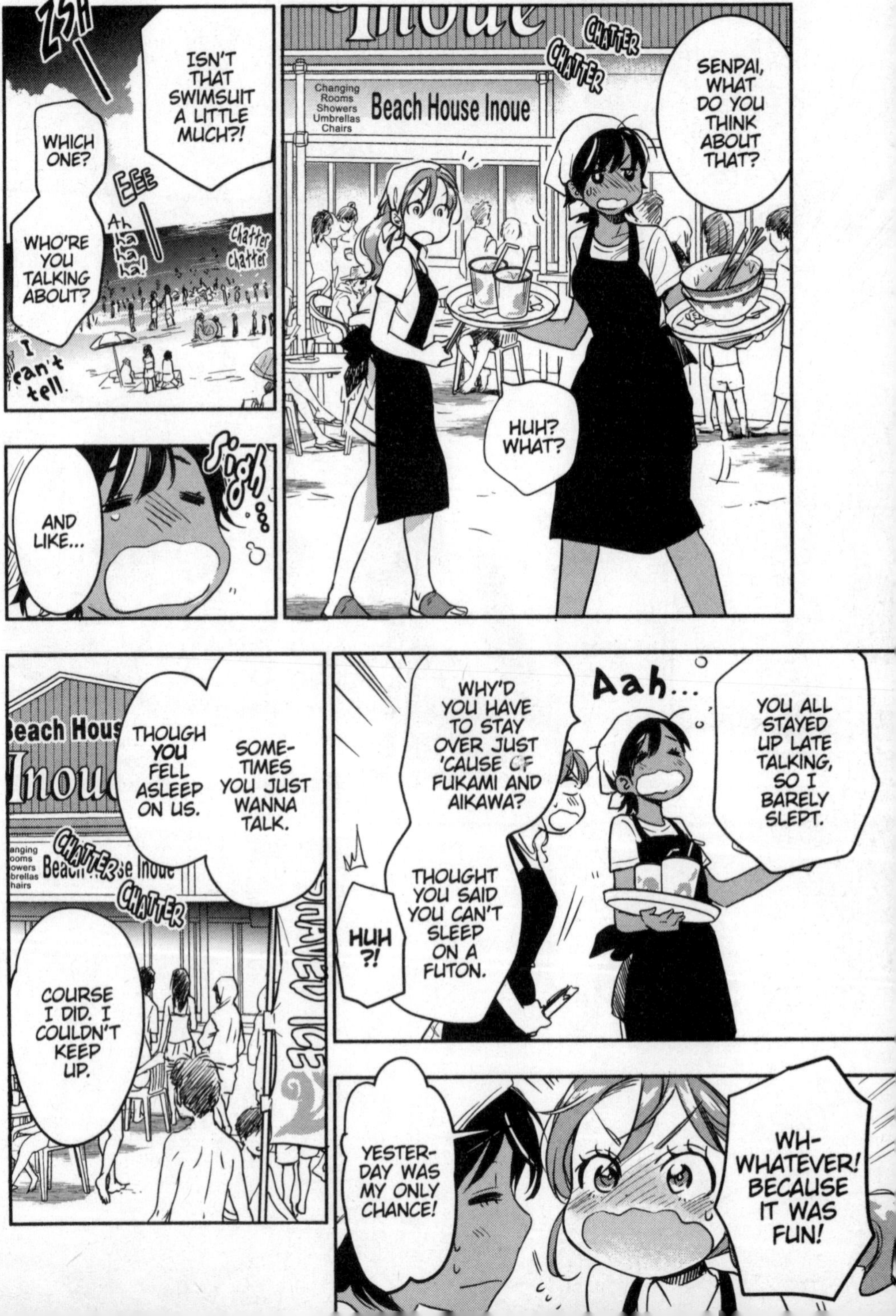
Inoue
Changing Rooms Showers Umbrellas Chairs
Beach House Inoue
CHATTER CHATTER
SENPAI, WHAT DO YOU THINK ABOUT THAT?
HUH? WHAT?
ZSH
ISN'T THAT SWIMSUIT A LITTLE MUCH?!
WHICH ONE?
EEE
Ah ha ha ha!
Chatter chatter
WHO'RE YOU TALKING ABOUT?
I can't tell.
Sigh
AND LIKE...
YOU ALL STAYED UP LATE TALKING, SO I BARELY SLEPT.
Aah...
WHY'D YOU HAVE TO STAY OVER JUST 'CAUSE OF FUKAMI AND AIKAWA?
THOUGHT YOU SAID YOU CAN'T SLEEP ON A FUTON.
HUH?!
WH-WHATEVER! BECAUSE IT WAS FUN!
YESTER-DAY WAS MY ONLY CHANCE!
SOME-TIMES YOU JUST WANNA TALK.
THOUGH YOU FELL ASLEEP ON US.
CHATTER CHATTER
COURSE I DID. I COULDN'T KEEP UP.

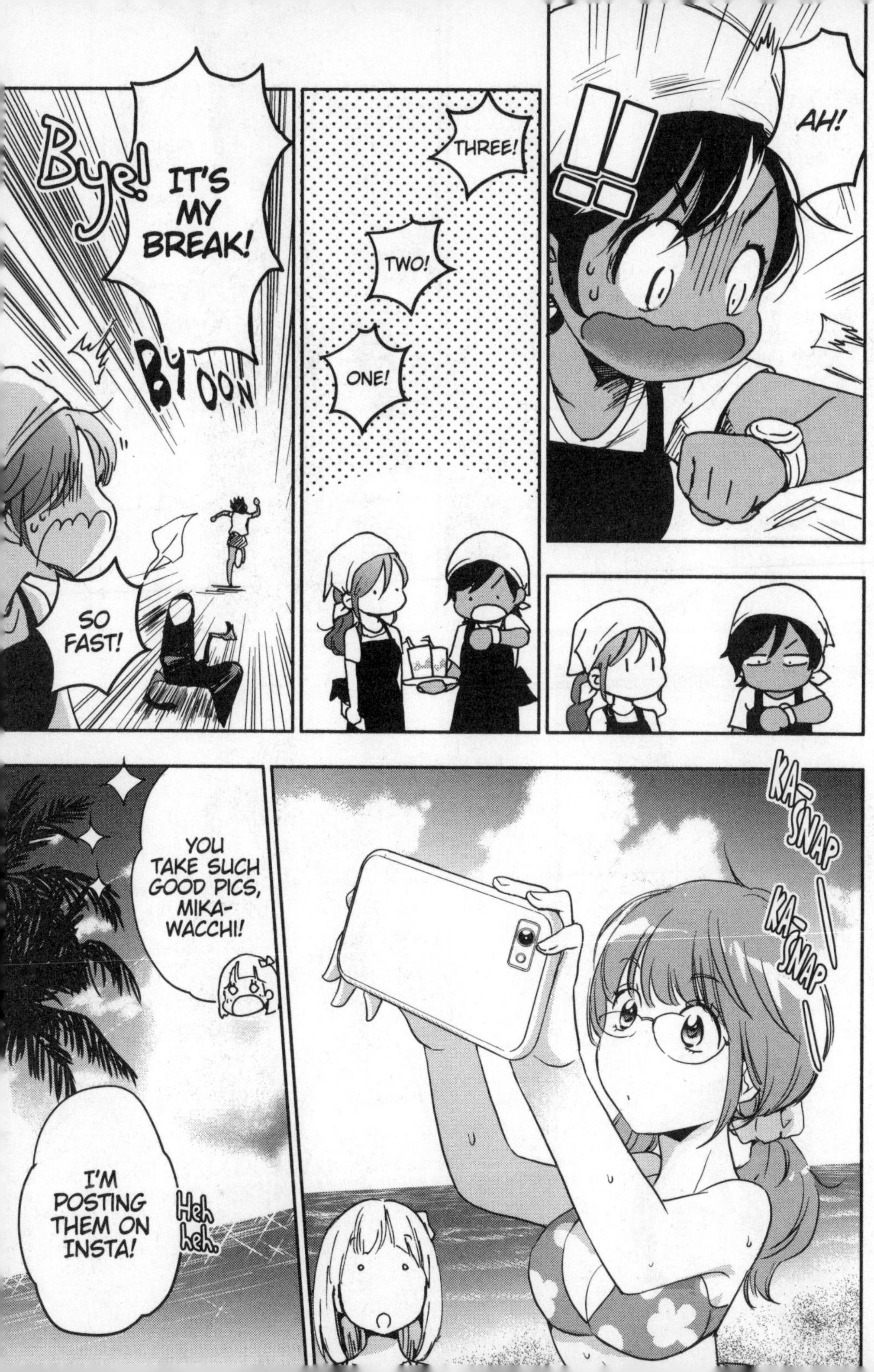
!!
AH!
THREE!
TWO!
ONE!
Bye!
IT'S MY BREAK!
BYOON
SO FAST!
KA-SNAP—
KA-SNAP—
YOU TAKE SUCH GOOD PICS, MIKA-WACCHI!
I'M POSTING THEM ON INSTA!
Heh heh.

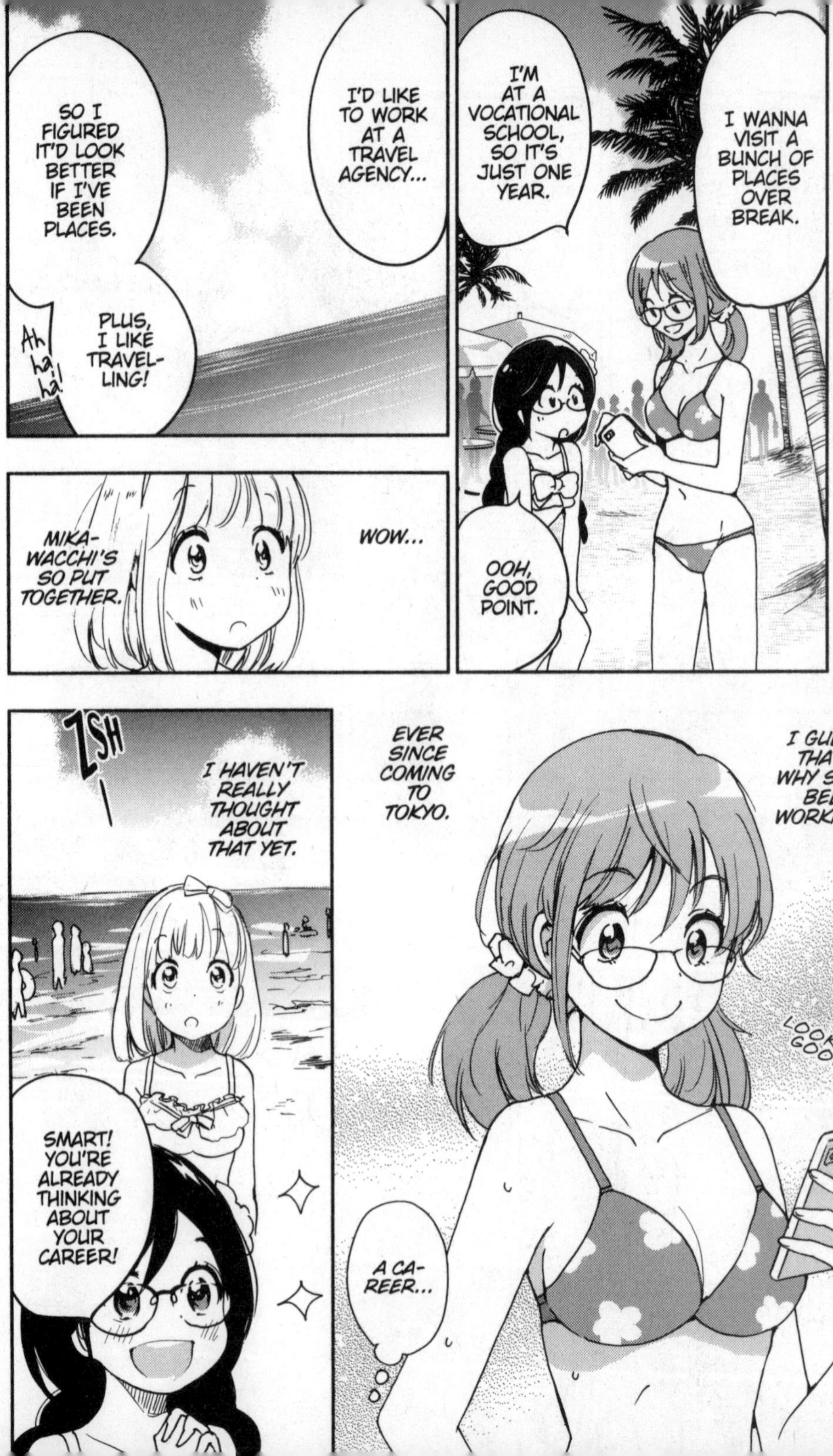
I WANNA VISIT A BUNCH OF PLACES OVER BREAK.
I'M AT A VOCATIONAL SCHOOL, SO IT'S JUST ONE YEAR.
OOH, GOOD POINT.
I'D LIKE TO WORK AT A TRAVEL AGENCY...
SO I FIGURED IT'D LOOK BETTER IF I'VE BEEN PLACES.
PLUS, I LIKE TRAVEL-LING!
Ah ha ha!
WOW...
MIKA-WACCHI'S SO PUT TOGETHER.
I GUESS THAT'S WHY SHE'S BEEN WORKING...
EVER SINCE COMING TO TOKYO.
LOOKING GOOD!
A CA-REER...
ZSH
I HAVEN'T REALLY THOUGHT ABOUT THAT YET.
SMART! YOU'RE ALREADY THINKING ABOUT YOUR CAREER!

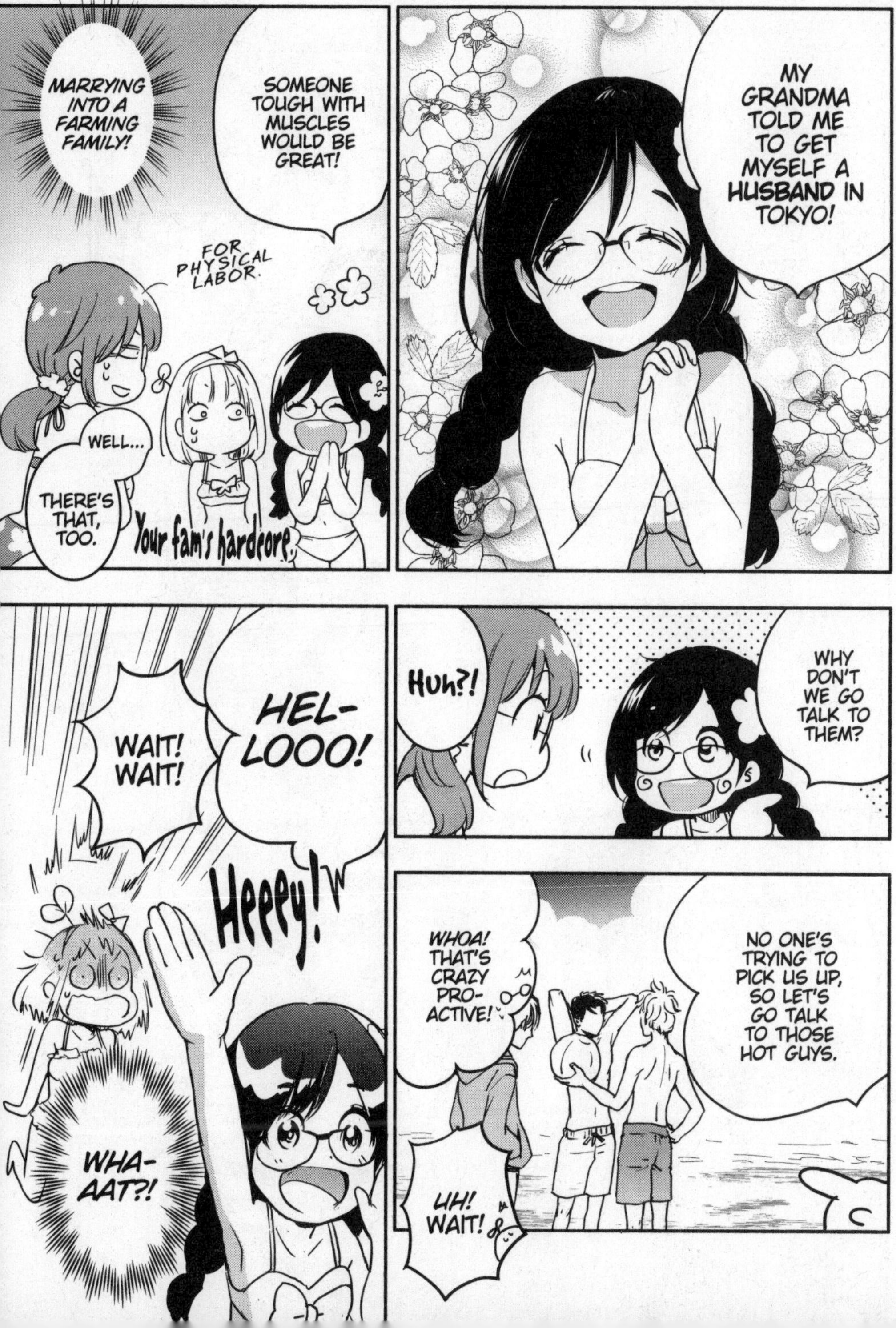
MY GRANDMA TOLD ME TO GET MYSELF A HUSBAND IN TOKYO!
SOMEONE TOUGH WITH MUSCLES WOULD BE GREAT!
MARRYING INTO A FARMING FAMILY!
FOR PHYSICAL LABOR.
WELL...
THERE'S THAT, TOO.
Your fam's hardcore.
WHY DON'T WE GO TALK TO THEM?
Huh?!
NO ONE'S TRYING TO PICK US UP, SO LET'S GO TALK TO THOSE HOT GUYS.
WHOA! THAT'S CRAZY PRO-ACTIVE!
UH! WAIT!
HEL-LOOO!
WAIT! WAIT!
Heppy!
WHA-AAT?!

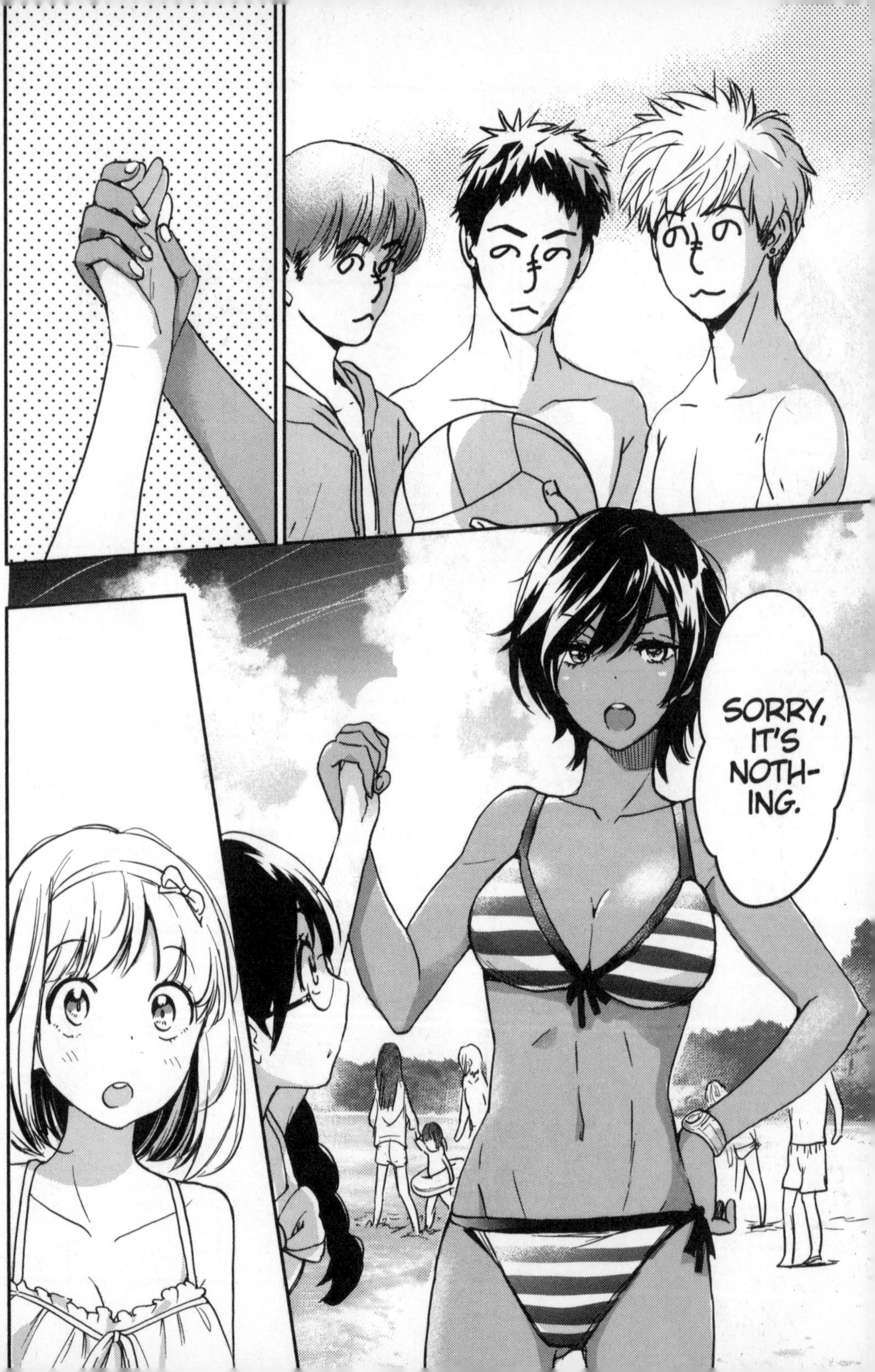
SORRY, IT'S NOTH-ING.

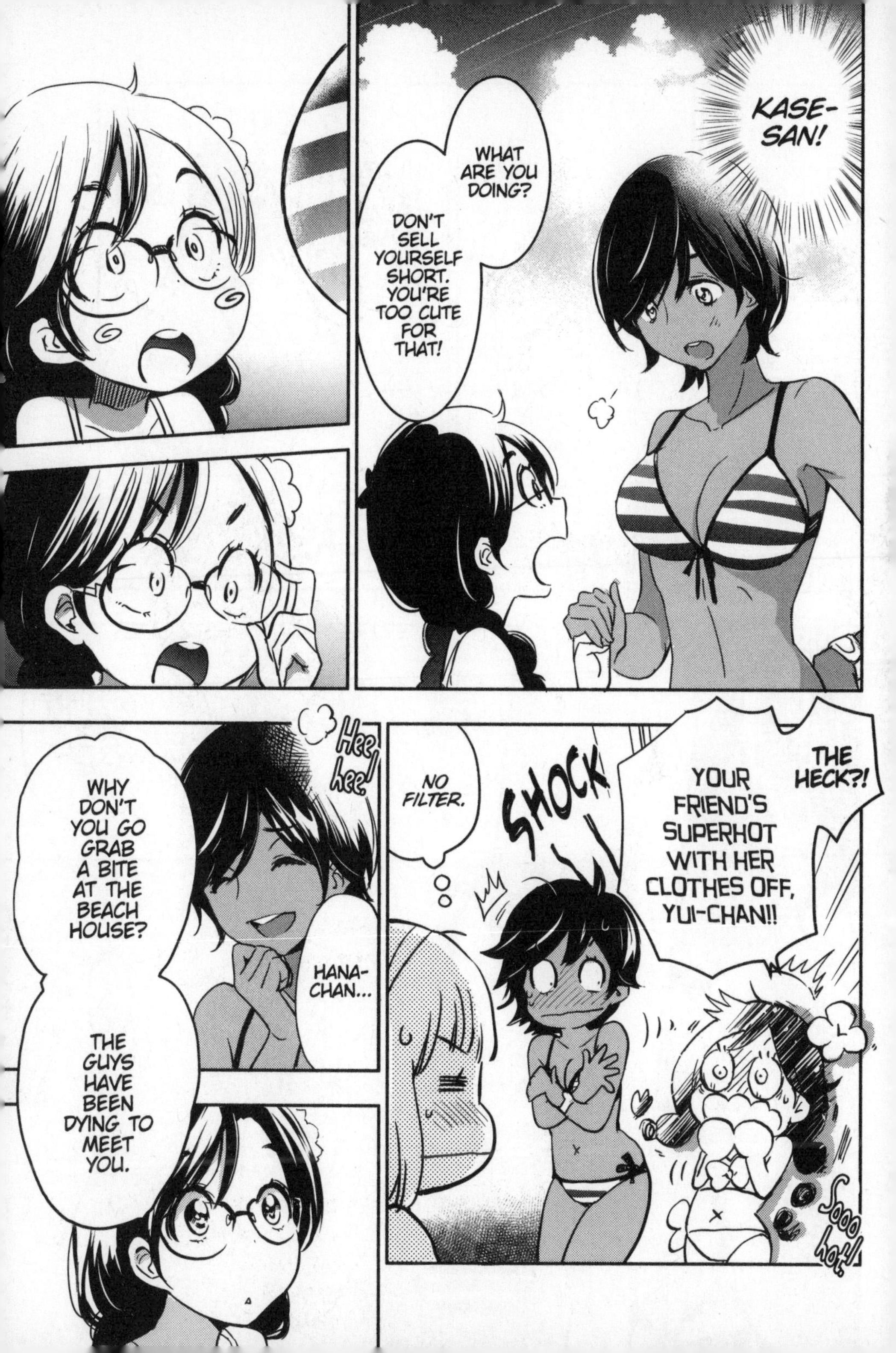
KASE-SAN!
WHAT ARE YOU DOING?
DON'T SELL YOURSELF SHORT. YOU'RE TOO CUTE FOR THAT!
THE HECK?!
YOUR FRIEND'S SUPERHOT WITH HER CLOTHES OFF, YUI-CHAN!!
SHOCK
NO FILTER.
Sooo hot!!
Hee hee!
WHY DON'T YOU GO GRAB A BITE AT THE BEACH HOUSE?
HANA-CHAN...
THE GUYS HAVE BEEN DYING TO MEET YOU.

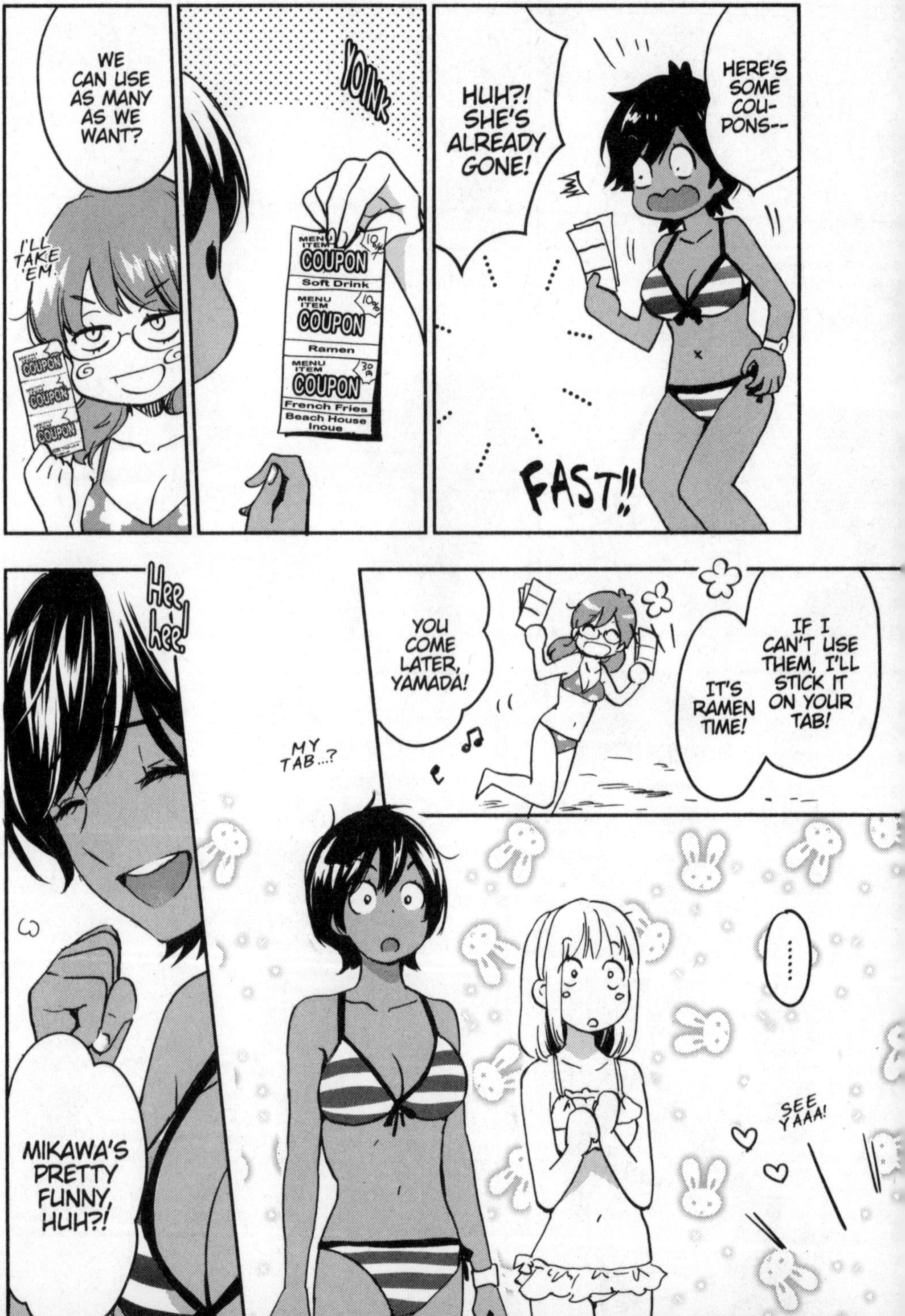
HERE'S SOME COU-PONS--
HUH?! SHE'S ALREADY GONE!
FAST!!
YOINK
MENU ITEM COUPON
Soft Drink
MENU ITEM COUPON
Ramen
MENU ITEM COUPON
French Fries
Beach House Inoue
WE CAN USE AS MANY AS WE WANT?
I'LL TAKE 'EM.
IF I CAN'T USE THEM, I'LL STICK IT ON YOUR TAB!
IT'S RAMEN TIME!
YOU COME LATER, YAMADA!
MY TAB...?
......
SEE YAAA!
Hee hee!
MIKAWA'S PRETTY FUNNY, HUH?!

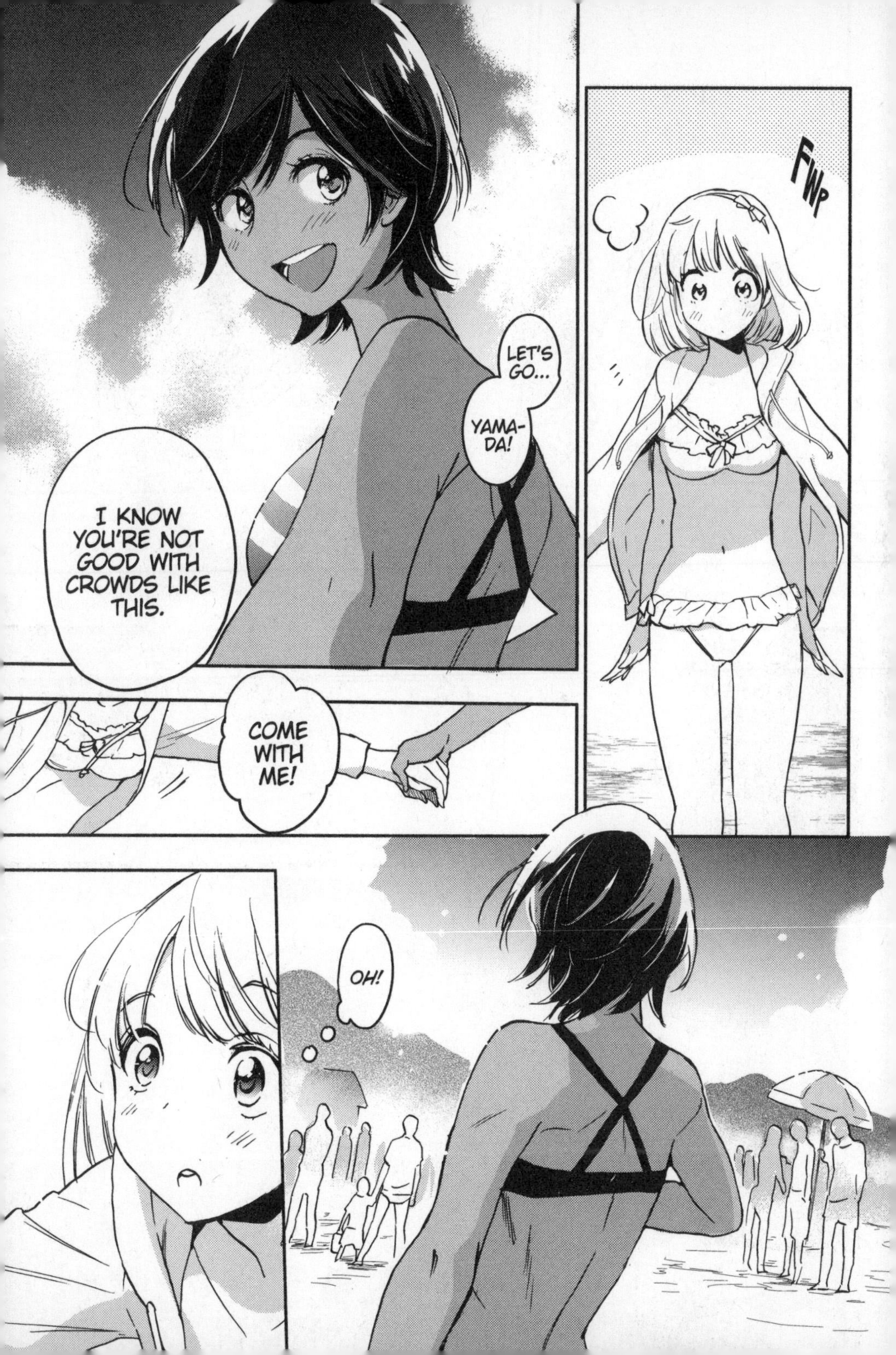
FWP
LET'S GO... YAMADA!
I KNOW YOU'RE NOT GOOD WITH CROWDS LIKE THIS.
COME WITH ME!
OH!

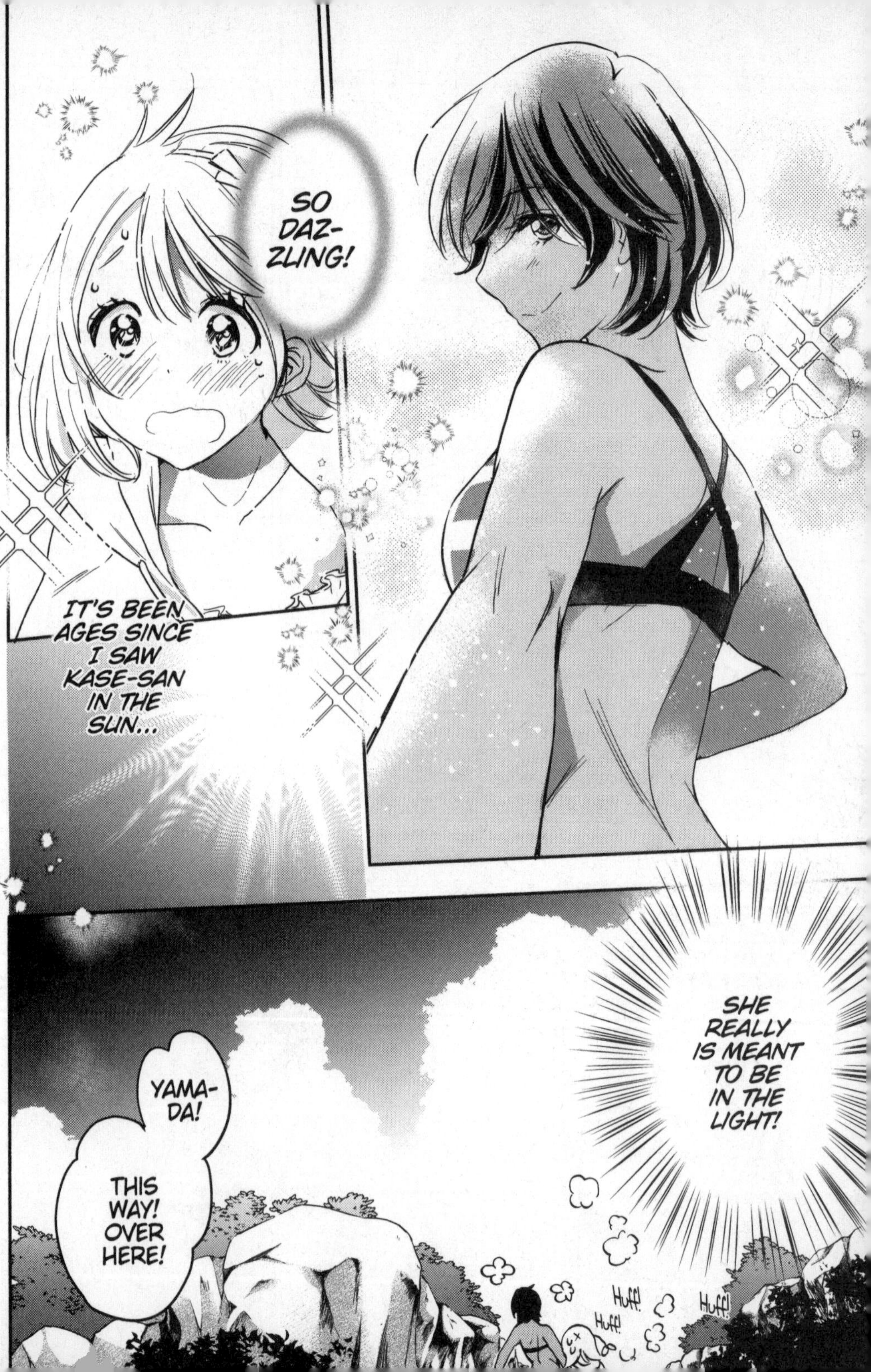
SO DAZ-ZLING!
IT'S BEEN AGES SINCE I SAW KASE-SAN IN THE SUN...
SHE REALLY IS MEANT TO BE IN THE LIGHT!
YAMA-DA!
THIS WAY! OVER HERE!
Huff!
Huff!
Huff!

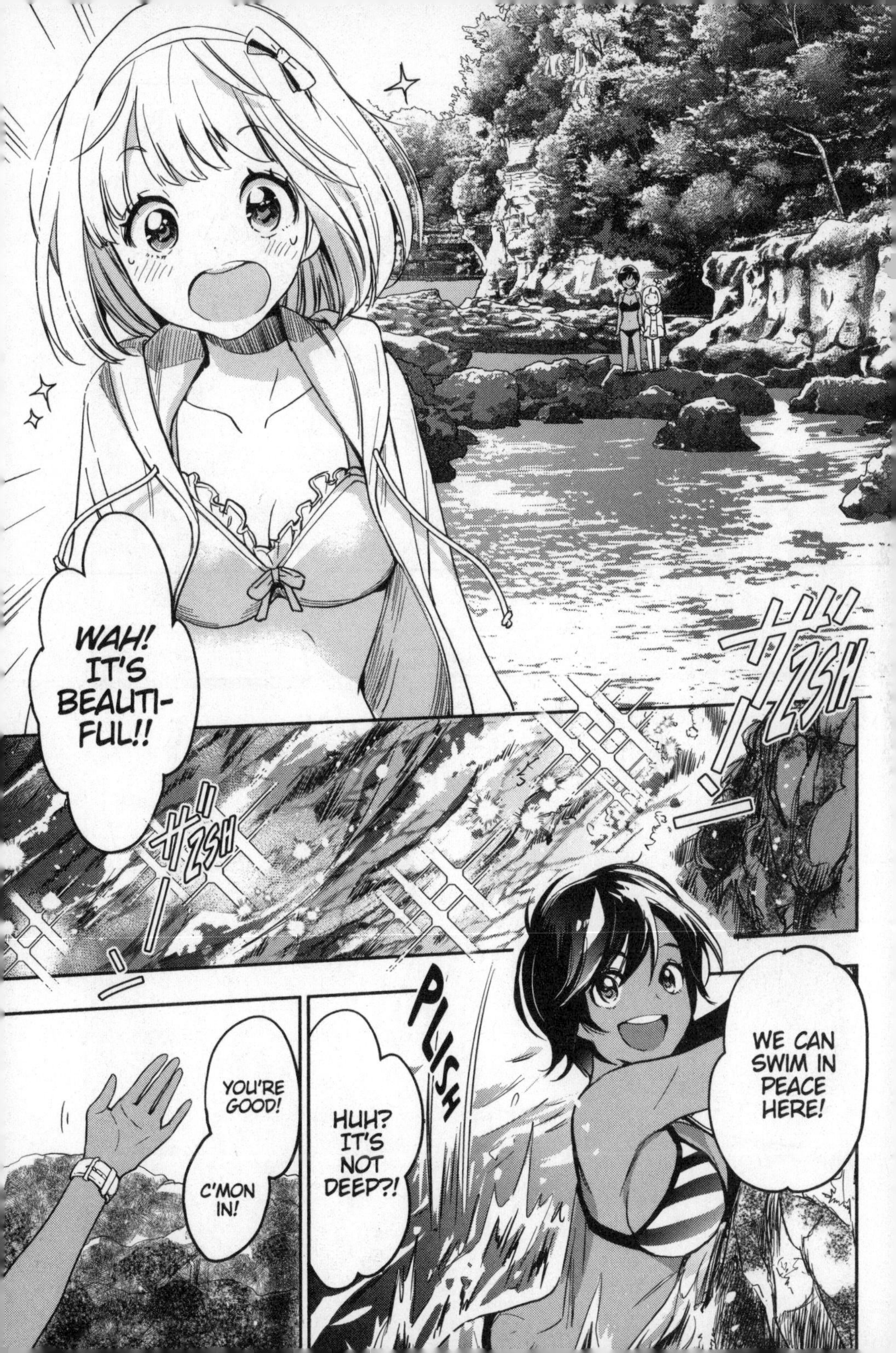
WAH! IT'S BEAUTI-FUL!!
WE CAN SWIM IN PEACE HERE!
PLISH
HUH? IT'S NOT DEEP?!
YOU'RE GOOD!
C'MON IN!

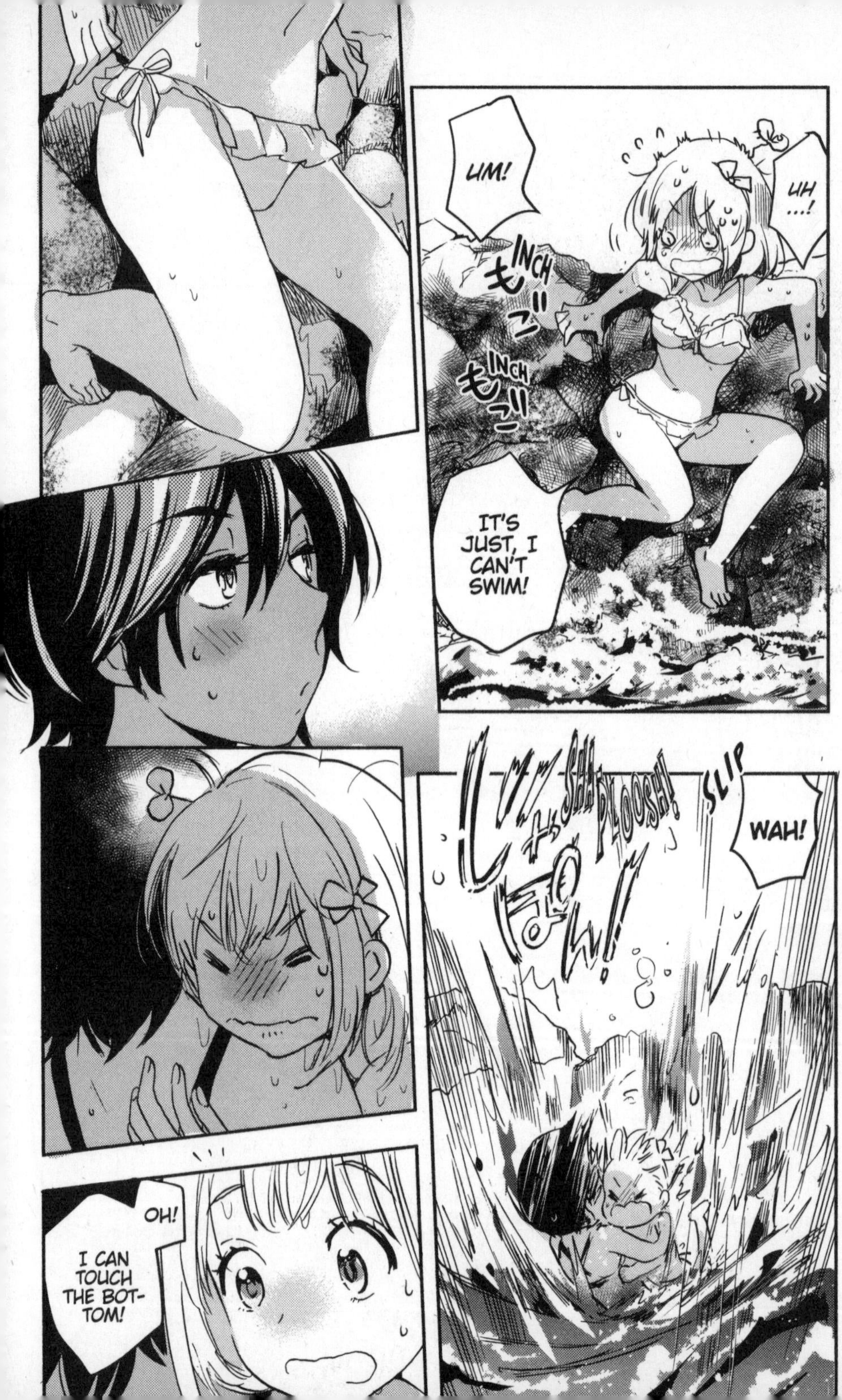
UH ...!
UM!
INCH
INCH
IT'S JUST, I CAN'T SWIM!
WAH!
SLIP
SHA PLOOSH!
OH!
I CAN TOUCH THE BOT-TOM!

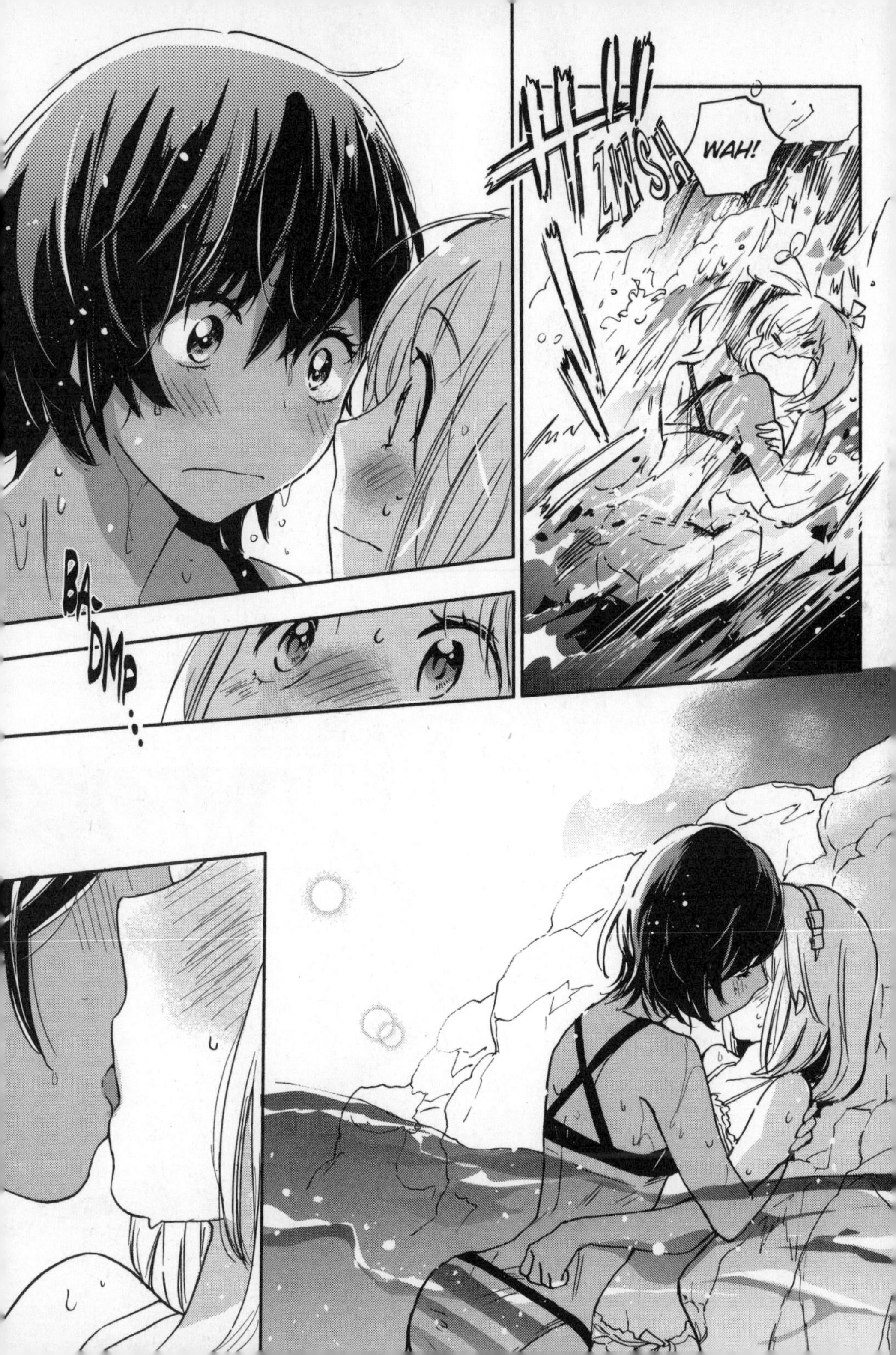
WAH!
ZWSH
BA-DMP...

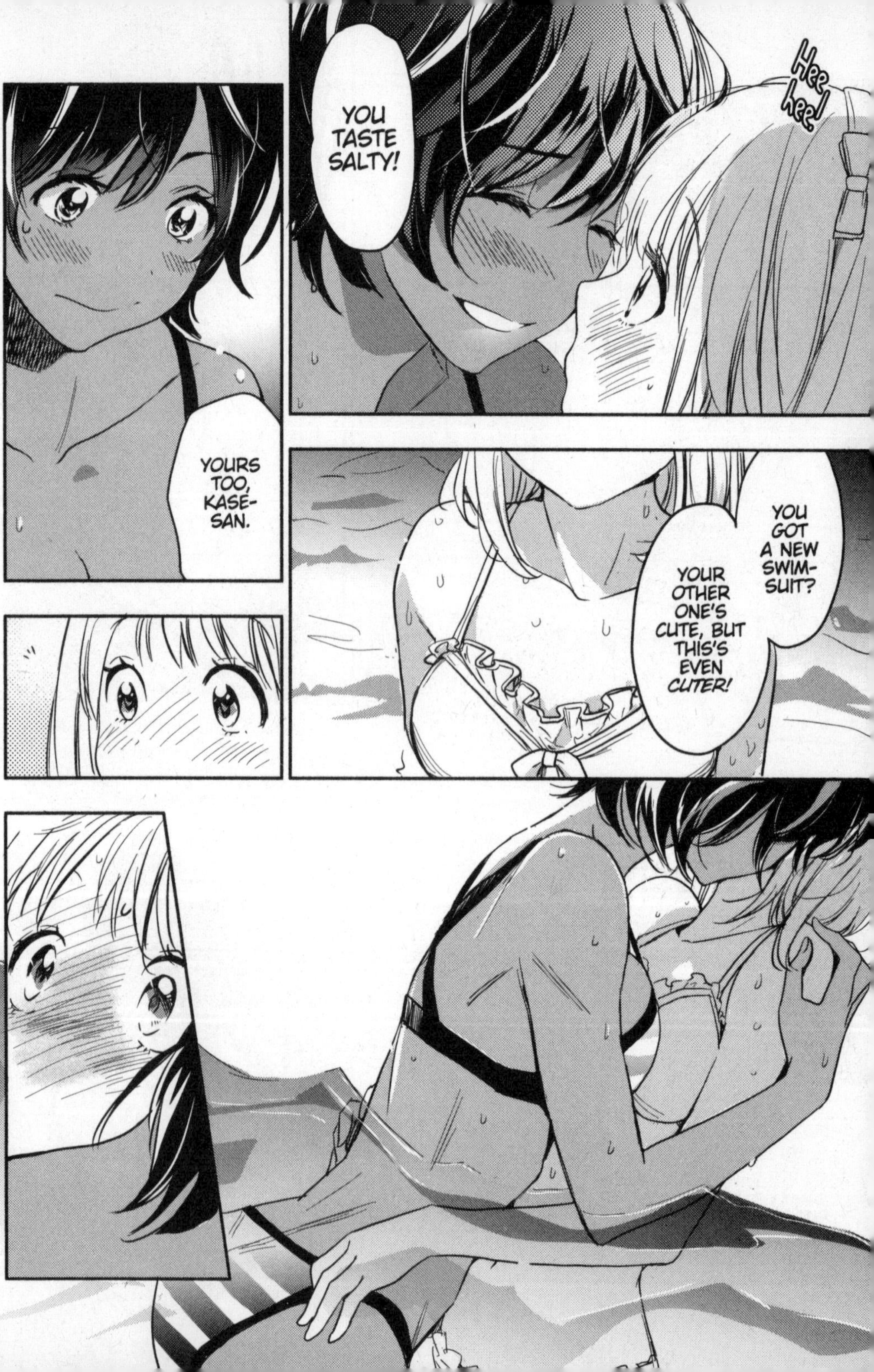
Hee hee!
YOU TASTE SALTY!
YOURS TOO, KASE-SAN.
YOU GOT A NEW SWIM-SUIT?
YOUR OTHER ONE'S CUTE, BUT THIS'S EVEN CUTER!

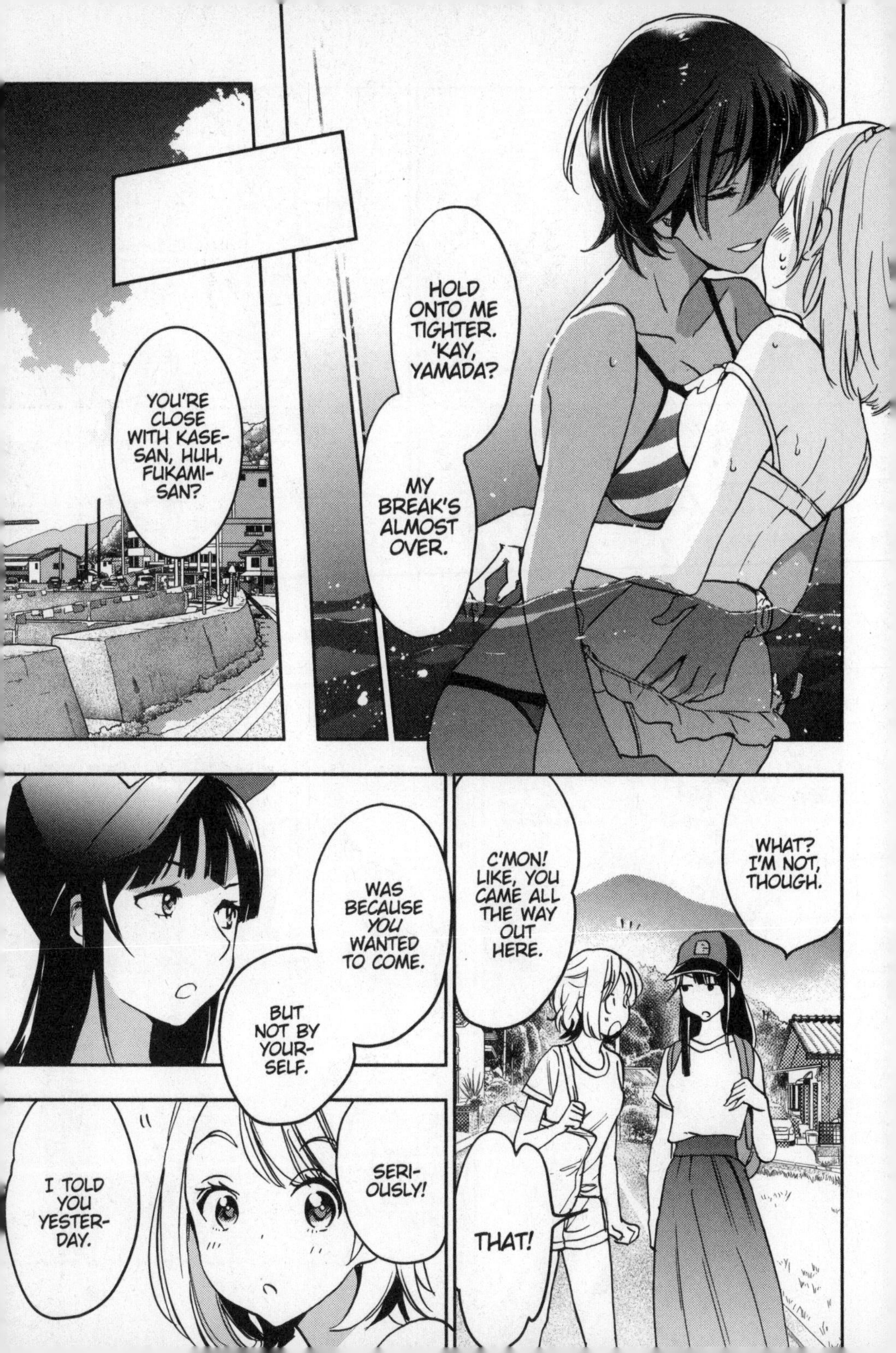
HOLD ONTO ME TIGHTER. 'KAY, YAMADA?
MY BREAK'S ALMOST OVER.
YOU'RE CLOSE WITH KASE-SAN, HUH, FUKAMI-SAN?
WHAT? I'M NOT, THOUGH.
C'MON! LIKE, YOU CAME ALL THE WAY OUT HERE.
THAT!
WAS BECAUSE *YOU* WANTED TO COME.
BUT NOT BY YOURSELF.
SERIOUSLY!
I TOLD YOU YESTERDAY.

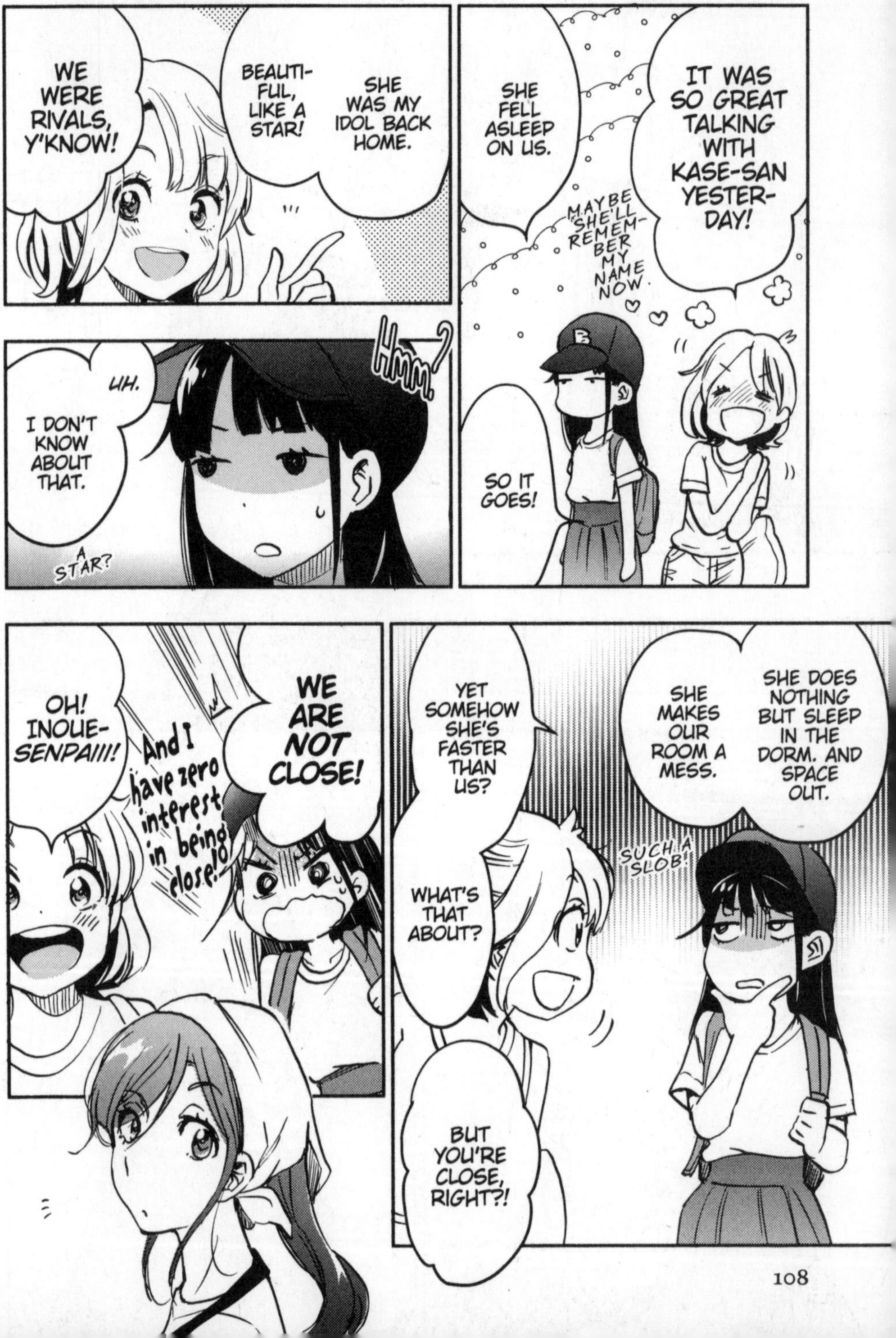
IT WAS SO GREAT TALKING WITH KASE-SAN YESTERDAY!
SHE FELL ASLEEP ON US.
MAYBE SHE'LL REMEMBER MY NAME NOW.
SO IT GOES!
SHE WAS MY IDOL BACK HOME.
BEAUTIFUL, LIKE A STAR!
WE WERE RIVALS, Y'KNOW!
Hmm?
UH.
I DON'T KNOW ABOUT THAT.
A STAR?
SHE DOES NOTHING BUT SLEEP IN THE DORM. AND SPACE OUT.
SHE MAKES OUR ROOM A MESS.
SUCH A SLOB!
YET SOMEHOW SHE'S FASTER THAN US?
WHAT'S THAT ABOUT?
BUT YOU'RE CLOSE, RIGHT?!
WE ARE NOT CLOSE!
And I have zero interest in being close!!
OH! INOUE-SENPAI!!!

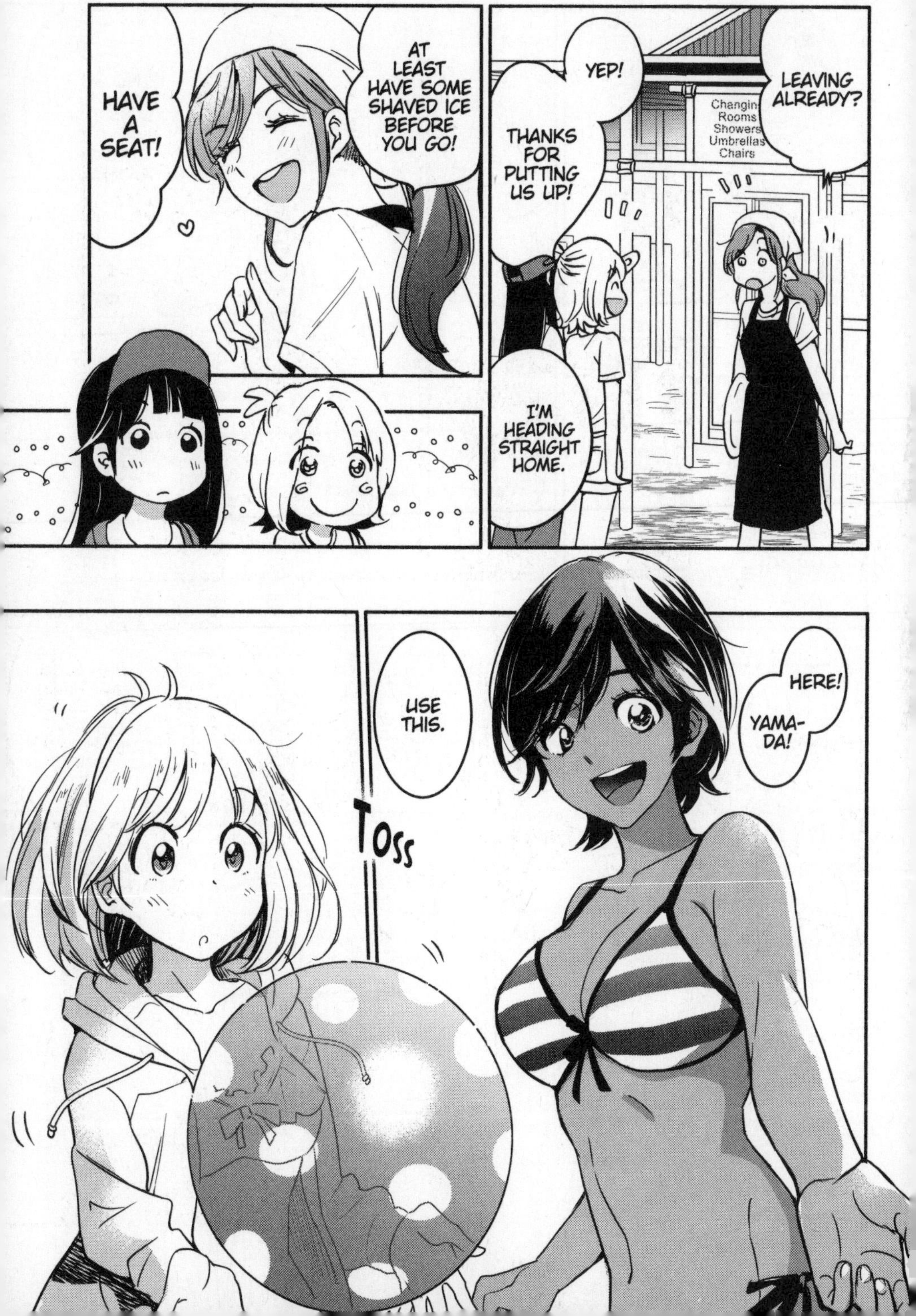
LEAVING ALREADY?
YEP!
Changin-
Rooms
Showers
Umbrellas
Chairs
THANKS FOR PUTTING US UP!
I'M HEADING STRAIGHT HOME.
AT LEAST HAVE SOME SHAVED ICE BEFORE YOU GO!
HAVE A SEAT!
HERE!
YAMA-DA!
USE THIS.
TOSS

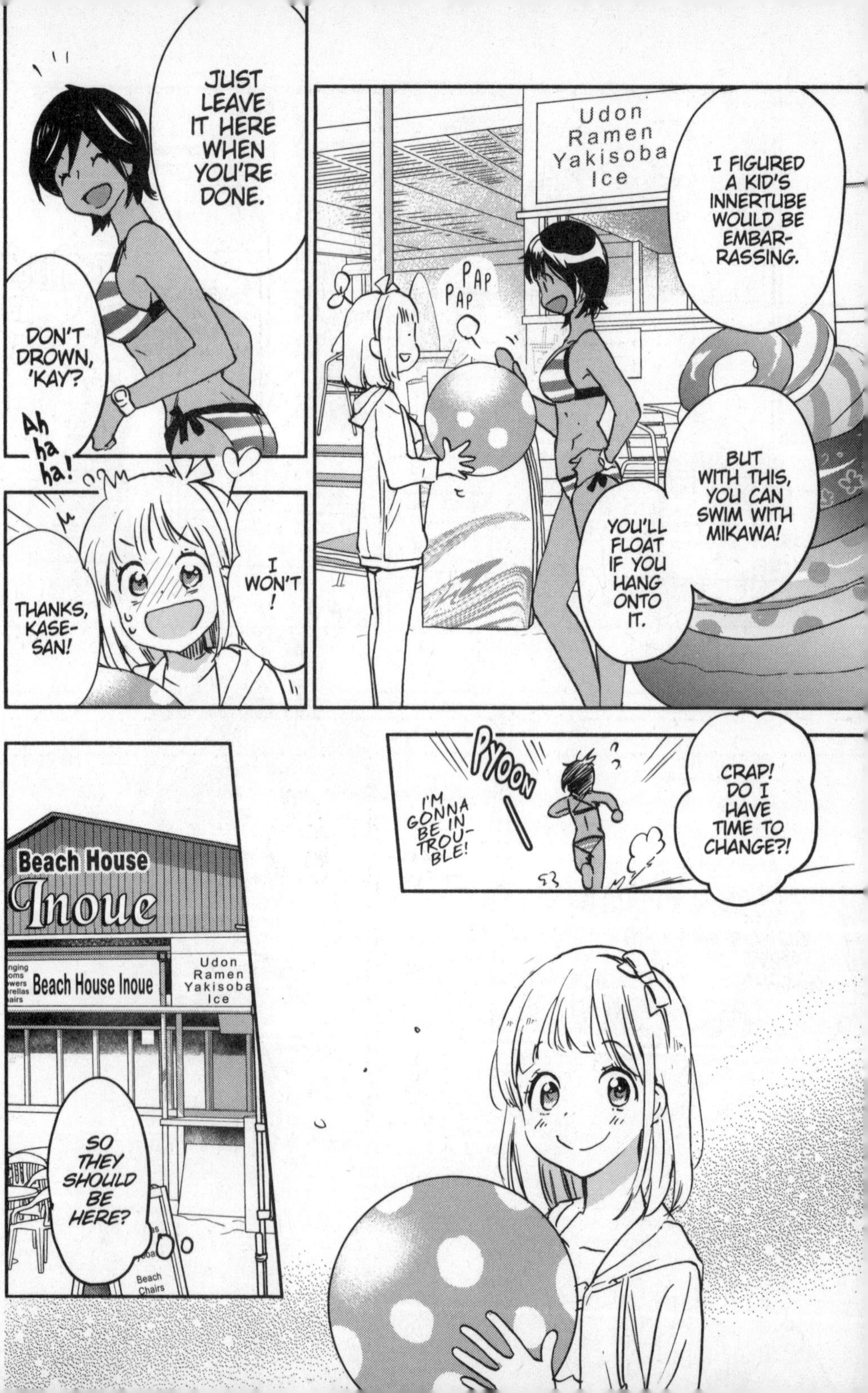

Udon
Ramen
Yakisoba
Ice
I FIGURED A KID'S INNERTUBE WOULD BE EMBAR-RASSING.
PAP PAP
BUT WITH THIS, YOU CAN SWIM WITH MIKAWA!
YOU'LL FLOAT IF YOU HANG ONTO IT.
JUST LEAVE IT HERE WHEN YOU'RE DONE.
DON'T DROWN, 'KAY?
Ah ha ha!
I WON'T!
THANKS, KASE-SAN!
CRAP! DO I HAVE TIME TO CHANGE?!
PYOOON
I'M GONNA BE IN TROU-BLE!
Beach House Inoue
Beach House Inoue
Udon
Ramen
Yakisoba
Ice
Beach Chairs
SO THEY SHOULD BE HERE?

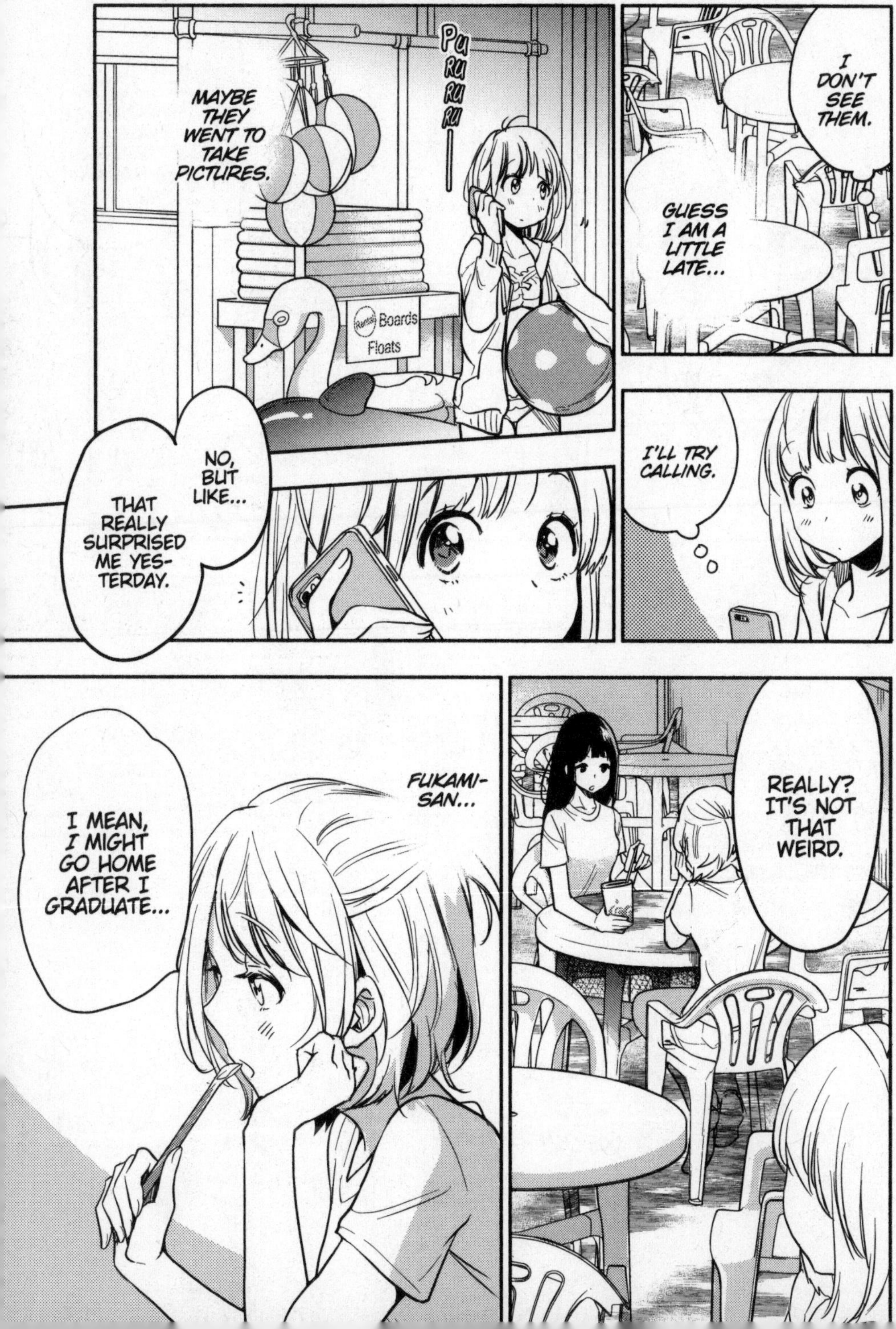
I DON'T SEE THEM.
GUESS I AM A LITTLE LATE...
PURURURU—
MAYBE THEY WENT TO TAKE PICTURES.
Rental Boards
Floats
I'LL TRY CALLING.
NO, BUT LIKE...
THAT REALLY SURPRISED ME YESTERDAY.
REALLY? IT'S NOT THAT WEIRD.
FUKAMI-SAN...
I MEAN, I MIGHT GO HOME AFTER I GRADUATE...

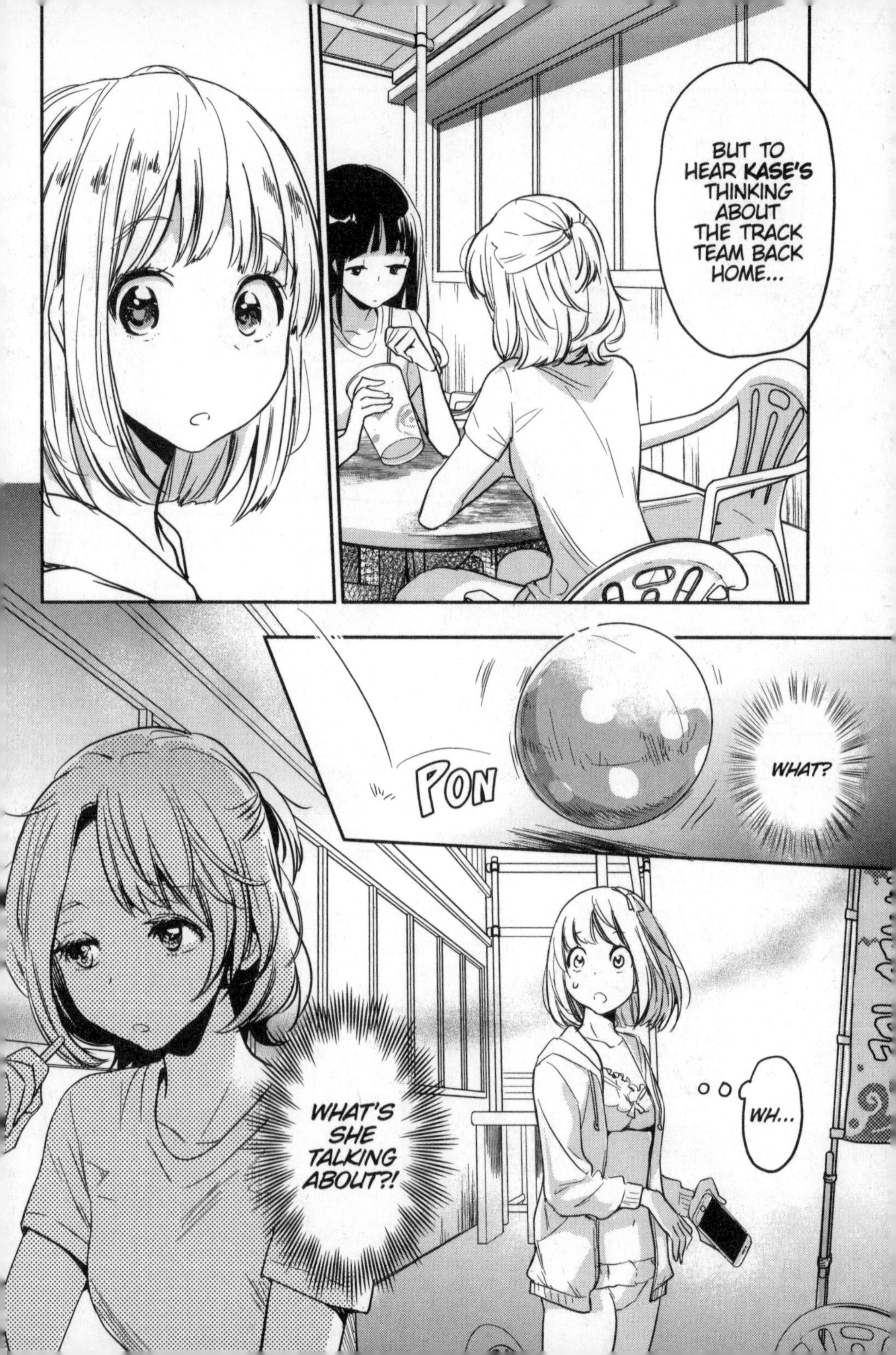
BUT TO HEAR KASE'S THINKING ABOUT THE TRACK TEAM BACK HOME...
WHAT?
PON
...WH...
WHAT'S SHE TALKING ABOUT?!

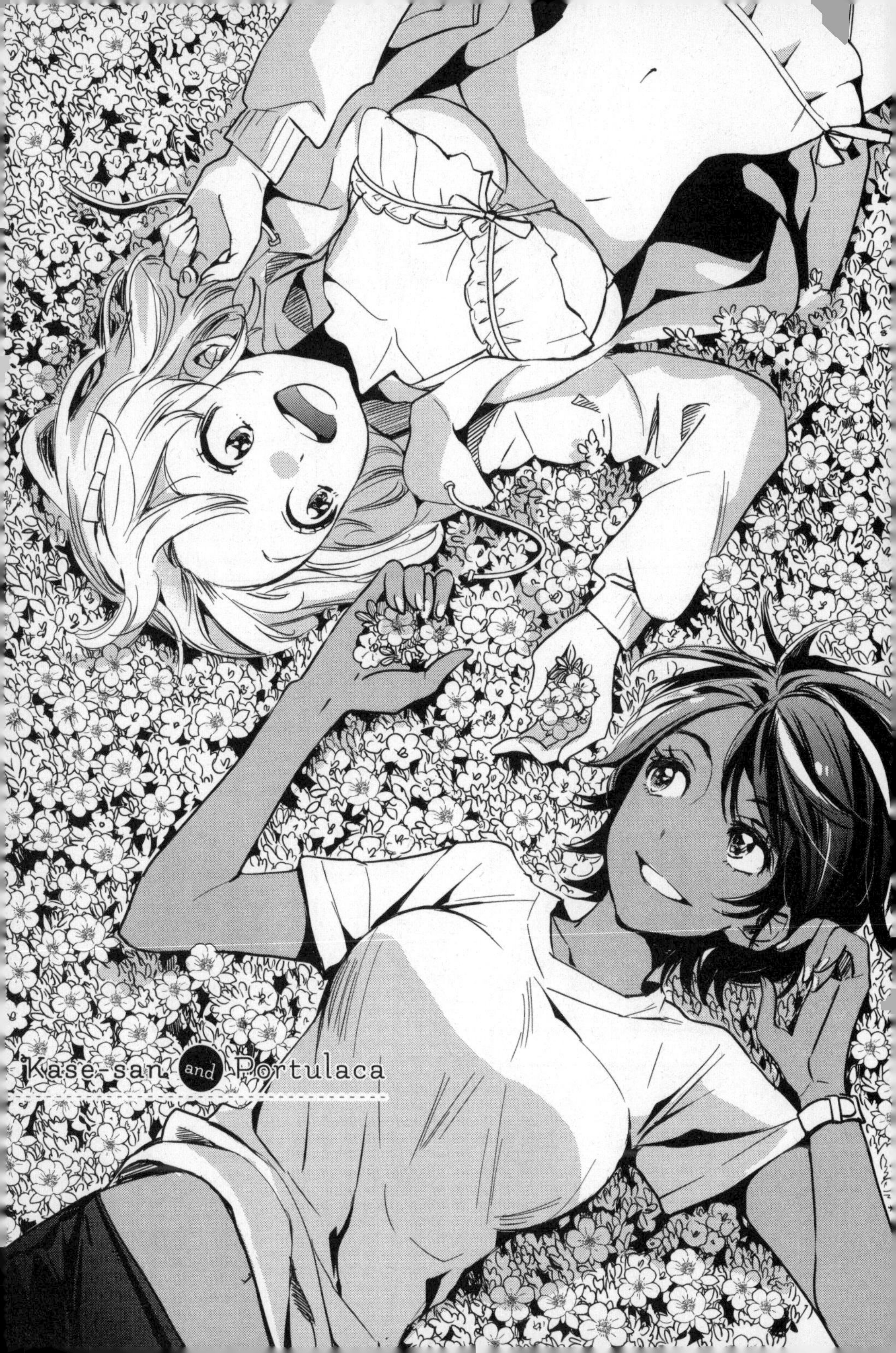
Kase-san and Portulaca

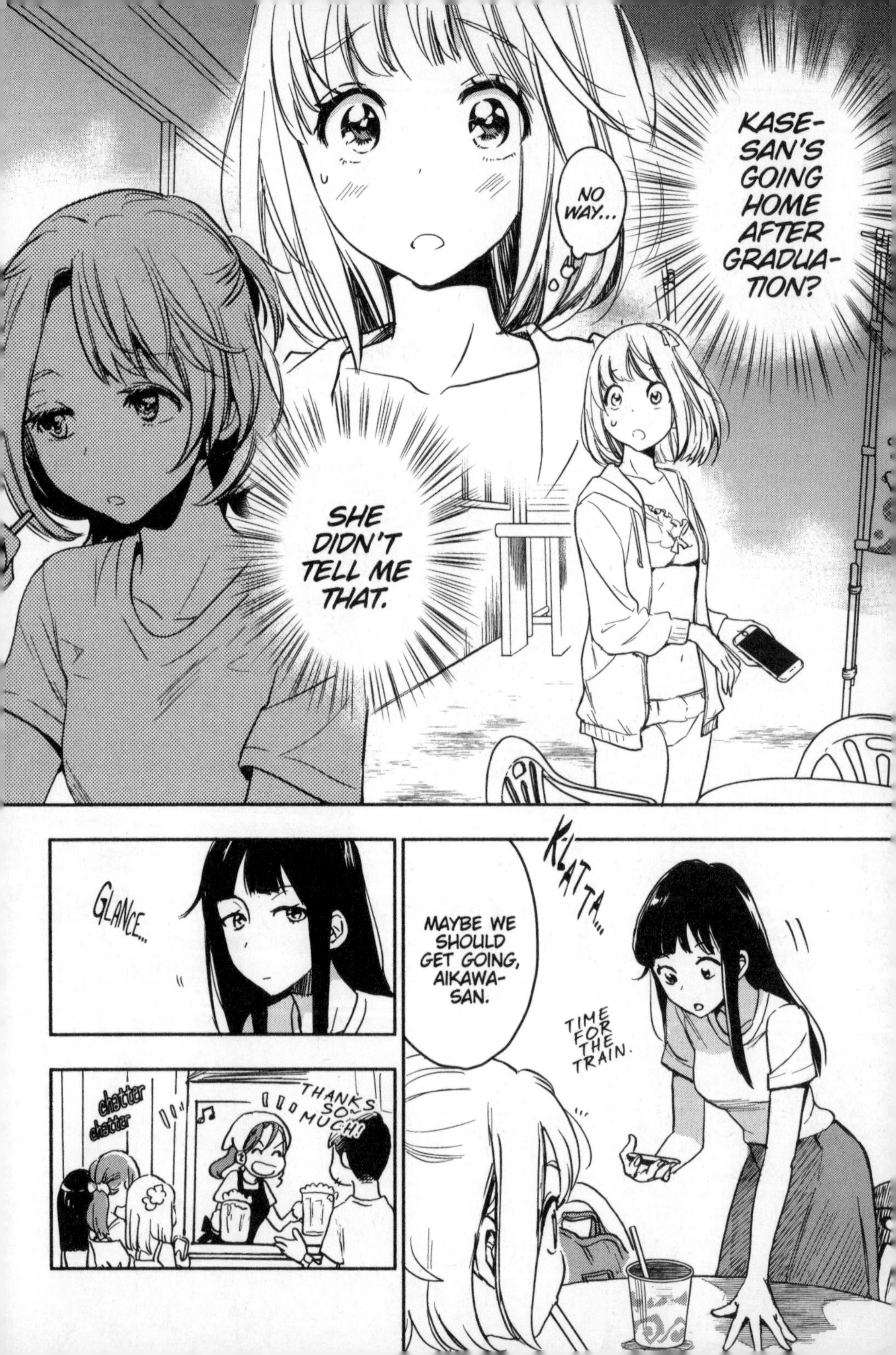
KASE-SAN'S GOING HOME AFTER GRADUATION?
NO WAY...
SHE DIDN'T TELL ME THAT.
KLATTA...
MAYBE WE SHOULD GET GOING, AIKAWA-SAN.
TIME FOR THE TRAIN.
GLANCE...
THANKS SO MUCH!
chatter chatter

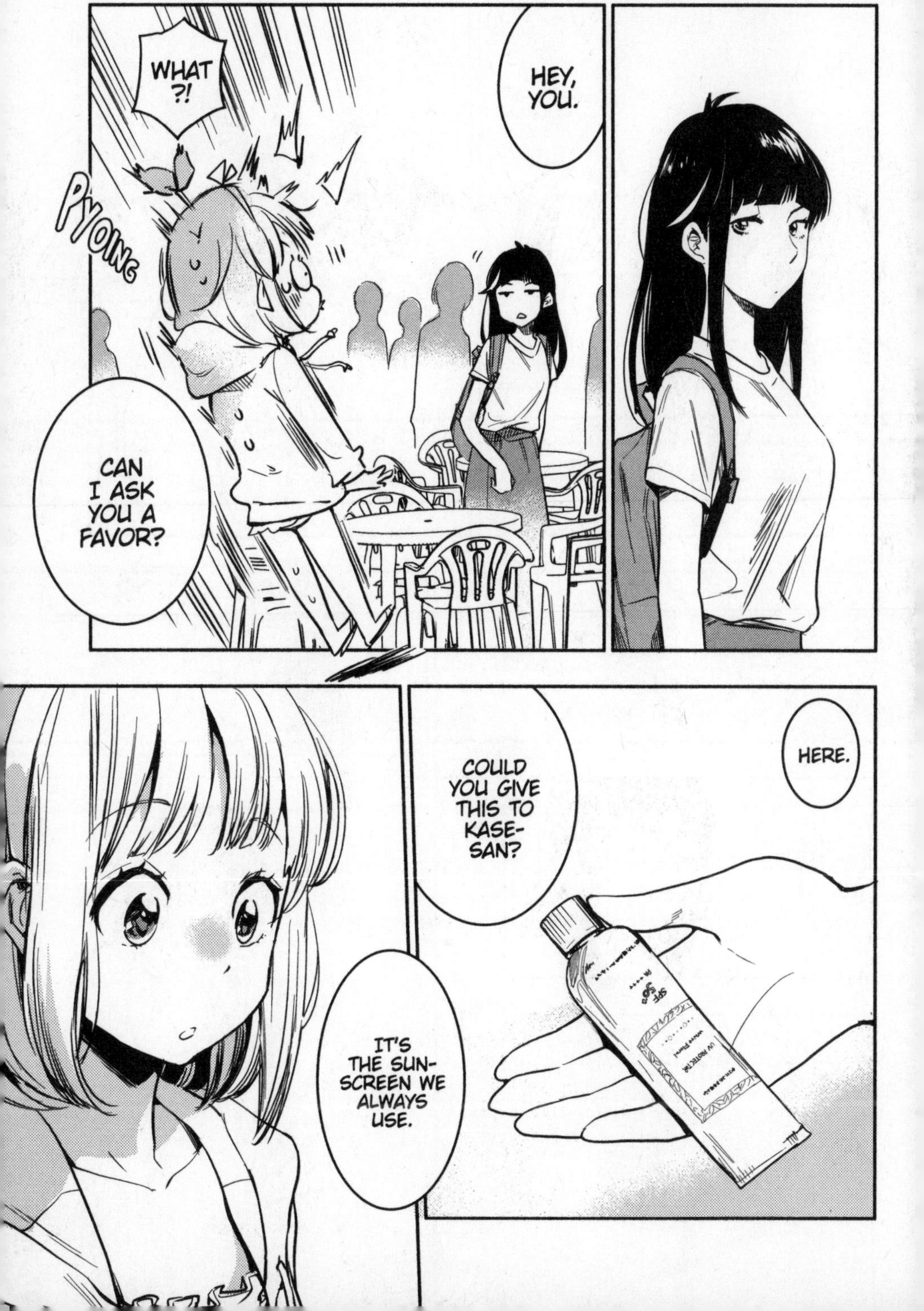
HEY, YOU.
WHAT?!
PYOING
CAN I ASK YOU A FAVOR?
HERE.
COULD YOU GIVE THIS TO KASE-SAN?
IT'S THE SUN-SCREEN WE ALWAYS USE.

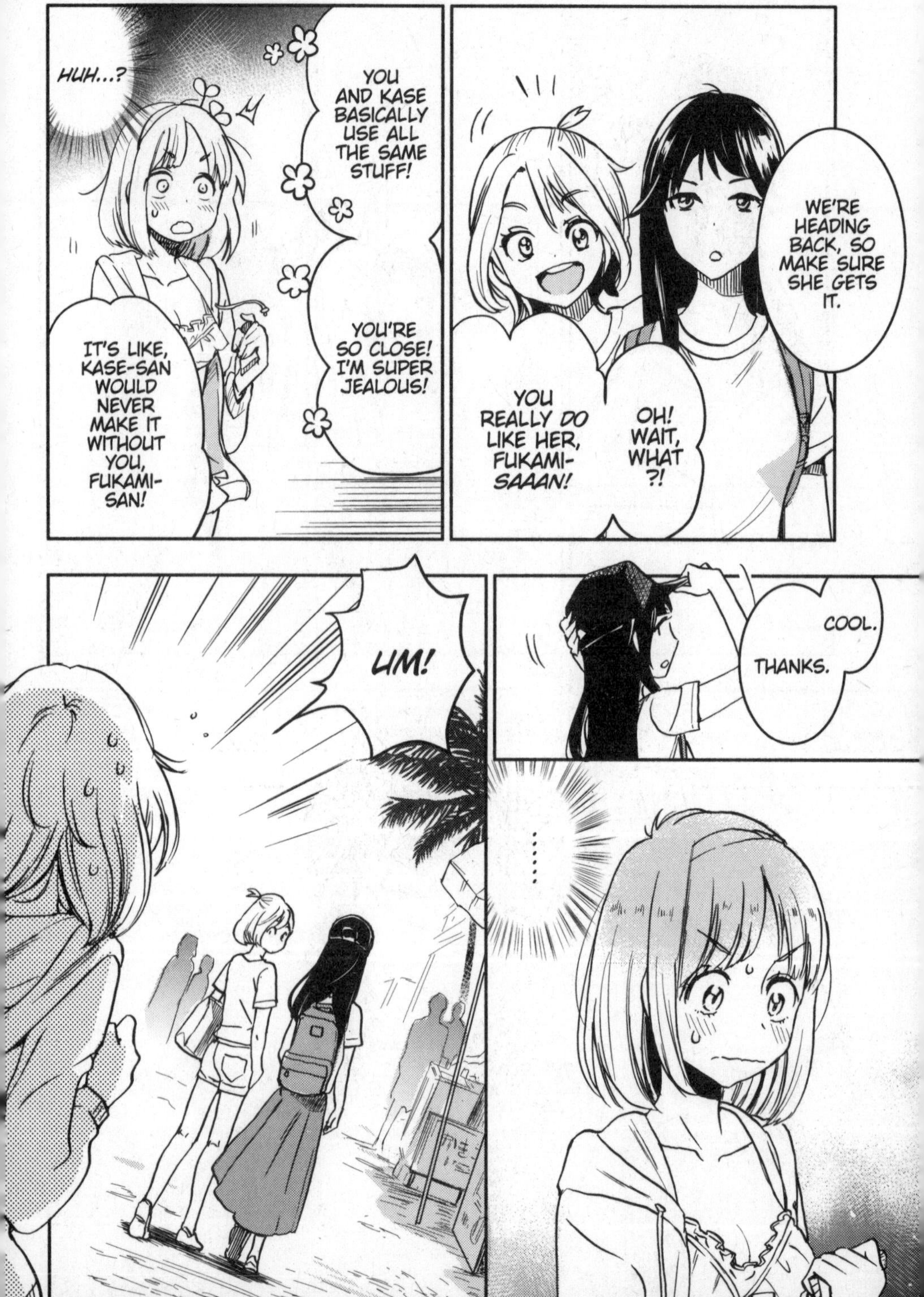
WE'RE HEADING BACK, SO MAKE SURE SHE GETS IT.
OH! WAIT, WHAT?!
YOU REALLY *DO* LIKE HER, FUKAMI-*SAAAN!*
YOU AND KASE BASICALLY USE ALL THE SAME STUFF!
HUH...?
YOU'RE SO CLOSE! I'M SUPER JEALOUS!
IT'S LIKE, KASE-SAN WOULD NEVER MAKE IT WITHOUT YOU, FUKAMI-SAN!
COOL.
THANKS.
......
UM!

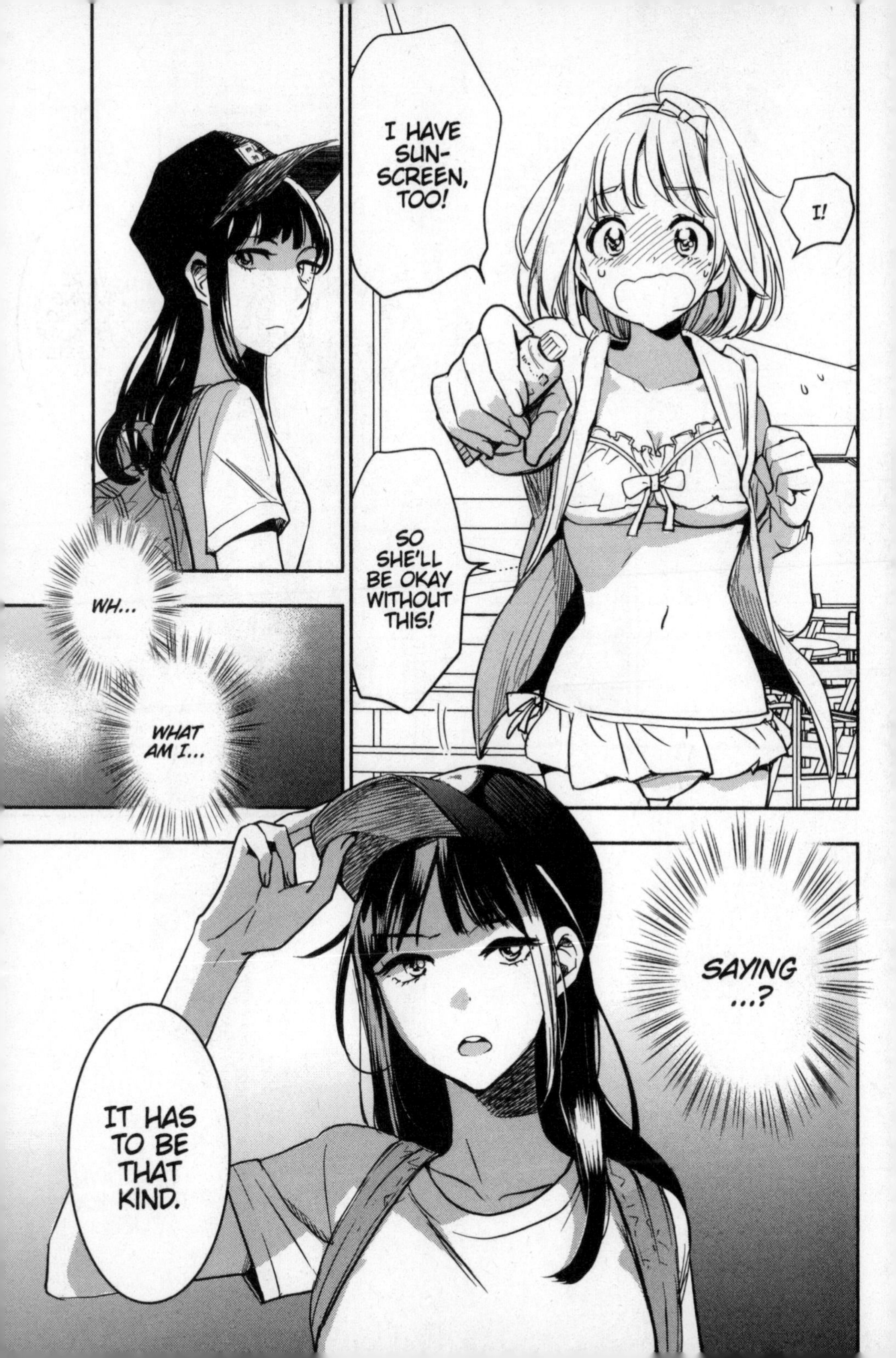
I!
I HAVE SUN-SCREEN, TOO!
SO SHE'LL BE OKAY WITHOUT THIS!
WH...
WHAT AM I...
SAYING ...?
IT HAS TO BE THAT KIND.

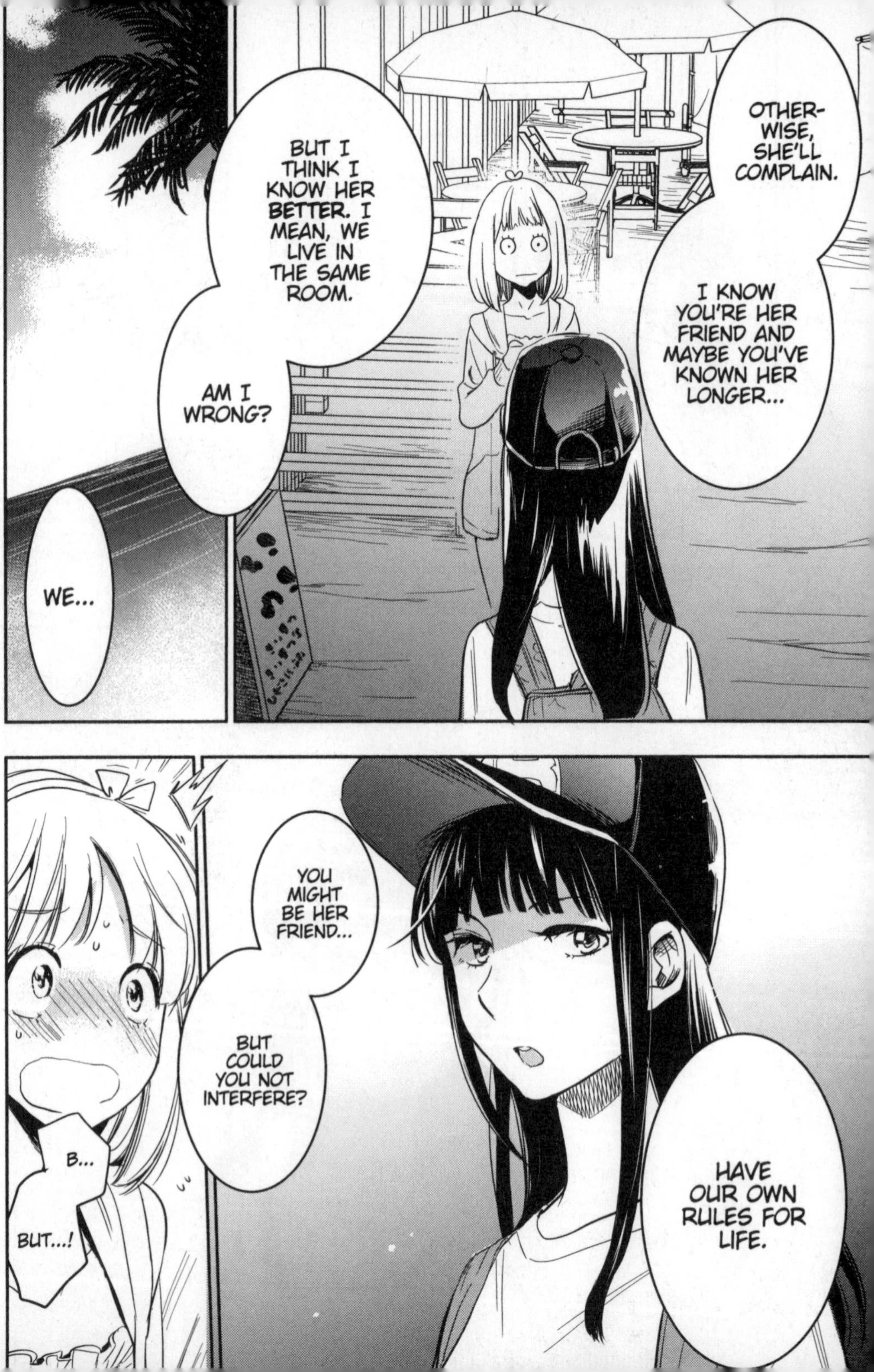
OTHER-WISE, SHE'LL COMPLAIN.
I KNOW YOU'RE HER FRIEND AND MAYBE YOU'VE KNOWN HER LONGER...
BUT I THINK I KNOW HER BETTER. I MEAN, WE LIVE IN THE SAME ROOM.
AM I WRONG?
WE...
HAVE OUR OWN RULES FOR LIFE.
YOU MIGHT BE HER FRIEND...
BUT COULD YOU NOT INTERFERE?
B...
BUT...!

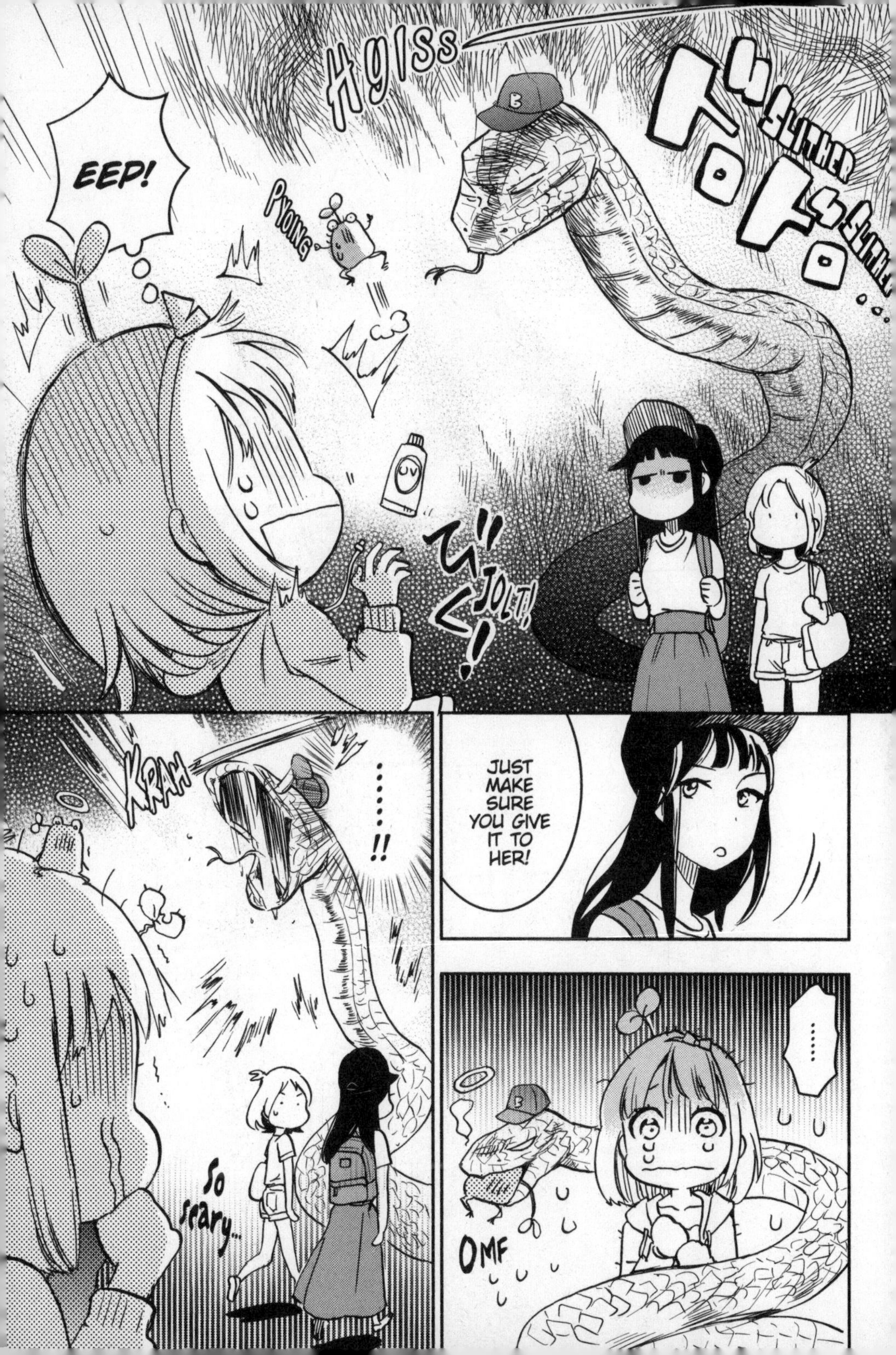
SLITHER
SLITHER...
HGISS
PYONG
EEP!
JOLT!
JUST MAKE SURE YOU GIVE IT TO HER!
......
OMF
KRAH
......!!
So scary...

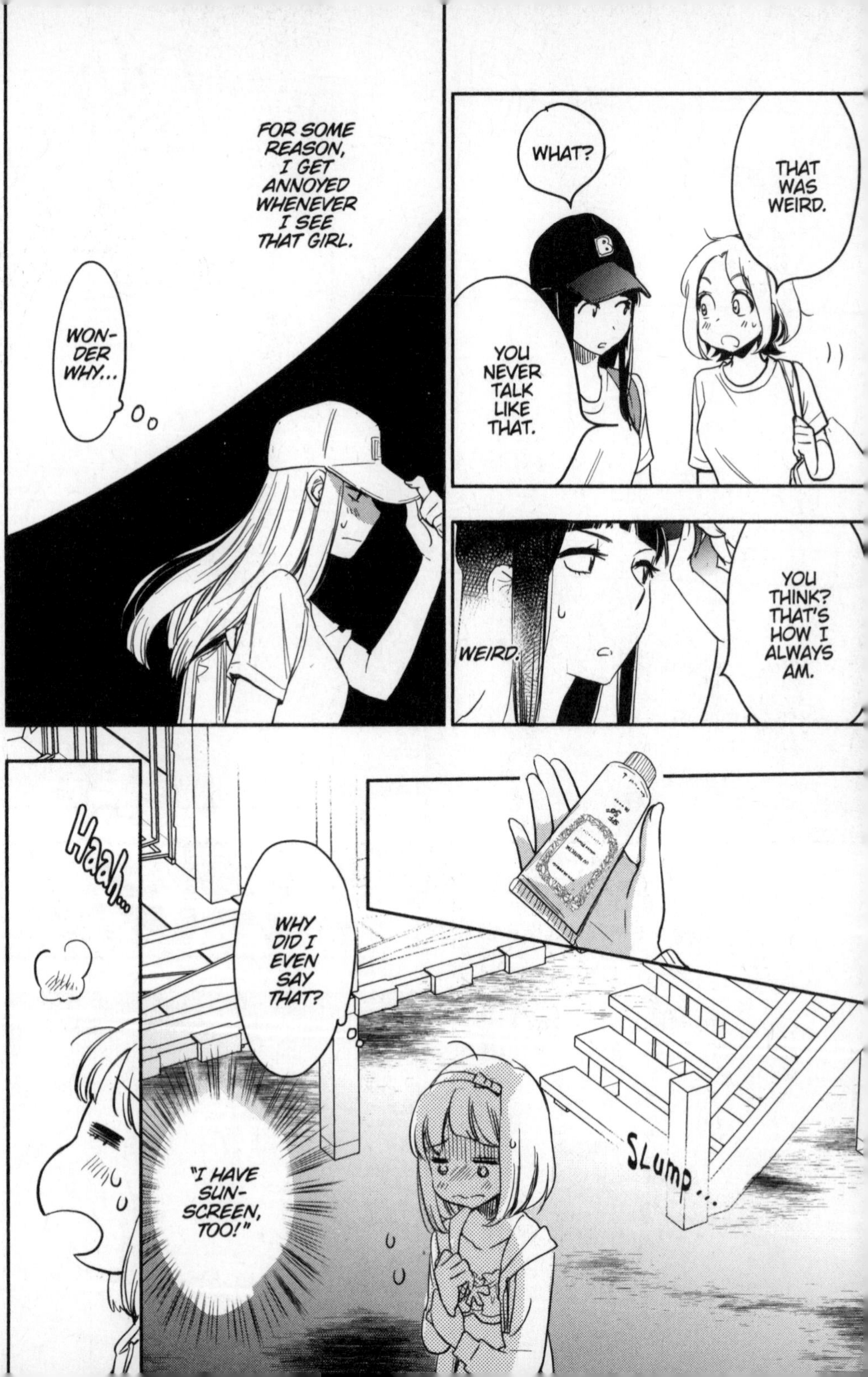
THAT WAS WEIRD.
WHAT?
YOU NEVER TALK LIKE THAT.
YOU THINK? THAT'S HOW I ALWAYS AM.
WEIRD.
FOR SOME REASON, I GET ANNOYED WHENEVER I SEE THAT GIRL.
WONDER WHY...
WHY DID I EVEN SAY THAT?
SLump...
"I HAVE SUN-SCREEN, TOO!"
Haah...

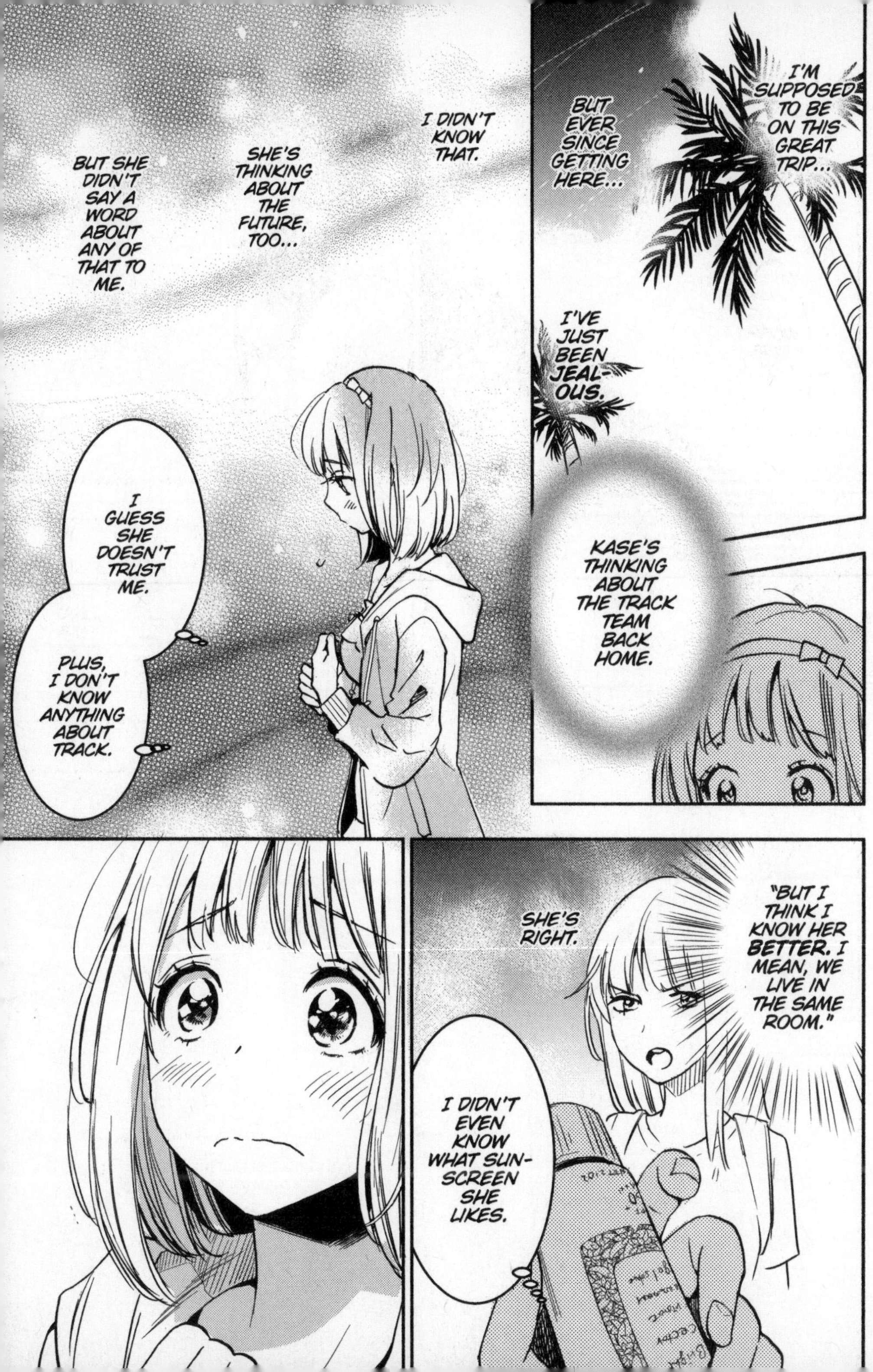
I'M SUPPOSED TO BE ON THIS GREAT TRIP...
BUT EVER SINCE GETTING HERE...
I'VE JUST BEEN JEAL-OUS.
KASE'S THINKING ABOUT THE TRACK TEAM BACK HOME.
I DIDN'T KNOW THAT.
SHE'S THINKING ABOUT THE FUTURE, TOO...
BUT SHE DIDN'T SAY A WORD ABOUT ANY OF THAT TO ME.
I GUESS SHE DOESN'T TRUST ME.
PLUS, I DON'T KNOW ANYTHING ABOUT TRACK.
"BUT I THINK I KNOW HER **BETTER**. I MEAN, WE LIVE IN THE SAME ROOM."
SHE'S RIGHT.
I DIDN'T EVEN KNOW WHAT SUN-SCREEN SHE LIKES.

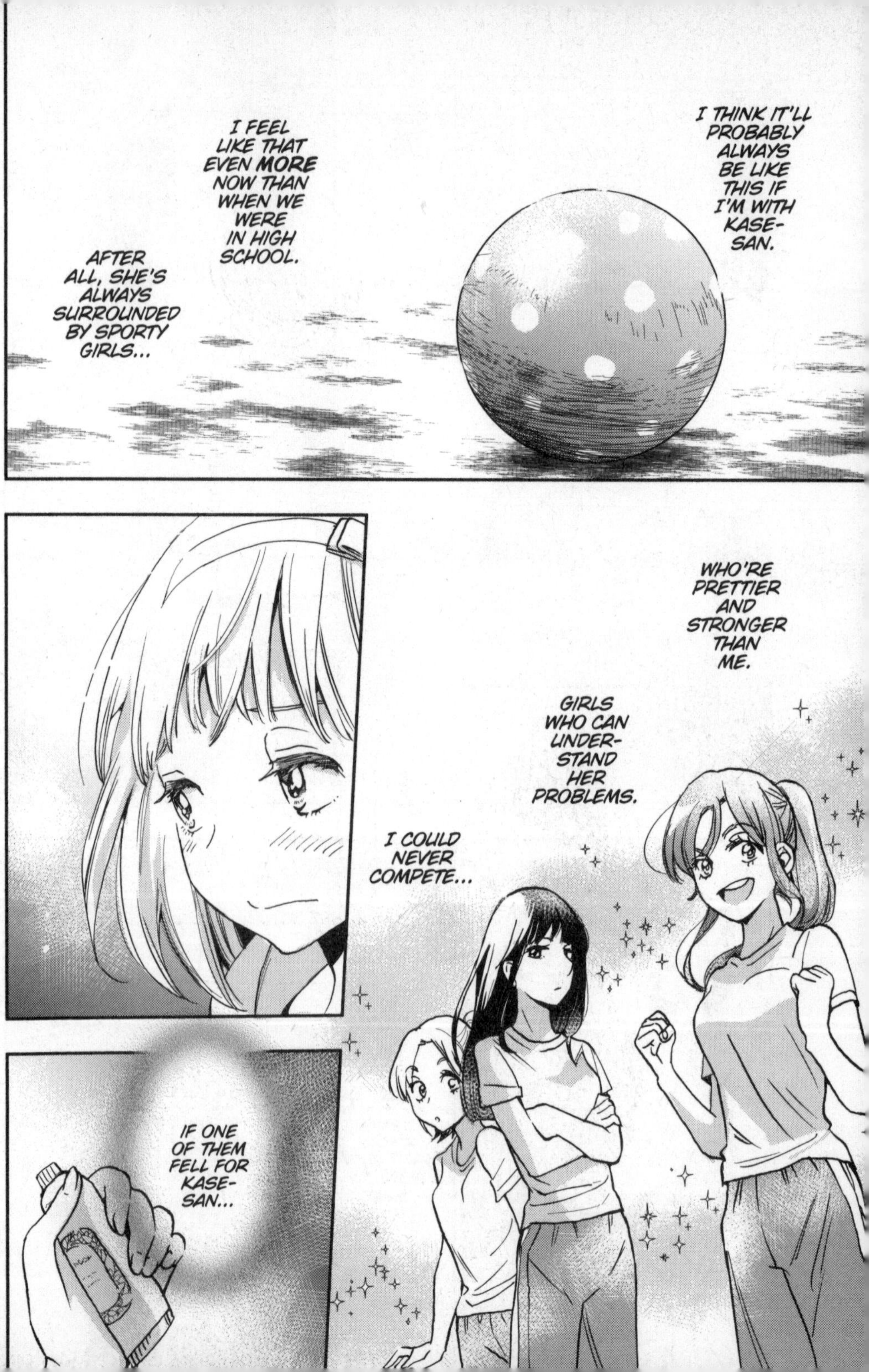
I THINK IT'LL PROBABLY ALWAYS BE LIKE THIS IF I'M WITH KASE-SAN.
I FEEL LIKE THAT EVEN MORE NOW THAN WHEN WE WERE IN HIGH SCHOOL.
AFTER ALL, SHE'S ALWAYS SURROUNDED BY SPORTY GIRLS...
WHO'RE PRETTIER AND STRONGER THAN ME.
GIRLS WHO CAN UNDERSTAND HER PROBLEMS.
I COULD NEVER COMPETE...
IF ONE OF THEM FELL FOR KASE-SAN...

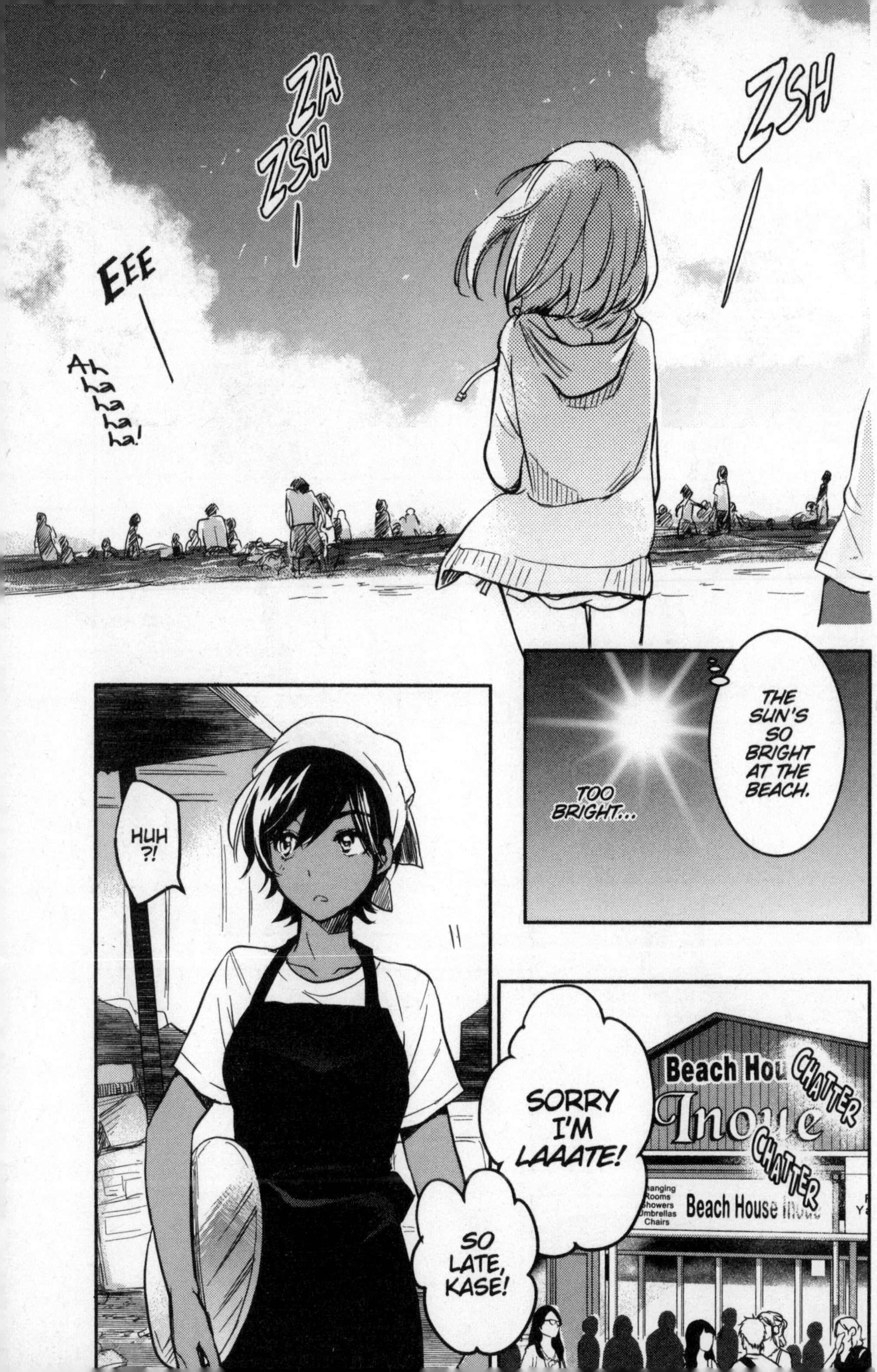
ZSH
ZA ZSH
EEE
Ah ha ha ha ha!
THE SUN'S SO BRIGHT AT THE BEACH.
TOO BRIGHT...
SORRY I'M LAAATE!
CHATTER CHATTER
Rooms
Chairs
Beach House
SO LATE, KASE!
HUH ?!

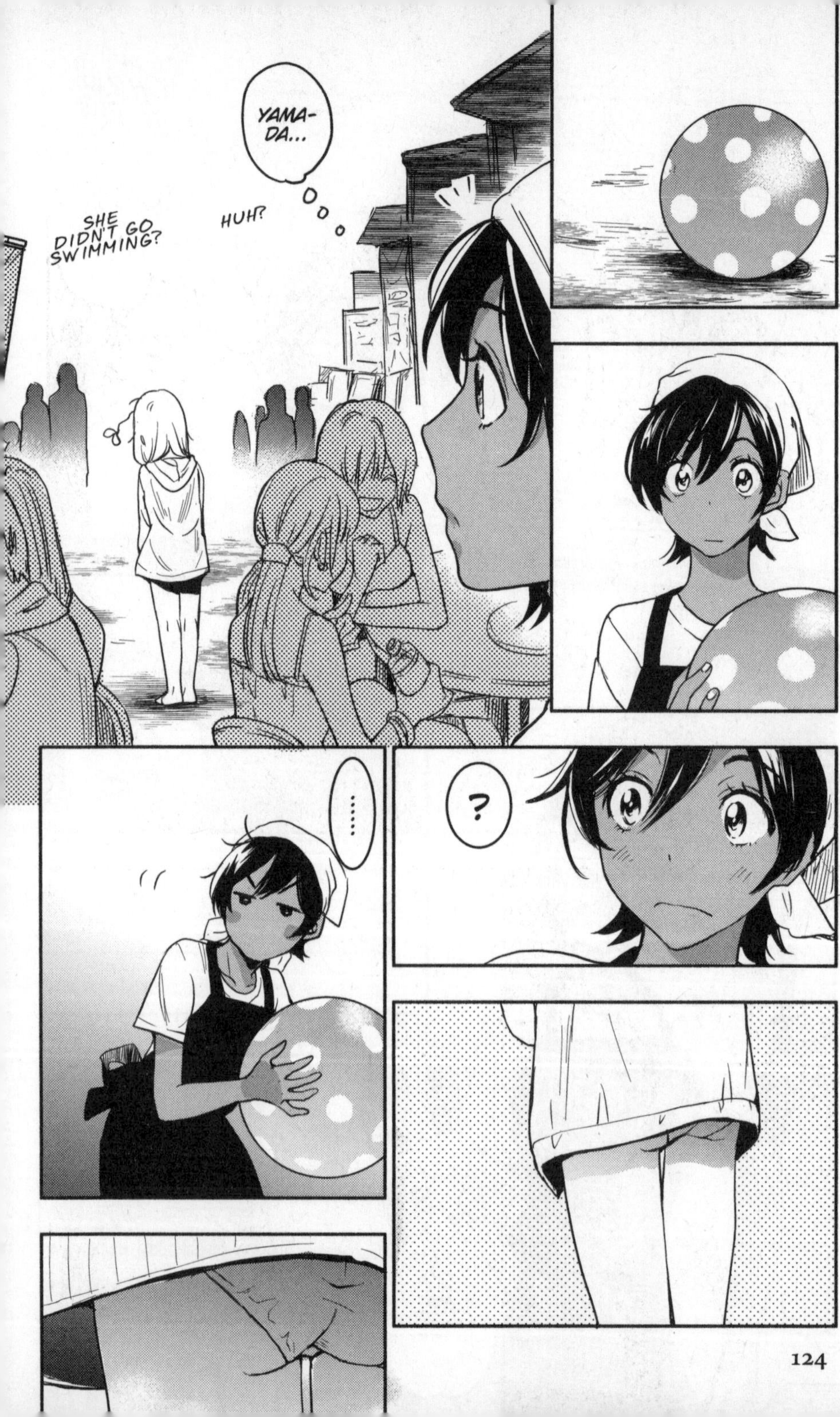

YAMA-DA...
HUH?
SHE DIDN'T GO SWIMMING?
?
......

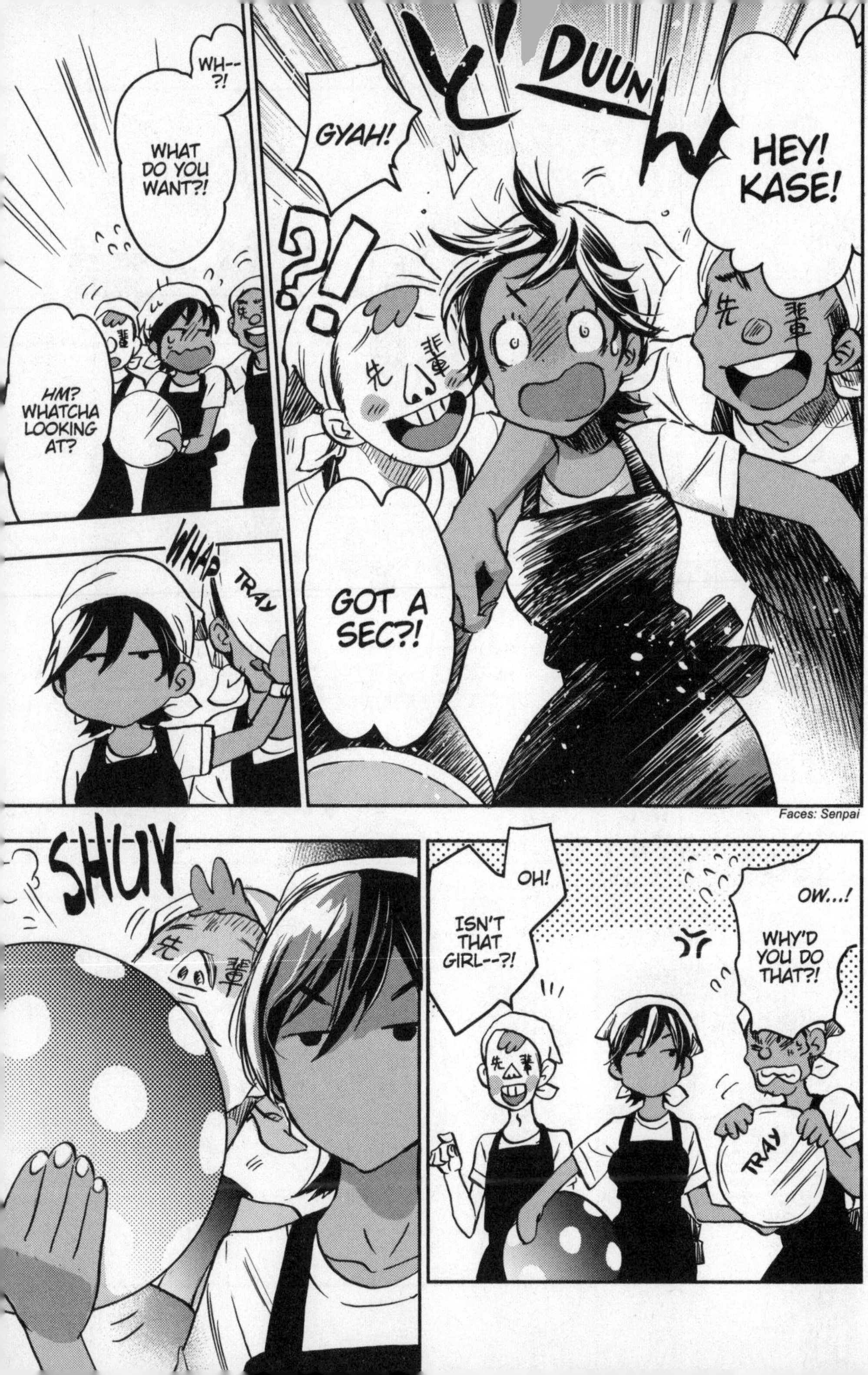
HEY! KASE!
DUUN
GYAH!
?!
GOT A SEC?!
WH--?!
WHAT DO YOU WANT?!
HM? WHATCHA LOOKING AT?
WHAP
TRAY
Faces: Senpai
OW...!
WHY'D YOU DO THAT?!
OH!
ISN'T THAT GIRL--?!
TRAY
SHUV

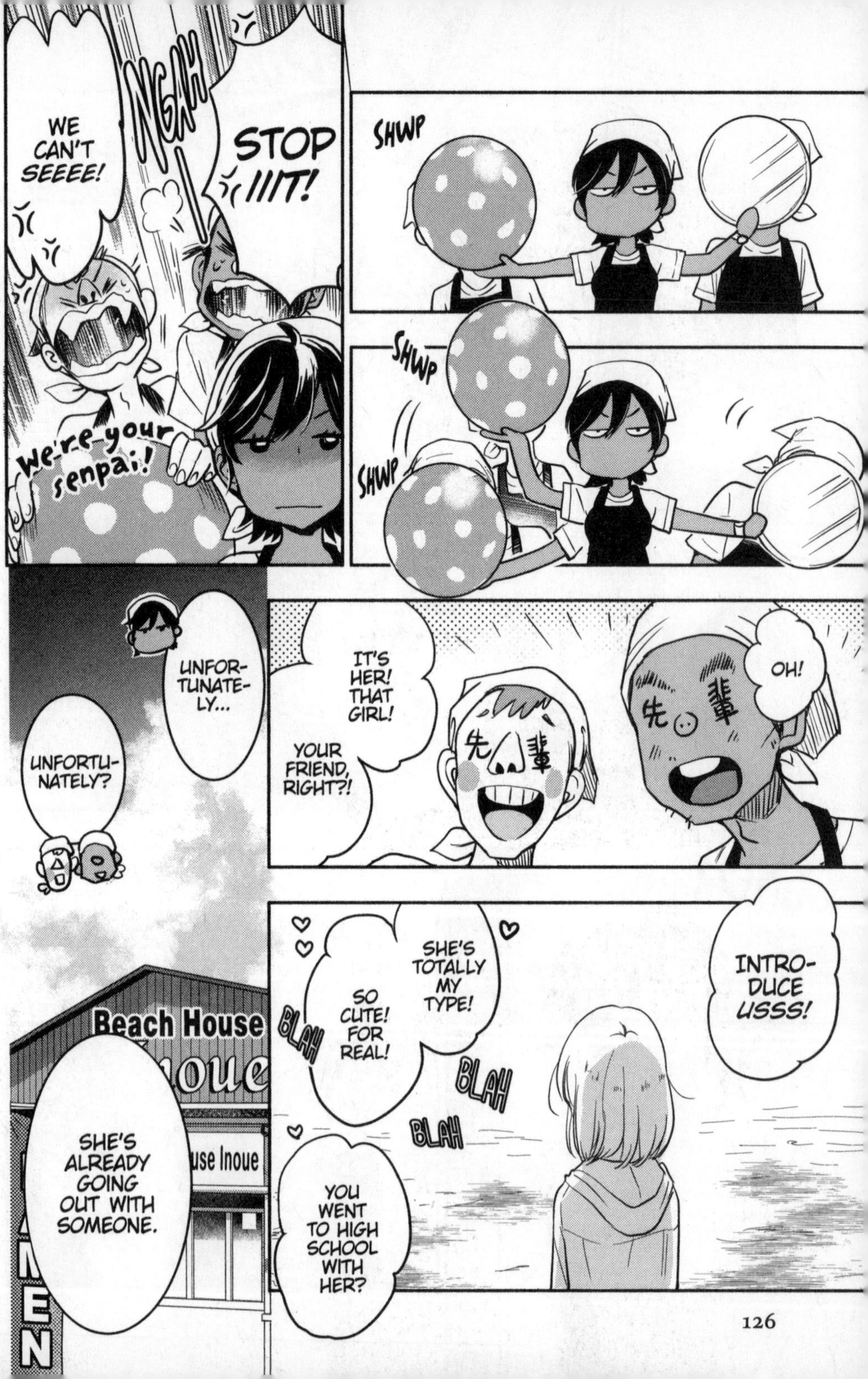
SHWP
SHWP
SHWP
STOP IIIIT!
NGAH
WE CAN'T SEEEE!
We're your senpai!
OH!
IT'S HER! THAT GIRL!
YOUR FRIEND, RIGHT?!
INTRO-DUCE USSS!
SHE'S TOTALLY MY TYPE!
SO CUTE! FOR REAL!
BLAH
BLAH
BLAH
YOU WENT TO HIGH SCHOOL WITH HER?
UNFOR-TUNATE-LY...
UNFORTU-NATELY?
Beach House
Inoue
use Inoue
SHE'S ALREADY GOING OUT WITH SOMEONE.
MEN

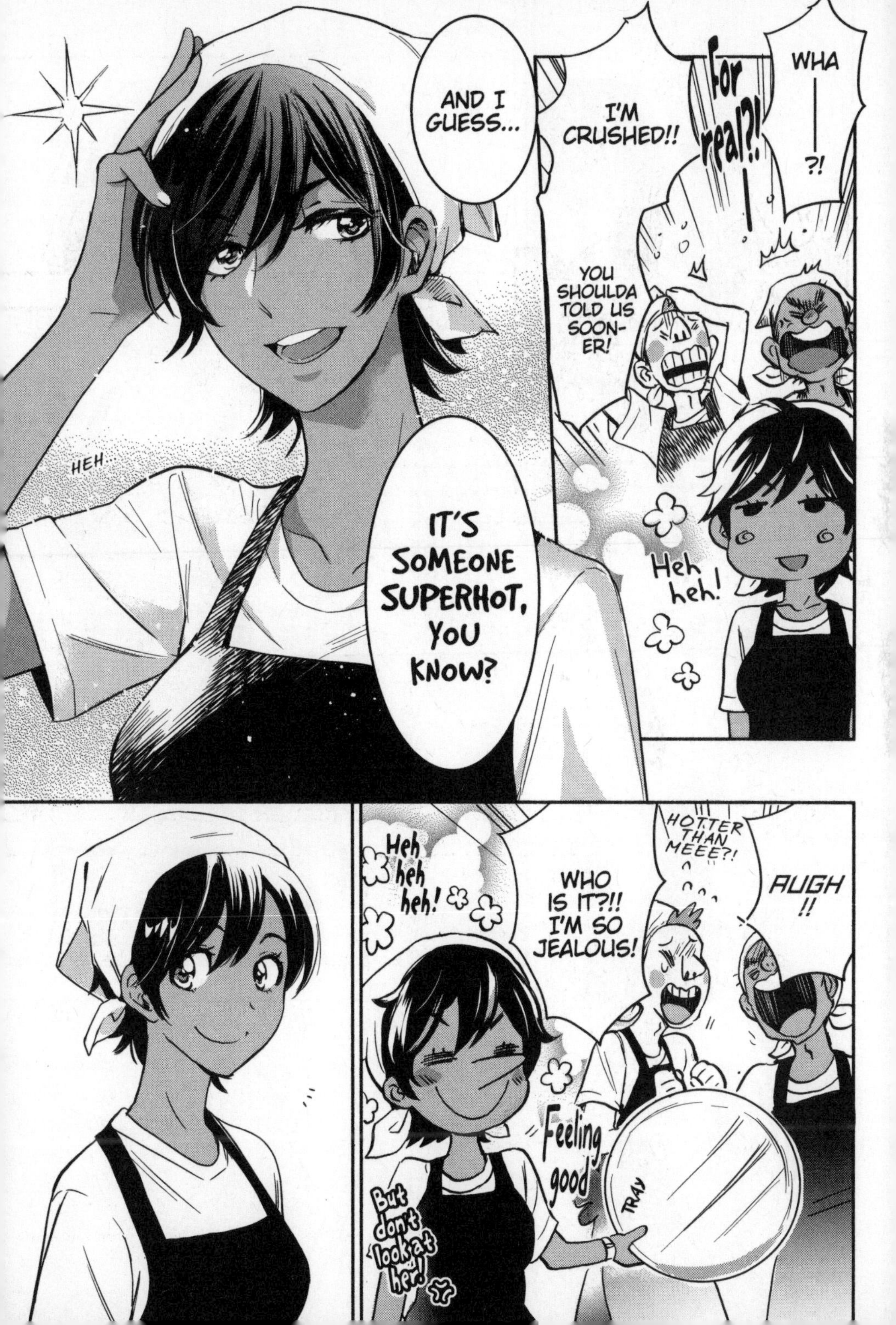
WHA—?!
For real?!!
I'M CRUSHED!!
YOU SHOULDA TOLD US SOONER!
Heh heh!
AND I GUESS...
HEH...
IT'S SOMEONE SUPERHOT, YOU KNOW?
HOTTER THAN MEEE?!
AUGH!!
WHO IS IT?!! I'M SO JEALOUS!
Heh heh heh!
Feeling good
TRAY
But don't look at her!

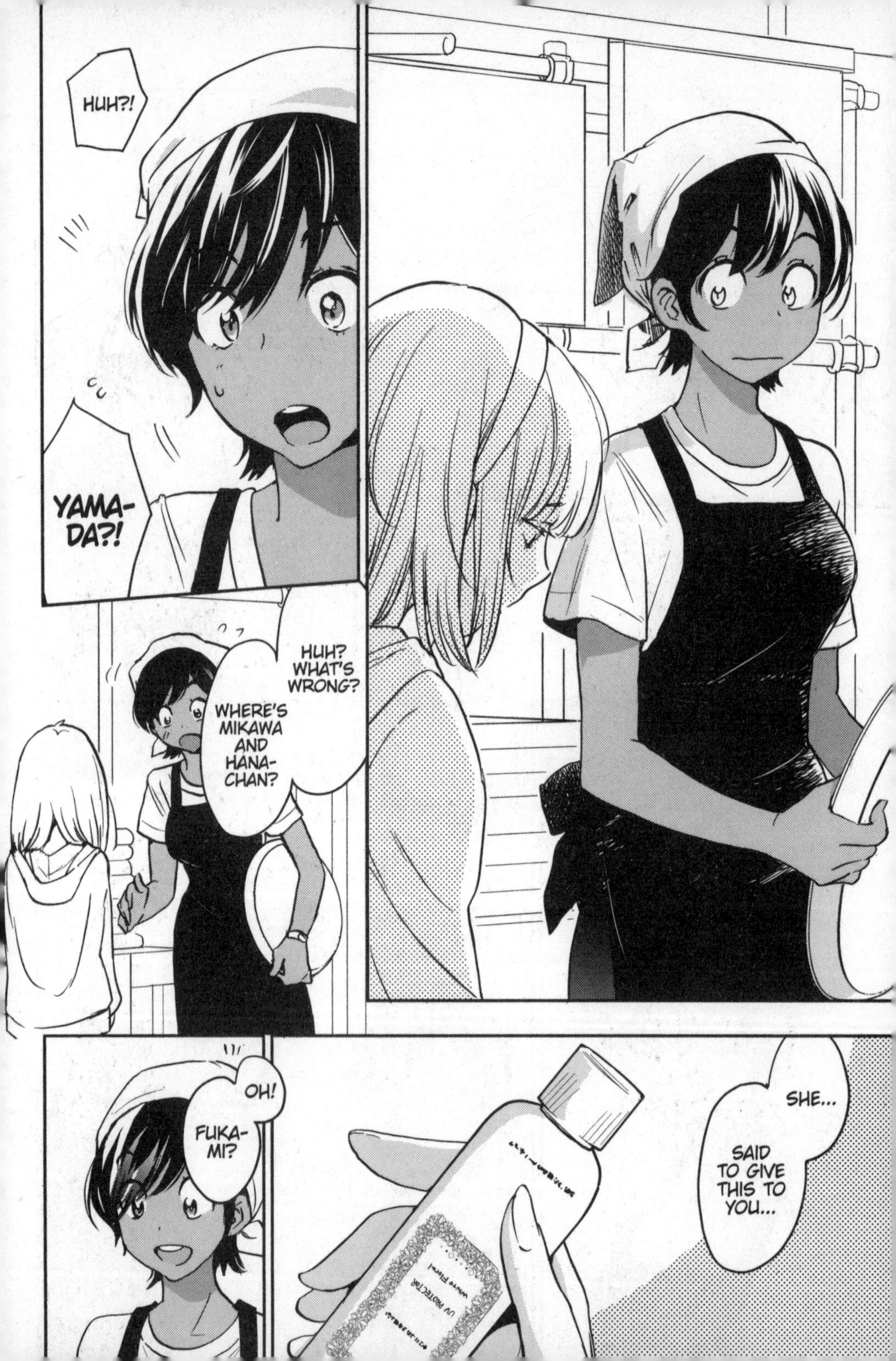
HUH?!
YAMADA?!
HUH? WHAT'S WRONG?
WHERE'S MIKAWA AND HANA-CHAN?
SHE...
SAID TO GIVE THIS TO YOU...
UV PROTECTOR
OH!
FUKAMI?

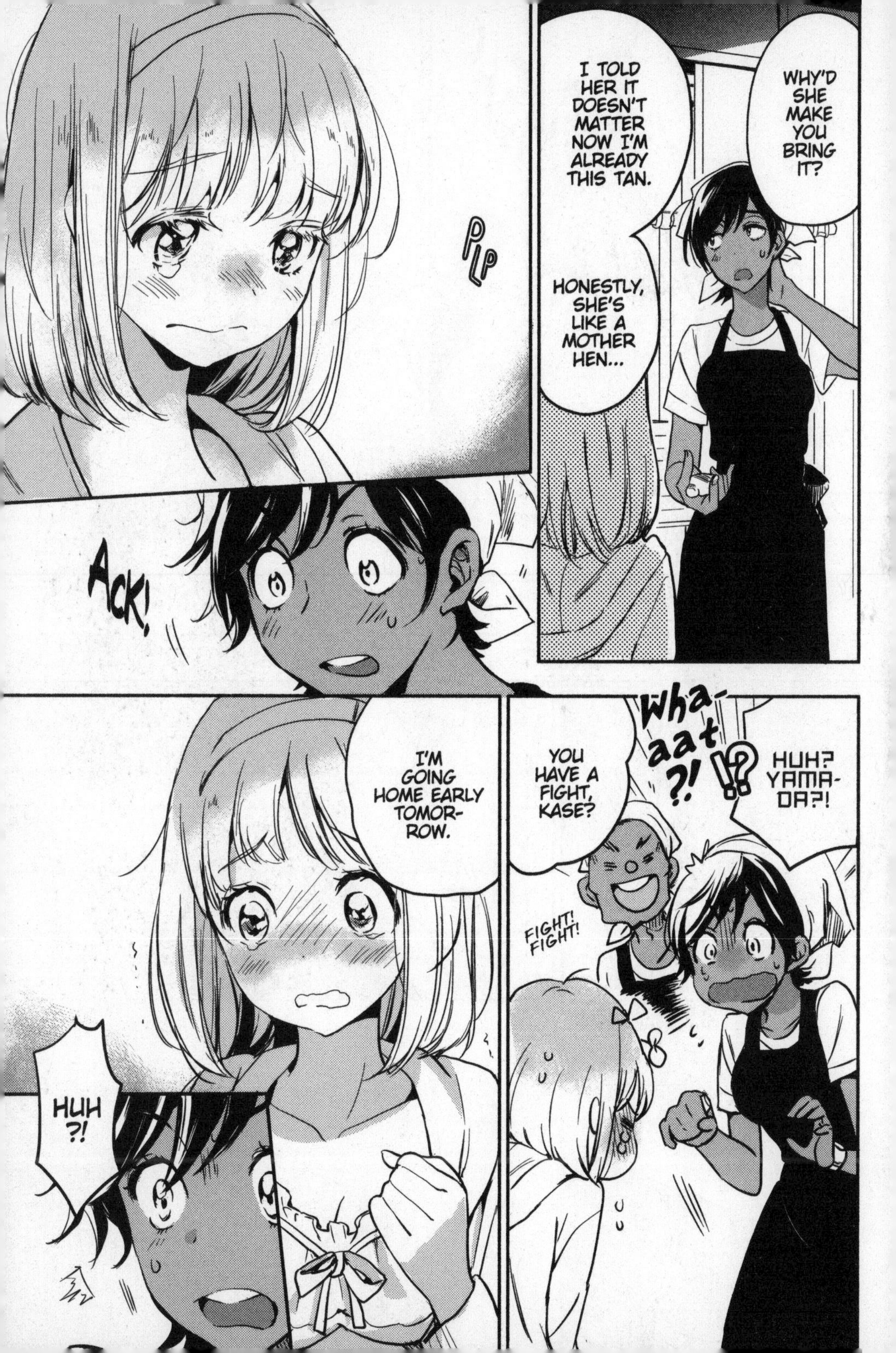
WHY'D SHE MAKE YOU BRING IT?
I TOLD HER IT DOESN'T MATTER NOW I'M ALREADY THIS TAN.
HONESTLY, SHE'S LIKE A MOTHER HEN...
PLP
ACK!
HUH? YAMA-DA?!
Wha-aat?!!?
YOU HAVE A FIGHT, KASE?
FIGHT! FIGHT!
I'M GOING HOME EARLY TOMOR-ROW.
HUH?!

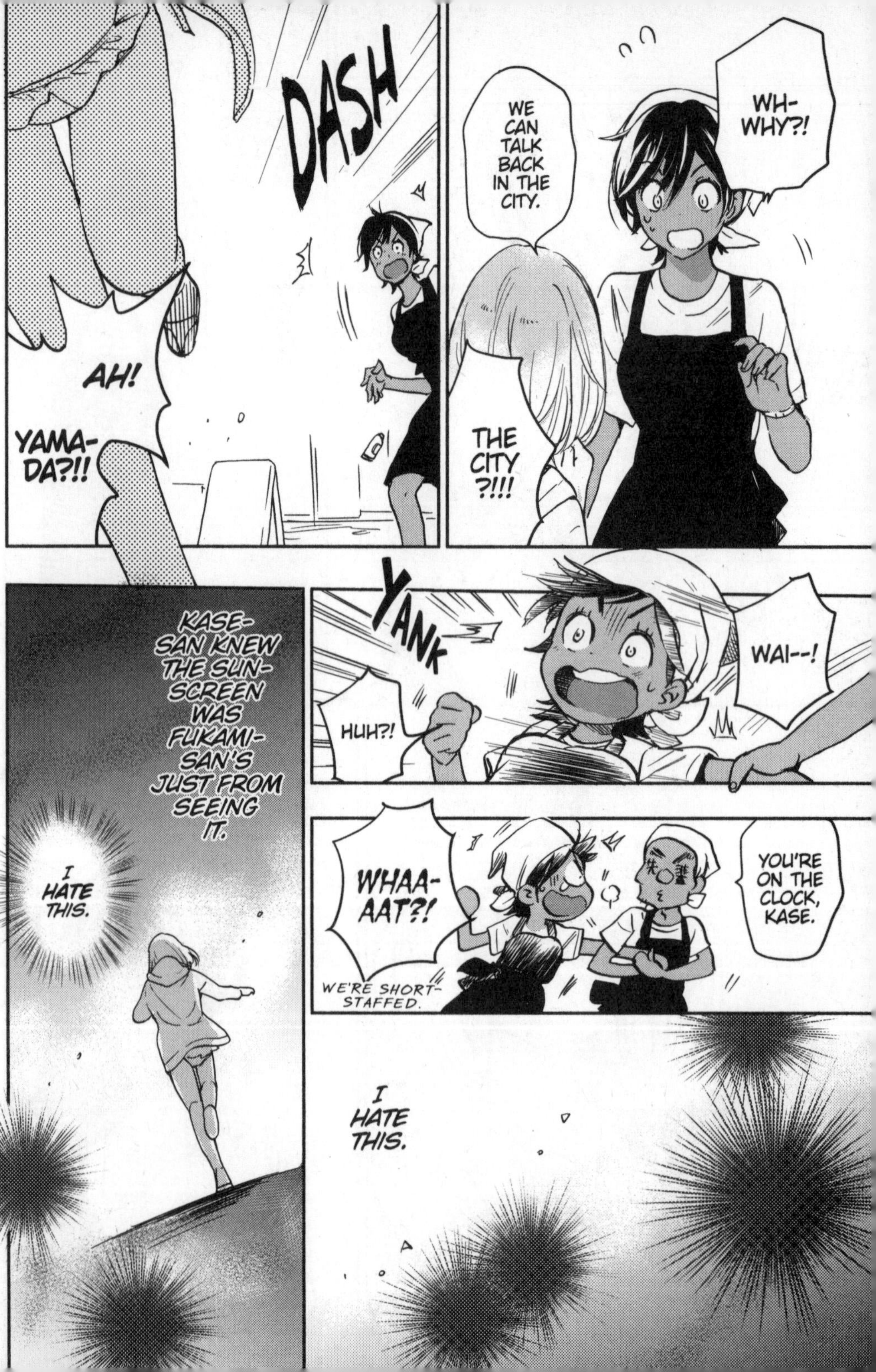
WH-WHY?!
WE CAN TALK BACK IN THE CITY.
THE CITY?!!!
DASH
AH!
YAMADA?!!
WAI--!
YANK
HUH?!
YOU'RE ON THE CLOCK, KASE.
WHAA-AAT?!
WE'RE SHORT-STAFFED.
I HATE THIS.
KASE-SAN KNEW THE SUN-SCREEN WAS FUKAMI-SAN'S JUST FROM SEEING IT.
I HATE THIS.

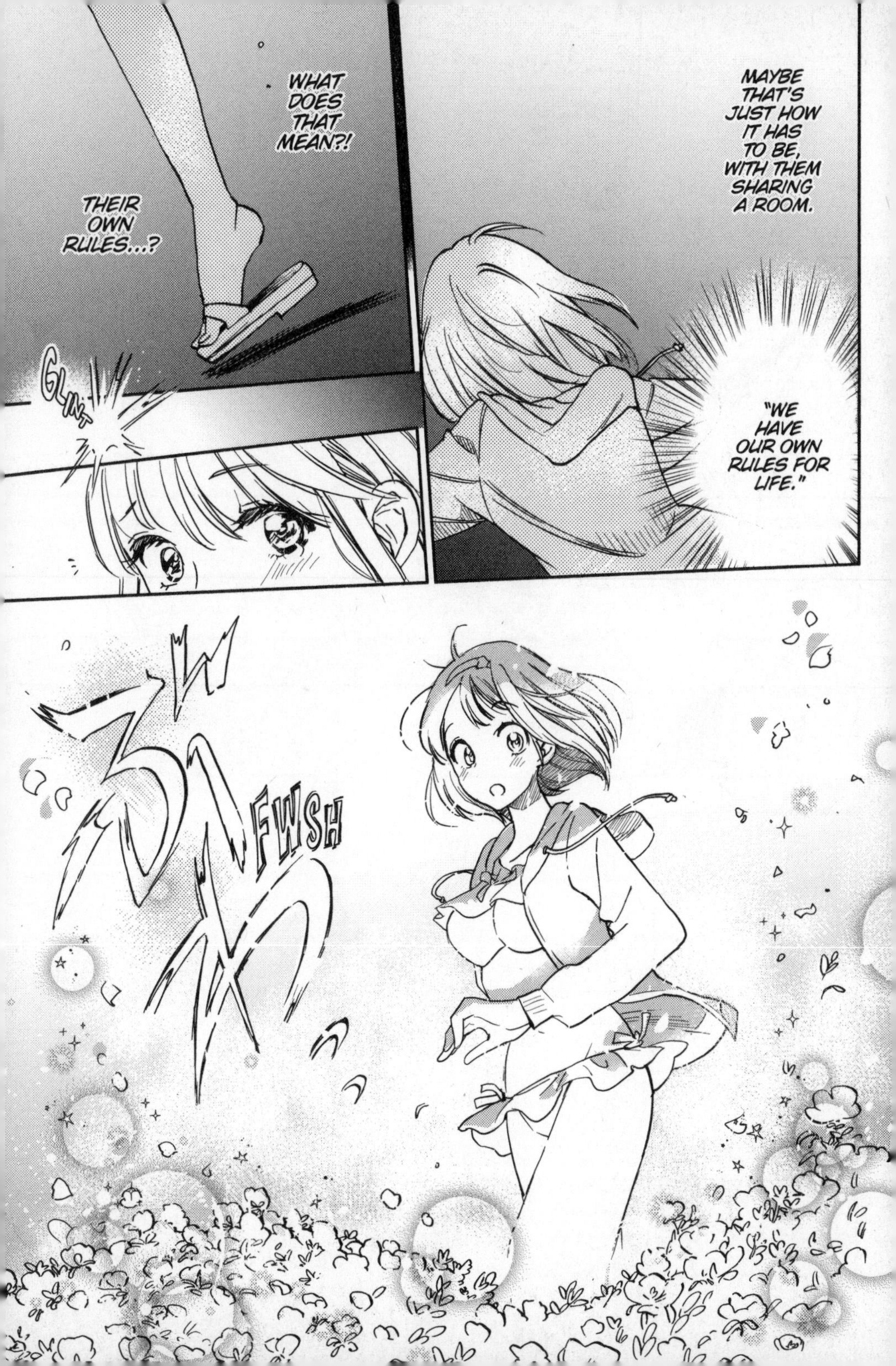
MAYBE THAT'S JUST HOW IT HAS TO BE, WITH THEM SHARING A ROOM.
"WE HAVE OUR OWN RULES FOR LIFE."
WHAT DOES THAT MEAN?!
THEIR OWN RULES...?
GLINT
FWSH

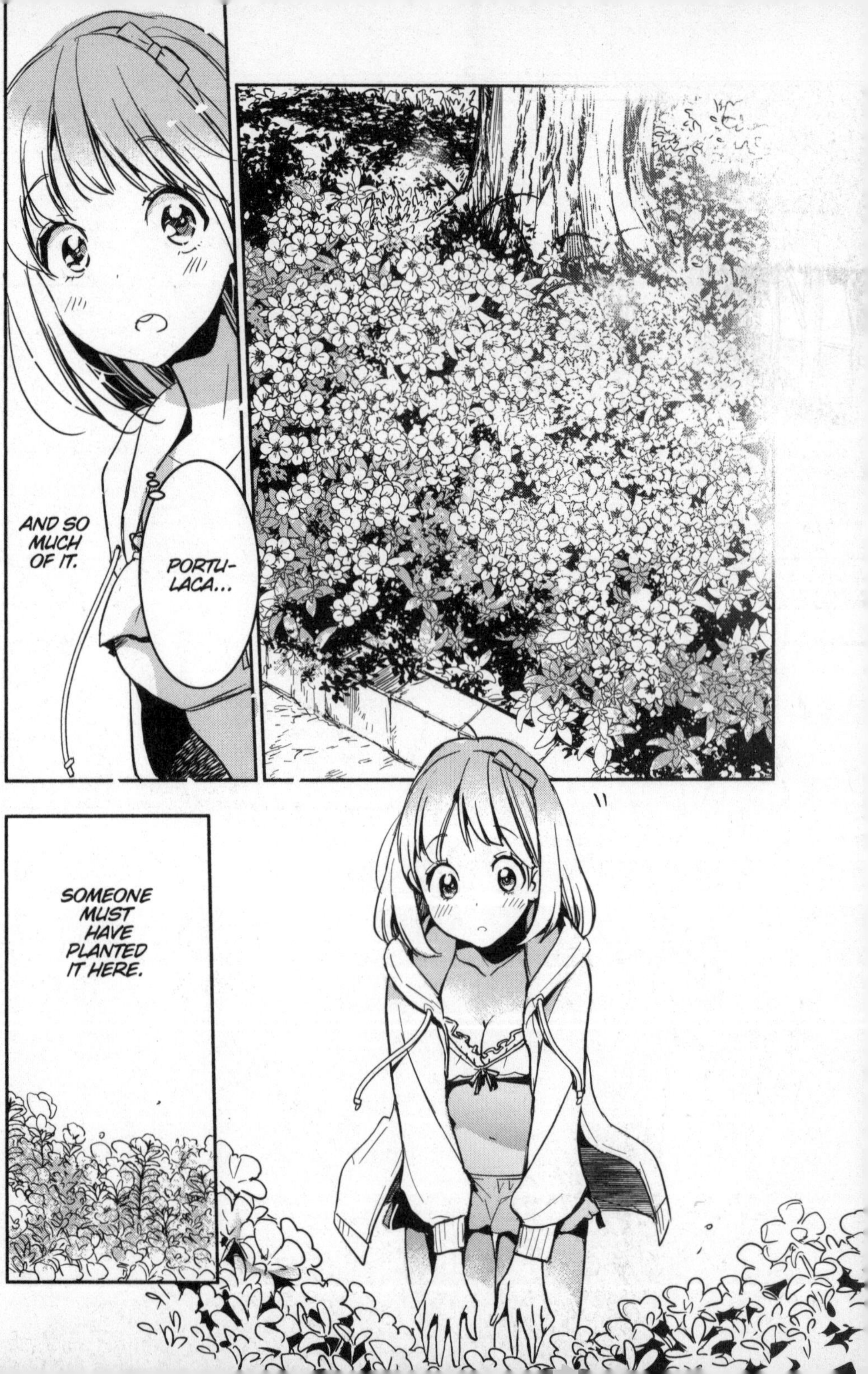
PORTU-LACA...
AND SO MUCH OF IT.
SOMEONE MUST HAVE PLANTED IT HERE.

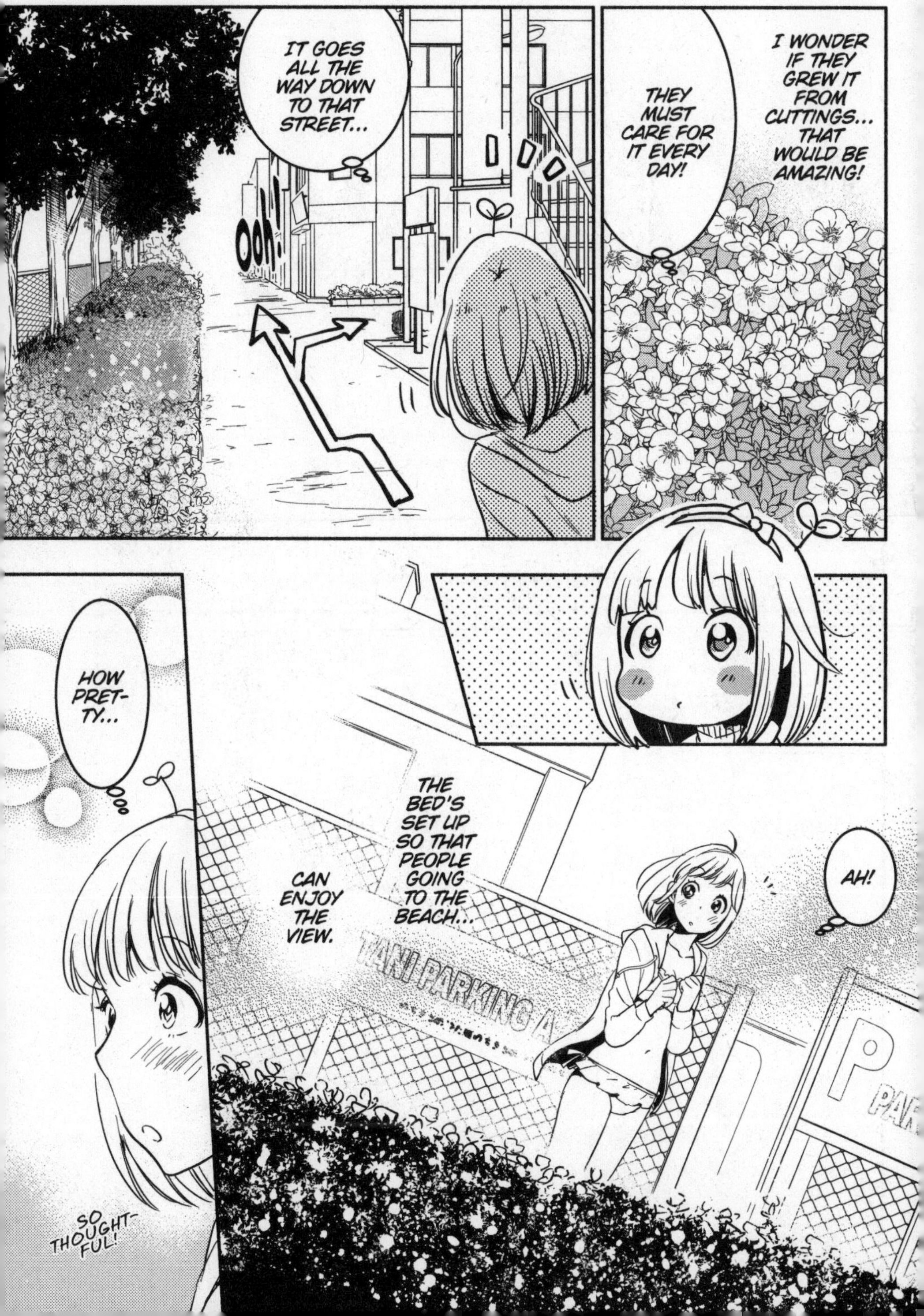
I WONDER IF THEY GREW IT FROM CUTTINGS... THAT WOULD BE AMAZING!
THEY MUST CARE FOR IT EVERY DAY!
IT GOES ALL THE WAY DOWN TO THAT STREET...
Ooh!
AH!
THE BED'S SET UP SO THAT PEOPLE GOING TO THE BEACH...
CAN ENJOY THE VIEW.
TANI PARKING A
P
PAR
HOW PRETTY...
SO THOUGHTFUL!

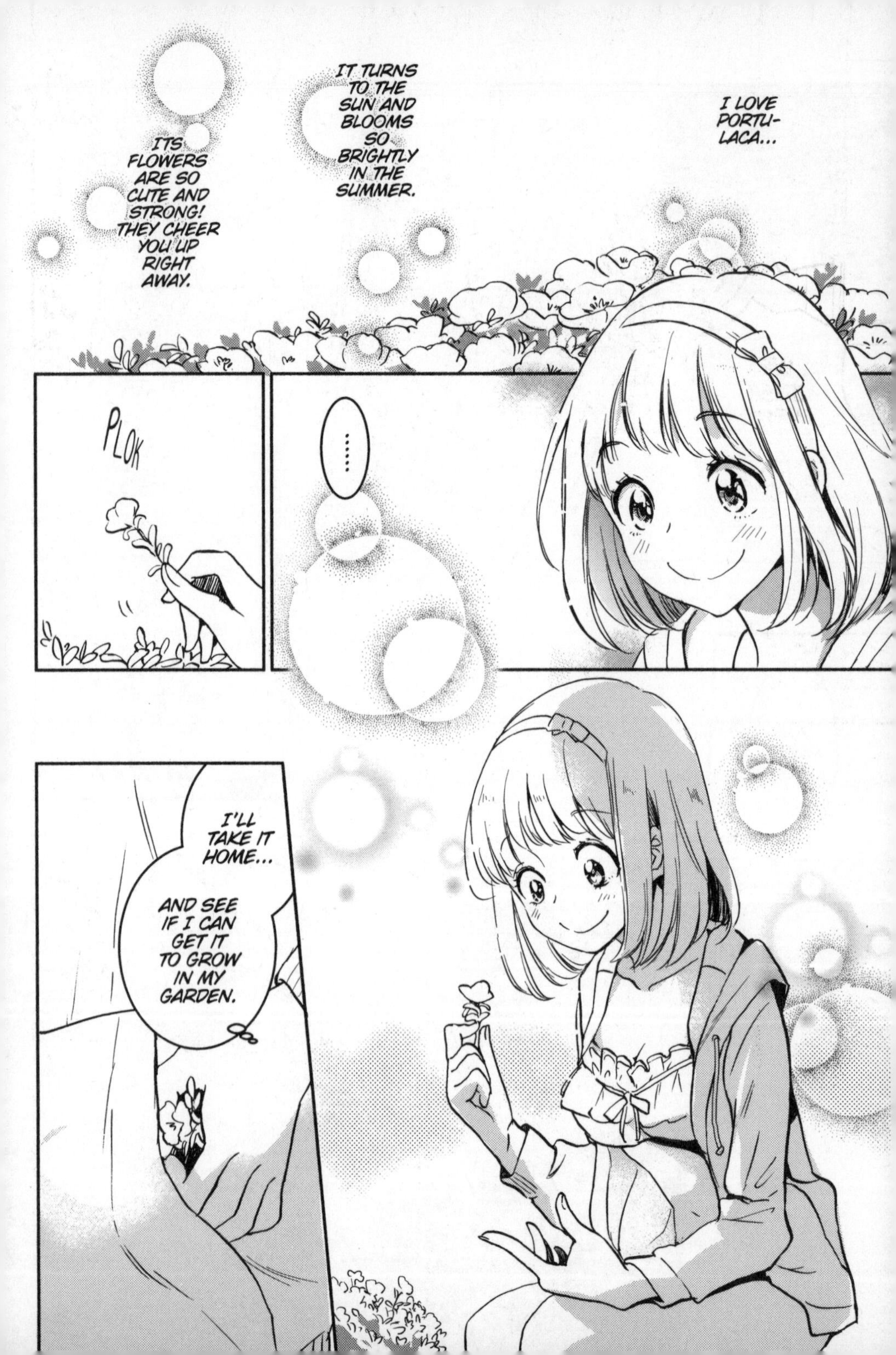
I LOVE PORTU-LACA...
IT TURNS TO THE SUN AND BLOOMS SO BRIGHTLY IN THE SUMMER.
ITS FLOWERS ARE SO CUTE AND STRONG! THEY CHEER YOU UP RIGHT AWAY.
......
PLOK
I'LL TAKE IT HOME...
AND SEE IF I CAN GET IT TO GROW IN MY GARDEN.

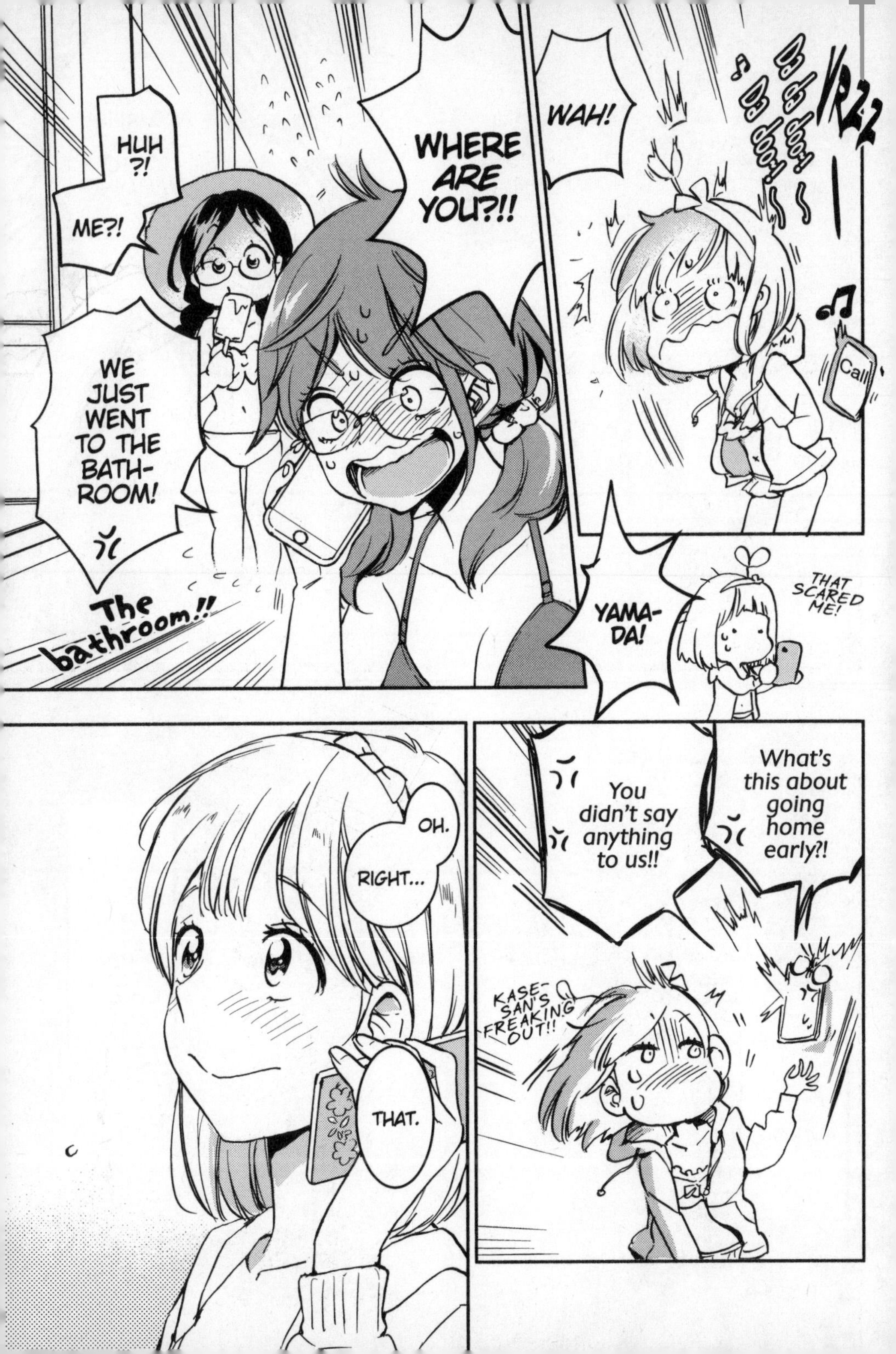
VRZZ—
Da da doo!~
Da da doo!~
WAH!
Call
YAMA-DA!
THAT SCARED ME!
WHERE ARE YOU?!!
HUH?! ME?!
WE JUST WENT TO THE BATH-ROOM!
The bathroom!!
What's this about going home early?!
You didn't say anything to us!!
KASE-SAN'S FREAKING OUT!!
OH. RIGHT...
THAT.

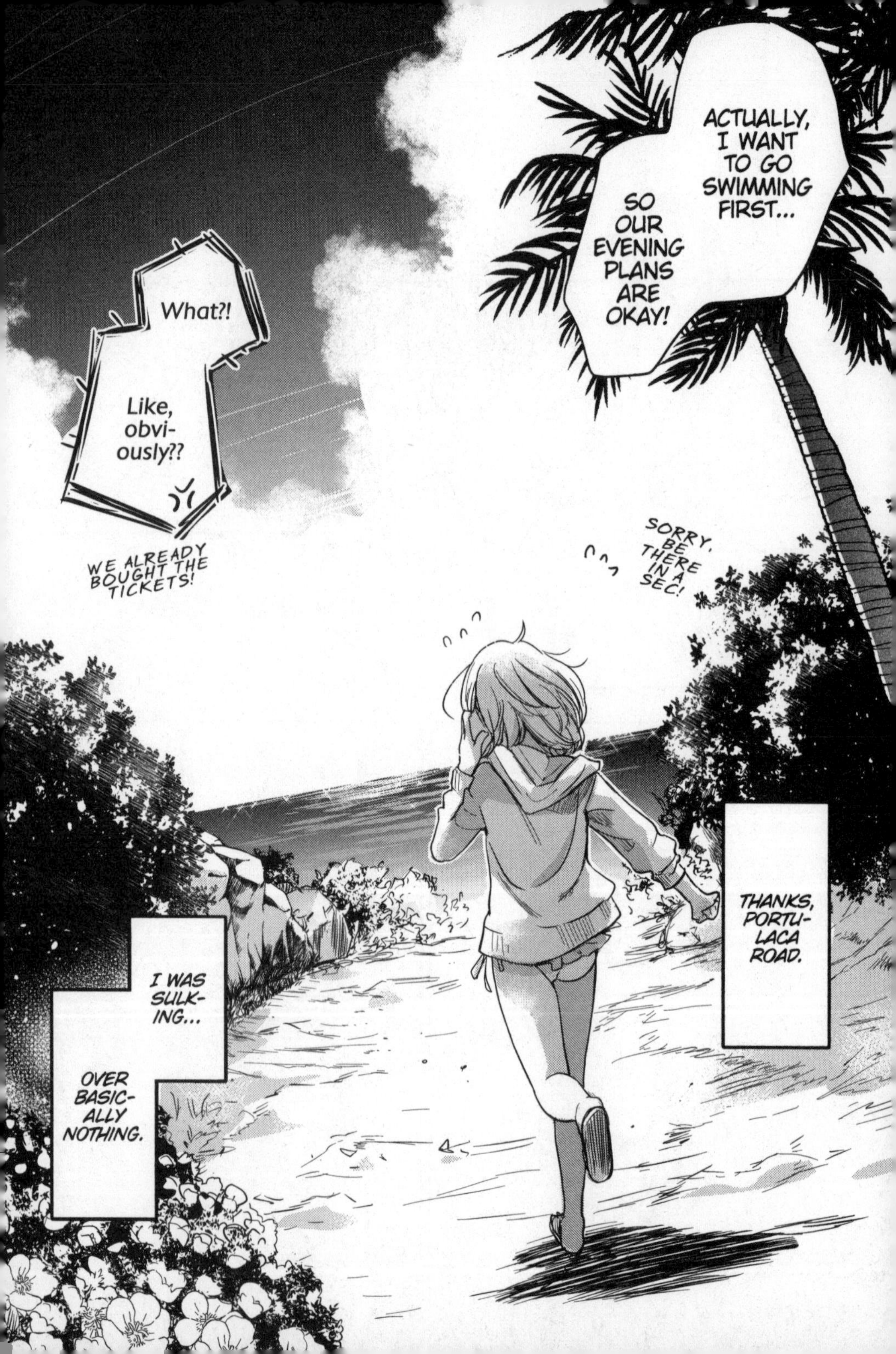
ACTUALLY, I WANT TO GO SWIMMING FIRST...
SO OUR EVENING PLANS ARE OKAY!
What?!
Like, obviously??
WE ALREADY BOUGHT THE TICKETS!
SORRY, BE THERE IN A SEC!
THANKS, PORTULACA ROAD.
I WAS SULKING...
OVER BASICALLY NOTHING.

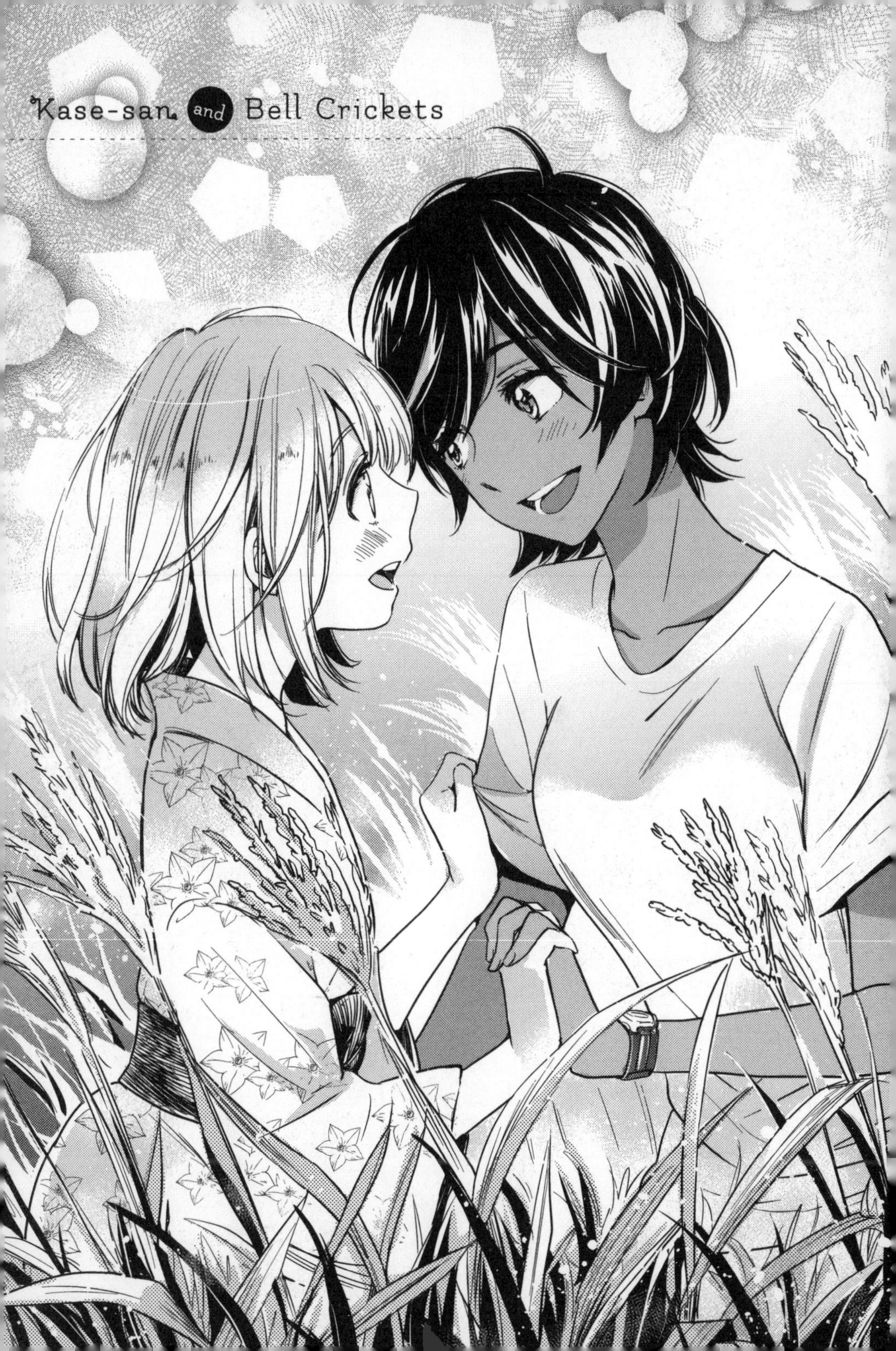
Kase-san and Bell Crickets

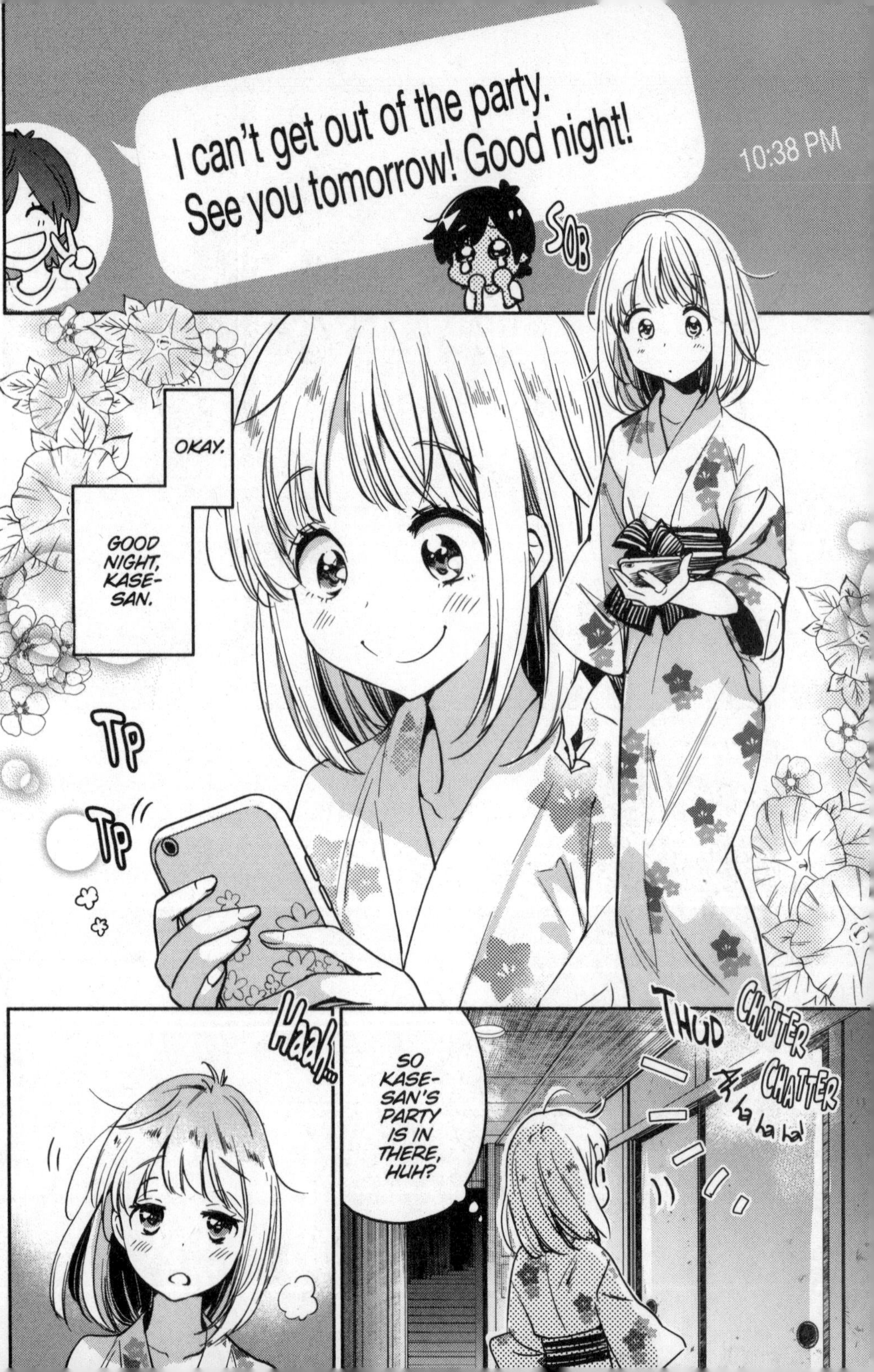

I can't get out of the party.
See you tomorrow! Good night!
10:38 PM
SOB
OKAY.
GOOD NIGHT, KASE-SAN.
Tp
Tp
THUD
CHATTER
CHATTER
ha ha ha!
SO KASE-SAN'S PARTY IS IN THERE, HUH?
Haah...

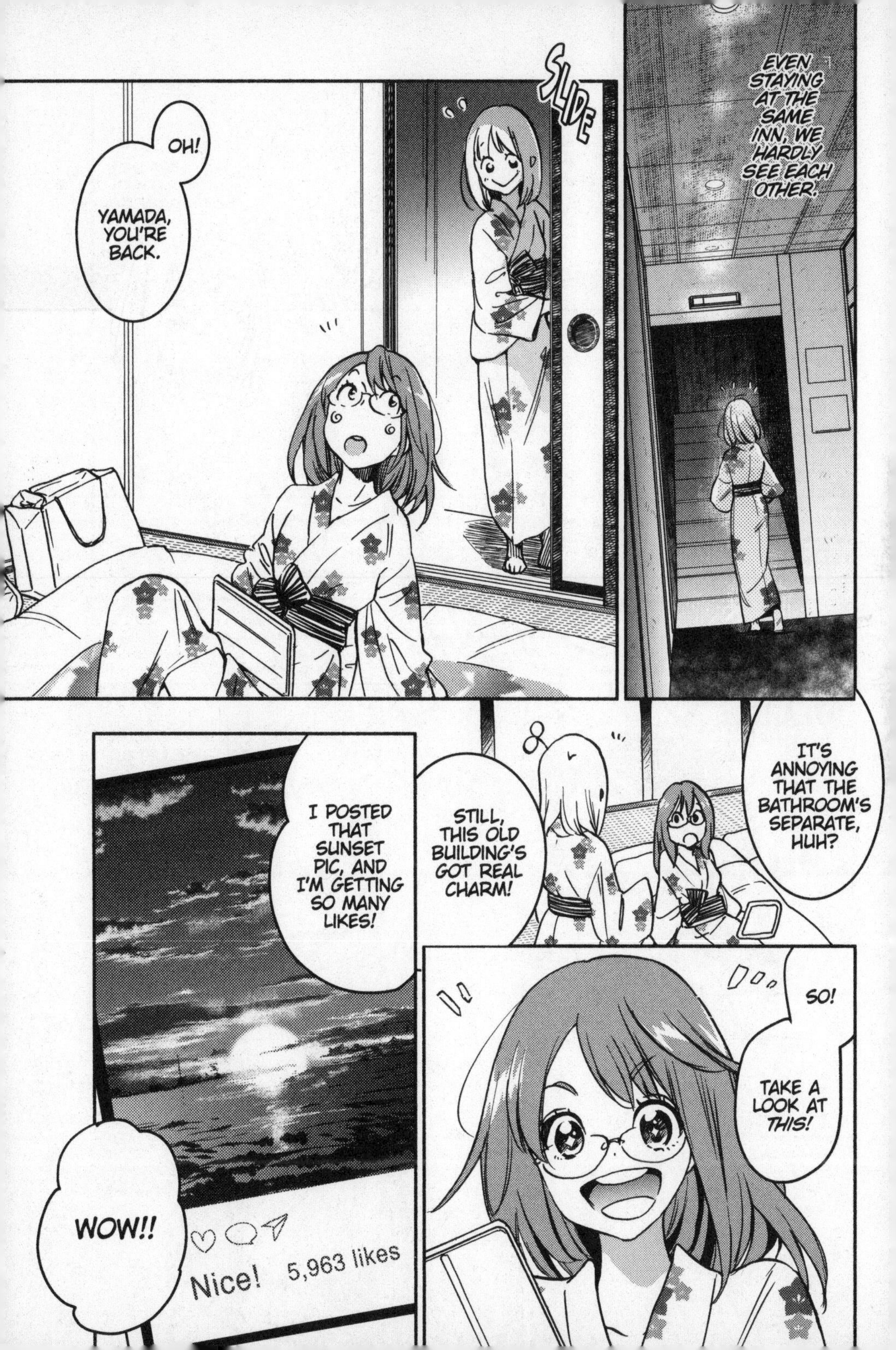
EVEN STAYING AT THE SAME INN, WE HARDLY SEE EACH OTHER.
SLIDE
OH!
YAMADA, YOU'RE BACK.
IT'S ANNOYING THAT THE BATHROOM'S SEPARATE, HUH?
STILL, THIS OLD BUILDING'S GOT REAL CHARM!
I POSTED THAT SUNSET PIC, AND I'M GETTING SO MANY LIKES!
SO!
TAKE A LOOK AT THIS!
Nice! 5,963 likes
WOW!!

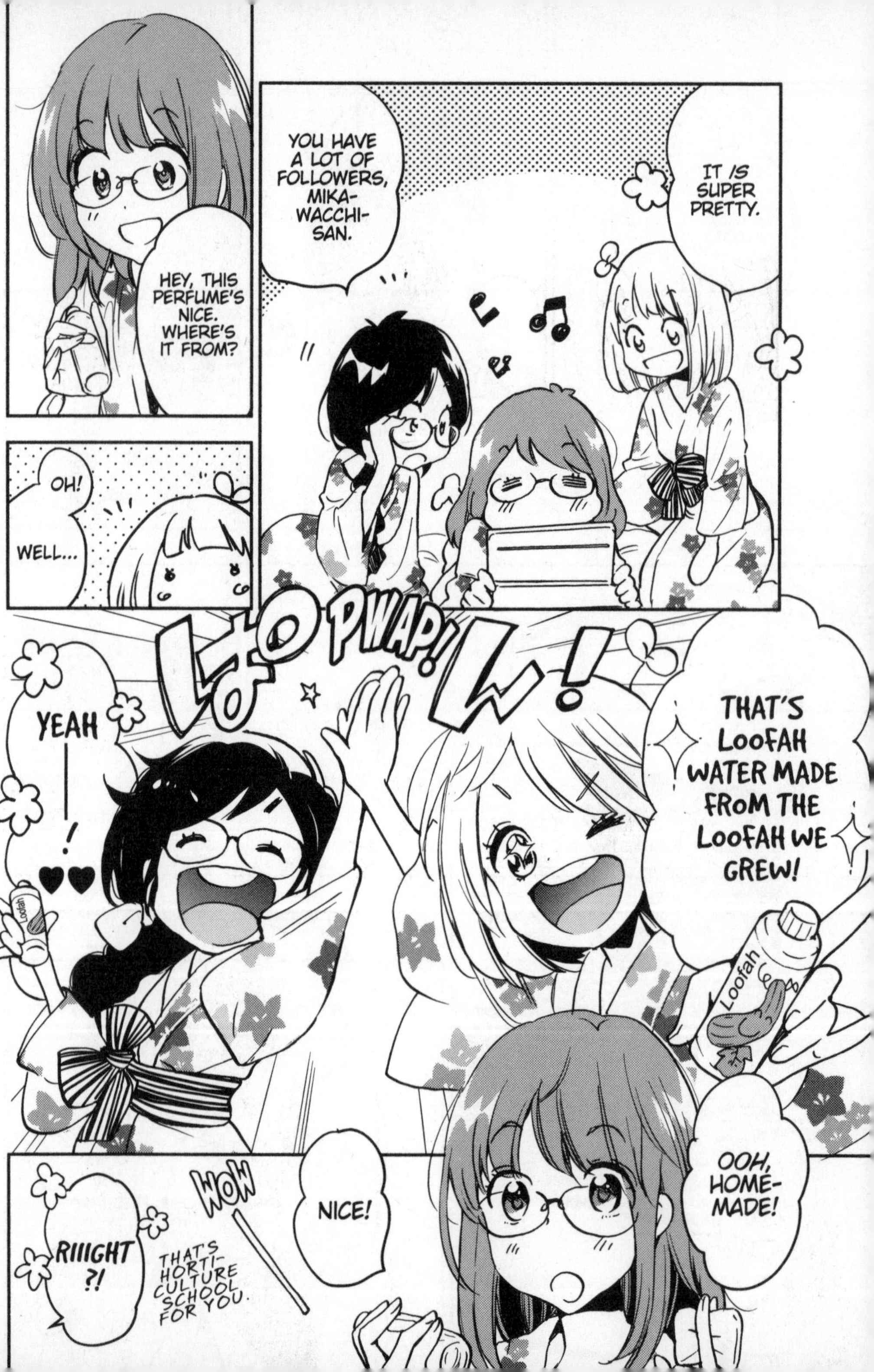
IT IS SUPER PRETTY.
YOU HAVE A LOT OF FOLLOWERS, MIKA-WACCHI-SAN.
HEY, THIS PERFUME'S NICE. WHERE'S IT FROM?
OH!
WELL...
PWAP!
THAT'S LOOFAH WATER MADE FROM THE LOOFAH WE GREW!
YEAH—!
Loofah
Loofah
OOH, HOME-MADE!
NICE!
WOW
RIIIGHT?!
THAT'S HORTI-CULTURE SCHOOL FOR YOU.

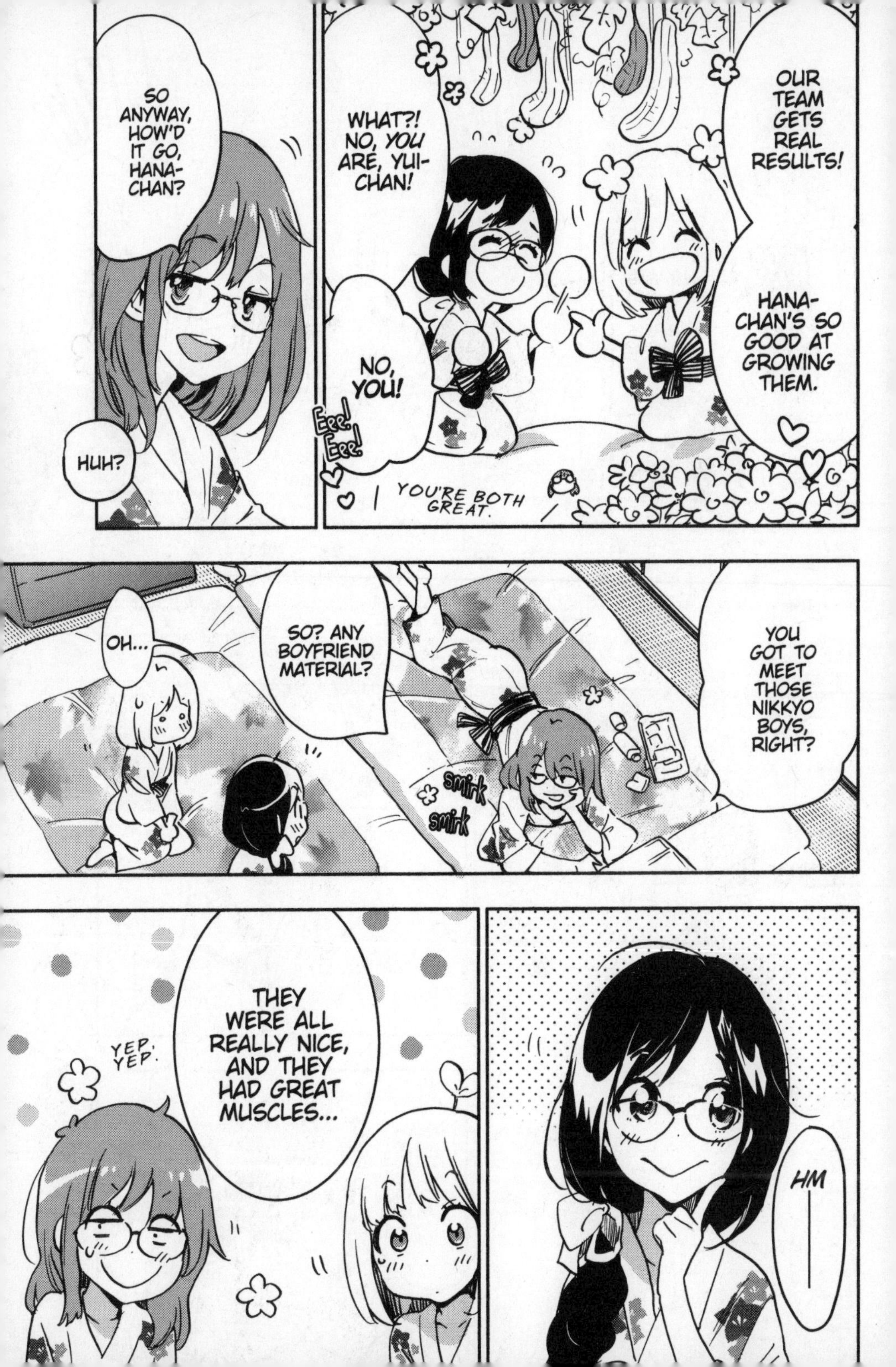
OUR TEAM GETS REAL RESULTS!
HANA-CHAN'S SO GOOD AT GROWING THEM.
WHAT?! NO, YOU ARE, YUI-CHAN!
NO, YOU!
Eee! Eee!
YOU'RE BOTH GREAT.
SO ANYWAY, HOW'D IT GO, HANA-CHAN?
HUH?
YOU GOT TO MEET THOSE NIKKYO BOYS, RIGHT?
smirk smirk
SO? ANY BOYFRIEND MATERIAL?
OH...
HM
THEY WERE ALL REALLY NICE, AND THEY HAD GREAT MUSCLES...
YEP. YEP.

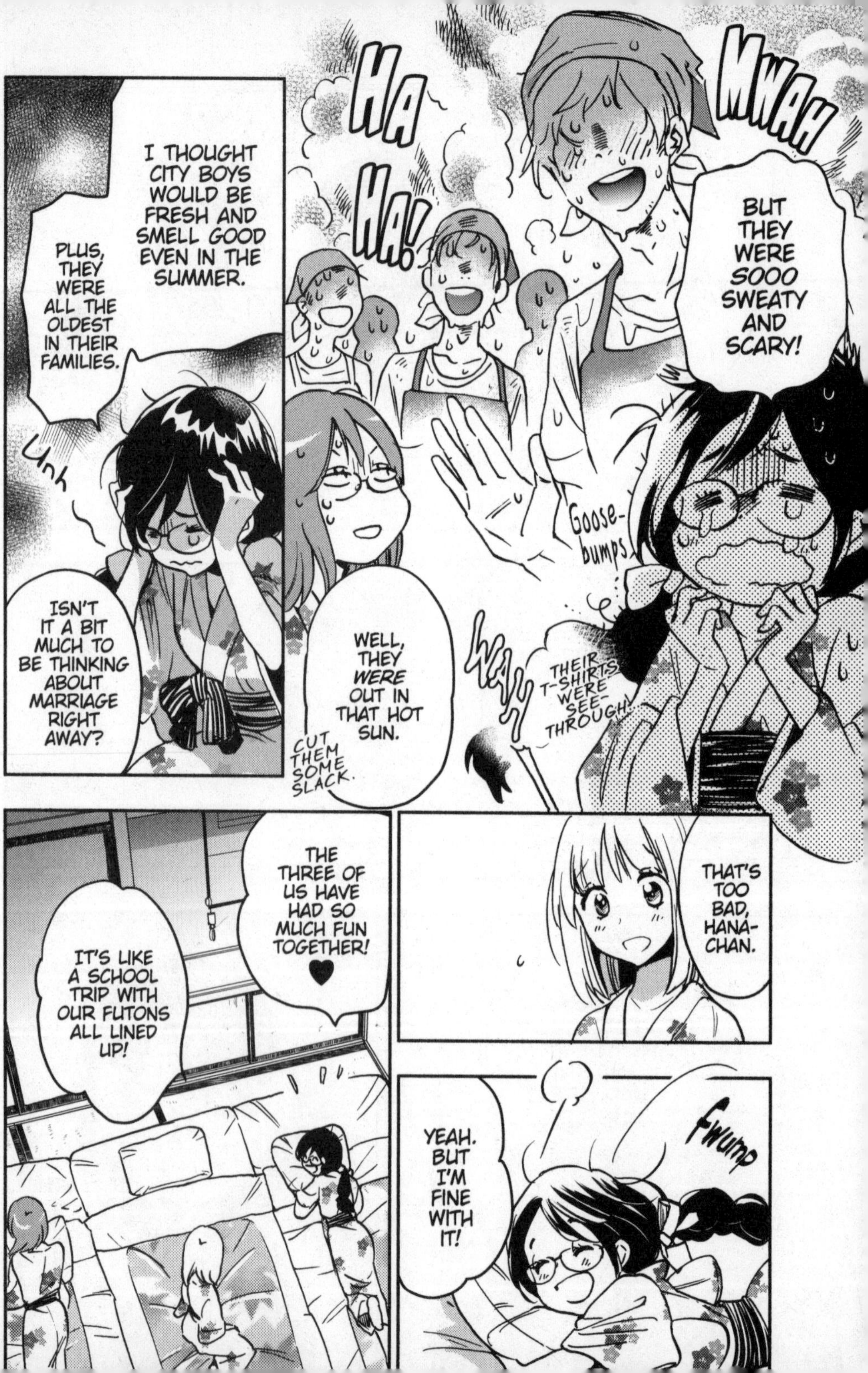
MWAH
HA HA!
BUT THEY WERE SOOO SWEATY AND SCARY!
Goose-bumps
THEIR T-SHIRTS WERE SEE-THROUGH!
WAAH
I THOUGHT CITY BOYS WOULD BE FRESH AND SMELL GOOD EVEN IN THE SUMMER.
PLUS, THEY WERE ALL THE OLDEST IN THEIR FAMILIES.
Unh
WELL, THEY WERE OUT IN THAT HOT SUN.
CUT THEM SOME SLACK.
ISN'T IT A BIT MUCH TO BE THINKING ABOUT MARRIAGE RIGHT AWAY?
THAT'S TOO BAD, HANA-CHAN.
Fwump
YEAH. BUT I'M FINE WITH IT!
THE THREE OF US HAVE HAD SO MUCH FUN TOGETHER! ♥
IT'S LIKE A SCHOOL TRIP WITH OUR FUTONS ALL LINED UP!

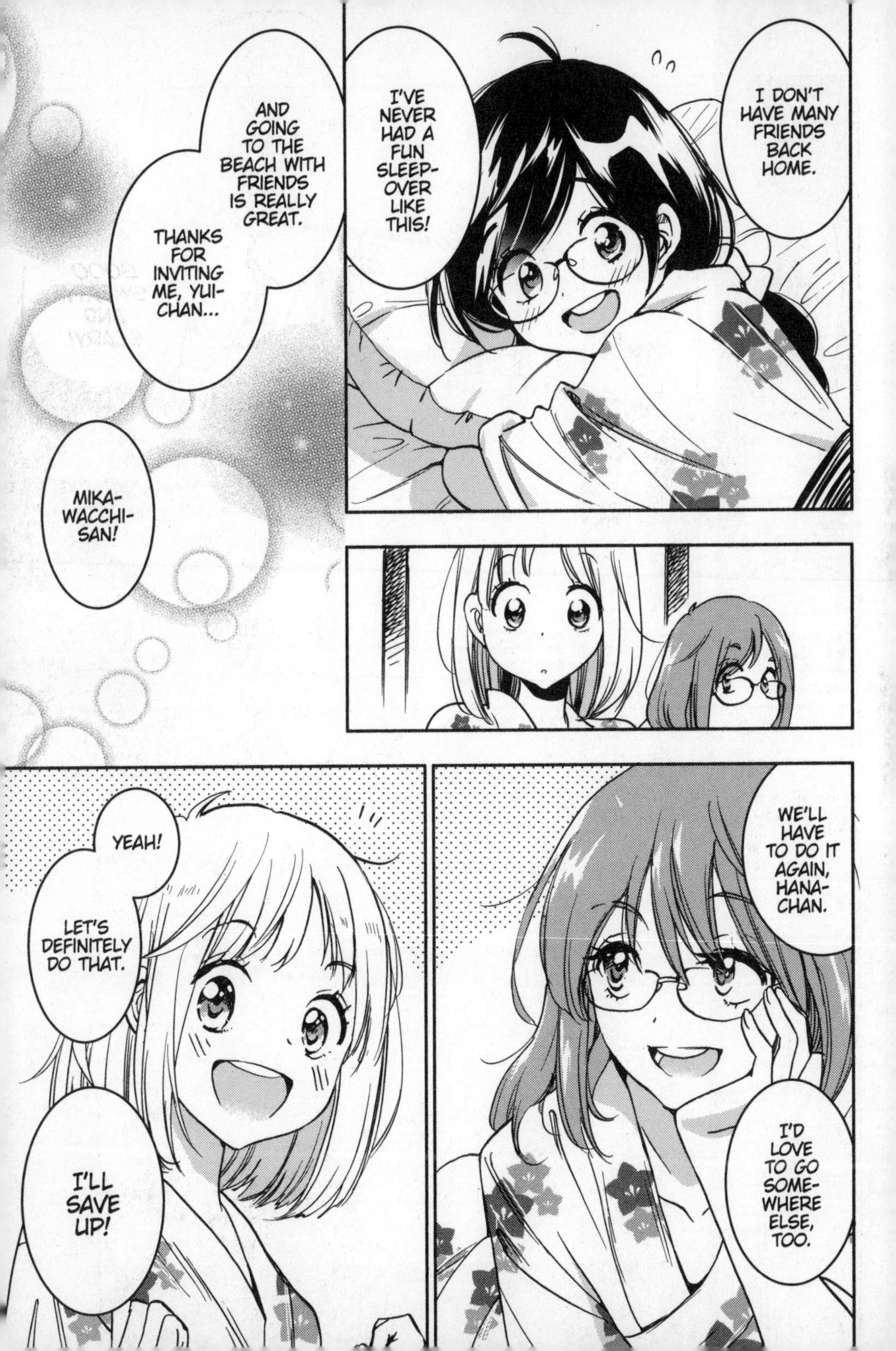
I DON'T HAVE MANY FRIENDS BACK HOME.
I'VE NEVER HAD A FUN SLEEP-OVER LIKE THIS!
AND GOING TO THE BEACH WITH FRIENDS IS REALLY GREAT.
THANKS FOR INVITING ME, YUI-CHAN...
MIKA-WACCHI-SAN!
WE'LL HAVE TO DO IT AGAIN, HANA-CHAN.
I'D LOVE TO GO SOME-WHERE ELSE, TOO.
YEAH!
LET'S DEFINITELY DO THAT.
I'LL SAVE UP!

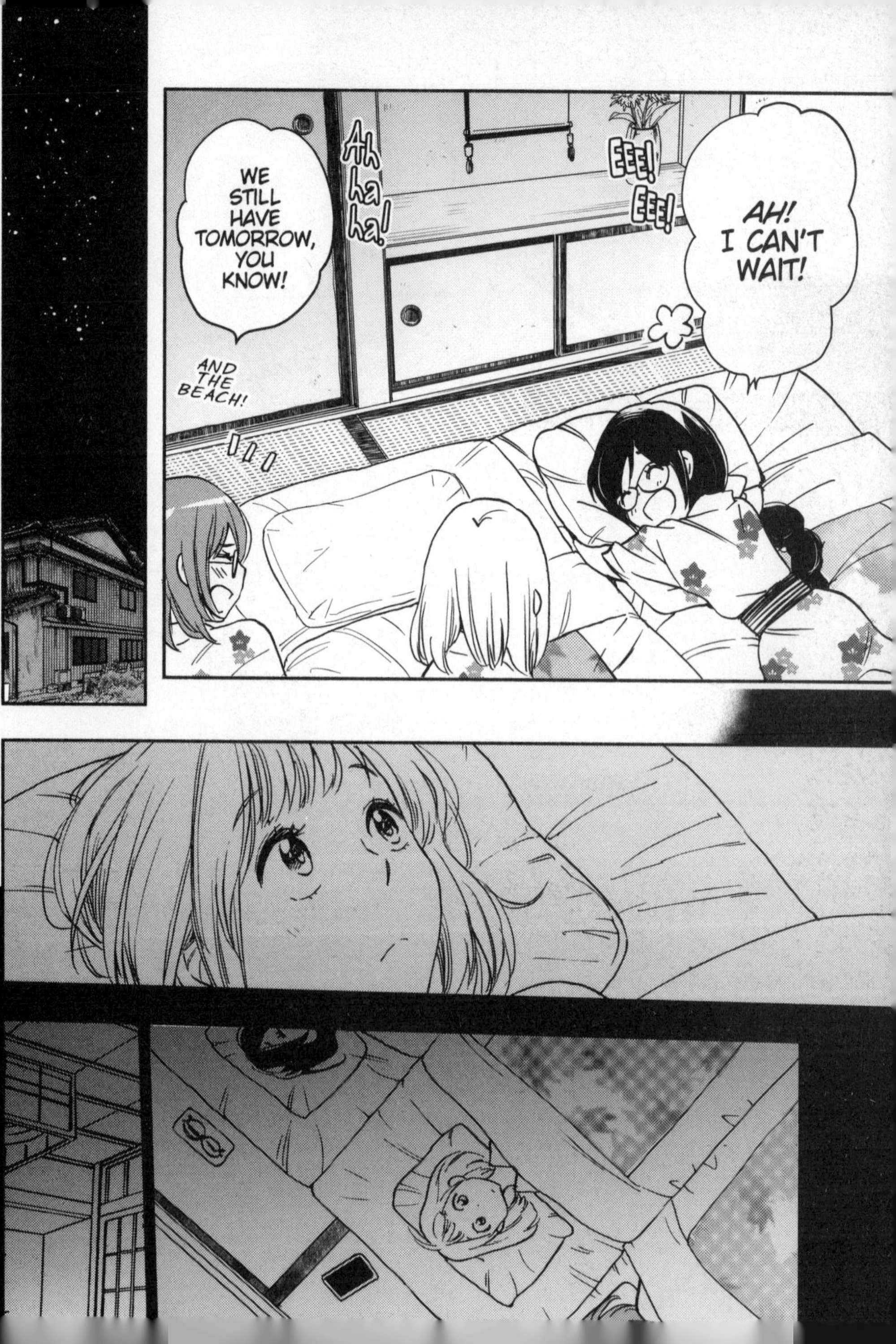
AH! I CAN'T WAIT!
EEE! EEE!
Ah ha ha!
WE STILL HAVE TOMORROW, YOU KNOW!
AND THE BEACH!

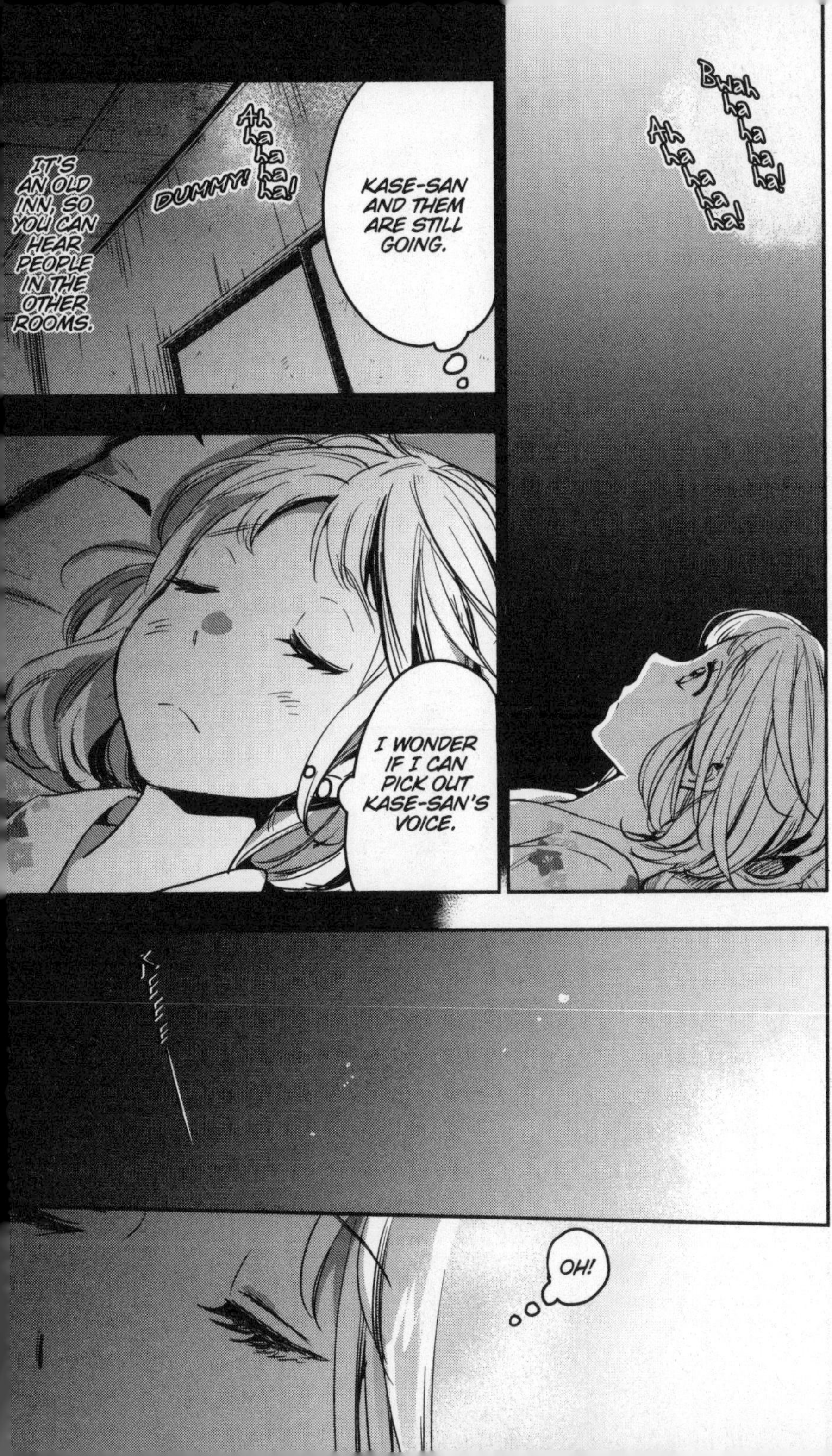
Bwah ha ha ha ha!
Ah ha ha ha ha!
KASE-SAN AND THEM ARE STILL GOING.
Ah ha ha ha ha!
DUMMY!
IT'S AN OLD INN, SO YOU CAN HEAR PEOPLE IN THE OTHER ROOMS.
I WONDER IF I CAN PICK OUT KASE-SAN'S VOICE.
OH!

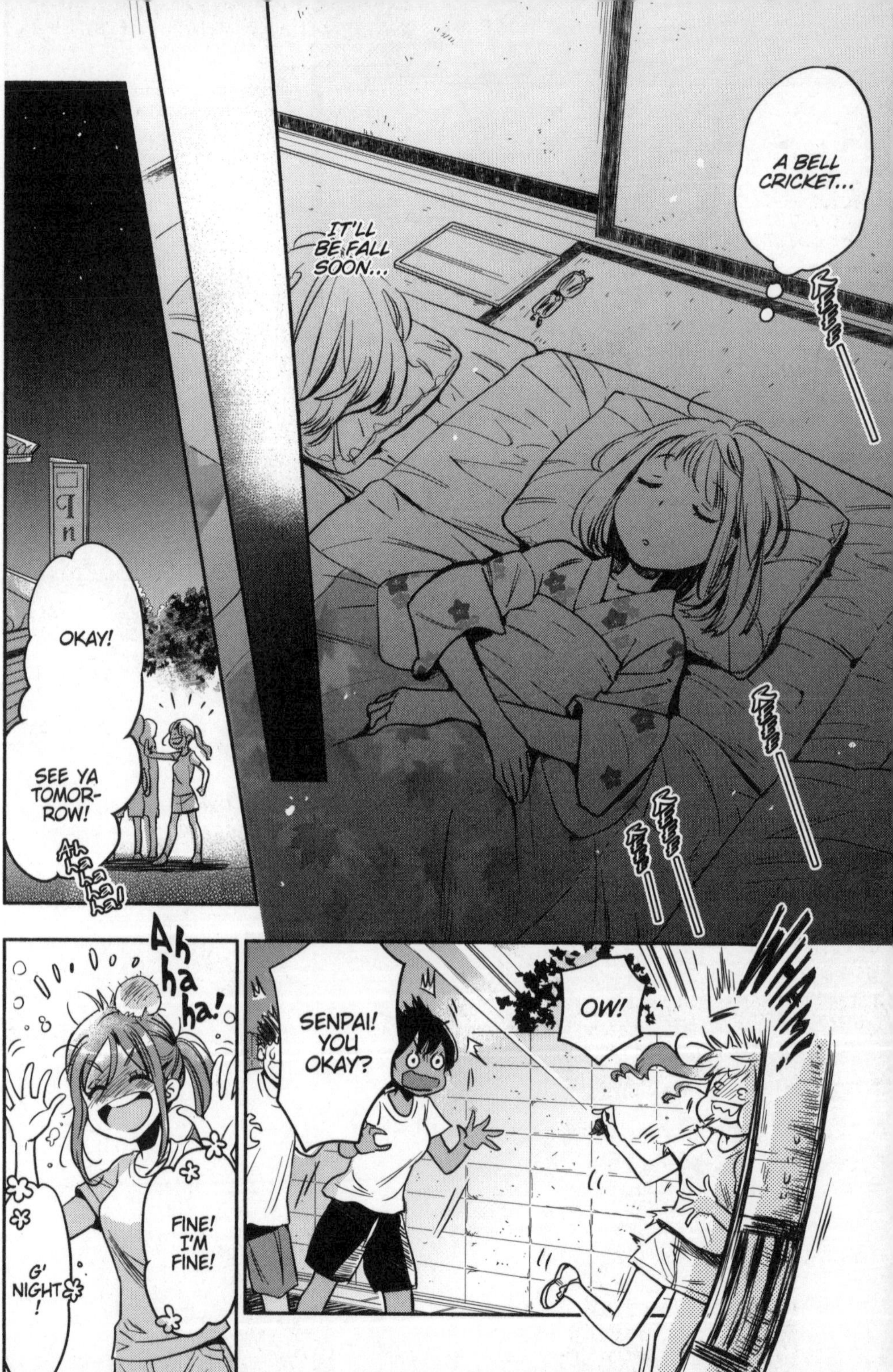
A BELL CRICKET...
IT'LL BE FALL SOON...
OKAY!
SEE YA TOMORROW!
Ahahahaha!
WHAM!
OW!
SENPAI! YOU OKAY?
Ahhaha!
FINE! I'M FINE!
G' NIGHT!

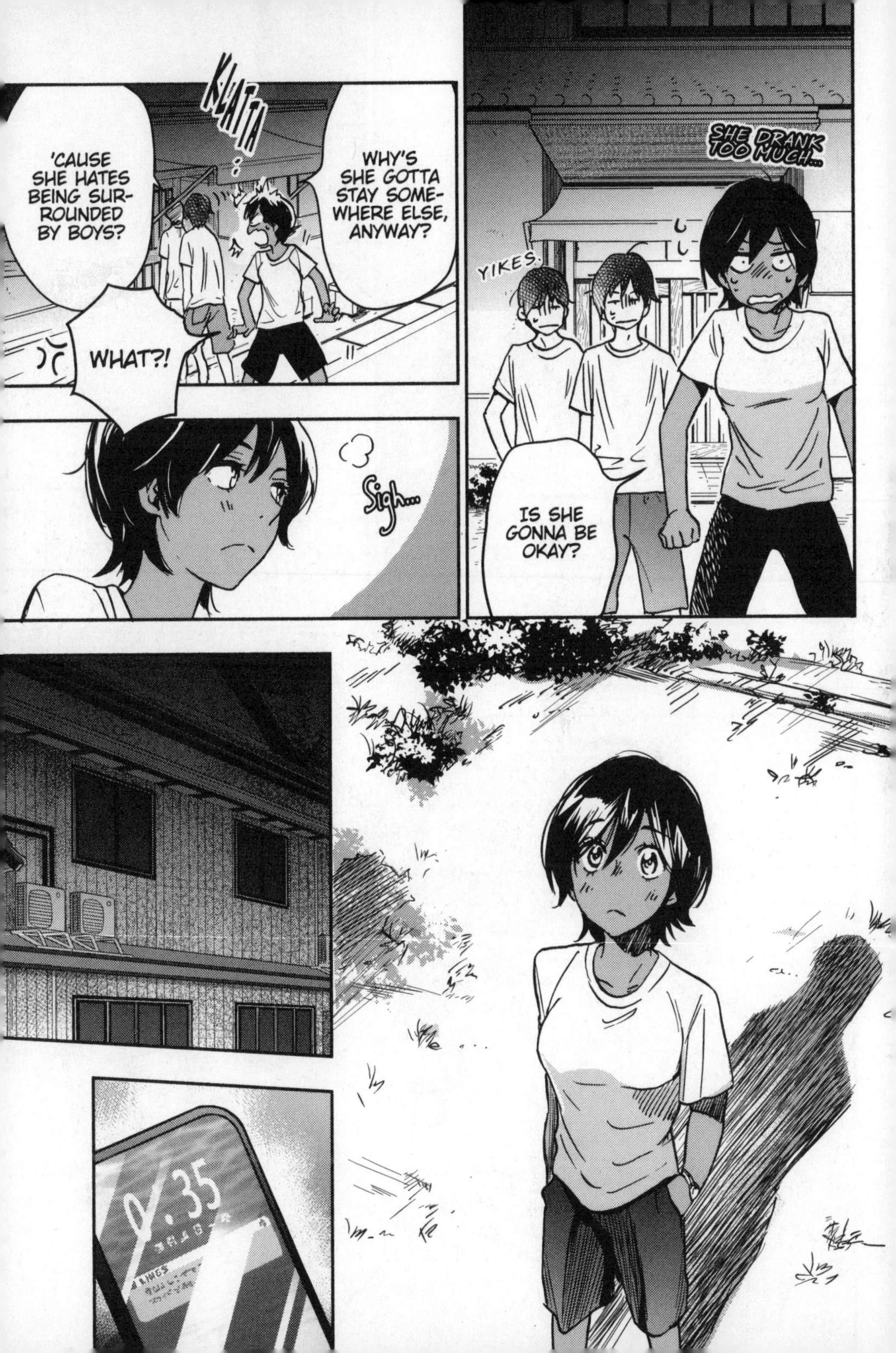
SHE DRANK TOO MUCH...
YIKES.
IS SHE GONNA BE OKAY?
WHY'S SHE GOTTA STAY SOME-WHERE ELSE, ANYWAY?
KLATTA
'CAUSE SHE HATES BEING SUR-ROUNDED BY BOYS?
WHAT?!
Sigh...
0:35

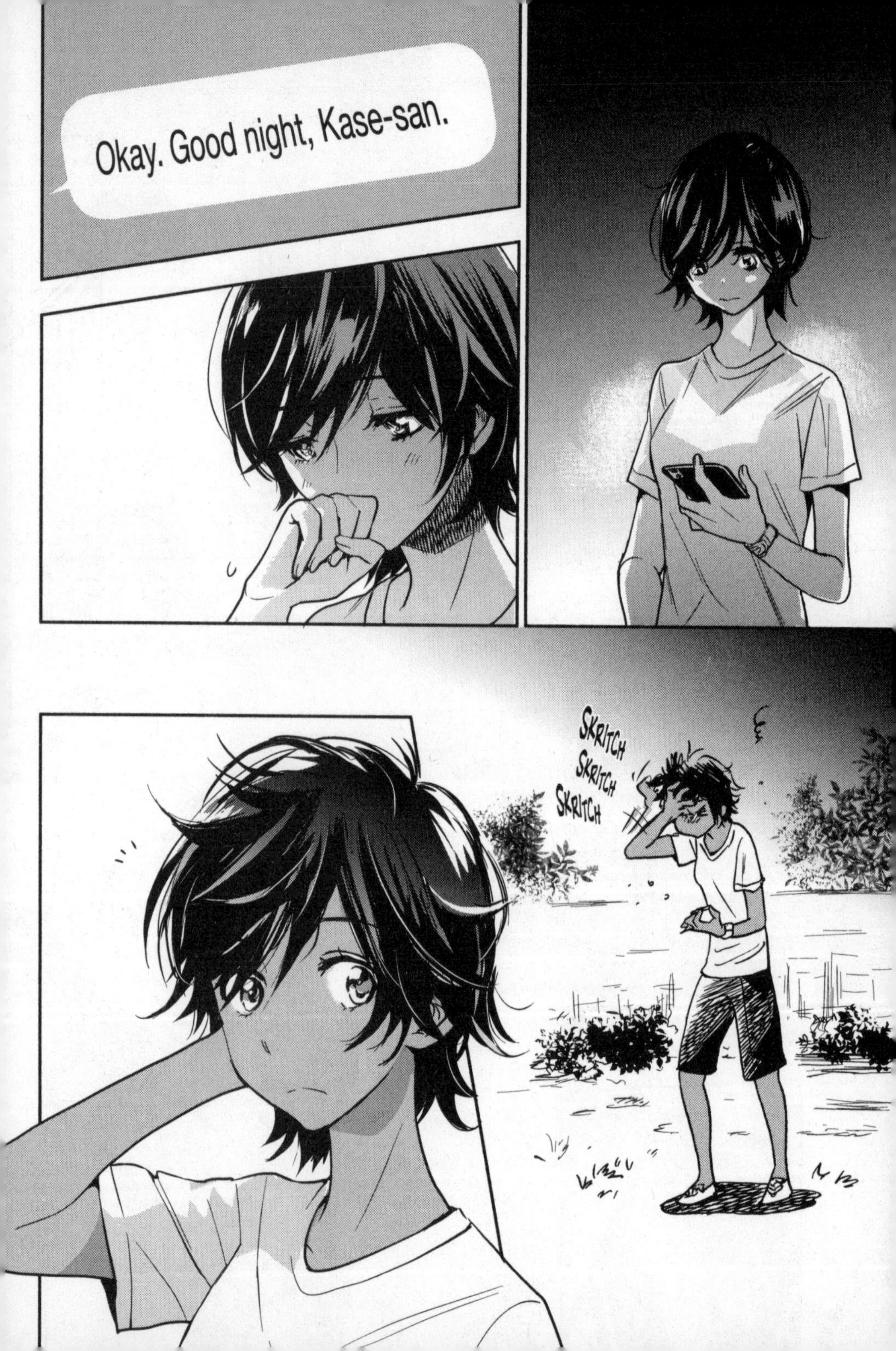
Okay. Good night, Kase-san.
SKRITCH SKRITCH SKRITCH

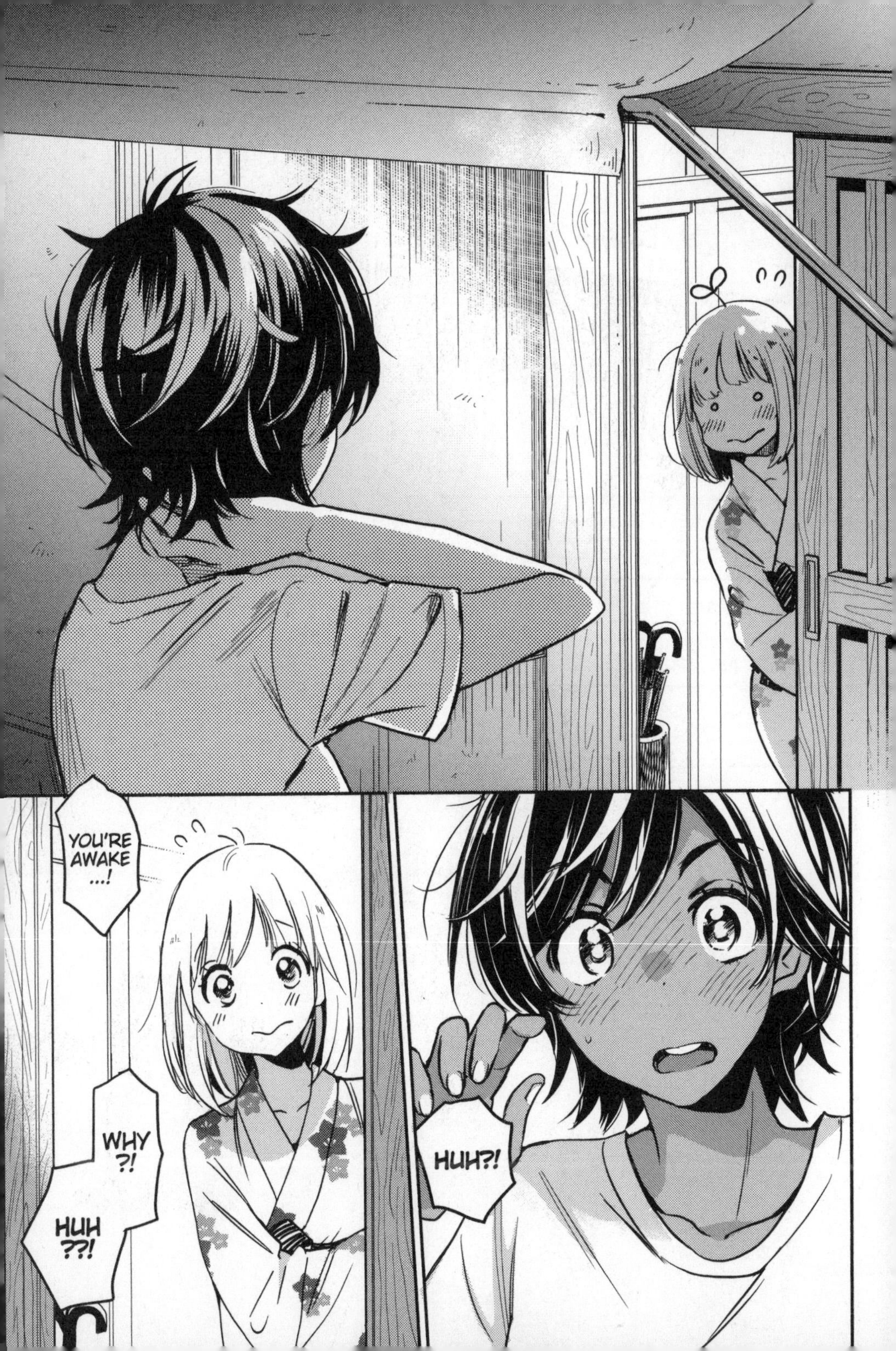
HUH?!
YOU'RE AWAKE ...!
WHY ?!
HUH ??!

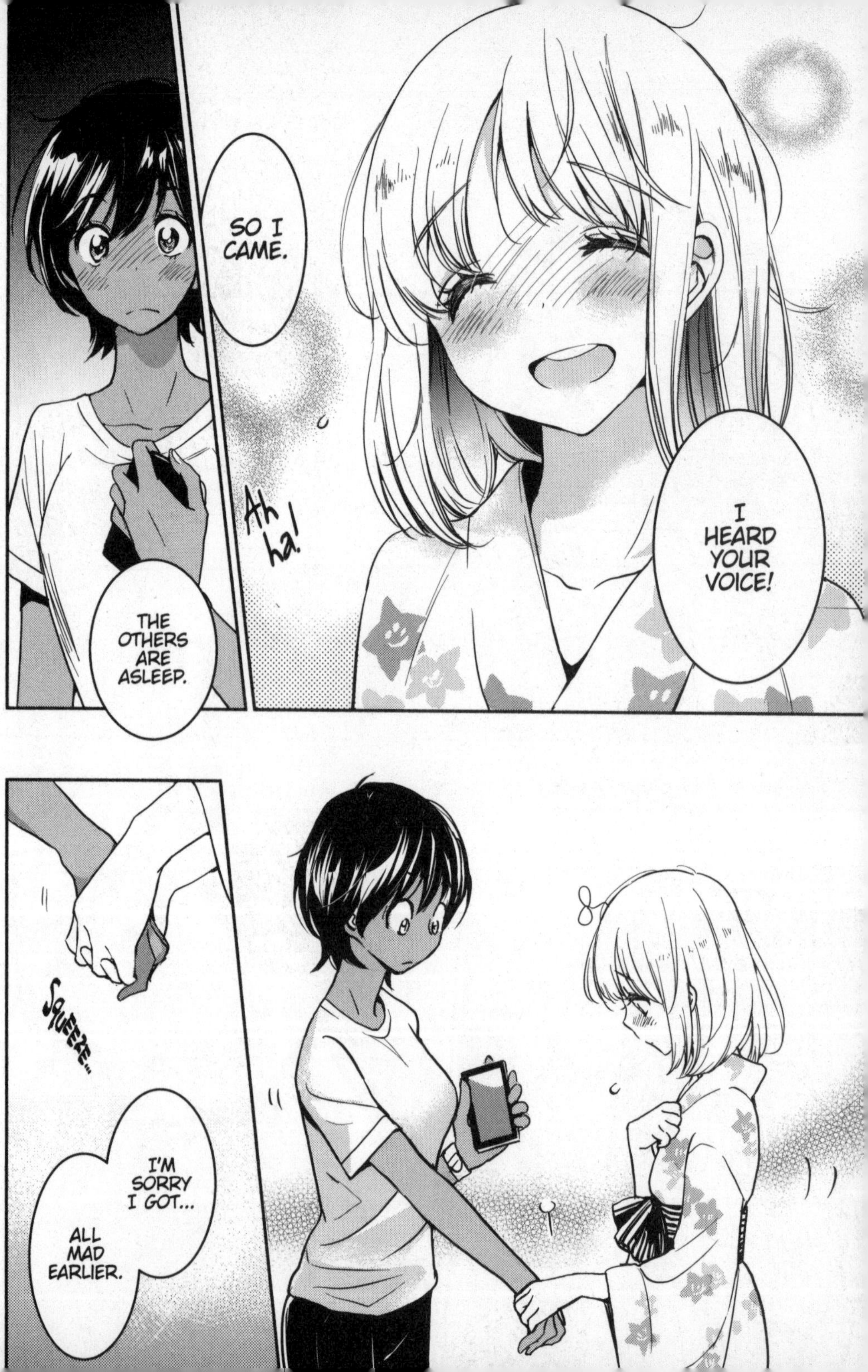
I HEARD YOUR VOICE!
Ah ha!
SO I CAME.
THE OTHERS ARE ASLEEP.
Squeeze...
I'M SORRY I GOT...
ALL MAD EARLIER.

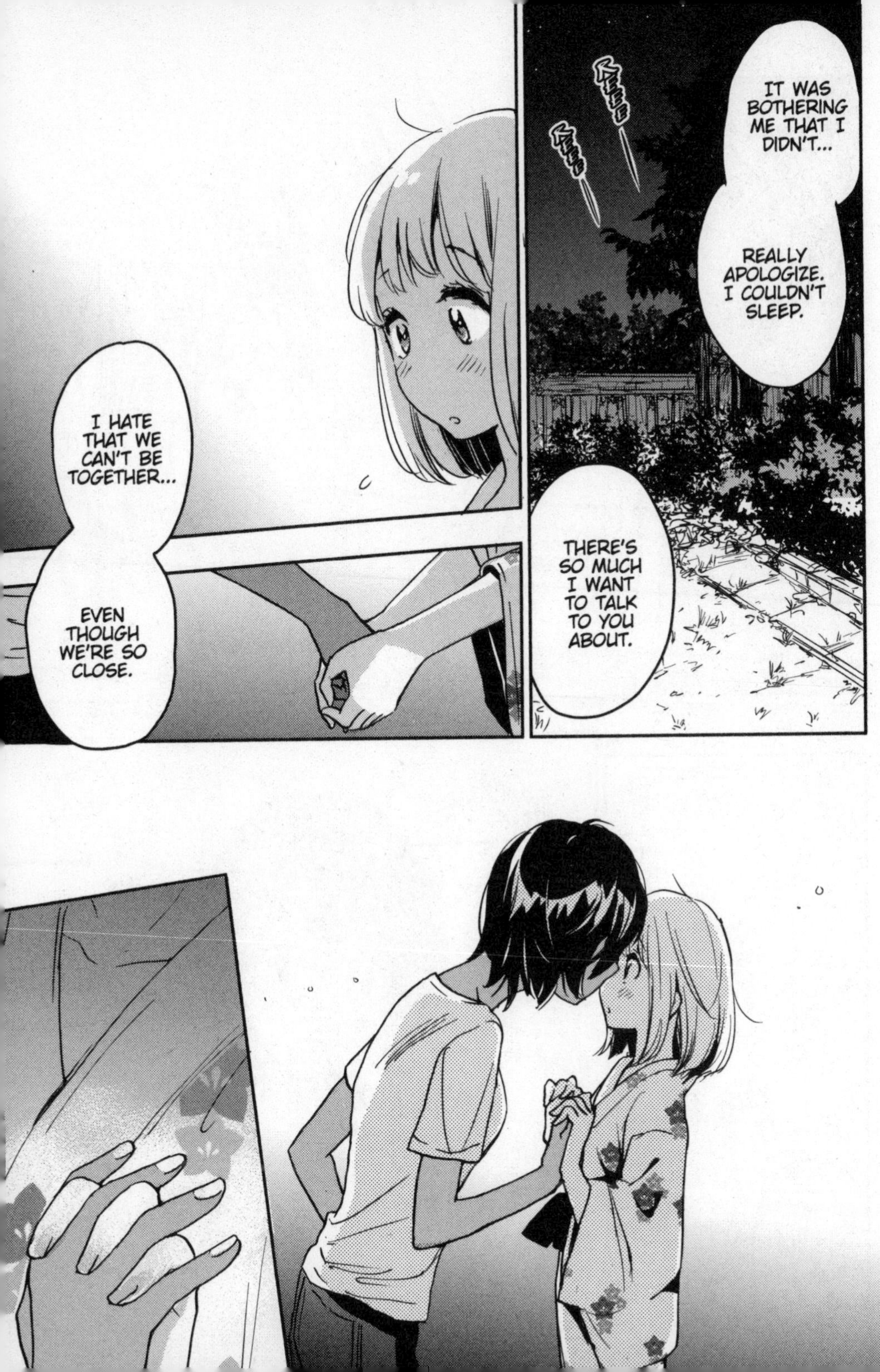
IT WAS BOTHERING ME THAT I DIDN'T...
REALLY APOLOGIZE. I COULDN'T SLEEP.
REEE
REEE
THERE'S SO MUCH I WANT TO TALK TO YOU ABOUT.
I HATE THAT WE CAN'T BE TOGETHER...
EVEN THOUGH WE'RE SO CLOSE.

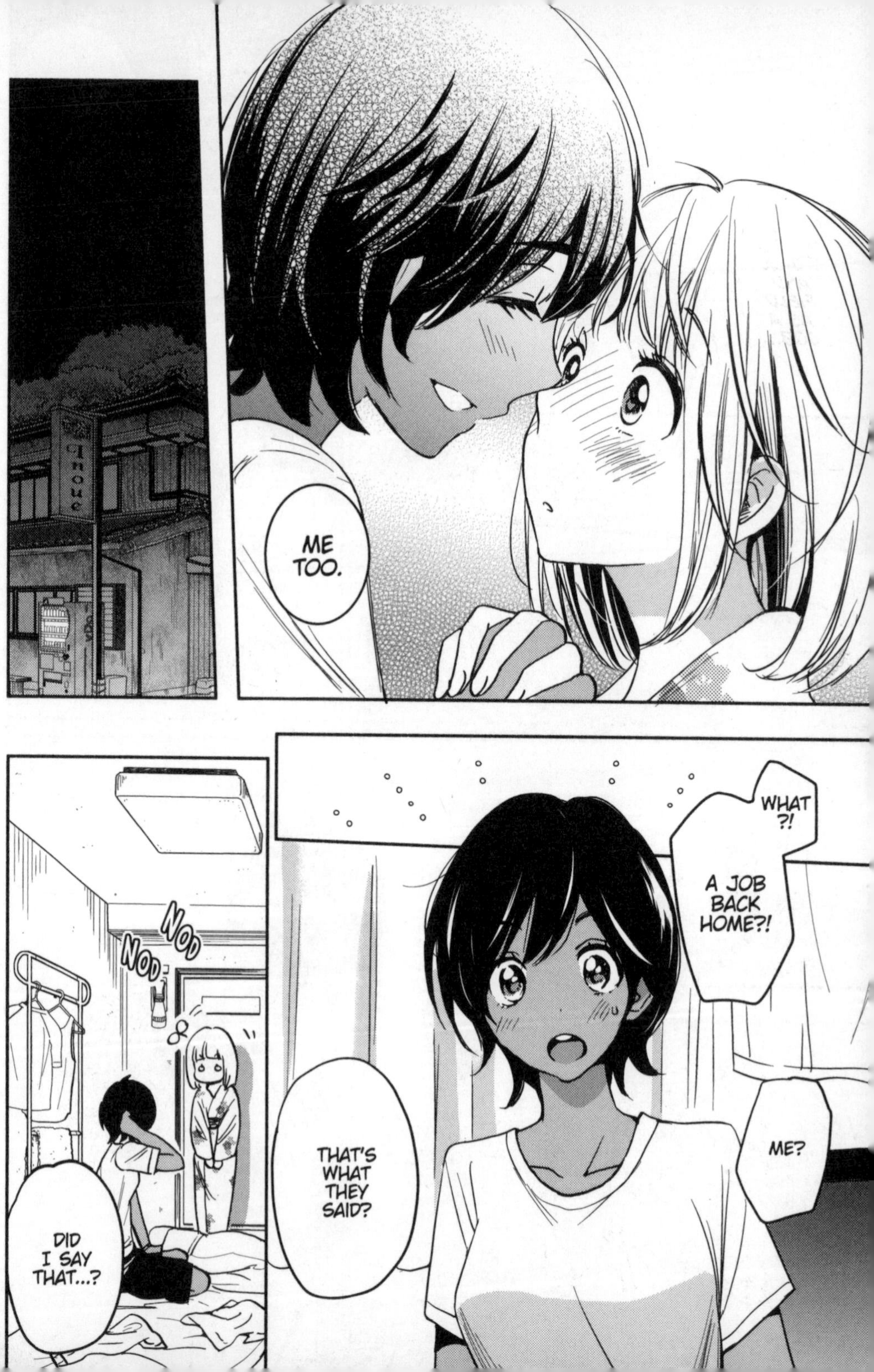
ME TOO.
WHAT ?!
A JOB BACK HOME?!
ME?
THAT'S WHAT THEY SAID?
NOD NOD
DID I SAY THAT...?

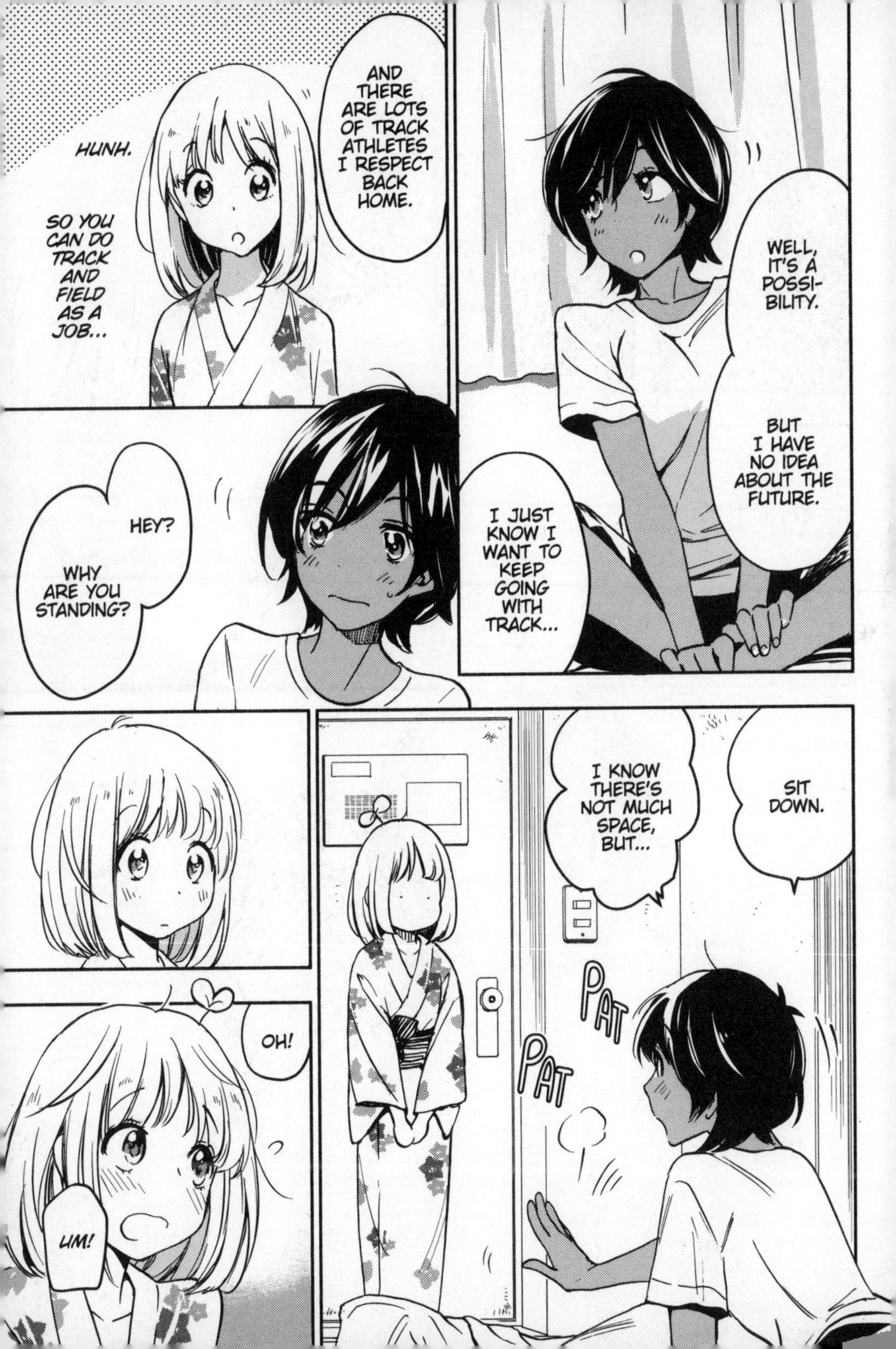
WELL, IT'S A POSSIBILITY.
BUT I HAVE NO IDEA ABOUT THE FUTURE.
I JUST KNOW I WANT TO KEEP GOING WITH TRACK...
AND THERE ARE LOTS OF TRACK ATHLETES I RESPECT BACK HOME.
HUNH.
SO YOU CAN DO TRACK AND FIELD AS A JOB...
HEY?
WHY ARE YOU STANDING?
SIT DOWN.
I KNOW THERE'S NOT MUCH SPACE, BUT...
PAT
PAT
OH!
UM!

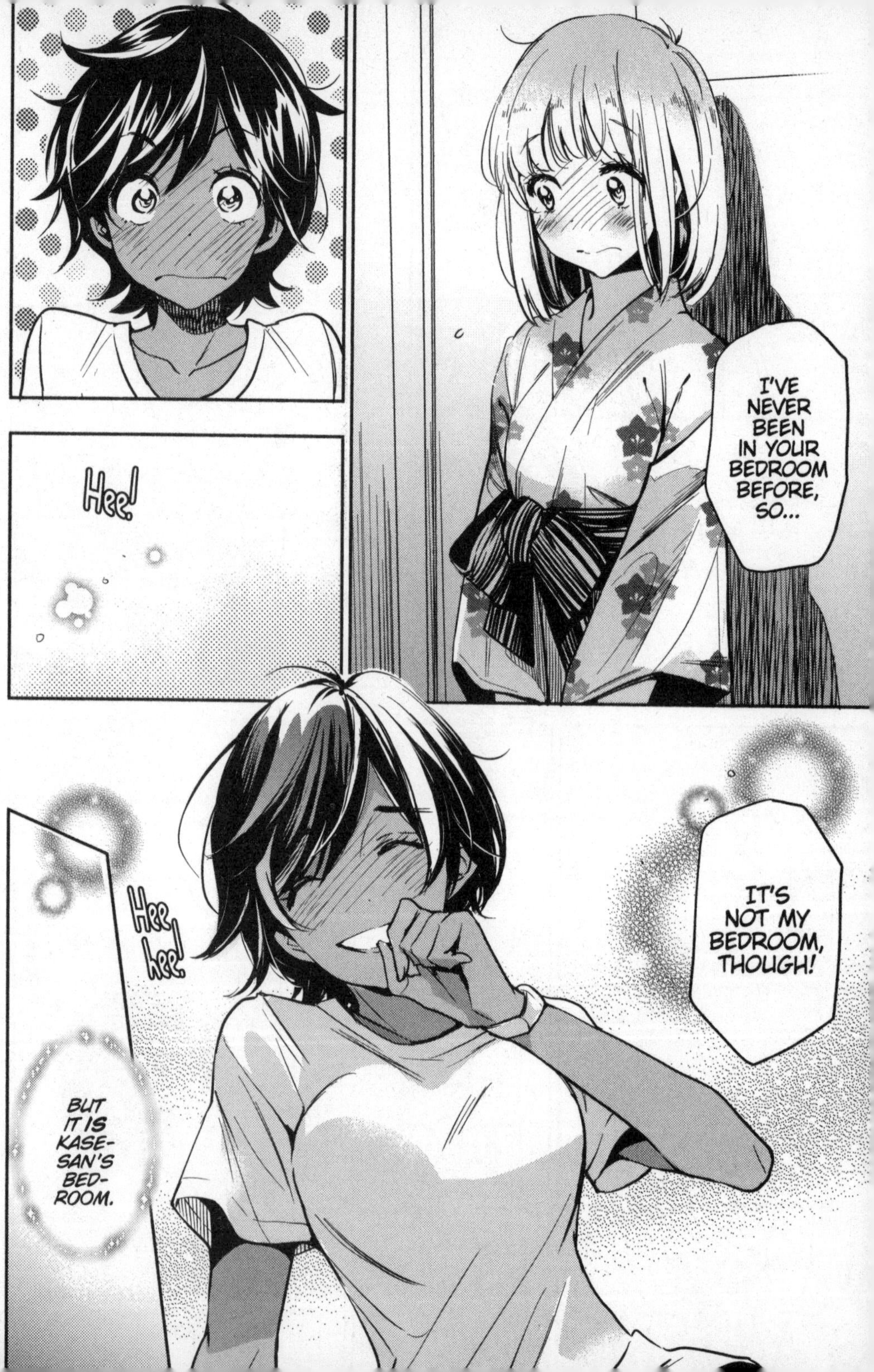
I'VE NEVER BEEN IN YOUR BEDROOM BEFORE, SO...
Hee!
IT'S NOT MY BEDROOM, THOUGH!
Hee, hee!
BUT IT IS KASE-SAN'S BED-ROOM.

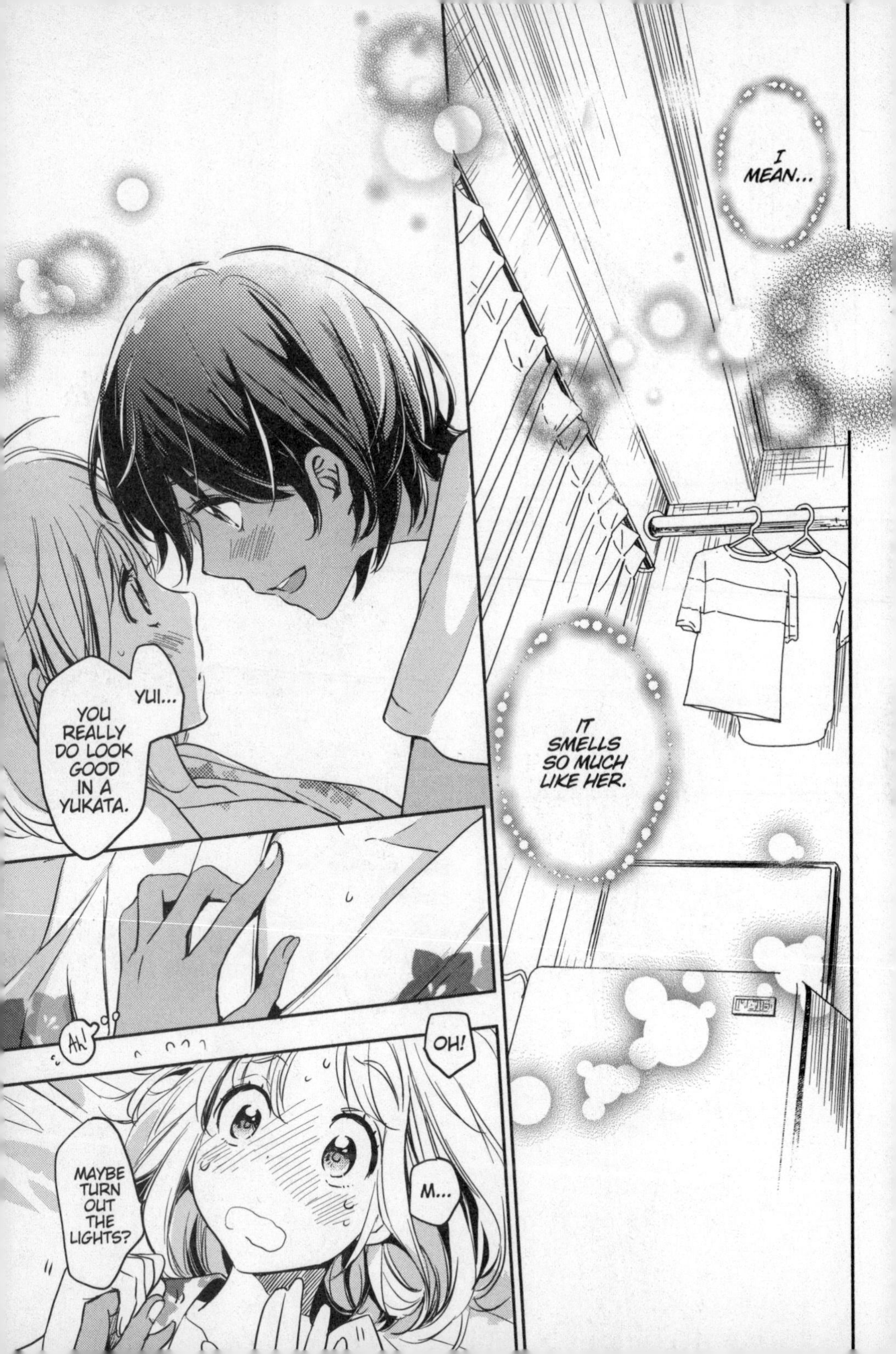
I MEAN...
IT SMELLS SO MUCH LIKE HER.
YUI... YOU REALLY DO LOOK GOOD IN A YUKATA.
Ah!
OH!
M...
MAYBE TURN OUT THE LIGHTS?

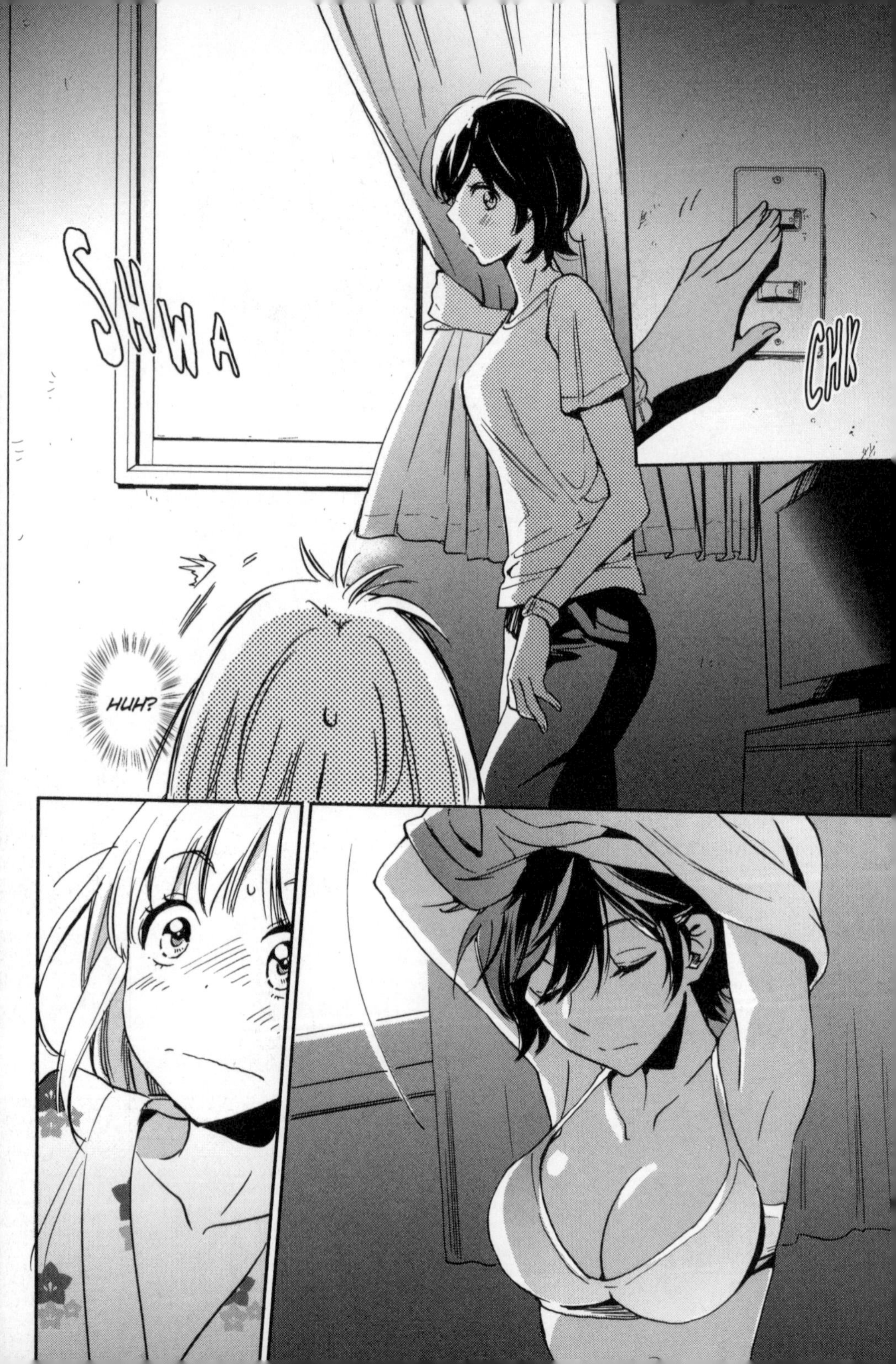
CHK
SHWA
HUH?

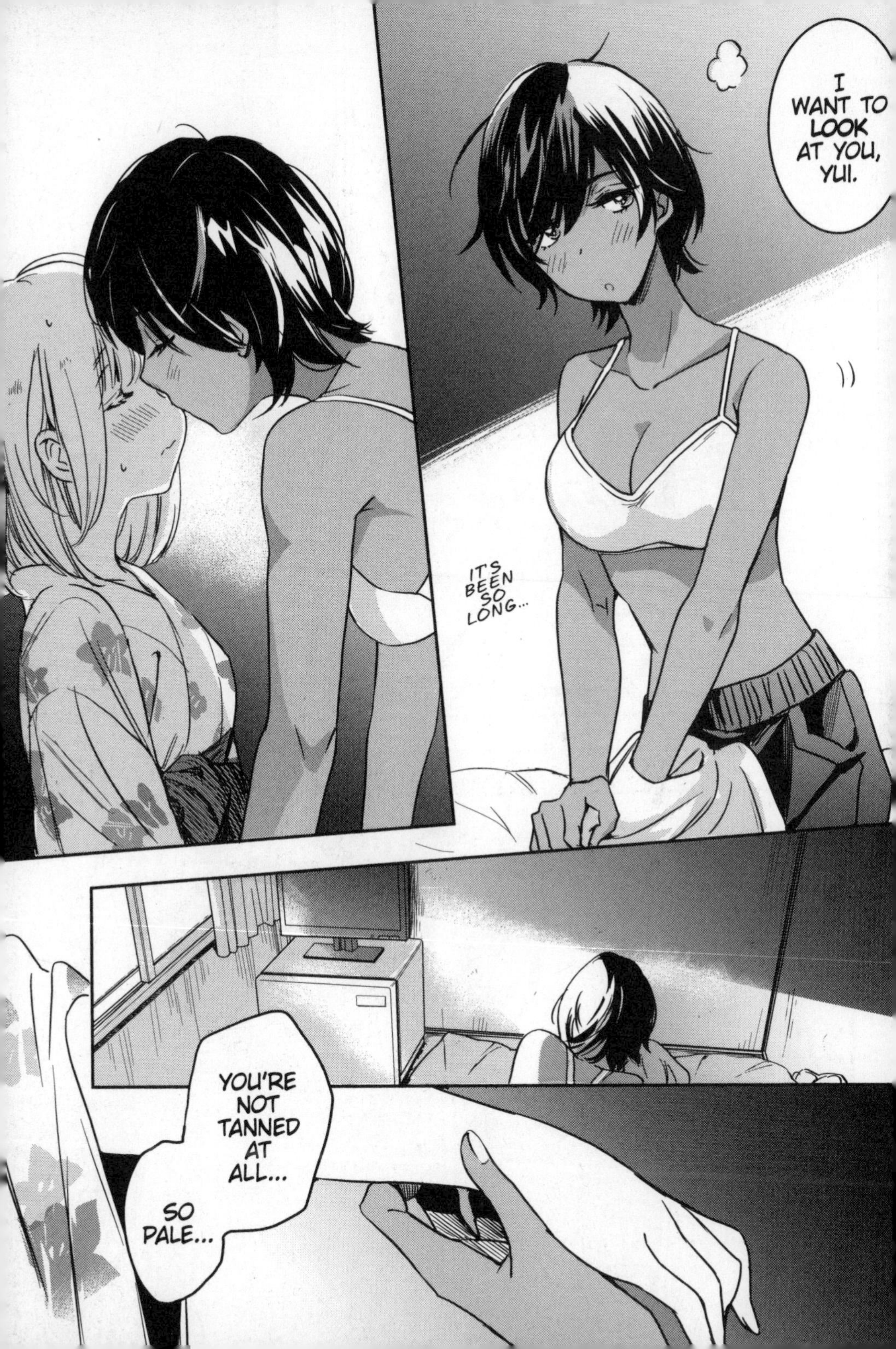
I WANT TO LOOK AT YOU, YUI.
IT'S BEEN SO LONG...
YOU'RE NOT TANNED AT ALL...
SO PALE...

YEAH, I ALWAYS WEAR SUN-SCREEN.
SUN-SCREEN...
AAH...
Mrph!
SQUEEZE
I DIDN'T WANT TO REMEMBER THAT.
AH!
!
FLINCH
THIS IT?

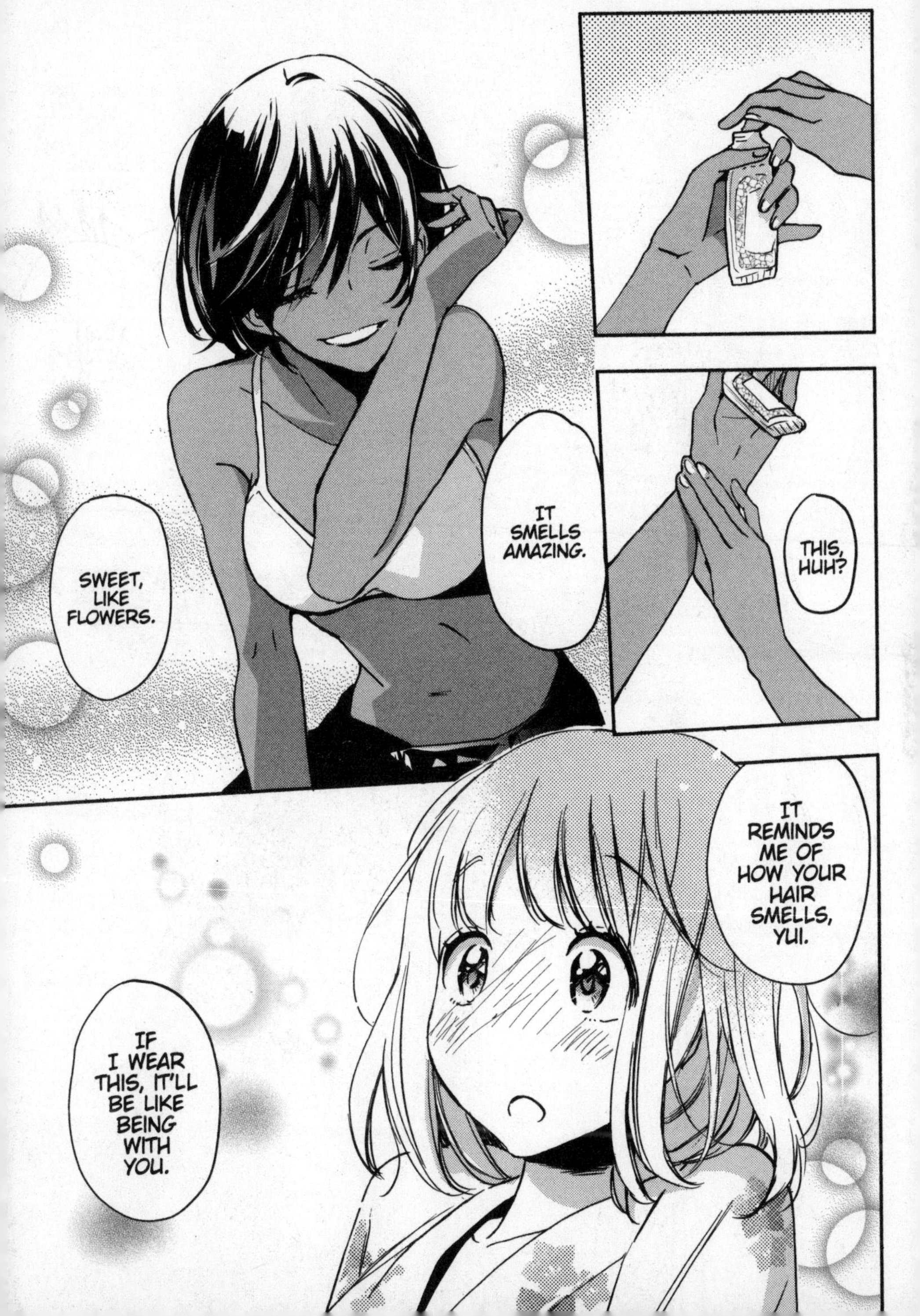
THIS, HUH?
IT SMELLS AMAZING.
SWEET, LIKE FLOWERS.
IT REMINDS ME OF HOW YOUR HAIR SMELLS, YUI.
IF I WEAR THIS, IT'LL BE LIKE BEING WITH YOU.

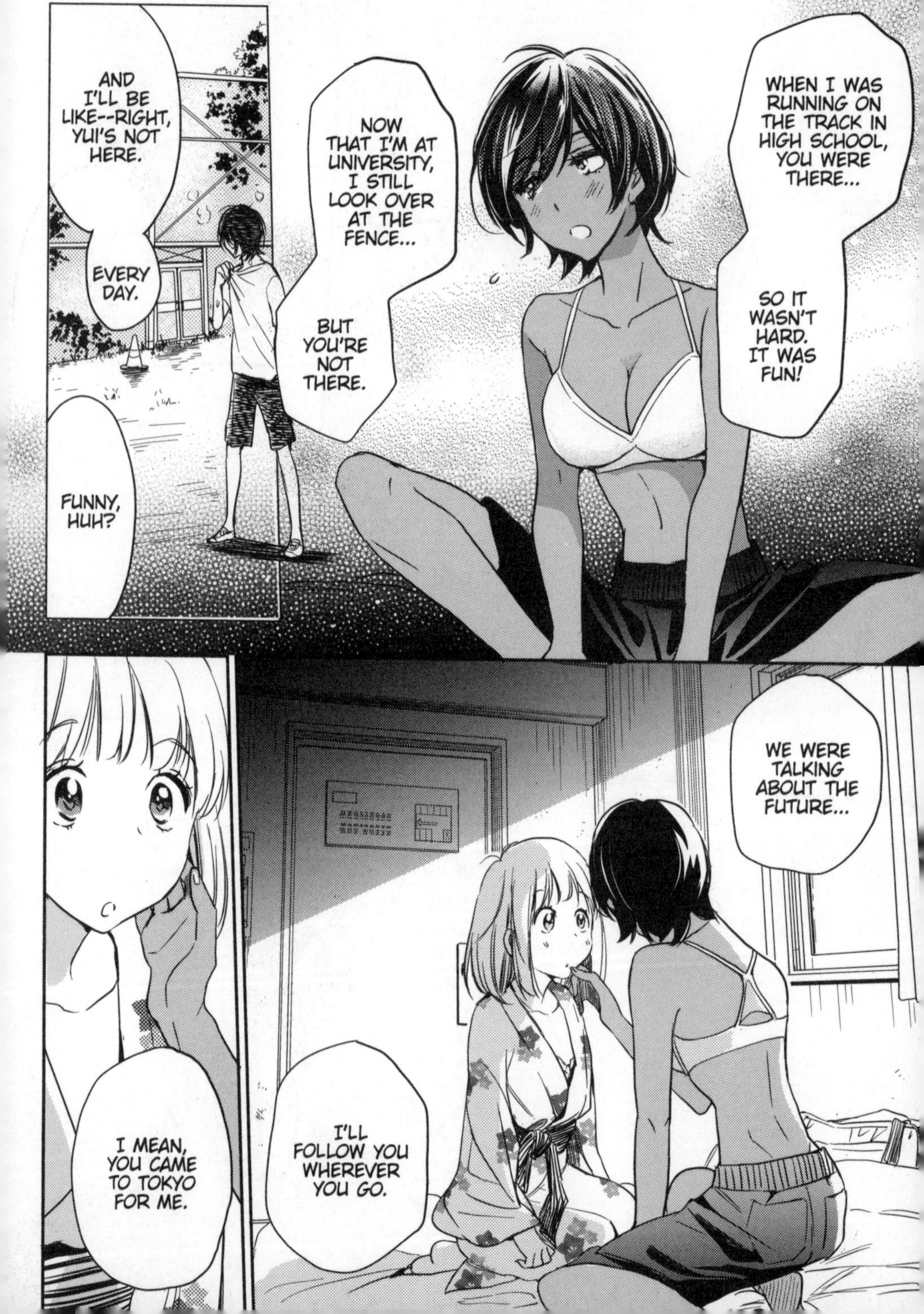

WHEN I WAS RUNNING ON THE TRACK IN HIGH SCHOOL, YOU WERE THERE...
SO IT WASN'T HARD. IT WAS FUN!
NOW THAT I'M AT UNIVERSITY, I STILL LOOK OVER AT THE FENCE...
BUT YOU'RE NOT THERE.
AND I'LL BE LIKE--RIGHT, YUI'S NOT HERE.
EVERY DAY.
FUNNY, HUH?
WE WERE TALKING ABOUT THE FUTURE...
I'LL FOLLOW YOU WHEREVER YOU GO.
I MEAN, YOU CAME TO TOKYO FOR ME.

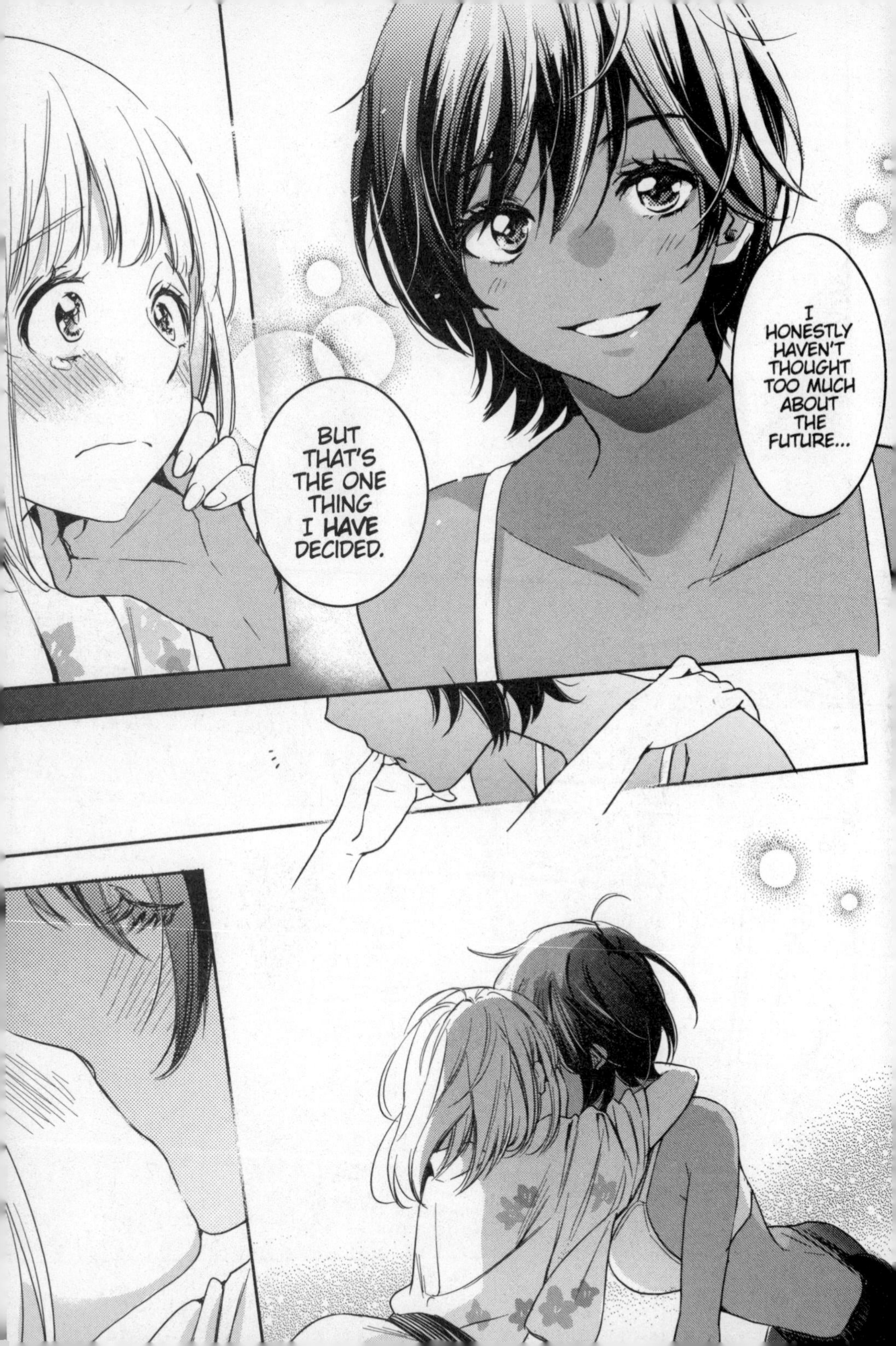
I HONESTLY HAVEN'T THOUGHT TOO MUCH ABOUT THE FUTURE...
BUT THAT'S THE ONE THING I **HAVE** DECIDED.

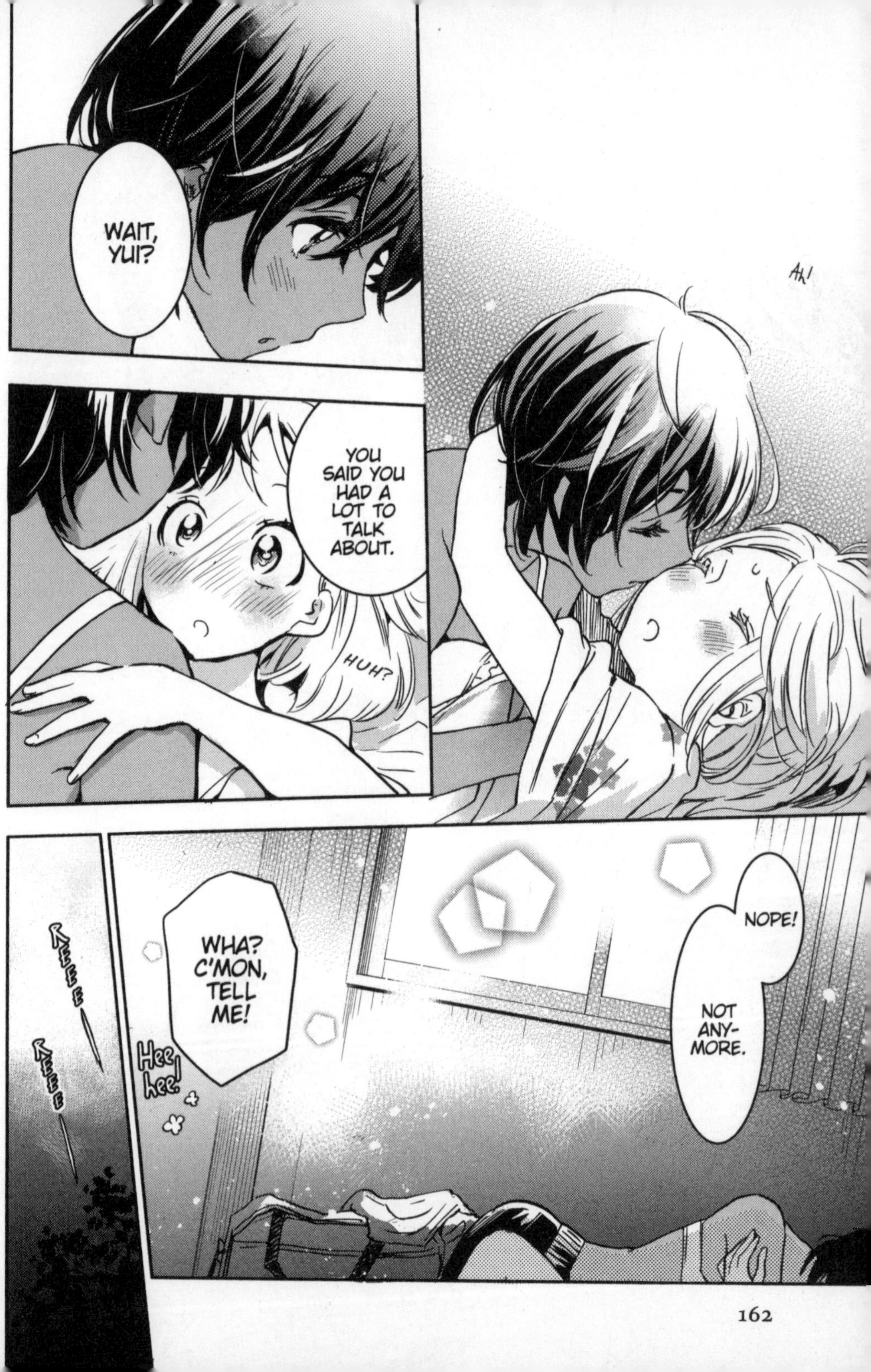
Ah!
WAIT, YUI?
YOU SAID YOU HAD A LOT TO TALK ABOUT.
HUH?
NOPE!
NOT ANYMORE.
WHA? C'MON, TELL ME!
Hee hee!
Reeee—
Reeee—

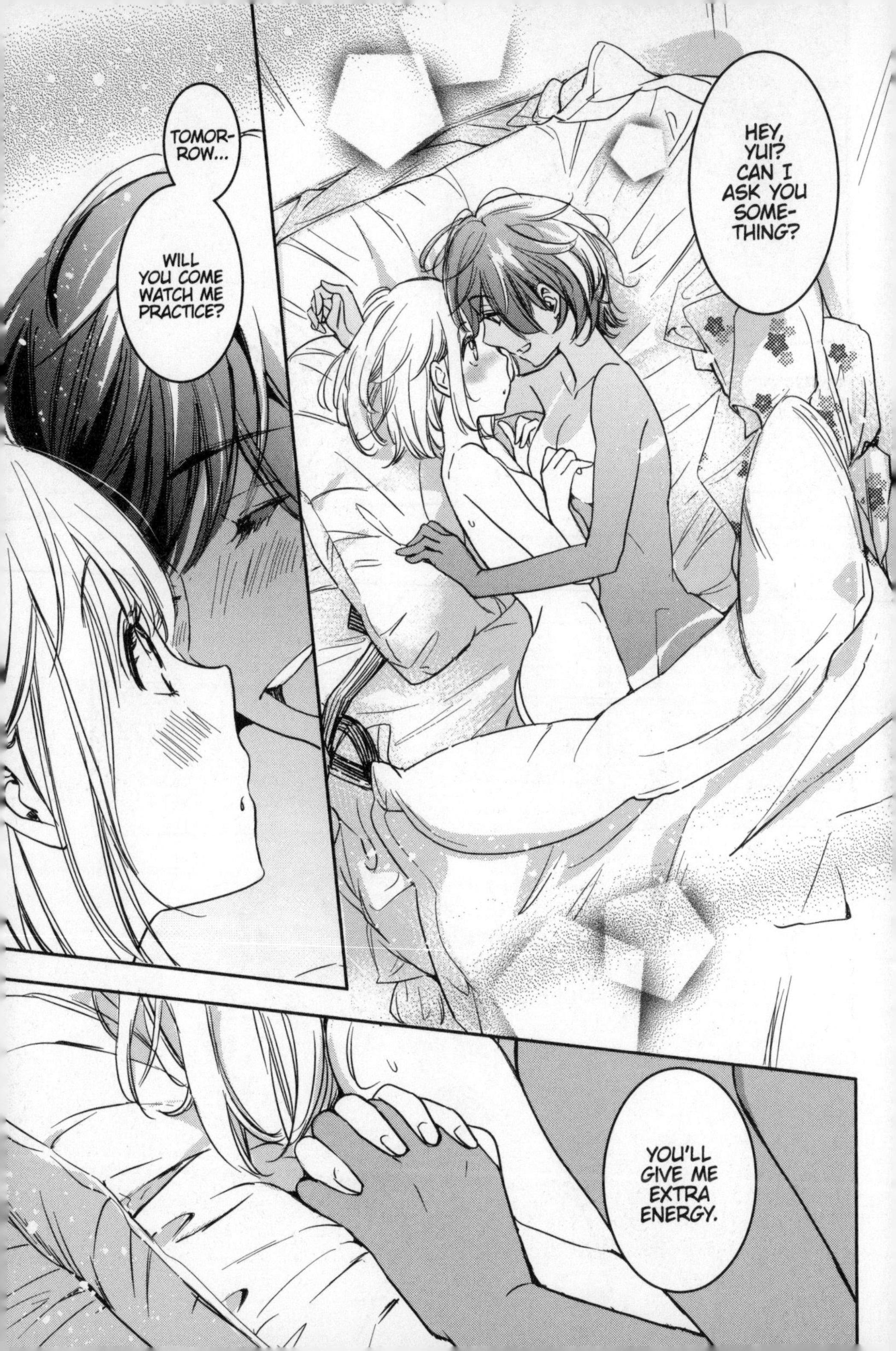
HEY, YUI? CAN I ASK YOU SOME-THING?
TOMOR-ROW...
WILL YOU COME WATCH ME PRACTICE?
YOU'LL GIVE ME EXTRA ENERGY.

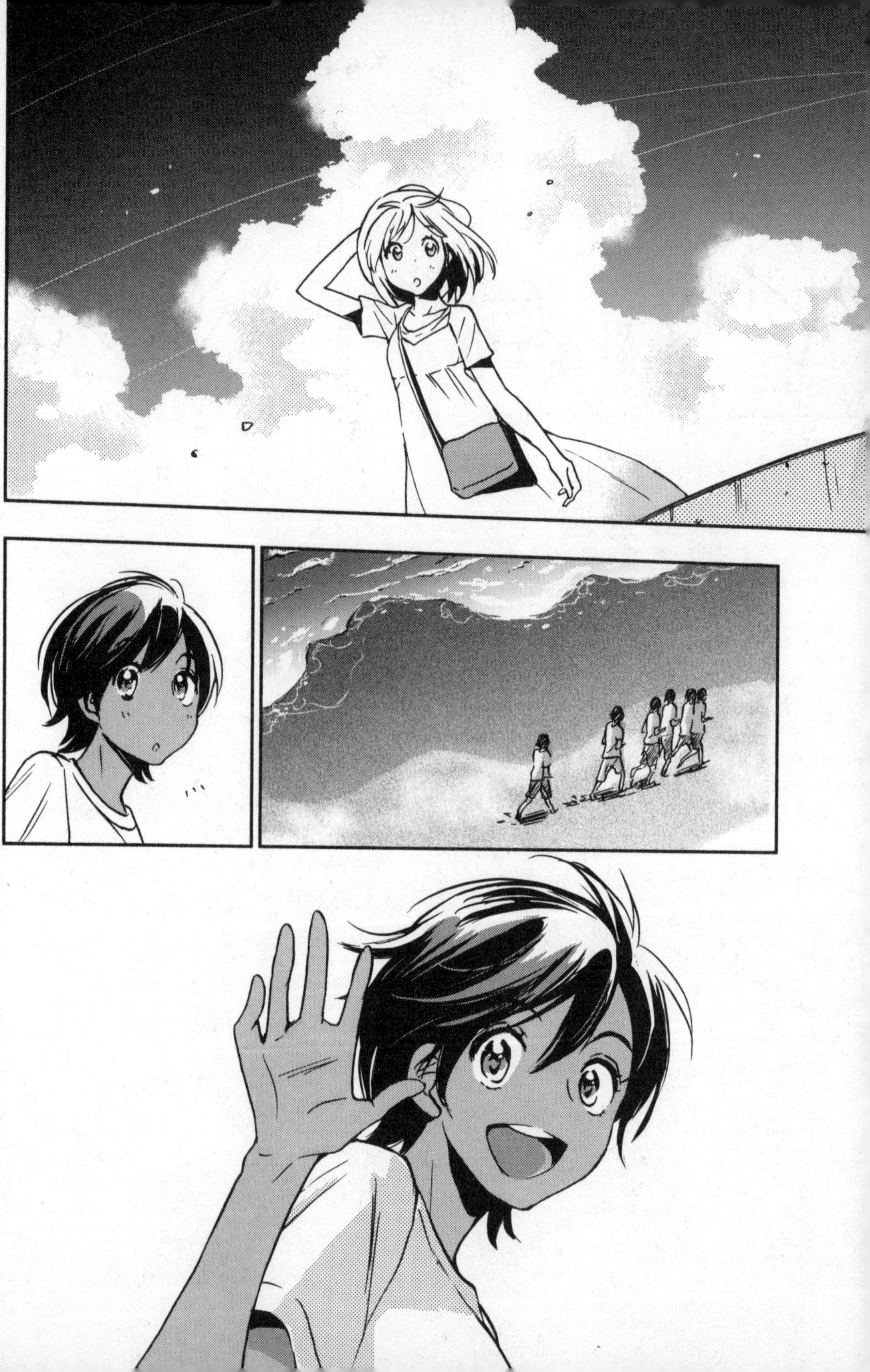

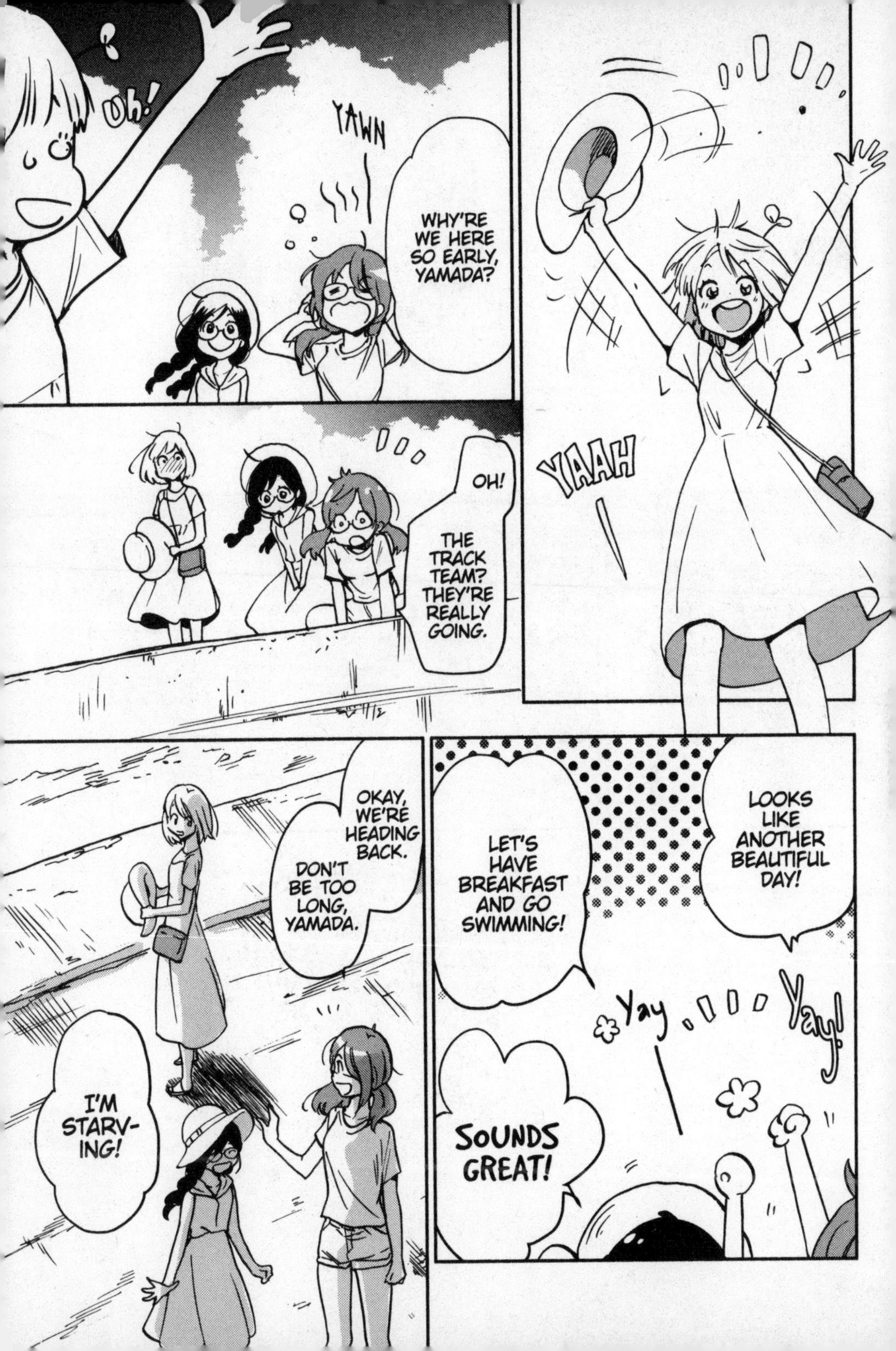YAAH
Oh!
YAWN
WHY'RE WE HERE SO EARLY, YAMADA?
OH!
THE TRACK TEAM? THEY'RE REALLY GOING.
LOOKS LIKE ANOTHER BEAUTIFUL DAY!
LET'S HAVE BREAKFAST AND GO SWIMMING!
Yay
Yay!
SOUNDS GREAT!
OKAY, WE'RE HEADING BACK.
DON'T BE TOO LONG, YAMADA.
I'M STARV-ING!

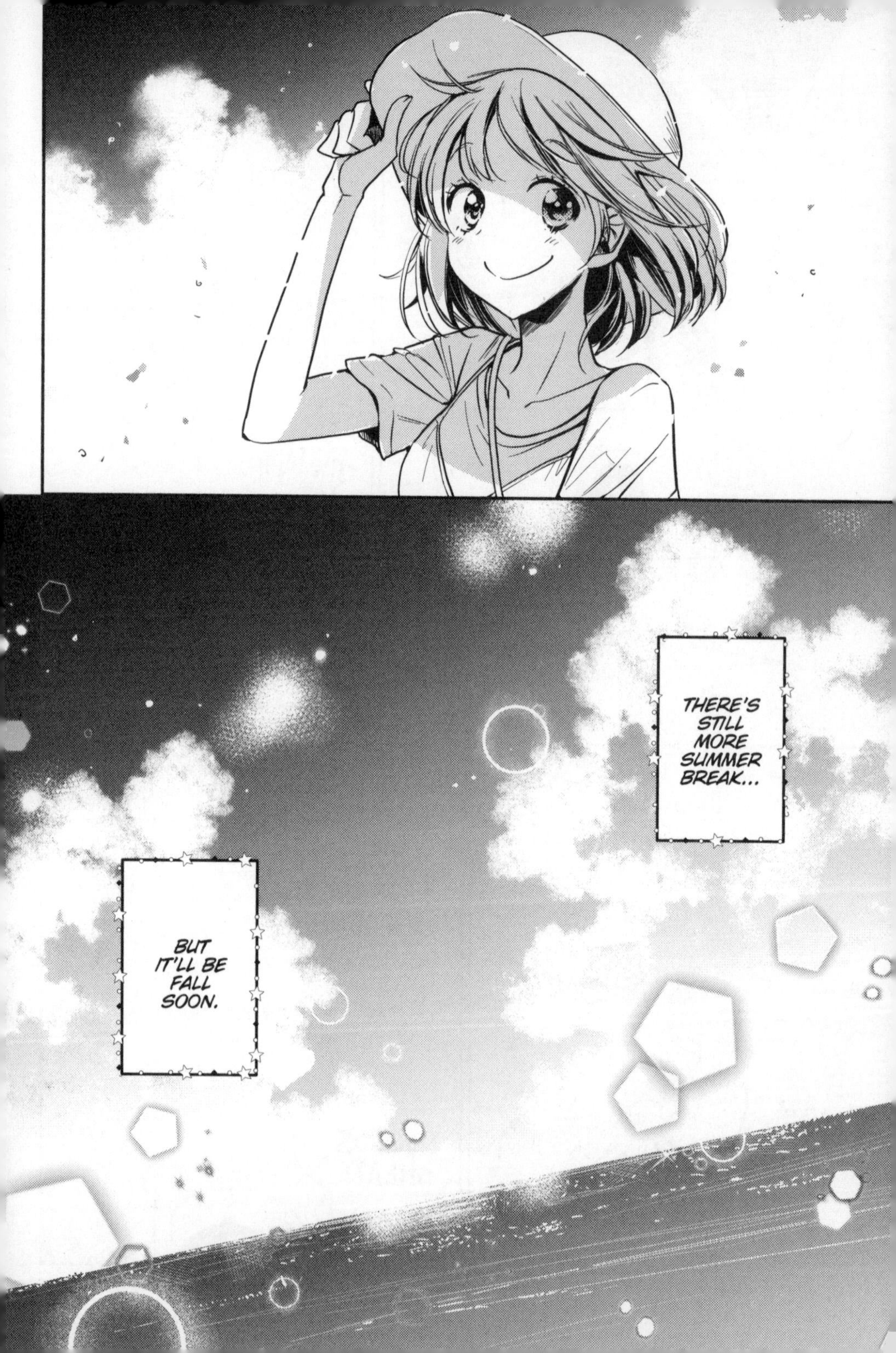
THERE'S STILL MORE SUMMER BREAK...
BUT IT'LL BE FALL SOON.

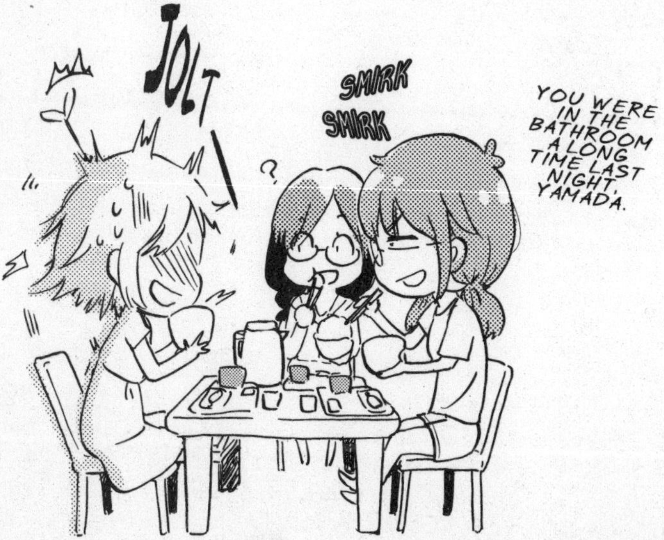
YOU WERE IN THE BATHROOM A LONG TIME LAST NIGHT, YAMADA.
SMIRK
SMIRK
?
JOLT

Kase-san and Yamada ②

# Kase-san and the Rival (Again)

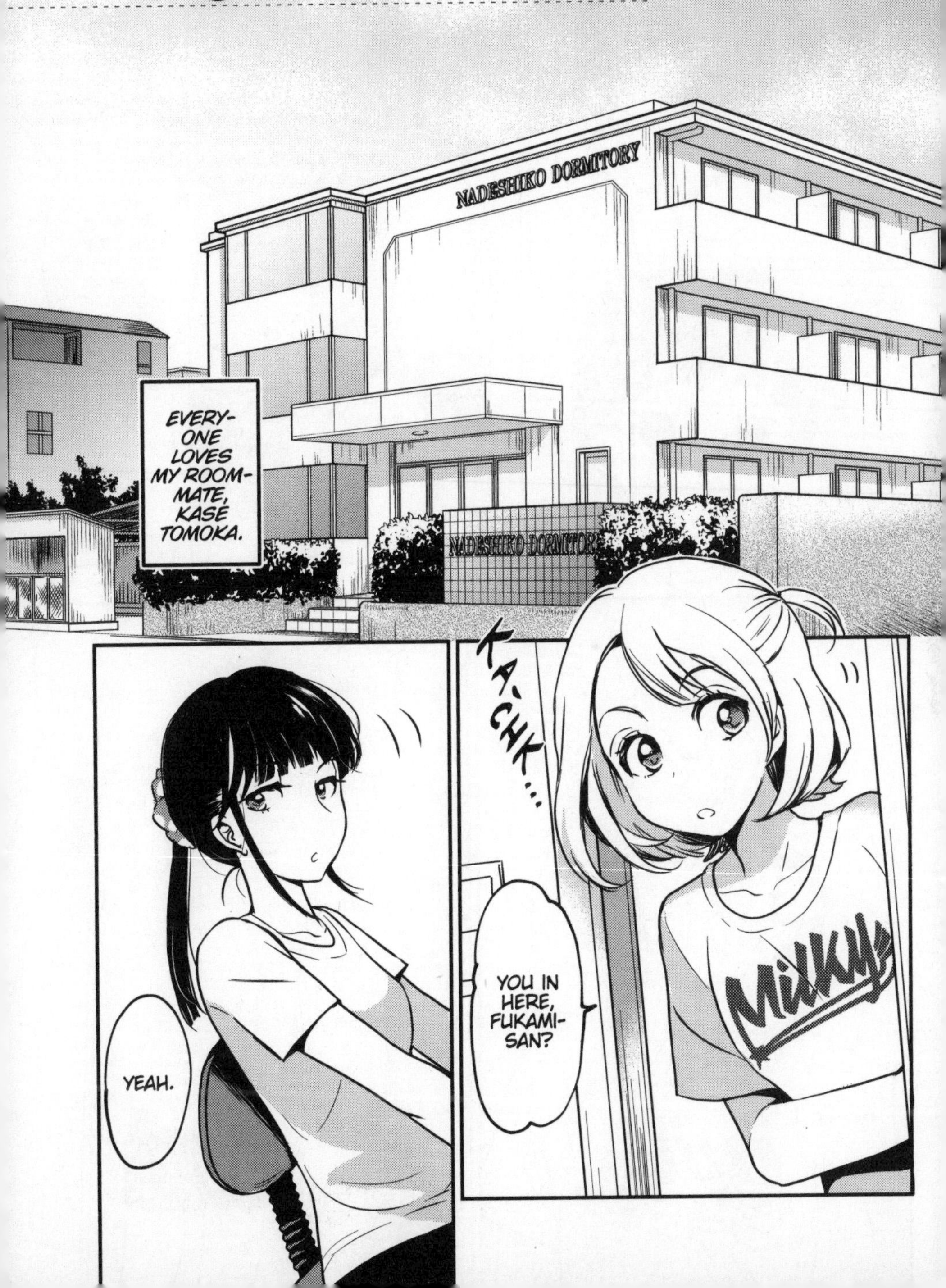
NADESHIKO DORMITORY
EVERY-ONE LOVES MY ROOMMATE, KASE TOMOKA.
NADESHIKO DORMITORY
KA-CHK...
YOU IN HERE, FUKAMI-SAN?
YEAH.

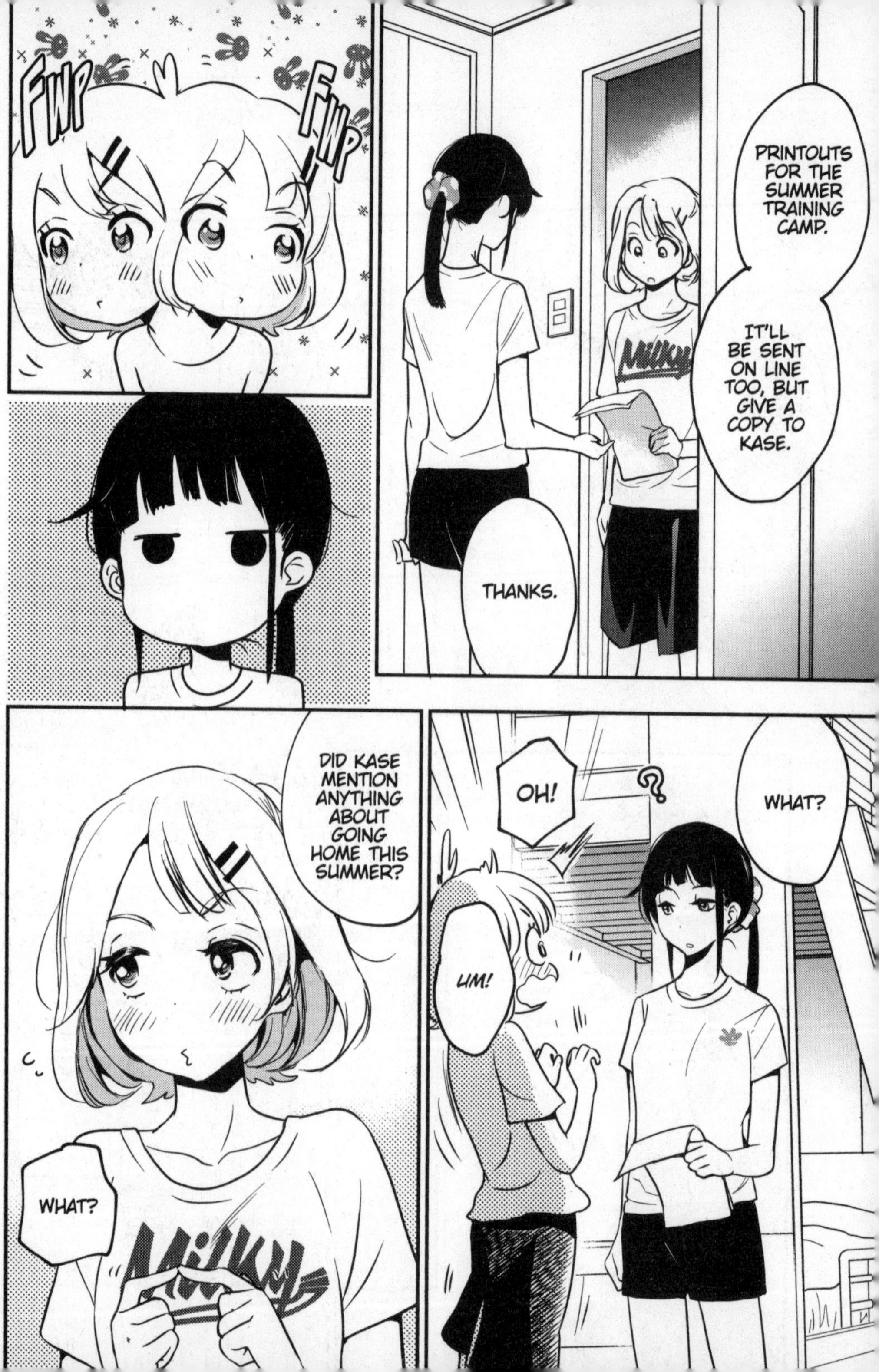
PRINTOUTS FOR THE SUMMER TRAINING CAMP.
IT'LL BE SENT ON LINE TOO, BUT GIVE A COPY TO KASE.
THANKS.
FWP
FWP
WHAT?
OH!
UM!
DID KASE MENTION ANYTHING ABOUT GOING HOME THIS SUMMER?
WHAT?

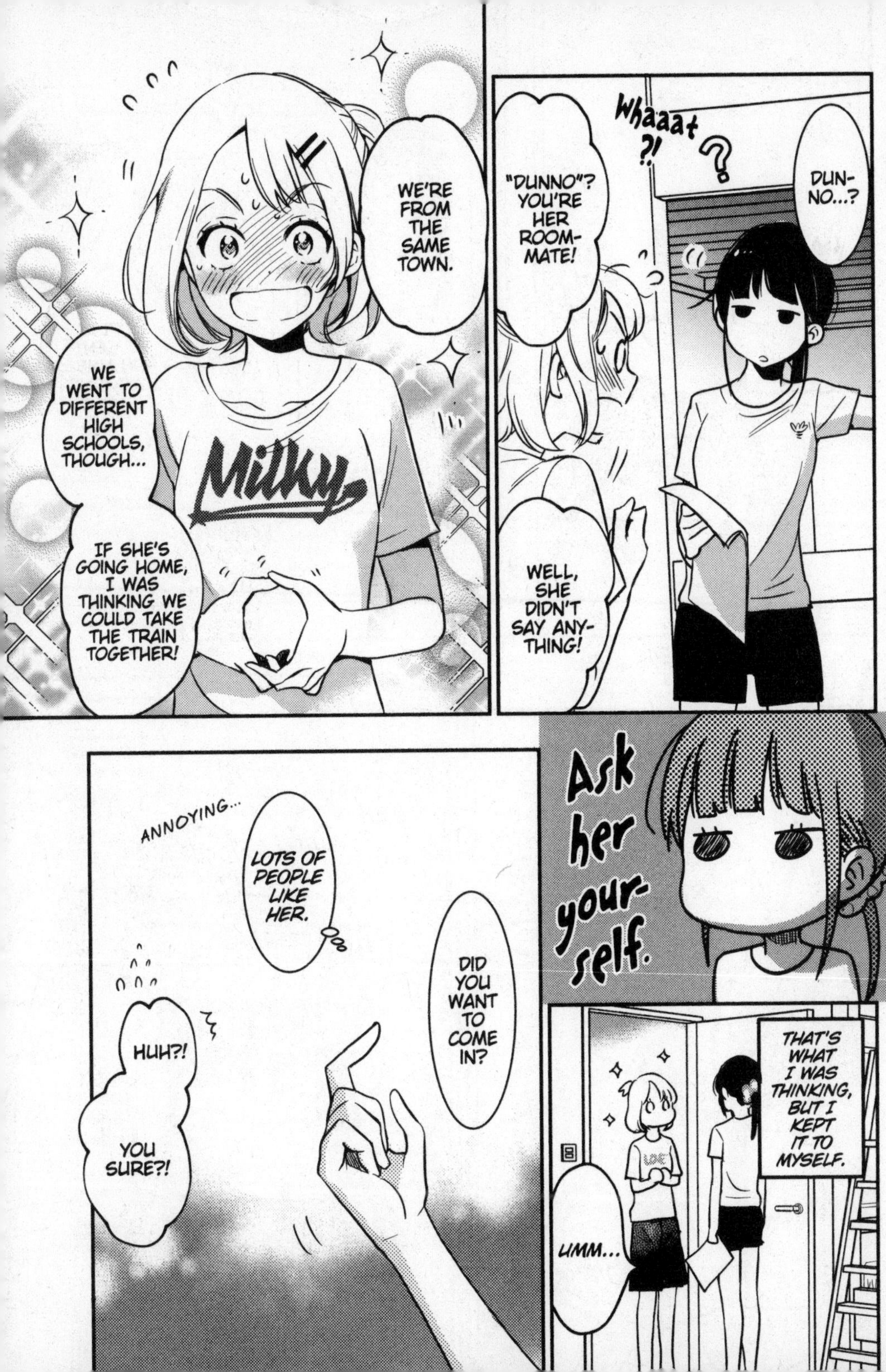
DUN-NO...?
Whaaat ?!
"DUNNO"? YOU'RE HER ROOMMATE!
WELL, SHE DIDN'T SAY ANYTHING!
WE'RE FROM THE SAME TOWN.
WE WENT TO DIFFERENT HIGH SCHOOLS, THOUGH...
IF SHE'S GOING HOME, I WAS THINKING WE COULD TAKE THE TRAIN TOGETHER!
Milky
Ask her yourself.
THAT'S WHAT I WAS THINKING, BUT I KEPT IT TO MYSELF.
UMM...
DID YOU WANT TO COME IN?
LOTS OF PEOPLE LIKE HER.
ANNOYING...
HUH?!
YOU SURE?!

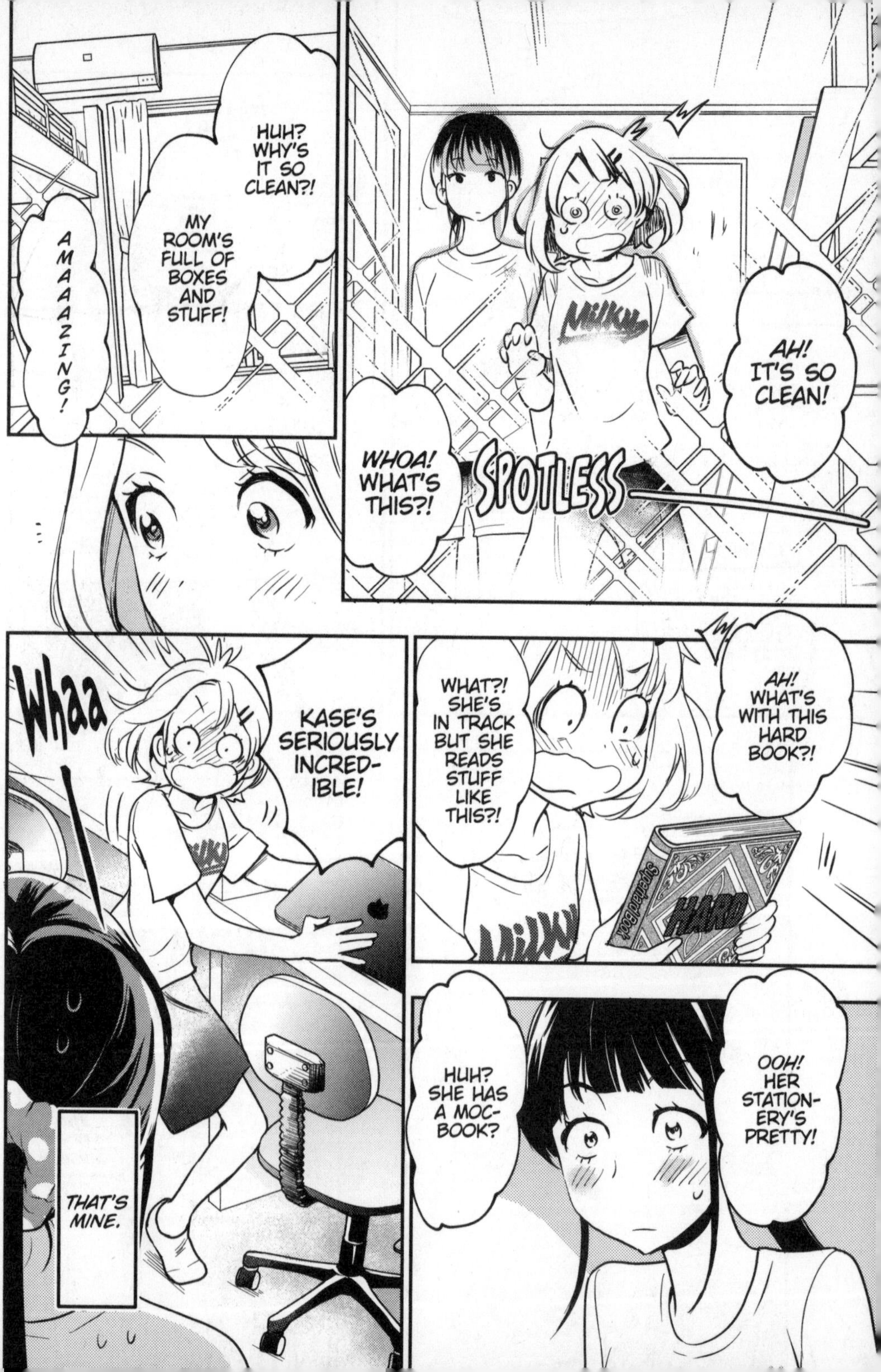
AH! IT'S SO CLEAN!
SPOTLESS
WHOA! WHAT'S THIS?!
HUH? WHY'S IT SO CLEAN?!
MY ROOM'S FULL OF BOXES AND STUFF!
AMAAAAZING!
AH! WHAT'S WITH THIS HARD BOOK?!
WHAT?! SHE'S IN TRACK BUT SHE READS STUFF LIKE THIS?!
Superhard Book
HARD
OOH! HER STATION-ERY'S PRETTY!
HUH? SHE HAS A MOC-BOOK?
KASE'S SERIOUSLY INCRED-IBLE!
Whaa
THAT'S MINE.

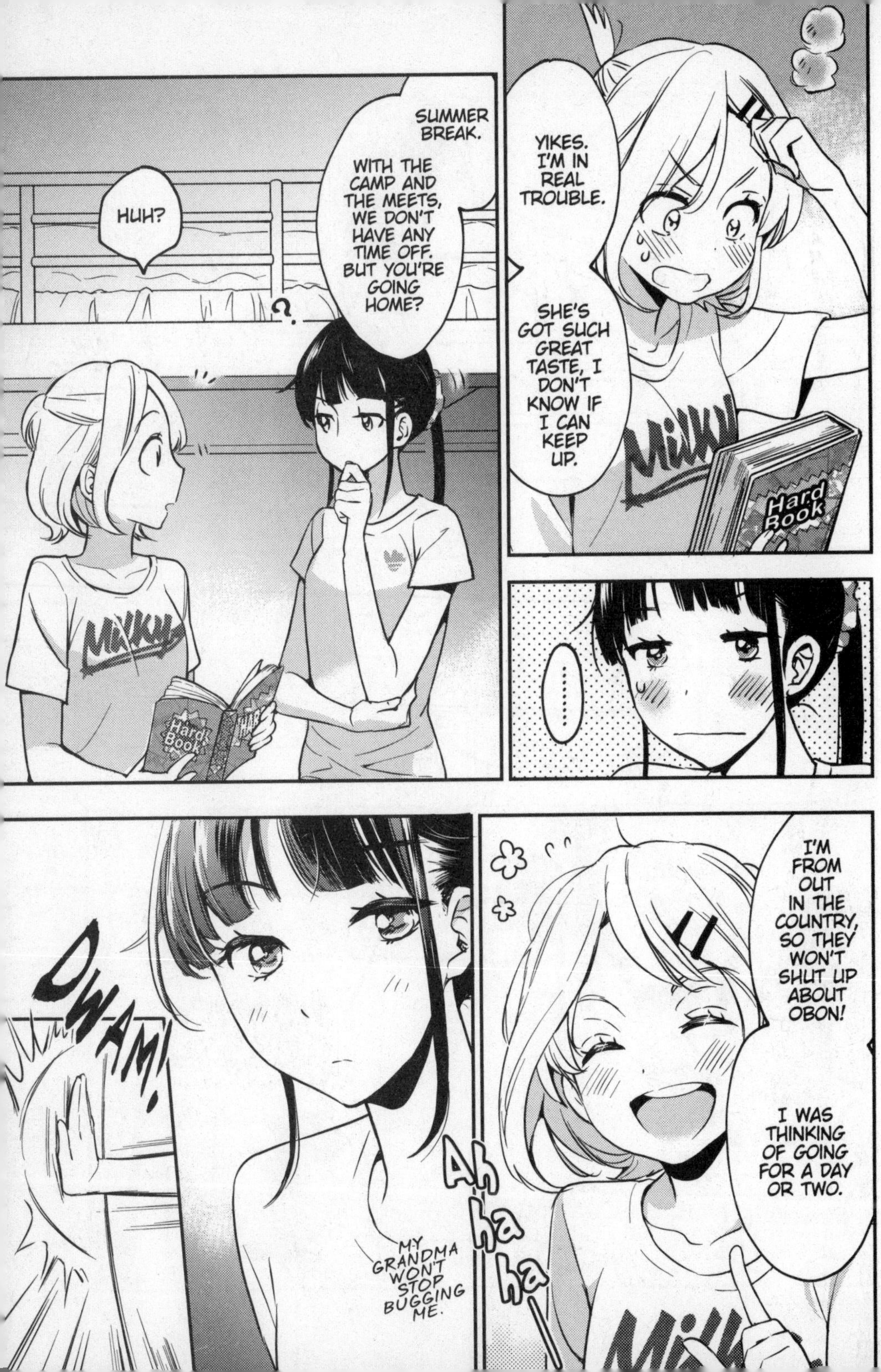
YIKES. I'M IN REAL TROUBLE.
SHE'S GOT SUCH GREAT TASTE, I DON'T KNOW IF I CAN KEEP UP.
Hard Book
......
SUMMER BREAK.
WITH THE CAMP AND THE MEETS, WE DON'T HAVE ANY TIME OFF. BUT YOU'RE GOING HOME?
?
HUH?
Hard Book
I'M FROM OUT IN THE COUNTRY, SO THEY WON'T SHUT UP ABOUT OBON!
I WAS THINKING OF GOING FOR A DAY OR TWO.
Ah ha ha
MY GRANDMA WON'T STOP BUGGING ME.
DWAM!

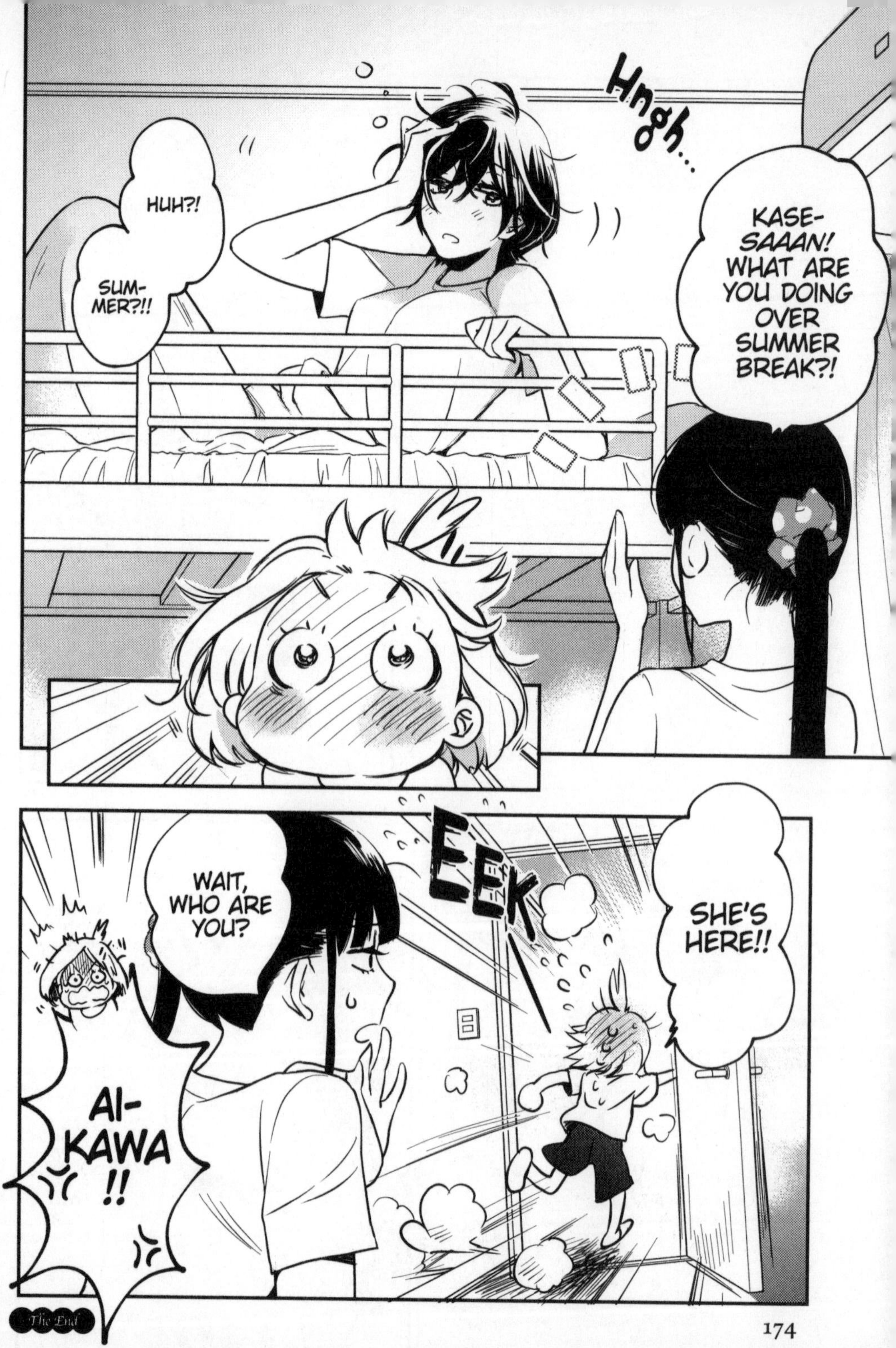
Hngh...
KASE-SAAAN! WHAT ARE YOU DOING OVER SUMMER BREAK?!
HUH?!
SUM-MER?!!
SHE'S HERE!!
EEK
WAIT, WHO ARE YOU?
AI-KAWA !!

The End

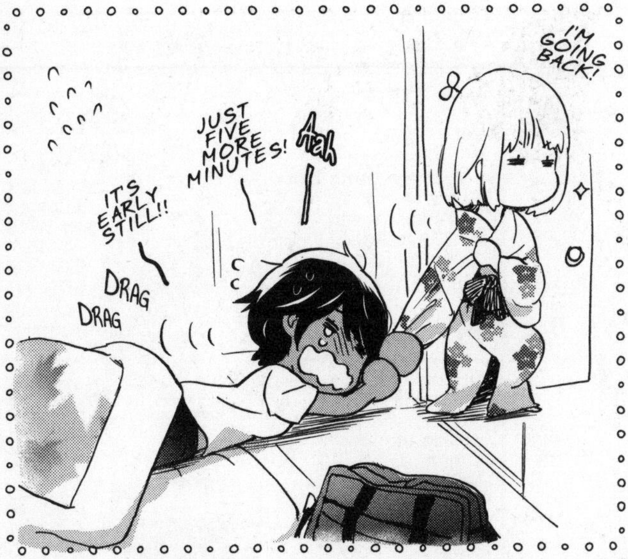
I'M GOING BACK!
Aah
JUST FIVE MORE MINUTES!
ITS EARLY STILL!!
DRAG
DRAG

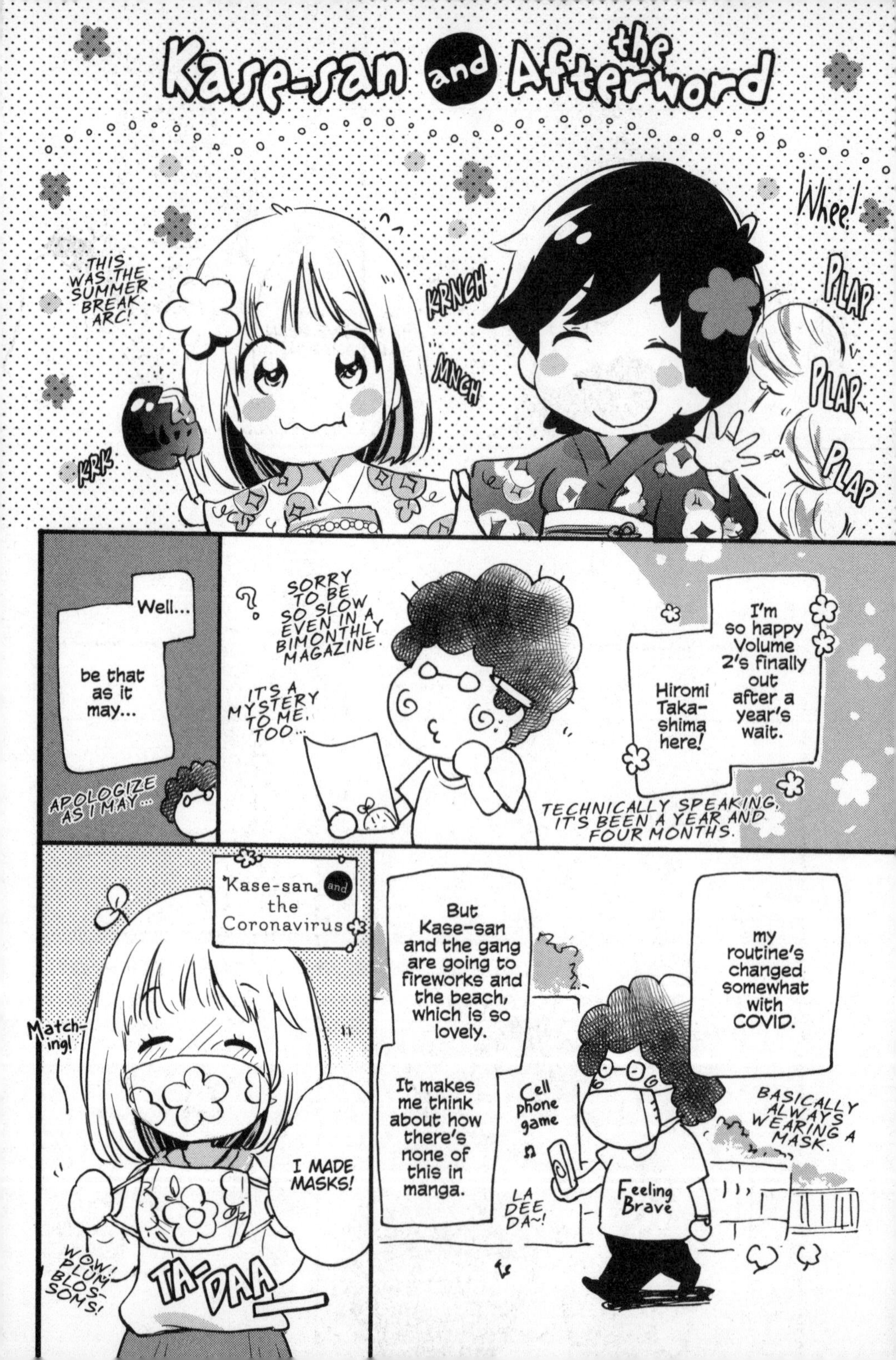
Kase-san and the Afterword
Whee!
PLAP
PLAP
PLAP
KRNCH
MNCH
THIS WAS THE SUMMER BREAK ARC!
KRK
Hiromi Takashima here!
I'm so happy Volume 2's finally out after a year's wait.
TECHNICALLY SPEAKING, IT'S BEEN A YEAR AND FOUR MONTHS.
SORRY TO BE SO SLOW EVEN IN A BIMONTHLY MAGAZINE.
IT'S A MYSTERY TO ME, TOO...
Well...
be that as it may...
APOLOGIZE AS I MAY...
my routine's changed somewhat with COVID.
But Kase-san and the gang are going to fireworks and the beach, which is so lovely.
BASICALLY ALWAYS WEARING A MASK.
It makes me think about how there's none of this in manga.
Cell phone game
LA DEE DA~!
Feeling Brave
Kase-san and the Coronavirus
Matching!
I MADE MASKS!
TA-DAA
WOW! PLUM BLOSSOMS!

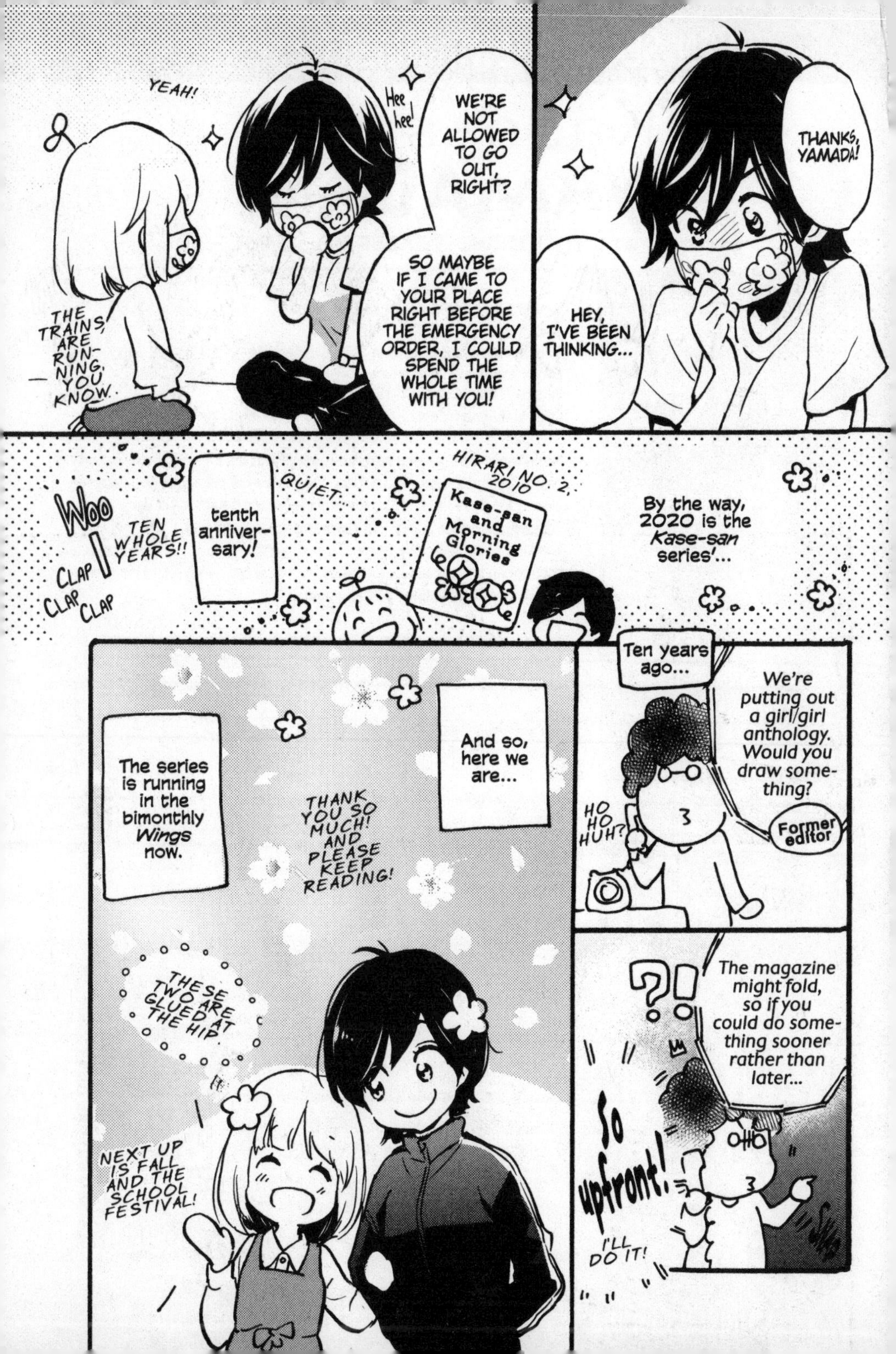

THANKS, YAMADA!
HEY, I'VE BEEN THINKING...
Hee hee!
WE'RE NOT ALLOWED TO GO OUT, RIGHT?
SO MAYBE IF I CAME TO YOUR PLACE RIGHT BEFORE THE EMERGENCY ORDER, I COULD SPEND THE WHOLE TIME WITH YOU!
YEAH!
THE TRAINS ARE RUNNING, YOU KNOW.
By the way, 2020 is the *Kase-san* series'...
HIRARI NO. 2, 2010
Kase-san and Morning Glories
QUIET...
tenth anniversary!
TEN WHOLE YEARS!!
Woo
CLAP CLAP CLAP
Ten years ago...
We're putting out a girl/girl anthology. Would you draw something?
Former editor
HO HO HUH?
The magazine might fold, so if you could do something sooner rather than later...
?!
So upfront!
I'LL DO IT!
And so, here we are...
The series is running in the bimonthly *Wings* now.
THANK YOU SO MUCH! AND PLEASE KEEP READING!
THESE TWO ARE GLUED AT THE HIP
NEXT UP IS FALL AND THE SCHOOL FESTIVAL!

SEVEN SEAS ENTERTAINMENT PRESENTS

# Kase-san and YAMADA

story & art by HIROMI TAKASHIMA Vol. 2

TRANSLATION
Jocelyne Allen

LETTERING
CK Russell

COVER DESIGN
Nicky Lim

PROOFREADER
B. Lillian Martin

COPY EDITOR
Dawn Davis

EDITOR
Jenn Grunigen

PRODUCTION ASSOCIATE
Christina McKenzie

PRODUCTION MANAGER
Lissa Pattillo

PREPRESS TECHNICIAN
Melanie Ujimori

PRINT MANAGER
Rhiannon Rasmussen-Silverstein

EDITOR-IN-CHIEF
Julie Davis

ASSOCIATE PUBLISHER
Adam Arnold

PUBLISHER
Jason DeAngelis



Seven Seas press and purchase enquiries can be sent to Marketing Manager Lianne Sentar at press@gomanga.com. Information regarding the distribution and purchase of digital editions is available from Digital Manager CK Russell at digital@gomanga.com.



ISBN: 978-1-64827-937-9
Printed in Canada
First Printing: February 2022
10 9 8 7 6 5 4 3 2 1

## READING DIRECTIONS

This book reads from ***right to left***, Japanese style. If this is your first time reading manga, you start reading from the top right panel on each page and take it from there. If you get lost, just follow the numbered diagram here. It may seem backwards at first, but you'll get the hang of it! Have fun!!

1
2
3
4
5
6
7
8
9

Follow us online: www.SevenSeasEntertainment.com

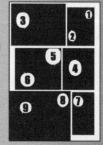